MILTON

Milton's contempt for women has been accepted since Samuel Johnson's famous *Life* of the poet. Subsequent critics have long debated whether Milton's writings were anti- or pro-feminine, a problem further complicated by his advocacy of "divorce on demand" for men. *Milton and Gender* reevaluates the charge that Milton was antifeminine, pointing out that he was not seen that way by contemporaries, but espoused startlingly modern ideas of marriage and the relations between the sexes. The first two sections of specially commissioned essays in this volume investigate the representations of gender and sexuality in Milton's prose and verse. In the final section, the responses of female readers ranging from George Eliot and Virginia Woolf to lesser-known artists and revolutionaries are brought to bear on Milton's afterlife and reputation. Together, these essays provide a thoroughly new perspective on the contested issues of femininity and masculinity, marriage and divorce in Milton's work.

CATHERINE GIMELLI MARTIN is Professor of English Literature at the University of Memphis. She is the author of *The Ruins of Allegory: Paradise Lost and the Metamorphosis of Epic Tradition* (1998).

MILTON AND GENDER

EDITED BY
CATHERINE GIMELLI MARTIN

CAMBRIDGE
UNIVERSITY PRESS

CAMBRIDGE UNIVERSITY PRESS
Cambridge, New York, Melbourne, Madrid, Cape Town, Singapore,
São Paulo, Delhi, Dubai, Tokyo

Cambridge University Press
The Edinburgh Building, Cambridge CB2 8RU, UK

Published in the United States of America by Cambridge University Press, New York

www.cambridge.org
Information on this title: www.cambridge.org/9780521123709

© Cambridge University Press 2004

This publication is in copyright. Subject to statutory exception
and to the provisions of relevant collective licensing agreements,
no reproduction of any part may take place without the written
permission of Cambridge University Press.

First published 2004
Third printing 2006
This digitally printed version 2009

A catalogue record for this publication is available from the British Library

Library of Congress Cataloguing in Publication data
Milton and gender / edited by Catherine Gimelli Martin.
p. cm.
Includes bibliographical references and index.
ISBN 0 521 84130 5
1. Milton, John, 1608–1674 – Political and social views. 2. Feminism and literature – England – History – 17th century. 3. Women and literature – England – History – 17th century. 4. Milton, John, 1608–1674 – Relations with women. 5. Milton, John, 1608–1674 – Characters – Women. 6. Sex role in literature. 7. Women in literature.
I. Martin, Catherine Gimelli.
PR3592.F45M7 2004
821'.4 – dc22 2004051860

ISBN 978-0-521-84130-6 Hardback
ISBN 978-0-521-12370-9 Paperback

Cambridge University Press has no responsibility for the persistence or
accuracy of URLs for external or third-party internet websites referred to in
this publication, and does not guarantee that any content on such websites is,
or will remain, accurate or appropriate.

Contents

List of illustrations — *page* vii
Notes on contributors — viii
Acknowledgments — xii
Abbreviations — xiii

Introduction: Milton's gendered subjects — 1
Catherine Gimelli Martin

PART I MASCULINITY, DIVORCE, AND MISOGYNY IN MILTON'S PROSE

1   The gender of civic virtue — 19
    Gina Hausknecht

2   The aesthetics of divorce: "masculinism," idolatry, and poetic authority in *Tetrachordon* and *Paradise Lost* — 34
    James Grantham Turner

3   Dalila, misogyny, and Milton's Christian liberty of divorce — 53
    Catherine Gimelli Martin

PART II THE GENDERED SUBJECTS OF MILTON'S MAJOR POEMS

4   The profession of virginity in *A Maske Presented at Ludlow Castle* — 77
    William Shullenberger

5   The genders of God and the redemption of the flesh in *Paradise Lost* — 95
    Marshall Grossman

6	Transported touch: the fruit of marriage in *Paradise Lost* John Rogers	115
7	The experience of defeat: Milton and some female contemporaries Elizabeth M. Sauer	133
8	Samson and surrogacy Amy Boesky	153
9	"I was his nursling once": nation, lactation, and the Hebraic in *Samson Agonistes* Rachel Trubowitz	167
10	"The Jewish Question" and "The Woman Question" in *Samson Agonistes*: gender, religion, and nation Achsah Guibbory	184

PART III GENDERED SUBJECTIVITY IN MILTON'S LITERARY HISTORY

11	George Eliot as a "Miltonist": marriage and Milton in *Middlemarch* Dayton Haskin	207
12	Saying it with flowers: Jane Giraud's ecofeminist *Paradise Lost* (1846) Wendy Furman-Adams and Virginia James Tufte	223
13	Woolf's allusion to *Comus* in *The Voyage Out* Lisa Low	254

Index 271

Illustrations

1. Jane Giraud, title page, *The Flowers of Milton* — page 224
2. Jane Giraud, family photo — 227
3. Jane Giraud, title page, *Floral Months of England* — 231
4. Jane Giraud, "Earth felt the wound," from *The Flowers of Milton* — 236
5. Jane Giraud, "Bower 1," from *The Flowers of Milton* — 238
6. Jane Giraud, "Bower 2," from *The Flowers of Milton* — 239
7. Jane Giraud, "Awake!" from *The Flowers of Milton* — 241
8. Jane Giraud, "Let us divide our labors," from *The Flowers of Milton* — 242
9. Jane Giraud, "Eve among her flowers," from *The Flowers of Milton* — 244
10. Jane Giraud, "Eve and the serpent," from *The Flowers of Milton* — 245
11. Jane Giraud, "Flowers were the couch," from *The Flowers of Milton* — 247
12. Jane Giraud, "Euphrasy and rue," from *The Flowers of Milton* — 248

Notes on contributors

AMY BOESKY is an Associate Professor of English at Boston College, Massachusetts. She is the author of *Founding Fictions: Utopias in Early Modern England*, and has published articles on Milton and other subjects in *Texas Studies in Language and Literature* (*TSLL*), *English Literary History* (*ELH*), *Milton Studies*, and *Modern Philology*. She is currently writing a book on time, technology, and the body in early modern England.

WENDY FURMAN-ADAMS is Professor of English at Whittier College, California. Her publications – many written collaboratively with Virginia Tufte – have dealt mainly with *Paradise Lost* as an illustrated poem and have appeared in such venues as *Milton Studies*, *Milton Quarterly*, and *Huntington Library Quarterly*. She also co-edited *Renaissance Readings: Intertext and Context* (with Maryanne Cline Horowitz), and *Riven Unities: Authority and Experience, Self and Other in Milton's Poetry* (with William Shullenberger). Her chapter in this volume is part of an ongoing collaborative book-length study, tentatively entitled "Revisions: Women Artists Reading Milton."

MARSHALL GROSSMAN is Professor of English at the University of Maryland. He is the author of *The Story of all Things: Writing the Self in English Renaissance Narrative Poetry* and *"Authors to Themselves": Milton and the Revelation of History*, and editor of *Aemilia Lanyer: Gender, Genre and the Canon*. His current projects are *The Seventeenth Century*, for the Blackwell Guide to English Literature series, and an edited collection of essays on reading and ethics in the Renaissance.

ACHSAH GUIBBORY is Professor of English at the University of Illinois, Champaign-Urbana. The author of numerous articles on seventeenth-century literature as well as *The Map of Time* and *Ceremony and Community from Herbert to Milton: Literature, Religion, and Cultural Conflicts in*

Seventeenth-Century England, she is writing a book on the uses of Judaism in seventeenth-century England and editing *The Cambridge Companion to John Donne*.

DAYTON HASKIN, Professor of English at Boston College, Massachusetts, is the author of *Milton's Burden of Interpretation* (Pennsylvania, 1994). He has written several essays on Milton and gender, including "Choosing the Better Part with Mary and with Ruth," in the collection called *Of Poetry and Politics: New Essays on Milton and His World*. A member of the Advisory Board for The Variorum Edition of John Donne, he has been working on the ways in which Donne is lodged in the literary history of the nineteenth and twentieth centuries.

GINA HAUSKNECHT is an Associate Professor of English at Coe College, in Cedar Rapids, Iowa where she teaches British Renaissance literature and gender studies. Her work on early modern masculinity includes a recent *Huntington Library Quarterly* article on husbands in Stuart marriage advice literature. She also has published in areas far afield from Milton: girls in contemporary popular culture, pedagogy, and technology, and Shakespearean adaptation and appropriation in central Europe and elsewhere.

LISA LOW is a Milton and Woolf scholar. She has published a number of articles on Virginia Woolf and is co-editor with Anthony Harding of *Milton, the Metaphysicals, and Romanticism*.

CATHERINE GIMELLI MARTIN is the author of *The Ruins of Allegory: "Paradise Lost" and the Metamorphosis of Epic Convention*, and the recipient of the Milton Society's James Holly Hanford Award (1999). She has also published numerous essays on Milton, Donne, Shakespeare, Marvell, and Bacon, often in conjunction with early modern science and philosophy. She is currently co-editing a volume commemorating the quadracentennial of Bacon's *Advancement of Learning: Advancement 2005*. Two completed book manuscripts are forthcoming: "Milton among the Puritans" and "Proteus Unbound: The Poetics of the Baconian revolution." She is a Professor of English at the University of Memphis and a 2003–2004 Francis Bacon Foundation Fellow at the Huntington Library.

JOHN ROGERS teaches English at Yale University. The author of *The Matter of Revolution: Science, Poetry, and Politics in the Age of Milton*, as well as other studies of seventeenth-century literary and cultural topics,

Rogers is currently writing a book about Milton's failure to write about the crucifixion, which examines the poet's literary and theological work in the context of early modern antitrinitarianism. The book is tentatively entitled "Milton's Passion."

ELIZABETH M. SAUER is Professor of English at Brock University, Canada, where she holds a Chancellor's Chair for Research Excellence. She has authored *Barbarous Dissonance and Images of Voice in Milton's Epics* and has just completed *Paper-protestations and Textual Communities in England*. She has also edited the following books: *Imperialisms: Historical and Literary Investigations 1500–1900*, co-edited with Balachandra Rajan; *Reading Early Modern Women*, co-edited with Helen Ostovich; *Books and Readers in Early Modern England: Material Studies*, co-edited with Jennifer Andersen; *Literature and Religion in Early Modern England*, co-edited with Jennifer Andersen (special issue of *Renaissance and Reformation*); *Milton and the Imperial Vision*, co-edited with Balachandra Rajan, and winner of the Milton Society of America Irene Samuel Award; and *Agonistics: Arenas of Creative Contest*, co-edited with Janet Lungstrum. Sauer has published in such journals as *Milton Studies* and *Prose Studies*, and was recently awarded a Social Sciences and Humanities Research Canada Council Grant (2003–6) to complete "Toleration and Milton's 'Peculiar' Nation." "Osiris and Urania: Milton and the Climates of Reading," edited by her, is in submission.

WILLIAM SHULLENBERGER is the Joseph Campbell Chair in the Humanities at Sarah Lawrence College, Bronxville, New York. He has published miscellaneous poetry, as well as essays in various collections and journals on Milton, Herbert, Donne, Vaughan, Wordsworth, Keats, and Dickinson, and has co-authored, with Bonnie Shullenberger, *Africa Time: Two Scholars' Season in Uganda*.

RACHEL TRUBOWITZ is Associate Professor at the University of New Hampshire, Durham. She has published essays on a variety of early modern topics. Her most recent publication is "Sublime/Pauline: Denying Death in *Paradise Lost*," in *Imagining Death in Spenser and Milton*, ed. Elizabeth J. Bellamy, Patrick G. Cheney, and Michael C. Schoenfeldt.

VIRGINIA JAMES TUFTE is Professor Emerita of English at the University of Southern California. Her publications include *The Grammar of Style*, *The Poetry of Marriage*, and *Changing Images of the Family*, in addition to her numerous articles on Milton (most, though not all, co-authored with Wendy Furman-Adams). She has written and produced a video-biography of Carlotta Petrina, who illustrated *Paradise Lost* in 1937. Tufte and Furman-Adams are working on a book-length study, "Re-Vision: Women Artists Reading Milton."

JAMES GRANTHAM TURNER teaches at the University of California, Berkeley, and has authored four books: *The Politics of Landscape: Rural Scenery and Society in English Poetry, 1630–60*; *One Flesh: Paradisal Marriage and Sexual Relations in the Age of Milton*; *Libertines and Radicals in Early Modern London: Sexuality, Politics, and Literary Culture, 1630–1685*; *Schooling Sex: Libertine Literature and Erotic Education in Italy, France, and England, 1534–1685*. He also co-edited, with David Loewenstein, *Politics, Poetics, and Hermeneutics in Milton's Prose*. His keynote address to the Milton Society of America, "Elisions and Erasures," appeared in *Milton Quarterly* 30 (1996).

Acknowledgments

This volume has profited from the helpful advice and encouragement of Joan Bennett, Stella Revard, David Loewenstein, and Victoria Kahn, who either suggested potential contributors or cogent revisions of the introductory chapter, or simply supplied much needed green flags at crucial junctures. Special thanks also go to Nigel Smith and Graham Parry, who organized the 1998 International Milton Symposium in York, England, where the core chapters of this volume were assembled. Not only the authors of these chapters – Amy Boesky, Dayton Haskin, Gina Hausknecht, and Rachel Trubowitz – but all of the subsequent contributors should also be thanked for their exceptional willingness to expand and revise their essays to fit the special requirements of this volume. Without exception, the collaborative process proved a richly rewarding and truly educational experience. And because the project was conducted with minimal institutional support, the internal support of my closest scholarly friends and relatives has been more invaluable than I can possibly say. In that category, William Shullenberger, Julie Solomon, Marshall Grossman, Wendy Furman-Adams, and Richard Martin stand out for reasons that they alone know best.

Abbreviations

AV	*Authorized Version*
CPW	*Complete Prose Works of John Milton*, gen. ed. Don M. Wolfe, 8 vols. (New Haven: Yale University Press, 1953–82)
CW	*The Works of John Milton*, ed. Frank Allen Patterson, 18 vols. (New York: Columbia University Press, 1931–38)
DDD	*Doctrine and Discipline of Divorce*
Hughes	Non-poetic prose citations or commentary
OED	*Oxford English Dictionary*
PL	*Paradise Lost*
PR	*Paradise Regained*
SA	*Samson Agonistes*

References to the prose works are given by volume and page number, references to *Paradise Lost* and *Paradise Regained* are given by book and line numbers. Unless otherwise noted, Milton's poetry is cited from Merritt Y. Hughes, *John Milton, Complete Poems and Major Prose* (New York: Odyssey Press, 1957).

Introduction: Milton's gendered subjects

Catherine Gimelli Martin

Milton's treatment of women, marriage, and divorce in his life and works has been subject to criticism almost as long as his major works themselves. Ever since Samuel Johnson's famous *Life* of the poet, the charge that the great advocate of mutuality in marriage bore a "Turkish contempt" for women has survived, and, in the twentieth century, actually thrived. Yet this claim would no doubt have astonished both the poet himself and his contemporaries, the most critical of whom regarded his views on women and marriage as libertine, not retrograde. As Ruth Mohl points out, the poet's early *Commonplace Book* also disproves "Milton's proverbial disesteem for women." Its many laudatory remarks upon the "weaker sex" include tributes to such admirable women as Queen Elizabeth, Tasso's heroine Sophronia, Lady Scroope, the wife of Edward I, Queen Martia, and the Countesse of Arundel. Even more significantly, these tributes characteristically counterbalance the "less complimentary . . . contentions of those writers who would discredit women altogether" (*CPW* 1:357). Yet then as now, these attitudes have proved far less controversial than his defense of divorce "at pleasure." His contemporaries considered this thesis no less scandalous than his defense of regicide: at worst, he was the spokesman of the radical new sect of divorcers; at best, his new notion of marriage as a spiritual rather than a physical bond seemed ludicrously utopian. Yet ironically, now that most moderns agree with Milton's once radical belief that the marriage is not a sacramental "seal" but a negotiable contract, his views on this and related gendered subjects are generally regarded as ultra-traditionalist, patriarchal, or masculinist rather than prophetic or progressive.

This volume aims to reconsider this and related charges in the light of the most recent developments in feminist theory. In the process, it will also reconsider why Johnson's high Tory insinuations about the innate hypocrisy of this notorious libertarian have been taken over by liberal feminists whose political agenda actually seems closer to Milton's own.[1] As several of this

1

book's contributors suggest, one reason may be that, with very few exceptions, his most hostile feminist critics have specialized in later literary epochs when the "woman question" was posed in quite different terms than it was in Milton's day. Nevertheless, the strongly argued positions of scholars like Christine Froula, Sandra Gilbert, and Susan Gubar have clearly left their mark upon mainline Milton criticism, which remains deeply divided over their conclusion that his works are staunchly antifeminist. Yet again, a great number of his works superficially seem to refute this critique: ten sonnets and an epitaph eloquently testify to his high esteem for female friends, acquaintances, and performers, including a beloved and deeply lamented late wife.[2] His first major poem idealistically incarnates feminine virtue in a youthful heroine and a water nymph who single-handedly fend off depraved masculine vice during the course of their atypical courtly masque. His later epic tributes to the mother of mankind and her true "daughter" Mary similarly laud the high intelligence and virtue of womankind, although his portrait of Eve is necessarily complicated by her role in initiating "man's first disobedience." Yet unlike John Donne, Milton does *not* present Adam's marriage to Eve as "our funeral," nor does he believe that her daughters follow her example in killing "us all . . . one by one" (*The First Anniversarie*, 106–7). On the contrary, Milton upholds the self-sufficient and the *almost* untarnished honor of womankind's "original" in much the same spirit that he cultivated cordial friendships with her daughters. Besides the subjects of his sonnets, these daughters include contemporaries like Lady Ranelagh – the brilliant sister of Robert Boyle, the mother of his pupil, Edward Jones, and quite probably a life-saving defender during the dark days of the early Restoration; his sister Anne Phillips and her two children, who similarly defended him during these years and long before; and at least two of his three wives.

Yet the negative side of the balance cannot be gainsaid: Milton's first marriage to Mary Powell was both a private and (in the wake of his divorce tracts) a public disaster, which, after an apparently uneasy reconciliation, finally left him a widower unable to cope with at least two of their three daughters. While the youngest of the three still harbored fond memories of her father when Johnson's contemporaries sought to reward her "national service" in assisting his literary endeavors, both the questionable nature of this less-than-voluntary service and the unquestionable resentment of the elder daughters continue to lend credence to Johnson's claims. Yet neither this failed "family romance" nor the high Tory critic himself ever cast so dark a shadow on Milton's idealistic literary portraits of women as his own divorce tracts. Written in the heat of emotion surrounding Mary's unexpected desertion after a month of marriage, these pamphlets betray strongly conflicted beliefs about the rights and responsibilities of women caught in failed marriages. All too often, their lofty sentiments about the "gladsome conversation" that sustains well-matched unions are undermined by bitter complaints about the "grinding" emotional and sexual stress suffered by ill-matched marriage mates – victims usually gendered male (*CPW* 2:258). Couched as they are in once widely shared biblical assumptions about the "natural" priority of the male in marriage, the divorce tracts strongly jar with modern sensibilities on that subject as well. The modern reader's perception of Milton's bias is further compounded by the biting sarcasm and obviously injured pride that repeatedly erupt in these treatises, although a good deal of this rhetoric originally seems to have been aimed at uncovering the unselfconscious hypocrisy of his male audience. Given their commonly held principle of Christian liberty, Milton attempts to startle these male contemporaries into realizing how inconsistent and unjust it is to subordinate God's "primary" creation (man) to his secondary creation (woman) by demanding that he endure a permanent state of marital discord and mental bondage. For as most readers would now agree, such purely physical unions can foster neither the emotional, the spiritual, nor (ironically) even the physical well-being of either party. Although this conclusion is hardly alien to modern feminists, most have found his argument not only unattractive but insincere. Like their many male sympathizers, they contend that Milton's passionate defensiveness shows that his "real" purpose was to convict either his first wife, women in general, or even heterosexuality in general of selfishly promoting male thralldom.

Yet, once again, the case cannot be considered closed. Not only did Milton's argument strongly appeal to contemporary feminists, who appreciated his subtle deployment of the logic of Pauline headship against itself, but they immediately put it to work in releasing themselves from domestic bondage.[3] Male readers, too, soon realized the power of this argument – and feared it, since it clearly threatened their traditional authority over their wives. In fact, even some of Milton's harshest modern critics readily concede that he was indeed trying to formulate an early version of "no fault" divorce. Yet since most of these critics remain convinced that these prophetic efforts were undermined by a potent combination of Pauline doctrine and Milton's own "masculinist" pride, his attempt to absolve divorce from all taint of sin is generally seen as a failure and the poet remains guilty as charged.[4]

Given the current state of the argument, the contributors to this volume are fully aware of the immense difficulty involved in decoding Milton's "real" views on gender. The task is obviously complicated not just by the density of his texts themselves but also by our vast distance from his social and intellectual milieu. This distance is proportionately increased in the wake of the strong influence that "second wave" or post-1970s feminism has generally exerted on literary studies, especially where women, marriage, and divorce are concerned. Writing in 1970, John Halkett could still safely conclude that both the divorce tracts and *Paradise Lost* presented consistently progressive views on the subject. Not very long afterward, most critics were ready to agree with the position presented in Sandra Gilbert and Susan Gubar's *Madwoman in the Attic* (1979): that Milton's views on women were at best inconsistent, and at worst, consistently masculinist. Since then, Diane McColley in *Milton's Eve* (1983) and Joseph Wittreich in *Feminist Milton* (1987) have forcefully challenged this consensus by deepening our critical awareness of the latent anachronisms lurking in the Gilbert/Gubar position, which fails to account for the long *durée* of literary history.[5] Reconsidering the long history of literary iconography surrounding Eve, McColley showed that Milton's portrait of our "grand mother" effectively reversed a thoroughly misogynistic tradition. Reconsidering the "reader responses" of eighteenth- and nineteenth-century women, Wittreich showed that they continued to regard Milton's female portraits as positive role models. However, as he also showed, from the mid nineteenth century onward, "first wave" feminists became increasingly suspicious of the "angel of the hearth" roles associated with Milton's Eve, and by the time "second wave" feminists came along in the 1970s, these suspicions had turned into active disdain.

Yet by now what we might call a "third wave" of feminist critics has become increasingly sensitized to the historical/particular conditions of marriage, divorce, and patriarchal domination in western culture, conditions which create a vast gulf between the social, legal, and political condition of seventeenth-century women and those of their Victorian daughters. Seventeenth- century women not only participated in the most radical phase of Reformation and early revolutionary culture in ways that Victorian women did not, but they also helped to initiate the wholesale rethinking of marriage and the family in which Milton actively participated. Since these gains were not lost until the neo-traditionalist reaction set in after the Restoration and especially after the eighteenth century, a less linear model of gender history would now seem to be in order. This volume not only seeks to take this more accurate historiography into account but also to explore alternatives to the heavily Freudian and implicitly anti-feminine accounts of gender dominance employed by critics like Gilbert, Gubar, and their "mentor" Harold Bloom. These alternatives range from Lacan's

Introduction: Milton's gendered subjects

rewriting of Freud (Shullenberger in this volume) to Heidegger's ontological mediations (Grossman in this volume).[6] Other contributors use other new theoretical tools to various ends, but all respond to a perceived need to reassess Milton's treatment of gendered subjects and subjectivity. In general, these newer accounts are directly or indirectly indebted to the productive rethinking of the organic, shifting, and interdependent economy of human selfhood, embodiment, and desire begun by French feminists and vigorously pursued by their American followers. By refusing to view femininity and masculinity as essentialist binary oppositions, theorists like Julia Kristeva and Luce Irigaray seminally foregrounded the linguistic processes that construct and mediate them over time.

Generally speaking, the authors whose work takes up the first two sections of this book pursue a wide range of variations on this basic linguistic approach – philosophical, spiritual, medical, and political – while those in the third section are more interested in documenting the responses of real historical women to Milton's life and art. Both groups thus produce a long overdue reexamination of the inaccurate assumptions, and, in some cases, even the historical-contextual "facts" implicit in second-wave feminism's view of the poet. The chapters in the first two sections generally accomplish this by considering how, when, and why gendered language interacts with and partially constructs its historical milieu, while those in the third and final section consider how and why Milton was "good for women" over the long *durée*. Although Julia Walker's 1988 volume on *Milton and the Idea of Woman* presented a considerable range of opinion on the latter topic, the strong influence of Gilbert and Gubar and/or of second-wave feminism on most of its writers left readers with the "traditional" misogynistic portrait of the poet largely intact. Since some of the current volume's contributors defend this portrait and others dispute it, this collection provides a broader ideological as well as textual spectrum of opinion on both Milton's poetry and his prose. A broader textual spectrum is supplied by devoting its first section to his prose works (with some attention to poetry), its second section to the major poems (with some attention to prose), and its final section to the historical responses of women readers from the early nineteenth century through Virginia Woolf. While no new consensus emerges here, the volume's pluralistic approach has the great advantage of allowing readers to make up their own minds about all of Milton's gendered subjects.

However, before briefly summarizing the various approaches taken by the volume's contributors, it will be useful to survey some of the twentieth-century scholarship on seventeenth-century women to which the present collection generally responds. In the earlier half of the century, before the onset of second-wave feminism and after the "first wave" of the suffragette era, Milton's civil war and gender politics had been largely rehabilitated from the Johnsonian critiques of T. S. Eliot and F. R. Leavis by a resurgence of Puritan scholarship. Relying especially on William and Malleville Hallers' work, historians began to link Milton's "proto-modern" view of marriage to the libertarian or radical wing of the Puritan movement. Michael Walzer's classic 1965 study of *The Revolution of the Saints* was typical in claiming that while Puritans officially upheld the traditional secondary status of women, their attitudes toward women and marriage were inherently progressive:

Puritan writers insisted upon the inferiority of the female, but nevertheless recognized in her the potential saint: "Souls have no sexes," wrote Robert Bolton. "In the better part they are both men." Marriage between two saints would be a "spiritual union" and not, in Milton's terms, "the prescribed satisfaction of an irrational heat." The new Puritan view of women, then, entailed a new view of marriage. Founded on a voluntary contract, it was directed in some fashion toward "healthful pleasures and profitable commodities." This was to make the choice of a partner far more important than it had ever been before – and a bad choice, as Milton was to learn, far more disastrous.

Yet Walzer is hedging here, since he knew that few if any Puritans followed Milton's sudden leap to the radical conclusion that "spiritual unions" implied: that marriage partners should be free to divorce whenever such unions were broken or never properly forged. Nor were they ready to follow him in grounding the marital partnership in mental and emotional conversation, but instead located the "new" feminine role in the wife's stronger but still traditional involvement in rearing and educating her children. Further, since the spiritual education of the child was still in the charge of fathers, Walzer far too facilely assumed that this new role would allow the "woman who thus directed her son . . . also [to] direct her husband," and that all women would be happy to become honorary male "souls."[7] Because he also forgot that, ironically *unlike* the Puritans, Milton was relatively uninterested in the wife's role as nurturer and deeply interested in her role as a true soul-mate, he led feminist critics to believe that the poet endorsed the obviously secondary, angel-of-the-hearth role commonly upheld by most of the godly.

This misperception was ably corrected by Halkett, but in the short run, his dissent from the Hallers seems not to have improved the situation. Arguing that Milton's position actually represented a considerable advance on the standard Puritan *and* Anglican view of marriage as mainly for the purposes of procreation and the avoidance of vice, Halkett unintentionally gave Milton's position an even stronger traditionalist cast. For in bypassing the religious manuals of the radical Puritans, Halkett's Milton instead relied upon the elite courtesy tradition of courtship and marriage associated with the Spanish humanist Ludovicus Vives and his royalist followers in England.[8] Although Halkett may have rightly considered these sources more enlightened than the religious manuals, he was not likely to convince a post-1970s feminist that male-authored and/or male-oriented how-to books on ideally "fitting" one's spouse for hearth and home represented a higher ideal. Nor would they be impressed by what Halkett considered Milton's most signal innovation in this tradition: his rejection of the traditional Augustinian view that "Solitariness" was "not a state of mind demanding remedy but a physical handicap" which could be removed by marriage.[9] According to the traditional view, if the marital remedy failed – if a spouse still found himself in a state of "inconsolable" loneliness – the situation was a simple fact of fallen humanity traceable to Eve's tragic inheritance; for ever since the fall, women have always proved more disobedient and less reliable than the male friends whom the disappointed husband should instead seek out.

Milton attempts to overturn this antifeminine tradition by redefining "solitude" as a spiritual rather than a physical condition. He can then argue that whenever a husband discovers that the mate to "whom he lookt to be the copartner of a sweet and gladsome society" has become an "image of melancholy despair," his spiritual impairment *demands* the previously unheard of remedy of divorce. For without it, his "unmeet" or conversationally inaccessible spouse will eventually become a physical curse rather than a blessing. Instead of helping him avoid sexual sin, she will become an "uncomplying discord of nature, or, as it oft happens, . . . an image of earth and phlegm" (*CPW* 2:254) that actually drives him into his neighbor's bed. Of course for moderns, neither this insulting description of unhappy wives nor Milton's "happier" alternative of complete compliance in marital harmony unsettle, but actually reinforce, his stereotypical misogynistic image despite the real improvements he made upon the older tradition. Yet as "sexist" as his rhetoric now seems to modern readers, Milton used precisely the same terms to describe conversationally inaccessible males like the interlocutor addressed in *Colasterion*. Calling his enemy a "fleamy clodd" indelibly fixated on physical "burning" as the only rationale for marriage, the poet sarcastically declares that not even this raging sexual fire will ever "expel the frigidity of his brain" (*CPW* 2:740).

Even so, Milton himself was so fixated on spiritual compatibility that many post-1970s feminists believed that he came dangerously close to demanding a perfect Stepford-type wife. As a result, even when insisting that his doctrine would free women as well as men, and even when reserving his sharpest sarcasm for male contemporaries who clung to the traditional view that women possessed neither the mental nor the spiritual ability to become true "mates," his divorce tracts remained under a deeper cloud than ever. In once again taking up these points in Milton's favor, however, recent scholarship on his sources has not only confirmed Halkett's earlier conclusions but questioned the Stepford-wife image as anachronistic. Although Milton did ground his views of companionate marriage primarily on the secular courtesy books, Gregory Chaplin shows that the erotic Platonic sources enthusiastically praised by the young Milton (Plato's *Phaedrus*, *Symposium*, and their Neoplatonic Italian and Spanish commentators) indeed helped to overturn a long antifeminine tradition of male bonding that continued as late as Montaigne's "On Friendship" and Sir Thomas Browne's *Religio Medici* (1646).[10] Moreover, in a period where silence was still the most "winning" word for women, Elaine Hobby shows that the emphasis on close heterosexual relationships was necessarily left to male courtesy book writers. Obeying traditional constrictions on their social roles, seventeenth-century women wrote about broader issues by alluding to practical matters rather than by joining in candid intellectual debate. The most outspoken of these women tended to be foreigners, aristocrats, or tutors to royalty such as Bathsua Makin, who, even when they did argue for active participation in the political world (usually under male pseudonyms), did not argue for suffrage. Thus as Hobby notes, so long as "Women were constrained by the requirement that they maintain a modest reputation[,] rallying forth with arguments about female excellences, or even female potential, was dangerous and perhaps for most women, unthinkable." In this social context, identifying with the causes of aristocratic women thus signaled a male author's approval of the most progressive female roles available to women during this period.[11]

Yet, as usual, several complex crosscurrents in Milton's writing about gender partially undermine Chaplin's or Hobby's positive reevaluations. In contrast to other liberal Protestants of his age and type, Milton does not anticipate the climate of the coming centuries by attempting to vindicate the feminine gender per se. In response to the *querelle des femmes* begun in 1615 by Joseph Swetnam's *Arraignment of Lewde, Idle, Froward, and Inconstant Women*, he produced no ringing defenses of women like those contributed by Rachel Speght (1617, 1622), Esther Sowernam (1617), or Constantia Munda (1617).[12] He also falls considerably short of the male defense of feminine virtue contributed by his political hero, Robert Greville, Lord Brooke, who clearly saw gender equality as a counterpart to religious toleration:

> Of the Chorus of Saints, the greatest number will bee found amongst the feminine sexe, because these are most naturally of affection, and so most apt to make knowledge reall. It is true, I confesse, these affections misguided, led them first into transgression; but these same affections after, carried them first to the grave, then to the sight of a Saviour, gave them the enwombing of Christ, who (in some sense) might have entertained our nature in another way (if he had so pleased;) and these affections will one day raise many of them into the sweet embraces of everlasting joy.[13]

A similar strain of apologetic appears in John Heydon's contemporary *Advice to a Daughter*, which agrees that women are generally superior to men in charity if also more "frail" in their tendencies toward "misguided affection."[14]

Yet Milton's great epics actually reinforce these defenses in several important respects. In *Paradise Lost*, Eve's worship is equally acceptable to a God who does not grant Adam any priority in offering him hymns of praise, and, as for Brooke, her role in the fall is counterbalanced by Mary's "enwombing" of Christ. Also as in Brooke, Eve's postlapsarian frailty is not so much "crooked" as overly affectionate, as we see from her overeager but "noble" desire to sacrifice herself for Adam, their posterity, or both. In *Paradise Regained*, the portrait of Mary is naturally even more positive and also less traditional insofar as she, not Joseph, serves as her Son's role model. Yet because *Paradise Lost* refuses the falling Eve the excuse of emotional frailty that both Greville and Heydon grant to the "feminine sexe" as a whole, Milton's position on women remains residually ambiguous. This ambiguity chiefly stems from his refusal to mollify either Eve's fall or Dalila's lapse by providing the sentimental justifications characteristic of more conservative contemporaries like John Dryden. Yet in rewriting Milton's Eve in *The State of Innocence* and in rewriting the femme fatale or Dalila role in *All for Love*, Dryden clearly illustrates how sentimentality often serves as a cloak for antifeminism. *Because* women are both emotionally and intellectually inferior to men, for Dryden a "Learned Wife" like Milton's Eve or Dalila is a notorious plague, not an authentic temptation. His most erotically tempting and excusable femme fatale thus turns out to be a silly, overly emotional, "harmless, household dove" like the Cleopatra of his *All for Love*.[15] This retraditionalizing of female roles stands in sharp contrast not only to Milton's strong literary women but also to the earlier efforts of female writers to defend themselves against Swetnam's outright misogyny.

Like Rachel Speght, later female contributors to the mid-century *querelle des femmes* like Bathsua Makin and Margaret Fell strongly espouse the spiritual, educational, *and* ecclesiological worth of women, even though none are willing to reject the Pauline doctrine of headship similarly accepted by the poet of *Paradise Lost*. They thus do *not* demand any broader rights for themselves than those given to Milton's unfallen Eve and (through a dream strangely reminiscent of Speght's) retained by her after the fall. The difference – if there is one – is that Speght's understanding of Eve's fall is actually less generous than Milton's. In her view, "Satan first assailed the woman, because where the hedge is lowest, most easy it is to get over, and she being the weaker vessel was with more facility to be seduced: like as a crystal glass sooner receives a crack than a strong stone pot."[16] Thus while she wittily elevates Eve's "clearer" and finer vessel over Adam's stony "pot," like Brooke, Speght at the same time concedes that the mother of mankind was far more frail than Milton ever made her.[17] In fact, since Milton puts the traditional idea that Eve was the weaker vessel into Satan's mouth (*PL* 9:480–85), it is not clear that he ever endorsed it. The unfallen Adam himself retracts his opinion of Eve's greater vulnerability in the wake of her Areopagitican claim to be "sufficient to have stood, though free to fall," a claim earlier maintained by none other than the Almighty himself (*PL* 3.99). After Adam's prediction proves false and Eve does succumb and "seduces" Adam into joining her, Milton's first husband is still unable to deny Eve's defensive plea that he might have fallen first had he found himself alone with the great Deceiver (*PL* 9.1145–53).

The only equally vigorous contemporary defense of womankind's equal capacity to handle "what was high" (*PL* 8.50) appears in Bathsua Makin's *Essay to Revive the Ancient Education of Gentlewomen, in Religion, Manners, Arts & Tongues* (1673), a work that seems partly inspired by Milton himself. Although we know little about Makin's life or literary influences, her *Essay* follows the lead of Milton's divorce tracts in describing Custom as a quasi-satanic deceiver which blocks both men and especially women from perfecting their intellectual abilities to "glorify God, and answer the end of [their] . . . creation, to be meet helps to [their] . . . husbands." Although strong disparagements of "mere" Custom had become fairly routine throughout the civil wars and especially in the wake of Thomas Sprat's *History of the Royal Society* (1667), Makin's definition of the essence of "meet help" as consisting first in "constant conversation," and *second* in caring for the common household concerns of "family and estate" strongly recalls the divorce tracts' atypical insistence that the physical side of marriage is secondary to spiritual conversation. Intriguingly, her supplementary point that the potential abuses of knowledge are no argument against its free and "necessary or very convenient" circulation also seems to echo the main argument of Milton's *Areopagitica*.[18] Because Makin's brother-in-law, John Pell, had been Milton's Cambridge classmate and remained an acquaintance through the Hartlib circle – a group containing some of *Areopagitica*'s strongest admirers – these probable echoes are quite possibly proof of a very early feminist's approval of Milton's position on women, education, and marriage.

As this example suggests, the "patriarchal" poet's literary influence on women now begins to seem far less overwhelmingly negative than Gilbert and Gubar once maintained. Like its editor, a number of other contributors to this volume critique their position, but, as noted above, others supplement it with new evidence. The full range of critical positions on these general issues is surveyed in the first section on Milton's prose representations of gender. Gina Hausknecht's chapter on "The gender of civic virtue" sets the stage for this discussion by reevaluating the linguistic implications of "masculinist" discourse. Her main argument is that while seventeenth-century writers typically understand "effeminacy" as the opposite of male virtue, at this time effeminacy was not at all equivalent to femininity but rather to immaturity, boyishness, or weakness. The next chapter by James Grantham Turner on "The Aesthetics of divorce: 'masculinism,' idolatry, and poetic authority in *Tetrachordon* and *Paradise Lost*" concedes that neither Milton's divorce tracts nor his epic oppose femininity to "male" virtue or integrity, but then argues that these works so strongly oppose spiritual freedom to "compulsive sexuality" that they effectively reassert the superior integrity of physical masculinity. The third chapter in this introductory triptych takes up this theme in both the divorce tracts and the tragedy of *Samson Agonistes* to argue the opposite case: that by stretching the parameters of Pauline doctrine to the limit, Milton makes both marital failure and spiritual freedom an equal opportunity affair. This chapter by the volume's editor also confronts the Johnsonian "myth" of Miltonic misogyny revived by Gilbert and Gubar, a myth to which a number of other chapters later return.

The second section centers on Milton's representation of women, gender, and femininity in the major poems, with additional attention to the major prose works. William Shullenberger's introductory chapter on Milton's earliest long poem, "The profession of virginity in *A Maske Presented at Ludlow Castle*," proposes that the masque ruptures the dramatic conventions of the genre in order to give his Lady powers normally associated with male ego-formation and selfhood. Marshall Grossman's following chapter on "The genders of God and the redemption of the flesh in *Paradise Lost*" surveys the quasi-Heideggerian ruptures and sutures that characterize the representation of divine "gender" in Milton's creation poetry. This study is followed by John Rogers's discussion of "Transported touch: the fruit of marriage in *Paradise Lost*," which innovatively uses Milton's *Christian Doctrine* to gloss his ambivalent epic representation of marriage. A final chapter on *Paradise Lost* by Elizabeth M. Sauer – "The experience of defeat: Milton and some female contemporaries" – surveys significant resonances between Milton's representation of the fall and the experience of radical women dissenters who similarly mourned their post-Restoration political defeat. This chapter is followed by three highly dialectical essays on *Samson Agonistes*, currently Milton's most controversial work. The positive pole of opinion is well represented by Amy Boesky's analysis of "Samson and surrogacy," which restates the traditional "regenerationist" view of the drama by discussing Samson as a quasi-maternal surrogate in the rebirth of his defeated people. Rachel Trubowitz and Achsah Guibbory challenge this view from two very distinct perspectives. In "'I was his nursling once': nation, lactation, and the Hebraic in *Samson Agonistes*," Trubowitz argues that Milton ultimately abandons the "feminine" cause of national identity for a more masculine universalism; while in "'The Jewish Question' and 'The Woman Question' in *Samson Agonistes*: Gender, Religion, and Nation," Guibbory more strongly stresses the negative side of the balance by arguing that the drama represents a distinctly anti-Judaic, antifeminine form of English nationalism.

The final section offers less conflicted but equally dialogic views on how later women writers related to Milton. In "George Eliot as a 'Miltonist': marriage and Milton in *Middlemarch*," Dayton Haskin surveys Eliot's transgendered and highly Miltonic views on divorce. He also cites what was to be a companion chapter in this volume, Anna Nardo's exploration of the mythical "Stories of Milton's Serviceable Daughters," which is now a chapter in Nardo's book-length study of Eliot and Milton.[19] Both authors explore the historical basis of the Gilbert/Gubar thesis, but Haskin's convincing rebuttal of their claim that Milton necessarily stifled literary daughters like George Eliot especially anticipates Lisa Low's reexamination of the same claim in her chapter in this volume on Virginia "Woolf's allusion to *Comus* in *The Voyage Out*." In between these two chapters, Wendy Furman-Adams and Virginia James Tufte's chapter on "Saying it with flowers: Jane Giraud's ecofeminist *Paradise Lost*" discusses positive appropriations of Milton's "ecofemininism" by the Victorian artist Jane Giraud. As Furman-Adams and Tufte show, Giraud was clearly in touch with "first-phase" modern feminism shared by Eliot, and, to a considerable extent, Woolf herself. As this brief summary indicates, all the chapters in this volume present powerful scholarly (re)evaluations of Milton's positions on nature and nationhood, modernity, marriage, divorce, and gender. Because many of the chapters included here were originally presented at the Sixth International Milton Symposium in York, England, in 1999, the editor would like to thank Graham Parry and Nigel Smith for presenting the forum where the core of the volume coalesced.

NOTES

1. Annabel Patterson usefully analyzes the unconscious "collusion" between Milton's conservative critics (Johnson, Coleridge, and T. S. Eliot) and his more liberal or even radical "apologists" in *Reading between the Lines* (Madison: University of Wisconsin Press, 1993) 244–52. On the gender question itself, hoewver, she largely concurs with the "masculinist" consensus on Milton (276–97).
2. Despite William Riley Parker's argument that this wife was Mary Powell, who also died in childbirth, most scholars continue to believe that the sonnet (usually numbered 23) refers to Milton's second wife, Katherine Woodcock, who died so tragically soon after their wedding.
3. On the infamous Mrs. Attaway who immediately used Milton's *Doctrine and Discipline of Divorce* to effect a spiritual divorce from her "unfit" spouse, see Nathaniel H. Henry, "Who Meant Licence When They Cried Liberty?" *Modern Language Notes (MLN)* 66 (1951): 509–13.
4. See, for instance, James Grantham Turner in this volume, and also in *One Flesh: Paradisal Marriage and Sexual Relations in the Age of Milton* (Oxford: Clarendon Press, 1987). Stephen Fallon acknowledges Milton's "no fault" concept of divorce in "The Spur of Self-Concernment: Milton in His Divorce Tracts" *Milton Studies* 38 ed. Albert C. Labriola and Michael Lieb (2000): 220–42. Yet he here also retreats from his more favorable reading of the divorce tracts in his earlier essay on "The Metaphysics of Milton's Divorce Tracts," in *Politics, Poetics, and Hermeneutics in Milton's Prose*, ed. David Loewenstein and James Grantham Turner (Cambridge: Cambridge University Press, 1990), 69–83.
5. John Halkett, *Milton and the Idea of Matrimony: A Study in the Divorce Tracts and "Paradise Lost"* (New Haven: Yale University Press, 1970); Sandra M. Gilbert and Susan Gubar, *The Madwoman in the Attic: The Woman Writer and the Nineteenth-Century Literary Imagination*, 2nd. edn. (New Haven: Yale University Press, 1984) 187–221. Diane McColley, *Milton's Eve* (Urbana: University of Illinois Press, 1983); and Joseph A. Wittreich, *Feminist Milton* (Ithaca: Cornell University Press, 1987).

6. For additional applications of Lacanian psychology (which both Kristeva and Irigaray at once employ and critique) to Milton, see Marshall Grossman, "The Rhetoric of Feminine Priority in *Paradise Lost*," *English Literary Renaissance* (*ELR*) 32 (2002), and chapter 6 in Catherine Gimelli Martin, *The Ruins of Allegory: "Paradise Lost" and the Metamorphosis of Epic Convention* (Durham: Duke University Press, 1998), 267–78.
7. Michael Walzer, *The Revolution of the Saints: A Study in the Origins of Radical Politics* (Cambridge, MA: Harvard University Press, 1965), 193.
8. Halkett, *Milton and the Idea of Matrimony*, 4–7, 24–30.
9. *Ibid.*, 14–16. His main thesis is further confirmed by James Grantham Turner's important study, *One Flesh*, which shows that Milton's thinking on marriage (if not on divorce) is much more liberal than that of most Protestant thinkers, mainline or mystical.
10. Gregory Chaplin, "'One Flesh, One Heart, One Soul': Renaissance Friendship and Miltonic Marriage," *Modern Philology* (*MP*) 99.2 (2001): 266–92. However, Chaplin overlooks Sir Thomas Browne's defense of this tradition in *Religio Medici*, part 2, section 9, which refers to woman as but the "rib and crooked piece of man" made only for his "twelfth part," while man is made for the "whole world."
11. Elaine Hobby, "A Woman's Best Setting-out is Silence: the Writings of Hannah Wooley," in *Culture and Society in the Stuart Restoration: Literature, Drama, History*, ed. Gerald Maclean (Cambridge: Cambridge University Press, 1995), 186, 188–89, 193–94.
12. These defenses are collected in *First Feminists: British Women Writers 1578–1799*, ed. Moira Ferguson (Bloomington: Indiana University Press, 1985).
13. Robert Greville, Lord Brooke, *The Nature of Truth* (London: R. Bishop, 1641), 68–69.
14. Quoted in Halkett, *Milton and the Idea of Matrimony*, 76, 78.
15. For Dryden's translation of Juvenal's Sixth Satire in "The Learned Wife," see *The Broadview Anthology of Seventeenth-Century Verse and Prose*, ed. Alan Rudrum, Joseph Black, and Holly Faith Nelson (Petersborough, Canada: Broadview Press, 2000), 1003. Given that Dryden's marriage was far less happy than any of Milton's, there seems little doubt that his translation choice clearly reflects his own view of women. His sentimentalized Cleopatra declares herself (and is accepted as) a "silly, harmless, household dove" in *All for Love* Act 4, sc.1, 92.
16. Rachel Speght, *A Muzzle for Melastomus, the Cynical Baiter of, and foul mouthed Barker against Eve's Sex* (1617), rpt. in *The Broadview Anthology*, 399. As Alinda Sumers points out in a forthcoming essay, Milton reverses this defense by making Eve more "earthy" but also more "graceful" than Adam in a wholly positive sense, since her origin in "cordial spirits warm" with "Life-blood" (*PL* 8.466–67) near his heart seems to give her a greater life force.
17. For a very different evaluation of Speght's position in relationship to Milton's, see Desma Polydorou, "Gender and Spiritual Equality in Marriage: A Dialogic

Reading of Rachel Speght and John Milton," *Milton Quarterly* 35.1 (2001): 22–32.
18. Bathsua Makin, *An Essay to Revive the Ancient Education of Gentlewomen, in Religion, Manners, Arts & Tongues*, in *The Broadview Anthology*, 425–27, 430.
19. Anna K. Nardo, *George Eliot's Dialogue with John Milton* (Columbia: University of Missouri Press, 2003.)

PART I

Masculinity, divorce, and misogyny in Milton's prose

CHAPTER 1

The gender of civic virtue

Gina Hausknecht

Throughout the political and ecclesiastical turmoil of the 1640s Milton observes and laments encroachments on liberty in church government, the family, and monarchy; again and again he deplores the loss of manhood which accompanies and characterizes acquiescence to these institutions. The ideal citizen of Milton's political prose is inevitably not just male but masculine in ways that are less about the performance of power over others than about individual choices between authority and submission. Such is the stuff of daily life in the free yet always hierarchical society which Milton envisions throughout the prose and poetry. The divorce tracts cast in domestic form the reconciliation of the theory of equal native liberty with the theory of naturally unequal capacities. In doing so, they anticipate the logical underpinnings of Milton's political vision in *The Tenure of Kings and Magistrates* and *Eikonoklastes* and, especially, the republicanism of *The Readie and Easie Way to Establish a Free Commonwealth*: in writing about both marriage and monarchy, Milton argues that consent alone legitimates binding human relationships. The implicit hero of these arguments is a figure near despair at his society's embrace of the tyranny of custom but adamant in his pursuit of a social organization founded on reason and liberty. This explicitly masculine heroism is, in Milton's terms, about courageous self-management and articulation, about the mind, and very specifically not about the body. Manliness represents for Milton the ability to discern correctly where one stands, when to submit and when to refuse, when and how to give consent. Because masculinity is formed through the exclusionary processes of opposition, it is inherently unstable, a tension felt perhaps most palpably in the divorce tracts' conflicted treatment of wives. Yet the oppositions Milton employs to construct a morally and ideologically freighted masculine ideal are not chiefly the familiar modern gender binary of male and female, and they do not preempt the possibility of women embodying that ideal.

The divorce and anti-monarchical tracts valorize the rational individual who stands against the reasonless restraints of his culture. The opening of *The Tenure* – "If men within themselves would be govern'd by reason, and not generally give up thir understanding to a double tyrannie, of Custom from without, and blind affections within, they would discerne better, what it is to favour and uphold the Tyrant of a Nation" (*CPW* 3:190) – echoes *The Doctrine and Discipline of Divorce*'s Custome and Error allegory and gives us the foundational Miltonic idea: if individuals can be freed from the shackles of inner and outer corruption, they will discover their capacity for rational self-rule. Reason is, for Milton, gendered: a free Commonwealth, he declares in *The Readie and Easie Way*, is "the noblest, the manliest, the equallest, the justest government" (*CPW* 7:424). This note is struck throughout the political prose: good citizens are manly; bad citizens are groveling and lack self-respect. Yet to be manly is not simply to be male. Manliness requires social and moral maturity. Men giving themselves up to be ruled by a king are described, with loathing, as "more like boyes under age then men" (*CPW* 7:427). Reason is a property of mature masculinity and masculinity is itself a virtue, characteristic not of biological sex but of merit.

Manliness, as Milton uses this and related terms in the prose, is about being transformed by desire, not for women or for sex or for dominance over others, but for liberty.[1] The seventeenth-century commonplace of the household as a miniature state encourages men to understand themselves as guardians and conservators of power, as in William Whately's typical formula: "a just, wise and mild government, is government indeed, causing the husband to be as it were a little God in the family, a weake resemblance of the large and unlimited soverigntie."[2] In Milton's exhortations, however, real men resist the guardians and conservators of power. The figure of the husband as a subject, not a ruler, points toward what is formally radical about the divorce tracts. In *The Doctrine* Milton laments the passivity of his age: "we literally superstitious through customary faintnes of heart, not venturing to peirce with our free thoughts into the full latitude of nature and religion, abandon our selvs to serve under the tyranny of usurpt opinions . . . and starting at every fals alarum, wee do not know which way to set a foot forward with manly confidence" (*CPW* 2:343). The phallic quality of the "free thoughts" which are capable of piercing through into the true liberty of "nature and religion" defines a manliness made potent by intellect and reason, not by household status. It is an image of sureness and fortitude that Milton will revisit in many other contexts. This is a vigorous manliness able to throw off custom's physically and mentally debilitating abjection, and it allows the Miltonic husband to reject the possibility of tyranny still implicit in Whately's formulation. Whately, conscious that husbands may over-exercise their authority, inveighs against the "mad violence of those tyrannous husbands" who will strike their wives before they have exhausted other options (170). Other writers who oppose wife-beating urge husbands to temper their tendency toward despotism: "Be very seldom in laying any command upon your wife; An intimation of what you would have done is enough between an husband and a wife," counsels Caleb Grantham, and Nathaniel Hardy explains that Ephesians 5.21–33 exhorts men to husbandly love "because that men are most apt to be defective in this, and likewise that this will teach them how to use their authority."[3] Milton is atypical among the marriage theorists in his lack of investment in the husband-as-ruler trope. So, while the conventional wisdom of Stuart marriage advice warns of the dangers of authoritarian husbands, for Milton the embrace of conventional wisdom means resigning oneself, cringingly, to the confinement of authoritarianism. Far from granting the husband power, marriage in its customary form makes him servile, timid, and lacking in "manly confidence."

John Tosh writes of the psychodynamics of masculinity, "Any identity, and especially an insecure one, is partly constructed in juxtaposition to a demonized 'other' – an imagined identity composed of all the relevant negatives, and pinned onto its nearest approximation in the real world."[4] The logic of our gender binary suggests that those manly attributes heralded as the indicators of liberty in Milton's prose stand in opposition to feminine ones; such logic typifies contemporary Milton criticism but does not adequately reflect Milton's own use of gender categories. Milton imagines the opposite of masculinity as boyishness or bestiality much more often than as femininity or effeminacy. In describing emasculation, *Eikonoklastes* is full of vituperative animal imagery and both *The Tenure* and *The Readie and Easie Way* conclude with bestial imagery; near the end of *The Readie and Easie Way* Milton argues the goal of monarchy is to ensure that the people are "softest, basest, vitiousest, servilest, easiest to be kept under; and not only in fleece, but in minde also sheepishest" (*CPW* 7:460). In a typical move at the end of *The Tenure*, Milton, marshalling all of what Tosh calls "the relevant negatives," renders his enemies infirm, impotent, and, finally, animal:

if there come a truth to be defended, which to them . . . seemes not so profitable, strait these nimble motionists, can finde no eev'n leggs to stand upon: and are no more of use to reformation throughly performd . . . then if on a sudden they were strook maime, and crippl'd . . . they would have *Scripture*, they would have *reason* also made to halt with them for company; and would putt us off with impotent conclusions, lame and shorter then the premises. (*CPW* 3:255–56)

In the final phrases of the book, the Presbyterian ministry is dehumanized in comparisons to locusts and, revisiting a favorite metaphor, to "a pack of hungrie Church-wolves" obeying "the meer suggestion of thir Bellies" (*CPW* 3:257–58). Unrighteous men are, for Milton, not even men. In *Areopagitica*, he argues that censorship strips them of their manhood: "What advantage is it to be a man over it is to be a boy at school, if we have only scapt the ferular, to come under the fescu of an *Imprimatur*? if serious and elaborat writings, as if they were no more then the theam of a Grammar lad under his Pedagogue must not be utter'd without the cursory eyes of a temporizing and extemporizing licencer" (*CPW* 2.531). As the passage continues to object to the licensers' reduction of an adult writer to a schoolboy, it offers a characteristically Miltonic definition of manhood and male valor by associating "fidelity" with intellectual work rather than courtly or military allegiance:

When a man writes to the world, he summons up all his reason and deliberation to assist him; he searches, meditats, is industrious, and likely consults and conferrs with his judicious friends; after all which done he takes himself to be inform'd in what he writes, as well as any that writ before him; if in this the most consummat act of his fidelity and ripenesse, no years, no industry, no former proof of his abilities can bring him to that state of maturity, as not to be still mistrusted and suspected . . . it cannot be but a dishonor and derogation to the author, to the book, to the priviledge and dignity of Learning. (*CPW* 2.532)

In several places Milton does reach for a word specifically opposite to "masculine" but even then he employs negative terms like "unmanly" and "unmaskuline" more often than any version of "effeminacy." The word "feminine" is used pejoratively only once, in its only appearance in the prose, in *Eikonoklastes*, when Milton rages against Henrietta Maria's "Feminine usurpation" (*CPW* 3:421). Indeed, Milton seems at times to deliberately avoid the opposition of male and female. In *The Tenure* when Milton alludes to John Gauden's pro-monarchical tract, *The Religious and Loyal Protestation*, he doesn't pit "feminine" against "masculine" as Gauden does: Gauden tells Parliament, "the world shall see your power bounded with Loyalty, sanctified with Piety, and sweetened with Pitty, not foolish and *feminine*, which I would have below you, but *masculine*, Heroick, truly Christian and Divine" (*CPW* 3:191, note 3). In attacking Gauden, Milton warns against "the unmaskuline [*sic*] Rhetorick of any puling Priest or Chaplin" (*CPW* 3:195). The descriptor "unmaskuline" is far more to the point for Milton, more profound an insult than the invocation of femininity. Milton's political thought is intensely androcentric. While the poet turns his attention to girls, women, and wives, the prose polemicist can exercise his extraordinarily capacious historical, social, and religious vision without very often catching a glimpse of women. Even where we might expect women to be distinguished from men, they are easily subsumed under the male generic. For example, *The Tenure*'s explanation of the origins of civil authority omits any mention of women, excluding the female even from the Edenic reference: the vulnerability that wreaks havoc on the state of nature derives not from Eve but from "the root of *Adams* transgression" (*CPW* 3:199). Milton's political imagination is entirely concerned with the right forms of male social performance.

Although Milton's deeply masculinist – and Latinist – thinking about gender assumes an inherent connection between virility and virtue, between the *vir* and *virtus*, the feminine is not in itself conceptually problematic for Milton. Femininity throughout the oeuvre is abstractly associated with a series of desirable qualities – qualities which are, indeed, necessary to manliness: justice, virtue, and eloquence are all frequently figured as female in the prose as in much of the poetry. For example, in *The Reason of Church Government* manliness is associated with both attributes of the mother-daughter pairing of eloquence and virtue (*CPW* 1:746). It is only femininity in actual women that Milton finds dangerous and corrupting and only when it slips from women into men. Contained femininity poses no threats, as we will see again in the later poetry. The fear and disgust that permeates Milton's prose writing is of contagion.

Effeminacy, the manifestation of such contagion, is associated (in the few places where Milton invokes it) with lack of discipline, with poor management of self and other, and, especially, with having too much power or undeserved authority. Prelates, magistrates, and courtiers are all effeminizing agents. Milton sounds a recurrent theme in his own work and in a broader social discourse about the slippery slope from domestic corruption to public weakness: the fear that personal mismanagement makes men unfit for rational political participation. This fear pervades the divorce and antimonarchical tracts and spurs *Eikonoklastes*'s bitter denunciation of Charles's reliance on his wife. *Eikonklastes* alludes to copious examples of "how great mischeif and dishonour hath befall'n to Nations under the Government of effeminate and Uxorious Magistrates" (*CPW* 3:421) and to how the Prince of Wales has been spoiled by the "soft effeminacies of Court" (*CPW* 3:571).

In *Of Reformation*, one of Milton's earliest prose invocations of gender roles shows how the prelates have "hamstrung the valour of the Subject by seeking to effeminate us all at home" (*CPW* 1:588). Effeminacy indicates the loss of self-control that produces licentiousness and, consequently, willing enslavement, sexual abjection, even bestiality:

> Well knows every wise Nation that their Liberty consists in manly and honest labours, in sobriety and rigorous honour to the Marriage Bed, which in both Sexes should be bred up from chast hopes to loyall Enjoyments; and when the people slacken, and fall to loosenes, and riot, then doe they as much as if they laid downe their necks for some wily Tyrant to get up and ride. (*CPW* 1:588)

This passage goes on to refer to Herodotus' account of how Cyrus was unable to defeat the Lydians militarily, but conquered them by effeminizing them, forcing on them a culture of song and dance; in Herodotus' account, Croesus tells Cyrus "you will soon see them turned to women instead of men" (*CPW* 1:588, n. 56). Cyrus' strategy, like the prelates' *Book of Sports*, produces a nation of weak-minded and weak-bodied libertines. The prelates are panders, preparing and "suppling" the English people for "Forreigne Invasion or Domestick oppression" (*CPW* 1:588, n. 56). The corruption of the Sabbath by "gaming, jigging, wassailing, and mixt dancing" (*CPW* 1:589) is a prelatical maneuver to "despoile us both of *manhood* and *grace* at once" (*CPW* 1:588). Manhood is, like grace, a condition of being, susceptible to corruption and reduction. Laud began his climb toward absolute power by "having first brought us to a servile *Estate* of *Religion*, and *Manhood*" (*CPW* 1:594).

To resist such corruption, a boy must be bred up right. In *Of Education* Milton advises that the pedagogical design must

> lead and draw them in willing obedience, enflam'd with the study of learning, and the admiration of vertue; stirr'd up with high hopes of living to be brave men, and worthy patriots, dear to God, and famous to all ages. That they may despise and scorn all their childish, and ill-taught qualities, to delight in manly, and liberall exercises: which he who hath the Art, and proper eloquence to catch them with, what with mild and effectuall perswasions, and what with the intimation of some fear, if need be, but chiefly by his own example, might in a short space gain them to an incredible diligence and courage: infusing into their young brests such an ingenuous and noble ardor, as would not fail to make many of them renowned and matchlesse men. (*CPW* 2:384–85)

A chief component of what is being taught in Milton's imagined school is manliness itself, aligned with the intellect and the will. Manliness here is defined in terms of the typically Miltonic balance of liberality and discipline. The life of the mind – the life of auto-didacticism, intellectual labor, and rational endeavor – is, unexpectedly, an active life, heroized in epic terms, characterized by "incredible diligence and courage" and "noble ardor." Unmanliness, then, is implicitly associated with sloth, laziness, and lack of vigor, as it will be again, for example, in the frequent disparaging references to courtiers in *Eikonoklastes*. Manliness is associated with effective rhetoric and its concomitant social control, as it was earlier in *The Reason of Church Government*, where in the opening passage of the preface Milton cites the lesson learned from Plato, that "persuasion certainly is a more winning, and more manlike way to keepe men in obedience then feare" (*CPW* 1:746).

Manliness is not yet, not for Milton, about rugged individualism, but about enmeshment in social relations and therefore, necessarily, it is concerned with forms and means of obedience. Although "the intimation of some fear" may need to be mixed in with "mild and effectuall perswasions," the "delight in manly ... exercises" is a function of "willing obedience." It is "chiefly by his own example" (*CPW* 2:385) that the instructor will guide his students. Just as it is manly to obey a good leader, it is manly of the leader to rule by intellect rather than arms, and manliness confers the rhetorical gifts that inspire obedience. In tracing how boys may become men, Milton looks to classical republicanism for the models of virtuous citizenship his own era lacks. As Martin Dzelzainis has argued, *Of Education* "represents something very close to a 'republican moment' for Milton."[5] Milton uses manliness to describe, and prescribe, participatory government.

If Milton's political language is pervasively masculinist and his arguments about liberty focused principally on men, it may well indicate that hierarchies between men and women concern him much less centrally than hierarchies between men. Anthony Fletcher urges us to "investigate fully and deeply the ways in which authority over women sustained men's sense of themselves as men"[6] in the early modern period, and we need to do this; but equally crucial to Milton's work are the ways in which authoritative relations with other men sustain his sense of masculinity. In the anti-monarchical tracts at either end of the interregnum, Milton consistently uses manliness to talk about servility and rectitude and, particularly, to name which forms of loyalty are servile and which forms are courageous. Although *Eikonoklastes* is unstinting in the scorn it pours on Charles, Milton devotes most of his attention to the perilous manliness of the governed rather than the governor. The recuperative energies of the anti-monarchical tracts are directed toward the people themselves to stir up "the old English fortitude and love of Freedom" (*CPW* 3:344).

The Tenure associates manliness with those who resist monarchy, servility with those who, in 1649, embrace it: "For indeed none can love freedom heartilie, but good men; the rest love not freedom, but licence; which never hath more scope or more indulgence then under Tyrants" (*CPW* 3:190). Milton turns to Sallust's *Catiline* for the convenient measure of virtue provided by this principle: "Hence it is that Tyrants are not oft offended, nor stand much in doubt of bad men, as being all naturally servile; but in whom vertue and true worth most is eminent, them they feare in earnest, as by right thir Maisters, against them lies all thir hatred and suspicion" (*CPW* 3:190). However, among those who opposed Charles in the first civil war, some joined in merely "as a noveltie, and for a flash hot and active," and are therefore unwilling to pursue the conflict to its righteous conclusion, "through sloth or inconstancie, and weakness of spirit either fainting . . . or through an inbred falshood and wickednes" (*CPW* 3:192). As he had before in the divorce tracts, in *The Tenure* Milton asserts that incontinent men will follow their "hot" impulses yet are ultimately weak and incapable, lacking the "fortitude and Heroick vertue" which distinguish "sincere and real men" (*CPW* 3:191).

The language about manliness in *Eikonoklastes* is fiercer and cruder than that of *The Tenure* as Milton's contempt for and frustration with Charles's supporters mounts in the wake of the regicide and of the popularity of the *Eikon Basilike*. Of all the prose writings, only in *History of Britain* does Milton use as much explicitly gendered language as he does in *Eikonoklastes* and there are more accusations about effeminacy here than anywhere else in Milton's work. The recurrent references to immaturity and the plethora of bestial images used to represent Charles, his courtiers, and his sympathizers are familiar tropes in Milton's gender vocabulary by late 1649. Charles is immature, even as he accuses Parliament of being so (*CPW* 3:466) and he seeks to infantilize the nation (*CPW* 3:469). While Milton deplores *Eikon Basilike*'s using animal images to describe the English people (*CPW* 3:396–7), he is liberal in his own deployment of such imagery: courtiers and clergymen are "Apes" (*CPW* 3:370), "Wolves" (*CPW* 3:489), "Foxes" (*CPW* 3:521); the people, in a recurrent analogy, are beasts (*CPW* 3:488, 601). Yet another means of "othering" Charles is by insisting on the foreignness of his court to account for the "low dejection and debasement of mind" which Milton "cannot willingly ascribe to the natural disposition of an Englishman" (*CPW* 3:344). Finally, Milton pits the category "slave" against "man" throughout *Eikonoklastes*, as he will again in *Pro Populo Anglicano*

Defensio. Manhood in *Eikonoklastes* is linked exclusively with liberty and all of its opposites are used to demonstrate the various manifestations of servility:

> that people that should seek a King, claiming what this Man claimes, would shew themselves to be by nature slaves, and arrant beasts; not fitt for that liberty which they cri'd out and bellow'd for, but fitter to be led back again into thir old servitude, like a sort of clamouring & fighting brutes, broke loos [*sic*] from thir copyholds, that know not how to use or possess the liberty which they fought for. (*CPW* 3:581)

Milton objects strenuously to Charles's use of the figure of the "good Man" who refuses to break the law, arguing rather that under tyranny citizens "should stand up like Men and demand thir Rights and Liberties." To claim, as Charles does, that the people may not use "*unlawfull and irreligious meanes*" to combat tyranny is "the artificialest peece of fineness to perswade men into slavery that the wit of Court could have invented" (*CPW* 3:392).

One manifestation of Charles's corruption is his reliance on women. The royalist conception of manly behavior itself is imitative of women, Milton suggests. He accuses Charles of modeling his speeches and comportment at his trial on the example of his grandmother "from whome he seems to have learnt, as it were by heart, or els by kind, that which is thought by his admirers to be the most vertuous, most manly, most Christian, and most Martyr-like" (*CPW* 3:597). Effeminacy is linked with foreignness: Milton's disdain for Henrietta Maria, the effeminizing force, is integral to his distaste for her religion. The letters taken from Charles at Naseby "reveal'd his endeavours to bring in forren Forces, Irish, French, Dutch, Lorrainers, and our old Invaders the Danes upon us, besides his suttleties and mysterious arts in treating: to sumn up all, they shewd him govern'd by a Woman" (*CPW* 3:538) – the logic of this sentence makes "woman" metonymic for Catholic. Finally, though, for all the fury it marshalls against the late king and his immediate circle, *Eikonoklastes* closes with an image which perhaps suggests its deepest concern, the Circean image of a "credulous and hapless herd, begott'n to servility" who "hold out both thir eares with such delight and ravishment to be stigmatiz'd and board through in witness of thir own voluntary and beloved baseness" (*CPW* 3:601). It is the surrender of their native rights, the "voluntary" debasement, that signifies for Milton the crucial loss of liberty.

After *Eikonoklastes* Milton uses little explicitly masculinist language until the next work to address the prospect of such voluntary debasement on a national scale, *The Readie and Easie Way.* In the long introductory passage which builds to the decentering of human authority by the abstract construct of reason, support for restoration is represented as unmasculine. The idolatry which Milton associates with monarchy is unmanly: in a free Commonwealth "they who are greatest . . . yet are not elevated above thir brethren . . . may be spoken to freely, familiarly, friendly, without adoration" (*CPW* 7:425). This recurrent theme of *The Readie and Easie Way* is expanded upon in the second edition (quoted here), which further deplores the debasement of the people by monarchy. Soon after, in the poetry, Milton will attempt to illustrate how natural hierarchies can exist without elevation or adoration. One of the most disturbing things about a king, or perhaps about Charles II, is the pageantry which surrounds him, stripping both him and his people of dignity: the king "who for any thing wherin the public really needs him, will have little els to do, but to bestow the eating and drinking of excessive dainties . . . to pageant himself up and down in progress among the perpetual bowings and cringings of an abject people, on either side deifying and adoring him for nothing don that can deserve it" (*CPW* 7:426). This passage builds in intensity to the declaration that "[c]ertainly then that people must needs be madd or strangely infatuated, that build the chief hope of thir common happiness or safetie on a single person," and to its central point: "The happiness of a nation must needs be firmest and certainest in a full and free Councel of thir own electing, where no single person, but reason only swaies" (*CPW* 7:427). No sooner has Milton made this claim, the heart of his argument not just about monarchy but about all of the social organizations which he addresses, than he calls on expressly masculinist language:

And what madness is it, for them who might manage nobly thir own affairs themselves, sluggishly and weakly to devolve all on a single person; and more like boyes under age then men, to committ all to [a king], how unmanly must it needs be, to count such a one the breath of our nostrils, to hang all our felicity on him, all our safetie, our well-being, for which if we were aught els but sluggards or babies, we need depend on none but God and our own counsels, our own active vertue and industrie. (*CPW* 7:427)

He goes on to express contempt for those men who are willing "basely and besottedly to run their necks again into the yoke which they have broken" (*CPW* 7:428). As in *Eikonoklastes*, "base" and "besotted" are key terms for defining the opposite of a mature and responsible masculinity. Just as the physical posture of erectness will recur in the later poetry as an image of moral rectitude, the possibility of passion without the loss of reason becomes a recurrent theme.

The gender of civic virtue

Milton makes two sets of distinctions in *The Readie and Easie Way*. One is between "unmanly" adherents to customary forms of power and those who are courageous enough to stand firm against the restoration of monarchy; the second is a parsing of the latter group into those who are "rightly qualifi'd" to rule and those who will live profitably under that rule although they will not participate in shaping it. In proposing that the "Grand Councel" should be perpetual and that elections be "refined," "permitting only those of them who are rightly qualifi'd" (*CPW* 7:442–43) to vote, Milton requires his utopic citizens to assent to a permanent set of rulers not of their choosing; consent is not to be based on individual choice precisely but on willingness to assent to the choice of others clearly more fit to decide. In this there is a distinct sense in which the people, the "rude multitude" (*CPW* 7:442), are given the same subject position in relation to authority which Milton wishes to accord to wives.

Because manliness resides in reasoned discourse, it is at risk wherever men may not negotiate rationally, hence the threat to English manhood posed by monarchy in insufficiently mixed forms of government and, no less, by marriage in a culture that prohibits divorce. The individual who suffers under these arrangements is, by virtue of how Milton conceives of liberty, gendered male: the injustice to which Milton addresses himself in his divorce writings is specifically that of the husband shackled by a bad marriage, a figure who bears a strong resemblance to the citizen shackled by bad government. Yet the heart of the argument, that marriage must be truly consensual in order to be legitimate, is, in *Tetrachordon*, explicitly inclusive of wives: "And why should not consent be heer understood with equity and good to either part, as in all other freindly covnants, and not be strain'd and cruelly urg'd to the mischeif and destruction of both?" (*CPW* 2:612). Equally important, the argument is founded in natural law: "if mariage be but an ordain'd relation, as it seems not more, it cannot take place above the prime dictats of nature" (*CPW* 2:621). The divorce tracts' discourse of sexual difference is not, as Mary Nyquist argues, ideologically seamless but is, in fact, radically unstable. The clearly articulated ideology of inherent female subservience is constantly threatened by Milton's belief that natural law renders inessential and relative any merely "ordain'd" relationship. In Nyquist's account, by prioritizing woman's creation in the image of man, Milton thereby renders her ontologically, permanently subordinate.[7] Yet in one of the few places where *Tetrachordon* rallys the kind of zeal for the wronged wife that it usually reserves for the husband, it asserts that the subordination of one human to another is always conditional: "the wife also, as her subjection is terminated in the Lord, being her self the redeem'd of Christ, is not still bound to be the vassall of him, who is the bondslave of Satan: she being now neither the image nor the glory of such a person, nor made for him, nor left in bondage to him" (*CPW* 2:591). Milton's real passion is not for rescuing the wife of a libertine but for reforming an injurious institution. His interest lies in the institution rather than the individual, in the concept of liberation in marriage; it is this exercise of civic virtue that leads, incidentally as it were, to the extension of rights to wives.

Just as the divorce tracts demote the function of sexual intercourse in marriage, they demote the function of sexuality in masculinity, casting manliness as self-control and moral rectitude, and associating rampant sexual appetite with its absence. In *The Doctrine*'s prefatory letter Milton argues that a well-ordered state will produce well-regulated men, a disordered state the opposite: "in what a degenerat and fal'n spirit from the apprehension of native liberty, and true manlines, I am sure ye find: with what unbounded licence rushing to whordoms and adulteries needs not long enquiry" (*CPW* 2:227). Sexual disorder is a natural consequence of the fall away from liberty but Parliament can repair the damage: "places of prostitution wil be lesse haunted, the neighbours bed lesse attempted, the yoke of prudent and manly discipline will be generally submitted to" (*CPW* 2:230). The divorce tracts, which, in James Turner's words, seem "almost to indict the existence of sexuality itself"[8] give the performance of citizenship rather than that of sex or sexuality precedence in providing the essential characteristics of manliness: "the agrieved person shall doe more manly, to be extraordinary and singular in claiming the due right whereof he is frustrated, then to piece up his lost contentment by visiting the Stews, or stepping to his neighbours bed" (*CPW* 2:247). "[T]he due right whereof he is frustrated" is not, as one might expect from the ubiquitous language of "due benevolence" in seventeenth-century marriage literature, the husband's sexual right but precisely his right to leave a sexual relationship degraded by lovelessness. Manliness is posited in *Tetrachordon* as the courage to articulate that right, the moral brilliance to demand justice: "And if men want manlinesse to expostulate the right of their due ransom . . . they may sit hereafter and bemoan themselves to have neglected through faintnesse the onely remedy of their sufferings, which a seasonable and well grounded speaking might have purchas'd them"(*CPW* 2:585). Only vigorous intellectual work renders a person sufficiently virile to right the wrongs of custom and bad law.

In one of the most radical and perhaps most anxious passages of the divorce tracts, *Tetrachordon* affirms the manliness of that pursuit of justice even as it asserts womens' right to the same justice:

The Law is to tender the liberty and human dignity of them that live under the Law, whether it bee the mans right above the woman, or the womans just appeal against wrong, and servitude. But the duties of marriage contain in them a duty of benevolence, which to doe by compulsion against the Soul, where ther can bee neither peace, nor joy, nor love, but an enthrallment to one who either cannot, or will not bee mutual in the godliest and the civilest ends of that society, is the ignoblest, and the lowest slavery that a human shape can bee put to. This Law therfore justly and piously provides against such an unmanly task of bondage as this. (*CPW* 2:625–26)

For Milton, justice liberates people from unmanliness. As this passage makes clear, both men and women may deserve such liberation. That is to say, liberty is gendered, not sexed. It is both associated with manliness and available to all who have a claim to it, regardless of physical sex. The assertion of "the mans right above the woman" does not erase the extension of the rights argument to women. Milton acknowledges woman's "just appeal against wrong, and servitude" and deplores compulsive sexual relations with reference to "human shape," not to male shape; this is an extraordinary granting of sexual integrity to women. Yet, no sooner has he done so than he recuperates justice for the purpose of freeing spouses from "unmanly ... bondage."

Similar cruxes appear in other passages of the divorce tracts: every time Milton grants rights to women, he invokes natural male superiority. The tracts shift from the gendered language of willed manliness and of character into the "sexed" language of biological absolutism when he is faced with the logical conflicts between gender hierarchy and inherent native liberty. As a result, Milton's most profound concession to wives is embedded in a defense of St. Paul's interpretation of Genesis 1:27, "in the image of God created he him." Remarkably enough, Milton asserts that gender hierarchy is inferior to other scales of human worth: "Not but that particular exceptions may have place, if she exceed her husband in prudence and dexterity, and he contentedly yeeld, for then a superior and more naturall law comes in, that the wiser should govern the lesse wise, whether male or female" (*CPW* 2:589). Making a claim that in practice would dramatically alter the legal status of wives, Milton here denies that all qualitative distinctions between human beings can be derived solely from gender differences. This explicitly rejects the logic that leads sermonizers like Thomas Gataker to insist, as a matter of natural priority, on female subservience regardless of capacity; the Christian wife is obliged "though she be her selfe of a greater spirit, and in some respect of better parts, though she bring much with her, though the maine estate come by her, yet to acknowledge her husband, as God hath appointed him, to be her superiour."[9] In marked contrast, Milton's elucidation of "a superior and more naturall law" than male prerogative is, perhaps, the most radical move he makes in the divorce tracts.[10] However, this assertion is immediately subsumed by "that which far more easily and obediently follows from this verse," the claim that "seeing woman was purposely made for man, and he her head" it cannot be right that the man "should so becom her thrall" (*CPW* 2:589).

The oscillation between "natural" and gendered hierarchies demonstrates the sense in which masculinity is, to use Mark Breitenberg's argument, inherently anxious. Breitenberg alerts us to "the ways in which early modern masculinity relies on a variety of constructions of woman as Other – on the perceived necessity of maintaining a discourse of gendered difference and hierarchy – that reveal in their most excessive moments a deeper suspicion that the model itself may be merely functional rather than descriptive of inherent truth."[11] The dynamic quality of the divorce tracts derives from their ambivalence about whether the truth lies more squarely with the discourse of gendered difference or of natural law. Because this is their central conflict, they are characterized by anxious reworkings of the same small but crucial patch of moral ground: women are at once naturally subordinate and naturally free, and men are always in danger of bondage to an inferior. Finally, though, *The Doctrine*'s title-page claim – the good of both sexes – is made good by the assignment of liberty to gender rather than to sex. Since Milton associates manliness with character rather than with biological sex, the libertarian argument against "an unmanly task of bondage" is able to include wives.

Because manliness involves negotiation of potentially conflicting responsibilities, its appearances in Milton's prose point toward some of the most vexed and most important passages of that work. Gender emerges in the prose where the contours of the lived experience of liberty are under discussion and Milton's most closely held principles are at stake. Milton associates manliness with the practices that characterize liberty in a civil society. Although Miltonists' discussions of gender focus almost exclusively on attitudes toward and representations of women in the work, Milton's gendered vocabulary suggests his own concern with men's navigation of the homosocial public world. He describes that world through a discourse of manliness in which privilege accrues to male gender, not male sex: men can be insufficiently masculine, and women are not unequivocally subordinate. The space opened up for gender does not preclude assumptions based on sex but it does indicate that those assumptions are not totalizing. It allows for a rational Eve in *Paradise Lost*. In *Comus*, it gives a teenage girl the moral and intellectual stamina not only to resist temptation bodily but to reject it with "seasonable and well grounded speaking" (*CPW* 2:585). It also provides an alternative explanation for the authority of bad men from that offered by absolutism or patriarchalism; real, legitimate authority is an attribute of manliness, which can be forfeited, but not of any immutable birthright, including male sex.

NOTES

I am grateful to Heather Dubrow for the generosity and insight with which she commented on an earlier version of this chapter. Many thanks to Quentin Skinner for his guidance in my thinking about the masculine qualities of virtue, including the ways in which the gender of civic virtue is "etymologically guaranteed" (private correspondence).

1. At issue here is not, in John Shawcross's words, "the psychodynamic aspects of the self that involve sexual attitudes and experiences and gender matters . . . basic to an understanding of an author, whose work may both reveal and hide that self," although the passages I treat here may well be interesting in terms of the psychodynamics described by Shawcross, *John Milton: The Self and The World* (Lexington: The University Press of Kentucky, 1993), 5. Rather, my study is specifically interested in Milton's attempts to represent and deploy masculinity for polemical purposes.
2. William Whately, *A Bride-Bush: Or, A Direction for Married Persons* (London, 1619), 113.
3. Caleb Grantham, *The Godly Mans Choice* (London, 1644), 93; Nathaniel Hardy, *Love and Fear The Inseperable Twins Of A Blest Matrimony* (London, 1653), 7.
4. John Tosh, "What Should Historians do with Masculinity? Reflections on Nineteenth-century Britain," *History Workshop Journal* 38 (1994): 196.
5. Martin Dzelzainis, "Milton's Classical Republicanism," in *Milton and Republicanism*, ed. David Armitage, Armand Himy, and Quentin Skinner (Cambridge: Cambridge University Press, 1995), 14.
6. Anthony Fletcher, *Gender, Sex and Subordination in England 1500–1800* (New Haven: Yale University Press, 1995), 346.
7. Mary Nyquist, "The Genesis of Gendered Subjectivity in the Divorce Tracts and in *Paradise Lost*," in *Re-membering Milton: Essays on the Texts and Traditions*, ed. Mary Nyquist and Margaret W. Ferguson (New York: Methuen, 1987).
8. James Grantham Turner, *One Flesh: Paradisal Marriage and Sexual Relations in the Age of Milton* (Oxford: Clarendon Press, 1987), 194.
9. Thomas Gataker, *Marriage Duties Briefely Couched Together* (London, 1620), 11.
10. See Matthew Jordan, *Milton and Modernity: Politics, Masculinity and "Paradise Lost"* (New York: Palgrave, 2001), for an important qualification: "whoever is the better reasoner, such an arrangement requires the agreement of the man" (14).
11. Mark Breitenberg, *Anxious Masculinity in Early Modern England* (Cambridge: Cambridge University Press, 1996), 11.

CHAPTER 2

The aesthetics of divorce: "masculinism," idolatry, and poetic authority in Tetrachordon *and* Paradise Lost

James Grantham Turner

"THOUGH I am not the only person in Sussex who reads Milton," wrote Virginia Woolf in a famous diary entry of September 1918,

> I mean to write down my impressions of *Paradise Lost* while I am about it. Impressions fairly well describes the sort of thing left in my mind. I have left many riddles unread. I have slipped on too easily to taste the full flavour . . . I am struck by the extreme difference between this poem & any other. It lies, I think, in the sublime aloofness & impersonality of the emotion. [Milton] deals in horror & immensity & squalor & sublimity, but never in the passions of the human heart. Has any great poem ever let in so little light upon ones own joys and sorrows? I get no help in judging life; I scarcely feel that Milton lived or knew men & women; except for the peevish personalities about marriage & the woman's duties. He was the first of the masculinists: but his disparagement rises from his own ill luck & seems even a spiteful last word in his domestic quarrels. But how smooth, strong & elaborate it all is! What poetry! . . . The inexpressible fineness of the style, in which shade after shade is perceptible, would alone keep one gazing in to it, long after the surface business in progress has been despatched. Deep down one catches still further combinations, rejections, felicities, & masteries.[1]

This is a fascinating response to Milton for several reasons. For one thing, it is not actually about *Paradise Lost* at all. Woolf says quite explicitly, in a tone of coolly amused detachment, that she has only read bits of the poem, and that she is only part-way through. Woolf is effectively responding to the tone and texture of a fragmented Modernist poem that she has created from this "slipping on" in Milton. She has abstracted those moments into which she can gaze like one suspended over a deep pool. A reading that accounts for every line could not possibly maintain that passion never enters the poem or that the feeling remains aloof and impersonal – an effect more akin to early Modernist predilections than to Milton's densely emotional poem. In some ways Woolf's is a rather conventional response: "joys and sorrows," "the passions of the human heart" – these phrases read like a parody, and the whole negative part is in any case borrowed almost verbatim from Johnson's *Life* of Milton. The part about masculinism (where "peevish personalities" run counter to the general remarks on "*im*personality") is much sharper and fresher, but it is still a variant on Johnson's infamous complaint about Milton's "almost Turkish contempt for women." For both traditional reasons (the dominance of Johnson's bogey) and avant-gardist reasons (a new Modernist aesthetic) Woolf expected, even wanted, to find aloofness in *Paradise Lost*; indeed, when she had finished she wrote to Lytton Strachey "I have read the whole of Milton, without throwing any light upon my own soul, but that I rather like."[2] This activist conception of the reading-process – *she*, rather than the poem, is now the subject of the verb "throw" – also plays its part in the diary-entry, where the whole package of conventional complaints is thrust aside to make way for the aesthetic response. The transition from ideology to art – "But what poetry!" – is not (as Sandra Gilbert argued in her influential "Reflections on Milton's Bogey") an intensification of the complaint against masculinism, a darkening of the page, but the glowing of an awakened judgment. Far from being diffident, vague, and abstract, as Gilbert asserted, Woolf's appreciation of those "further combinations, rejections, felicities & masteries" shows a critic intimate with the writing process and confident that she can recognize the special touches of a fellow-practitioner, even down to his "rejections"; she feels the shadow of phrases he might have used but did not.[3] Compared with this profound aesthetic reappropriation, the masculinist ideology is merely "surface business" soon "despatched," a diminutive blemish however "peevish" and "spiteful."

In the delicious suspension of reading, the aesthetic seems to form an autonomous realm for Woolf. The authority of poetry, shared and even recreated by the female author-critic, seems to sweep away the mean authority of sexual politics that excludes her. She may even find conventionally female qualities (smoothness, richness of work, aloofness) in the first of the masculinists. We know of course, and no one better than Woolf, that things are not so simple, that the material conditions of male dominance still restrict women's literary production. Gazing into the imaginary pool is not enough, even though Woolf does reappropriate and improve upon the waking moments of Milton's Eve by having herself gaze *past* the surface into the real depths. Woolf's sophisticated vision of aesthetic autonomy still does not do justice to the complex and often submerged interrelation of the ideological and the artistic. We might say it was wishful thinking or old-fashioned idealism. But to produce aesthetic autonomy in a context so acutely aware of masculinism, to enact its triumph in the very phrases of one's response, is itself a kind of political praxis.

Since Gilbert's powerful intervention, several generations of scholars, of both sexes and many ideological persuasions, have launched rescue missions on Milton's behalf.[4] A few key passages in the epic and the divorce tracts have become ammunition for these revisionist interpreters – in particular one very striking moment in *Tetrachordon* when Milton seems to imagine a household led by a superior woman. As Gina Hausknecht remarks in the previous chapter, this would be "the most radical move" if it were not "immediately subsumed" into a more masculinist argument. Having quoted St. Paul on the wife's absolute subjection, Milton goes on to allow exceptions "if she exceed her husband in prudence and dexterity, and he contentedly yeeld, for then a superior and more naturall law comes in, that the wiser should govern the lesse wise, whether male or female" (*CPW* 2:589). This passage, along with other tributes to the ideal of mutual companionship in the divorce tracts, is often cited to prove Milton's open-mindedness. I would like to restore it to its context – showing that it reinforces rather than mitigates his vehement masculinism – and then to use this episode as a key to the divorce tracts, which in turn are the front door to *Paradise Lost*. I will try to keep in view the crucial issue raised by Woolf's and Gilbert's responses: what *is* the relationship between poetics, biblical hermeneutics, and the ideology of masculine power?

Milton's "exception" to masculine rule is indeed astonishing, since he appears to grant supreme authority to the "superior and more naturall law . . . that the wiser should govern the lesse wise" – letting it override *both* the divine authority of St. Paul *and* the biological difference of sex, conventionally assumed to be the most "naturall" authority of all. The divorce tracts repeatedly stage this form of argument, in which conflicting texts or conflicting hermeneutic principles slug it out until one falls to the ground. They are not harmonized, despite the name *Tetrachordon* or "four-stringed lyre," nor are they negotiated or mediated: one must rule and all the others submit. The entire edifice of the divorce tracts is based on Milton's contention that a single line of Genesis (2:18 – "it is not good for man to be alone: let us make him a help like unto himself") constitutes the absolute and total definition, the "divine institution," of marriage and gender-relations. Every other line of Genesis, the Old Testament, and the Gospels – including Christ's rather inconvenient prohibition of divorce – must be ruthlessly subordinated to the primal master-definition or else rejected completely. Yet apparently St. Paul can override Genesis, the divorce-provision of Deuteronomy can override Christ, and the "more naturall law" can override everything.

The aesthetics of divorce

However the critics may use this passage, the reader of it in context does not have time to ponder what Milton meant by it, or on what authority he bases his "natural law." The entire sentence is a rhetorical booby-trap, which explodes the moment the curious reader touches it. The ostensible author's voice turns out to be a disguised objection, and the prevailing tones of wisdom, natural law, and anti-masculinism are themselves drowned out by another voice:

But that which far more easily and obediently follows from this verse, is that, seeing woman was purposely made for man, and he her head, it cannot stand before the breath of this divine utterance, that man the portraiture of God, joyning to himself for his intended good and solace an inferiour sexe, should so becom her thrall, whose wilfulnes or inability to be a wife frustrates the occasionall end of her creation, but that he may acquitt himself to freedom by his naturall birthright, and that indeleble character of priority which God crown'd him with.[5]

I am not sure that I would use the terms "easy" or "obedient" to describe this performance. Far from easy, the tone is apoplectic, the sentence-structure sprawling and breathless, the vocabulary tendentiously emotive. Moreover, does it "obediently follow . . ." from the verse under discussion, from Genesis 1:27? Is exegesis simply a humble leading-out of the true meaning of the Word? On the contrary: in the first chapter of Genesis *all* the human attributes are given to humanity in the plural, as a species including male and female. The plural gods (Elohim) say "Let us make man in our image, after our likeness: and let *them* have dominion over" the beasts and creeping things:

27. So the Elohim created man in their own image, in the image of Elohim created they him; male and female created they them.
28. And the Elohim blessed them, and said unto them "Be fruitful and multiply, and replenish the earth, and subdue it."

The "him" of 1:27 is a generic singular in the grammatical masculine, substituted for "them" on this one occasion so as not to end two lines with the identical word. Milton, however, scans the text according to his preconceived ideological agenda, now intensified by the collapse of his disastrous marriage; he is alert for anything that will assuage his sense of having been tricked, enslaved, deserted, and "unspeakably wrong'd," and falls hungrily on that isolated phrase "in the image of God created he *him*": "Had the Image of God bin equally common to them both, it had no doubt bin said, In the image of God created he them; but St. Paul ends the controversie by explaining that the woman is *not* primarily and immediatly the image of God . . ." (*CPW* 2:589, my emphases). Milton is not "obediently following" this verse in Genesis 1, but running it down with

St. Paul and Genesis 2 as his hounds. In the very act of forcing Scripture to obey him, however, he reconstitutes the issue of gender as a "controversie," and succeeds in making centuries of Pauline orthodoxy sound like "peevish personalities."

Throughout his reading of Genesis, Milton turns the "image of God" into an attribute of maleness, hiving it off from those qualities unmistakably attributed to "them" rather than "him." Thus the very next phrase, "male and female created he them" – the first mention of gender in the Bible, unmarked by any priority or subordination – is represented as a secondary phenomenon or minor addendum: "this contains *another* end of matching man and woman" – confusing the sequence of Scripture with the sequence of his own exposition – "the right and lawfulness of the marriage bed, though *much inferior* to the former end of her being his image and helpe in religious society" (2:592, my emphases). "Male and female" refers only to copulation, and thus this phrase is the "dregs" of the text, a "poor consideration" next to the nobility of the rest of the line. This is pure fantasy: we look in vain for any source of these ideas in the text, neither in chapter 1 – which proceeds to declare a blessing on sexuality of the most emphatic and explicit kind – nor in chapter 2, from which Milton deduced the temporal priority of "it is not good that man should be alone." Milton's own prior sense of sexual loathing, which bubbles out of every seam of the divorce tracts, here overrides the word of God itself. He even maintains that God made Adam and Eve "one flesh" in order to assure them that copulation is acceptable; otherwise it would seem an act of "pollution" (2:323). In an astonishing act of hubris, Milton injects pollution into the original state of Paradise, and into God's mind as He created humanity.

One would expect, then, that in his self-serving attempt to exclude gender from the "image of God" Milton would exclude *all* the qualities given in common to both sexes. He is not so consistent however. First he says that the image means "Wisdom, Purity, Justice, and rule over all creatures" (*CPW* 2:587), even though the first three are not mentioned in Genesis at all, the fourth is given explicitly to both male and female, and all of the above were lost at the fall anyway. At another point he equates it with "unity of mind and body," at another he says it means simply "holiness," and shortly afterwards he locates it in the physical body of flesh and blood, which shows that "there are left *some* remains of God's image in man" (*CPW* 2:591). In *De Doctrina* he refers to another of these faint survivals of the image, the ability to terrify animals. In *Paradise Lost*, when Satan first sees the innocent couple, the image of God shone in "*their* looks divine" (according to the narrator) and divine resemblance shines "in *them*" (according to Satan, who would like to find a difference).[6] What *is* this image in *Paradise Lost*? It is something palpable, a visible manifestation of "Truth, Wisdom, Sanctitude" and the source of "true authority." Does it survive the fall? No, says the archangel Michael in Book 11; the "image" of God vanished completely, though some obscure "similitude" does linger on (511–25). Yet in *Tetrachordon*, on the "true autoritie" of his own assertion, Milton equates the "portraiture of God" with irreducible biological maleness – "that indeleble character of priority which God crown'd him with" – and defines it in terms of domination, not over the creeping things that creep upon the earth, but over woman.

This is the primary definition of the Image that strikes down all the others, that strikes down the first chapter of Genesis and the pusillanimous voice of natural law and wisdom. Milton's refutation is intensely physical and performative. He is thinking quite literally of a false image like Dagon falling flat before the power of Truth, a mighty wind: "it cannot stand before the breath of this divine utterance." The "divine utterance" itself, however, does not say what Milton says it says. The only falling flat, the only triumph of one text over another, is performed here in this text by "the breath of *this* divine utterance," this stream of breath that I am now shaping and uttering to blow your house down. Milton's interpretation claims the authority of the Old Testament *ruach*, the divine breath, wind, or voice that creates the world in a few words and breathes life into clay, which withers the grass and cuts down the Assyrian in his pride. This is creation rather than interpretation, an "assertion" supported only by his own breath, by the rhetorical or poetic authority generated from within his own voice, driven by his own presuppositions about the masculine birthright and the heroism of divorce – opinions now fanned to white heat by his marital disasters. It is pure Miltonic invention, for example, which puts into the mind of Adam, at the very moment of meeting Eve, the terrible thought that "God would far sooner cut [the rib] quite off from all relation for [my] undoubted ease, than nail it into [my] body again, to stick forever a thorn in [my] heart" (*CPW* 2:602). Milton's strategy is the precise reverse of Woolf's: to override the status quo with a voice of inward, imaginative authority that will *promote* ideology, that will *restore* masculinism to a world perceived as hopelessly effeminate and corrupt.

This pattern, then, recurs throughout the divorce tracts: what appears to be exegetics dissolves into pure energetics, vehement and rhetorically powerful assertions substituted for the text they are supposed to explain.

In the process, a structure of argument based on hierarchy dissolves into indeterminacy. The "image of God" line in Genesis 1 is first declared the highest and most primordial, while the clause about "male and female" is thrust down to the "dregs"; the second line is as it were divorced, and the errant female part expelled as unclean. The whole of chapter 2 is therefore declared to be a commentary on this very phrase of chapter 1, "male and female created he them." Then chapter 2 is promoted *over* chapter 1, as if the later expansion of a part took precedence over the previous whole (an embarrassing assumption for someone who wants to prove Eve an inferior and occasional being). Further, chapter 2 is itself mutilated, since its culminating celebration of the union in one flesh and the happy sharing of nakedness is suppressed, and every other verse is made to bow to the single verse that Milton declares to be the Institution: "And the Lord said, it is not good that man should be alone; I will make him a help meet for him" (2:18).

The imagery at this point is literally patriarchal: the other verses of Genesis "must be led back to receive their meaning from those institutive words of God which give them all the life and vigor they have" (*CPW* 2:602). The metaphor seems to make Milton a nursemaid or governess, until you reflect that he is also the arbitrary authority who has promoted this one verse over the others. The logic of this "leading-out" is dubious, too. Verse 2:23, for example, comments on Adam's passionate recognition of woman as "flesh of my flesh": "therefore shall a man leave his father and his mother, and shall cleave unto his wife, and they shall be one flesh." *Therefore*, as we constantly remind our students, can only refer to the immediate precedent and must express a logical-causal relation; but Milton, invoking something he calls the "necessity of construction," insists that it can only refer to the Institution, five lines earlier. Yet when we *do* go back "obediently" to the key verse we find that, once again, it does not say what Milton claims. God declares that loneliness is bad and that he will make a help fit for or corresponding to the man – not a female *ezerah* or handmaiden, as in "Help Wanted," but an *ezer* as in "my help cometh even from the Lord." Milton inverts this by imposing a subordinationist reading. Obviously he is not alone in this interpretation – I wrote a whole book to show otherwise – but he goes further than anyone else in recreating Scripture in his own image, not only raising this verse to unwarranted prominence but rewriting it as a heady mixture of Love and Subjection. Yet, after all this, it turns out that he really wants Deuteronomy to be the master-text. The Mosaic law overrides "all that lost Paradise relates," since his key demand is the restitution of Old Testament divorce by simple and unilateral declaration of the husband – the ultimate fantasy of pure, performative verbal power.

Milton's house of Scripture turns out to be constructed like the staircase-house of M. C. Escher, a conundrum where everything is simultaneously above and below everything else. It is in any case built upon sand, since true authority is at crucial moments declared to reside not in an actual text at all, but in the invisible text of the Spirit, the "lively Sculpture" that is most deeply graven in the heart of Adam and his masculine descendants – what Milton earlier called "those unwritten lawes and Ideas which nature hath ingraven in us."[7] In the midst of strenuous biblical exegesis, despite all his denunciations of those who "make an Idol of marriage [by] advanc[ing] it above the word of God" (*CPW* 2:276), Milton reserves the right to override and expel the Scripture by personal intuition and declaration. For this, he was quite understandably attacked as a dangerous radical Antinomian.

I do not intend to generalize or theorize from this reading, arguing (for example) that the divorce tracts are pure textual play, disengaged from all reference except self-reference and so unrelated to the world. Rather, I would isolate specific deconstructive moments in Milton, points where contradiction bursts into view and invention works doubly hard to close the rifts. The very lack of foundation allows us to see the construction of an ideology under real and intense pressures, from the explosion of his marriage in the years of social conflict and civil war. Texts like *Tetrachordon* may not be interpretations of Scripture, but they are certainly interpretations, representations, reenactments of something very concrete. The real necessity they body forth is not the logical and exegetical "necessity of construction" (or its reverse), but the psychological and aesthetic necessity of giving vent and form to rage, anguish, and sexual humiliation, after the head-on crash of ideal and reality in marital collapse.

Milton's personal situation was both more horrific and more ridiculous than Woolf realizes when she accused him of petty irritation, "peevish" didacticism that "rises from his own ill luck & seems even a spiteful last word in his domestic quarrels." He had kept himself virgin for thirty-four years, to guarantee not only his future salvation but his future poetic gifts, had married a royalist teenager on sudden impulse without consulting his family, had lived with her for only a month – enough time for him to amass a vast stock of hideous images of copulation – and then found himself (as he perceived it) deserted without redress. One can no more keep Milton's "peevish personalities" out of the divorce tracts than one can keep his blindness out of *Paradise Lost*; his whole textual strategy is devoted to rewriting his own anguish as a national emergency and reinstalling his own dream of perfect marriage in the heart of the godly nation. His main logical premise (that if a marriage fails to live up to its Paradisal definition it is actually a non-marriage and must be annulled) only serves to usher in his ideal fantasy – a rapturous fusion of Plato and the Song of Solomon grafted onto the myth of Eve. This in turn sets off, by contrast, his violent denunciation of the defective wife. Time and again the level tones of exposition, the ostensible appeals to rational calm, ease and obedience, love and peace and mutual benefit, erupt into gushers of scalding anger:

"Cleav to a Wife," but let her *bee* a wife, let her *be* a meet help, a solace, not a nothing, not an adversary, not a desertrice; can any law or command be so unreasonable to make men cleav to calamity, to ruin, to perdition? ... "What therefore God hath joyned, let no man put asunder." But here the Christian prudence lies to consider what God *hath* joyn'd; shall we say that God hath joyn'd error, fraud, unfitnesse, wrath, contention, perpetuall lonelinesse, perpetuall discord? (*CPW* 2:605, 650, my emphases)

As in our original example, the mild voice of prudence is overthrown by pure rhetorical energy, heightened emotional pitch, and quickened pace – an *accelerando* of furious diction. This sequence of evils (error, fraud, unfitness, etc.) is clearly a miniature version of the Mary Powell saga as Milton constructed it, and appears over and over again in the divorce tracts, embroidered by accusations of putrid nullity or monstrous trickery, always directed against the wife and driven home with nervous protestations of the husband's innocence, and always blanketed in assurances that such a fate befalls "Millions" of the wisest men every day (*CPW* 2:603). If, however, the man is prudent and wise, as Milton constantly avers, how did he get involved in such an idiotic situation in the first place? If he is manly, active, heroic, always out to express his "true dignity" and to "acquit himself to freedom by his natural birthright" – as Milton continually claims – why is he so gullible and so passive, somehow not implicated at all in the act of choosing his wife, which is presented as an instantaneous "casualty" that "befalls him" like a piano dropping on his head?

For all their exegetical diligence, then, Milton's divorce tracts are at best dubious exegesis, and for all their rhetorical energy they are ineffective as public persuasion; they certainly fail to deliver their promised emotional reward – a "gentle stroking," a softening of bondage, a benefaction sweeter than wine and oil (*CPW* 2:245, 240). They do achieve more, though, than the Woolfian "peevish personalities" and "spiteful last word in his domestic quarrels," though they are certainly that. Their nervous tics, self-interruptions, and explosions of wounded innocence, their constant complaints about female usurpation, thralldom, succubean sorcery, and "grinding in the mill of a servile and undelighted copulation," are as it were hyper-ideological, straining masculinism to the limit and so revealing its contradictions. Their tautology and solipsism, their reliance on an authority that turns out to be the daughter of his *own* voice, the word of a God rewritten in his *own* image, brings them closer to pure poetry, to a kind of inner-directed art of violence.

It may be objected that I am dragging in aesthetic terms unnecessarily, labelling "poetic authority" what is merely rhetorical energy. I would argue, however, that Milton's flights are indeed poetic in seventeenth-century terms, not just for the cynical reason that his arguments are quite fictitious, but because, in his own words, they are more "sensuous and passionate" than other hermeneutics and more dependent on those properties of words that bring them closer to art than to exposition.[8] Milton never spelled out his theories in an *ars poetica*, but we can reconstruct his conception of verbal magic from poems like "At a Solemn Music": suitably enhanced by art, language gains a quasi-supernatural "power . . . Dead things with inbreathed sense able to pierce" (l.4). Trinity MS variants of the poem show that Milton associated this creative penetration with "equal raptures" and "happy spousal." In *Tetrachordon*, which means a four-stringed instrument, the Orphic poet tries to charm his way out of *un*equal raptures and *un*happy spousal.

The divorce tracts take us to the dark cellar where Milton's social anxieties and sexual fantasies mingled with the roots of his creativity. The divorce-campaign forced him to engage with and revise the text of Genesis, an essential stage in the shift towards *Paradise Lost* that perhaps started in these years of marital crisis. It forced him to abandon the apologetic, "left-handed," reference to his own prose and emphasize the language of poetic inspiration, to define the relations between manliness, liberty, and sexuality (as Hausknecht shows above), to generate a sustained text of headlong energy and daring originality, unified by focusing on the "prime institution of human existence" and locating the central area of human experience in the domestic. Above all, the divorce crisis forced him to confront the bodily stratum (beginning the move towards monism that flowers in *Paradise Lost*), and to articulate an imaginative vision of ideal marriage. In the 1640s, however, it is divorce, and not marriage, that represents the highest ideal, the most wonderful thing imaginable.

Paradise Lost ends with the protagonists painfully reconstructing their marriage and refusing the temptation to expel the other, but the divorce tracts, like *Samson Agonistes*, seek their consummation in cataclysmic violence, in what I called "a great sundering."⁹ As early as the *Apology for a Pomphlet*, written in the virginal years, we find not only an intensely romantic evocation of Platonic and chivalric Eros, but also a long and vividly imagined scene of Old Testament divorce, where the masculine Reformed church expels the female Popery, and she uses all her "whoorish cunning" to plant sentimental mementos and to lure him into "unclean wallowings" (*CPW* 1:942). (It is rather eerie to reflect that this was written *before* he met and married his Anglican wife.) In *De Doctrina* and *Tetrachordon* he proposes divorce as a "dear, noble and desirable cherishing of man's life," as a beneficial release of pent-up humors, a nature-cure for such problems as "frantick heresy," "blasphemous thoughts," "melancholy despair," "whordoms and adulteries," and "mutin[ies] against divine providence," as a "rule of perfection," and as "the highest commandment." He even equates it with the original act of divine creation, the "divorcing command" that first separated the universe from Chaos and will, must, separate John Milton from Mary Powell.¹⁰

In the light of this equation of divorce, creation, and the giving of life, we begin to notice other implications of those scenes of horror that run through all the divorce tracts – where the poor unwilling husband is locked in copulation with "something beneath man," tied like the victims of Mezentius to a rotting corpse, bound to "an image of earth and phlegm" (*CPW* 2:254, orig. "fleam"). *Image* here must mean an idol, a Dagon, a dead representation in the space where there should be his own "image and glory." The female is conceived not as another person, a partner in a mutual conversation, endowed with equal responsibilities and rights, but as an accessory ideal, a being who is simultaneously "occasional" and "inferior" and the pinnacle of an amorous dream, a Paradisal companion who embodies all the love promised by Plato, Ovid, St. Paul, Dante, Petrarch, and the romances (as the *Apology* tells us explicitly). Even more than Pygmalion, Milton longs for a wholly imaginary sexual partner authored, given life and vigor, by himself alone.

The horrors of the divorce tracts, as we would expect in a period of crisis both personal and political, belong to the history of radical iconoclasm as well as to the history of marital representation. Like Woolf's more subtle casting down of him as bogey, Milton's assertions (as he called his polemic works) are both text and praxis. In Milton's case, more precisely, they are texts that aspire to the condition of acts – acts of expulsion and acts of compensatory creation. Like his epic God, he wants to purge off the first revolted elements and then speak a new world into existence, a world where

Old Testament divorce *can* be carried out in the breath of a word, where God *does* bring perfect lovers together and *does* smite down the unfit and unwilling wife, the sorceress, the image of earth and phlegm.

I am aware of the paradox in all of this. I am painting Milton on the one hand as a violent iconoclast, on the other hand as an idolater and an overreacher for whom signification and authority are essentially "self-created, self-begot" – that is, as an embodiment of everything Milton himself most detested. I see him as "drunk with idolatry" (like the Philistines in *Samson Agonistes*), promoting his own intuitive masculinism over the word of God, blowing away the sexual and egalitarian lines of Genesis with "the single whiffe of a negative" – precisely what he attacked in the personal rule of Charles I (*CPW* 3:579). Isn't this just another partial or selective reading, like the Romantics' promotion of Satan or like Woolf's Modernist fragmentation, which I contrasted earlier to the thorough reading that accounts for all and only the lines of the text? I would answer by saying, firstly, that my assumptions are not necessarily anachronistic: psychomachia and dialogue were privileged forms in this period; rhetorical theory acknowledged that passion and *energia* had a signifying power of their own; and Pascal, of course, recognized that "le coeur a ses raisons que la raison ne connoit point." Secondly, I would say that a multiplex and contradictory model better suits the mind of Milton and the crisis of his age.

Milton is an anomalous creature, a Renaissance artist in a time of revolution, and we should expect signs of severe internal contradiction in him. The religious husband obedient to St. Paul had to love his own image as his own flesh in the sexual act; the religious radical had to cast down all graven images as a whoredom abominable to the Lord; the Platonist had to regard all imaginative creation (and potentially all graven images) as a higher form of sexual-erotic procreation, a birth-in-beauty. Milton dealt with this crisis by resorting to a kind of vitalistic dualism: for him these modes of iconophilia (the "image" of the sexual partner and the "image" of artistic creation) were indeed connected, but they existed in two opposite forms, one living and one dead, one supremely wonderful and the other utterly loathsome. Remember here that procreational "life and vigor," and the already-aesthetic idea that God makes the heart a "lively Sculpture," replace interpretation at the heart of *Tetrachordon*. Music, like the gods of Genesis, has the power to breath sense into "Dead things," and zealous preaching can "procreate" men, "making a kind of creation like to Gods, by infusing his spirit and likenesse into them."[11]

The idea of the Living Word, common to both Platonism and Christianity, is thus deepened until it breaks away even from the Scripture that creates its authority. At best, one could say that this created a new kind of artist, self-reliant and polyvocal: self-reliant because the "vital signs" of the true image could be established only by a corresponding vital energy in the words; polyvocal because containing a sort of proto-Whitmanesque multitude of contradictions. At worst, however (as Woolf sensed even in the smooth and impersonal splendors of *Paradise Lost*), this Miltonic solution brings about an extreme polarization of love and hatred for the opposite sex, an extreme "masculinism" that equates the image of God in man with male supremacy. If enforced by authority, this masculinism would be idolatrous both for the male (who assumes the role of God) and for the female (who is forced to worship maleness as divine). I have no objection to idolatry per se, in fact (as Woolf would say) I rather like it: what Judeo-Christians call idolatry is an essential forerunner of art and its appreciation. Yet I would want to distinguish between the productive kind of idolatry that inspires fresh images, and the sterile kind that reinstates the wooden idols of the tribe; and the masculinism of Milton (shared by most of his contemporaries) is of the second kind.

These speculations lead us to the heart of *Paradise Lost*. Many years ago now, my book *One Flesh* examined a number of connection-points between the divorce tracts and the epic, echoes of phrases or parallels of thought that prompt us to read one text against another. New interpretations can, however, still be generated out of this exchange, new readings of the struggle between erotic idealization and sexual abjection.[12] I will end with one such reading, fine-tuning my earlier account of the initial description of Adam and Eve (*PL* 4:288–318), which relates closely to Milton's mangling of Genesis in *Tetrachordon*.

Here, as I mentioned above, the image of God shines in Adam and Eve both – "in *their* looks divine" – but the genders are soon afterwards split apart in the notorious line "Hee for God only, shee for God in him." Coming from a close and suspicious reading of the divorce tracts, we should look for evasions and dissimulations; following Woolf's lead, we should gaze into the rich and elaborate poetic artifact, but also interrogate it. How, for example, does the condition ascribed to Eve differ from idolatry pure and simple: total devotion to a creature as if it embodied God? Not even St. Paul's tendentious revision of Genesis (that Eve was created for Adam and not vice versa) dared pretend that the female was made for the *God* in man. How does Milton authorize such a construction? He wants to persuade us that the image shone in them both, *but not to the same extent*: in fact he had said so in the crucial passage of *Tetrachordon* I analyze above. To mitigate St. Paul and to usher in the strange experiment with natural law and the dominion of the wiser female – just before the whole train of thought is blown off the rails by the breath of Milton's divine utterance – he says that "man is not to hold her as a servant, but receives her into a part of that empire which God proclaims him to, though not equally, yet largely, as his own image and glory: for it is no small glory to him, that a creature so like him should be made subject to him." This sounds quite moderate, until we reflect that it is a complete travesty of Genesis, where "empire" over the creatures is explicitly given to both male and female with no qualifications whatever, and the subjection of the woman is explicitly laid on as a punishment after the fall (3:16), and not mentioned before. Still, beside the ranting that erupts elsewhere in *Tetrachordon* it is a mild voice, and Milton is probably seeking to revive this tone when he echoes his own prose in the epic: the couple

> In naked Majestie seemd Lords of all,
> And worthie seemd, for in thir looks Divine
> The image of thir glorious Maker shone,
> Truth, Wisdom, Sanctitude severe and pure,
> Severe but in true filial freedom plac't;
> Whence true autoritie in men; though both
> Not equal, as their sex not equal seemd. (4:290–96)

The whole exegesis of the Image of God in *Tetrachordon* was so devious that we are bound to ask whether, here too, the appearance of logical connection and controlled structure will dissolve on closer inspection.

The crucial question is, how (and where) do the sexes get divided? "True authority" clearly should apply to both Adam and Eve as joint Lords of All, but the "whence" phrase, slung between two semi-colons, is unclear in its antecedent and its time-scale (does it mean then only or at all times?). This in turn makes us wonder about "men" in the phrase "whence true autoritie in men," which simultaneously refers back to *the two human beings Adam and Eve* and begins the process of whittling off the female share – with the immediate qualification "though both / Not equal . . . seem'd." Paradoxically, in the peevish *Tetrachordon* woman still rules the world "not equally, yet largely," whereas in *Paradise Lost*, where the representation of the female is infinitely more majestic, the adverbial particle and strict grammatical link is suppressed, so that "not equal" becomes a free-floating general epithet for the sexes, a sort of absolute ontological pronouncement. This free-standing authority is not allowed to remain, however, but is then tied to the explanatory devices held over by the contorted syntax. "Both not equal as their sex not equal seemed": *seemed* (a word pointedly repeated by the narrator here) enforces the subjective nature of these observations in a scene where the only observer is Satan; *their sex* sends us for explanation down to the visible anatomy of sexual difference.[13] The famous couplet about contemplation and valor versus soft attractiveness (itself a false parallelism sugared over by sheer sweetness of sound), and the famous "Hee for God only, shee for God in him," are both bracketed within this explanatory construction, as appendages of that "sex" whose sight is shared by Satan (without fig-leaf) and by the reader, in imagination.

Of all the primary and secondary sexual characteristics, it is hair that most eloquently signals this mystery; hair becomes a kind of radiant condensation of the image of God itself, the essential clue to what makes Adam and Eve Lords of All. Adam's proud forehead and parting "declar'd / Absolute rule"; Eve's lush curls "impli'd / Subjection, but required with gentle sway." The parallelism could not be closer, since in both phrases the line breaks after the verb of signification. What the words on the page say is that Adam rules over the beasts and creeping things sternly, and Eve gently; Adam *declares* his command and Eve *implies* hers. Each has a style of authority analogous to his or her genitalia, which cannot be described, and to his or her style of hair, which can: they are not "equal" in the sense of uniform or identical, but they are no more power-differentiated than, say, retrievers and spaniels. In a Paradisal context "equal" *should* be read as one of those words (like "wanton" or "error") that, by a deliberate semantic ploy of Milton's, retain their innocent, neutral, descriptive meaning in contrast to their fallen usage. Yet just as in *Tetrachordon* Milton had intruded an ideological "necessity" into the natural "construction" of Genesis, so here his hot breath forces male suprematism into the sentence, so that the subject of "required" becomes Adam – against all grammatical probability – and "subjection" rolls over so that it is Eve, and not the creeping things, who finds herself underneath. The disturbingly seductive phrases which close this long sentence ("yielded . . . yielded . . . with sweet reluctant amorous delay"), suspending time in a kind of heavy-lidded erotic daze, suspend judgment and "necessary construction" as well. To adapt Woolf's terms, Milton's poetic "felicities," his "combinations" of sensuous phrases in loose apposition, generate "rejections" of the egalitarian implications of Genesis 1, and thus subliminally associate the "mastery" of the poem with the mastering of Eve.

These ideological interventions are not always rigidly masculinist, however, nor do they always reveal a continuity or complicity between the divorce tracts and the epic. In the allusion to the genitals that follows Eve's "coy submission," for example, Milton denounces the "honor dishonorable" of fallen modesty – "mere shows of seeming pure." In the divorce tract *Colasterion* he had likewise attacked "dis-honourable honour" in the context of focusing on the genitals (*CPW* 2:728). His point was, however, utterly different: there, he was raging against the idea of giving sexuality importance in marriage; in the epic, he is celebrating sexuality. Bringing together these two uses of the same oxymoron only dramatizes the difference between the sensuous maturity of the great poem, and the narrow violence that frames the glowing idealism of the divorce tracts.

On the issue of female subordination and inferiority, again, echoes of the divorce tracts in *Paradise Lost* yield, not a simple continuity, but a complex pattern of combinations and rejections. In the divorce tracts, the rage against a sexual-reproductive definition of marriage led Milton to a higher ideal of gender-relations, a kind of mutual heterosexual "conversation" which diffuses erotic pleasure into every interchange; but though he liberates her from reproductive biology, he still assigns woman a subordinate and (to us) degrading role. The man is to go out into the real world, to study furiously, to fight for religion's sake; but it is hard for him to be "intense" all the time, so he needs to slip home once in a while for a little sensuous relaxation – "slackening his cords," as Milton puts it. The woman's "helpe in religion," quoted earlier, is thus defined in rather vulgar terms: she tones him up like a masseuse for his real achievements elsewhere, achievements that, ironically, consist of attacking "effeminate slackness" and "remissness" in bishops and royalist leaders. The same basic configuration occurs in this familiar passage that I am analyzing in *Paradise Lost* –

> For contemplation he and valour formed,
> For softness she and sweet attractive grace –

but here the context and the characterization blur these boundaries. In Paradise all life, all work, all arts, and all moral issues are domestic, in the praxis of which active and passive mingle; it is Eve who several times goes off to work and Adam who wants to stay close to her and cuddle. As the narrative develops, moreover, and they describe their earliest experiences and reactions to one another, we find that contemplation, action, and amorous fulfilment are not separated, but combined in both of them.

When Adam describes his longing for a partner in Book 8 (379–97), he does so in terms that evoke and refute the divorce tracts' model of unequal marriage. Though Adam is only a few minutes old, and though he is arguing against the supreme authority of God, he vehemently rejects the offer of an animal companion and insists that love cannot exist "in disparity / The one intense, the other still remisse" (386–87). This is the same image of musical strings, "intense" meaning taut and "remiss" meaning slack; but the equation of the junior partner with "slackening his cords" is now utterly rejected. Indeed, the whole notion of inequality is rejected – which is why this episode must be brought in to confront that "not equal" of Book 4: Adam refuses to be mated with an "inferior" (in contrast to the "inferior sex" of *Tetrachordon*), and demands of God "Among unequals what society / Can sort, what harmony or true delight?" (382–84). As in *Tetrachordon*, a more powerful realization of true marriage wells up, breathes forth, bursts out, overcomes the previous interpretation by sheer strength of imagination; but here the ideological drift is *away* from masculinism. God deliberately stimulates Adam's dramatic self-realization by pretending to argue against this vision of partnership; Adam's persistence thus reveals how deeply graven in human nature this desire for the equal is. The institution-verse, the keystone of Milton's authoritarian model in *Tetrachordon*, is now taken out of the mouth of God entirely, rewritten as the thought and utterance of Adam alone. This is still a scene of two males drawing up a contract about a female, but at the same time there is not a word in all this episode about occasionality, inferiority, or subordination.[14] The whole dynamics of visionary discovery, the whole pleasure of God when Adam demands what is already planned to complete his being, renders such traditional misogynist ideologies absurd. Two possibilities open up, both rather subversive. Either Adam has entirely rewritten this scene to hoodwink the listener and justify that erotic love for Eve which makes her seem his equal, the "wise" woman briefly evoked (and obliterated) in *Tetrachordon*; or Milton has created an imaginative and impassioned non-masculinist vision of primal equality, endorsed at the highest level – a vision that clashes, in some absolute and irresolvable way, with the hollow voices of masculine authority that sound throughout the poem.

It would be nice to conclude with a sort of psychomachia, rewriting *Paradise Lost* according to the Woolfian polarity of poetry and masculinism. On the one side the equal raptures and living words of egalitarianism, on the other side the Dead Things, male-suprematist statements discredited by their tone or context; a "smooth, strong & elaborate" vision of egalitarian ecstasy on one side, and "peevish personalities about . . . the woman's duties" on the other. Thus we could stress that the "not equal" of 4:296 is the hermeneutics of Satan, the subject of "seemed." Or that Eve sounds like an automaton, a real image of earth and phlegm, when she declares her own subordination in 4:635–38, in contrast to the soaring poetry she achieves immediately afterwards. Or that Adam's declaration of Eve's inferiority and distance from the image of God occurs in his shiftiest and most tainted speech before the fall. Or that the archangel Raphael embodies the worst

The aesthetics of divorce

aspects of the divorce tracts in his marital advice to [...] woman is inferior, less wise, a mere trick or show of s[...] 565–76). At one point, in fact, Raphael reveals his ina[...]ing of human gender by adopting a crudely sexual-procreationis[...] of creation: "Male he created thee, but thy consort / Female for race" is precisely the position that the divorce tracts attack most fiercely, unleashing upon it the Londoner's worst insults, "crabbed" and "rustic" (7:529–30).[15]

This comforting polarity would be an illusion, however. Clearly both sides are poeticized in Milton, both are bodied forth with rhetorical vehemence, seductive sensuousness, and vital energy. The rhetorical violence of the divorce tracts, struggling to find a form, allows us to see sex and gender as contested areas, as "controversies." In the great poem, Milton's concrete imaginative power allows us to see the unresolvable clash of two ideologies of gender – the ecstatic-egalitarian and the patriarchal-masculinist.[16] In terms of extrinsic authority, each claims the sanction of divine approval, and so each overrides the other – Escher's impossible staircase once again. In terms of poetic authority, each is brought to life at moments, made urgent and convincing. To adapt the passage with which this enquiry began, neither can stand before the breath of the other.

NOTES

1. Virginia Woolf, *The Diary*, vol. 1, ed. Anne Olivier Bell (San Diego, New York, and London: Harcourt Brace Jovanovich, 1979), 192–3.
2. Virginia Woolf, *The Letters*, ed. Nigel Nicolson and Joanne Trautman, vol. 2 (New York and London: Harcourt Brace Jovanovich, 1976), 282.
3. Sandra Gelbert, "Patriarchal Poetry and Women Readers: Reflections on Milton's Bogey," *PMLA* 93 (1978): 369–70.
4. Joan M. Webber, "The Politics of Poetry: Feminism and *Paradise Lost*," *Milton Studies* 14 (1980): 3–24, esp. 21–22 n. 6, and Diane McColley, *Milton's Eve* (Urbana: University of Illinois Press, 1983), 19 n. 6, pointed out glaring problems in Gilbert's reading of *Paradise Lost*; the opposite extreme from Gilbert was formulated in Joseph A. Wittreich's *Feminist Milton* (see review by James Grantham Turner in *Criticism* 21 (1989), 193–200, questioning most of his scholarly evidence). Since then the literature on Milton and gender has grown too vast to list in full, and will be familiar to readers of this volume; my apologies to anyone who feels unjustly omitted.
5. *CPW* 2:589–90; even before this violent turn, Milton's choice of "prudence and dexterity" as qualities of the putative female head show that he is only thinking of an artisanal household. For Milton's increasing tendency to blame the wife in *Tetrachordon* (including this passage), see Stephen M. Fallon, "The Spur of Self-Concernment: Milton in His Divorce Tracts," *Milton Studies* 38 (2000): 220–42.

6. CW 15:209, *PL* 4:291–2, 363–4.
7. *CPW* 1:764; for "engraving" see James Grantham Turner, "Elisions and Erasures" *Milton Quarterly* 30 (1996): 27–39.
8. *CPW* 2:403; for the context of erotic education, see James Grantham Turner, *Schooling Sex: Libertine Literature and Erotic Education in Italy, France, and England, 1534–1685* (Oxford: Oxford University Press, 2003), 48–49, 54–55.
9. In *One Flesh: Paradisal Marriage and Sexual Relations in the Age of Milton* (Oxford: Clarendon Press, 1987), 228; many points in this chapter have been expanded from this book. For the terroristic resonance of *SA*, see James Grantham Turner "Recent Studies in the English Renaissance," *SEL: Studies in English Literature 1500–1900* 41 (Winter 2001): 201 (written September 11, 2001).
10. *CPW* 2:240, 354, 254, 227, 667, 273.
11. *CPW* 1:721, cited in James Grantham Turner, "The Poetics of Engagement," in *Politics, Poetics and Hermeneutics in Milton's Prose*, ed. David Loewenstein and James Grantham Turner (Cambridge: Cambridge University Press, 1990), 264.
12. E.g. Henry Staten, *Eros in Mourning: Homer to Lacan* (Baltimore and London: Johns Hopkins University Press, 1995), ch. 6.
13. Alastair Fowler (reacting to Turner, *One Flesh*, 281) counters (over-literally) that Satan's view cannot possibly be represented since the narrator is Milton, using the word *God* and commenting on post-lapsarian shame; see his edition of *PL*, 2nd. edn. (London and New York: Longman, 1998), 237.
14. As Mary Nyquist emphasizes in "Gynesis, Genesis, Exegesis, and the Formation of Milton's Eve," in *Cannibals, Witches, and Divorce: Estranging the Renaissance*, ed. Marjorie Garber (Baltimore: Johns Hopkins University Press, 1987), 147–209.
15. Cf. Turner, *One Flesh*, 270.
16. I would still argue that my irreconcilable-contradiction model is the best solution to the question of Milton and gender, and that attempts to find a single, consistent pattern in Milton – or a consistent relation to a Scripture read as equally homogenous – are misguided, even fundamentalist; more sophisticated examples include Kent R. Lehnhof, "'Nor turnd I weene': *Paradise Lost* and Pre-Lapsarian Sexuality," *Milton Quarterly* 34 (2000): 67–83, and Desma Polydorou, "Gender and Spiritual Equality in Marriage: A Dialogic Reading of Rachel Speght and John Milton," *Milton Quarterly* 35 (2001): 22–32.

CHAPTER 3

Dalila, misogyny, and Milton's Christian liberty of divorce

Catherine Gimelli Martin

> Milton, the guardian and hierophant of sacred mysteries, [is] inalterably opposed to the "idleness and unmanly despair" of the false, effeminate creation ... however ... the image of the Miltonic father *being ministered to* hints that his powers are not quite absolute, that in fact he has been reduced to a state of dependence upon his female [literary] descendents [*sic*]. Blinded, needing tea and sympathy as well as secretarial help, the godlike bard loses at least some of his divinity and is humanized, even (to coin a term) Samsonized.
> —Sandra M. Gilbert and Susan Gubar, *The Madwoman in the Attic*

Although not specifically concerned with Milton's tragic drama, Gilbert and Gubar's *The Madwoman in the Attic* clearly implies that Milton's misogynistic hatred of all "effeminate creation" receives its final expression in Samson's "crushing" revenge upon Dalila and the full flower of her effeminate people. In return, his literary daughters are licensed to "Samsonize" the godlike bard lest they fall victim to his "bogey," the hierophant who makes women "at best a serviceable second" to masculine creation by associating the feminine principle with the satanic principle. From that perspective, the real hero of *Samson Agonistes* is Dalila, whose wrongs should be righted by critical daughters ready and willing to transvaluate the drama's fallen ethics.[1] Yet while their advice is specifically aimed at a female readership, Gilbert and Gubar are hardly unique in carrying on Samuel Johnson's old campaign against Milton's reputed misogyny, masculinism, paternalism, and elitism. Throughout the twentieth century, these charges have particularly surfaced in response to *Samson Agonistes*, a tragedy that ironically *seems* to celebrate the liberation of an oppressed, decentralized, kingless, and "effeminate" minority of Hebrew Danites from their powerful imperial oppressors. However, by following Johnson's example and overlooking the tragedy's supposedly "missing" middle, modern readers not only ignore the strikingly egalitarian spousal debate that casts Samson, not Dalila, in the role of tragic victim, but license Johnson's condescending dismissal of

53

the "unenlightened" poet.[2] Of course, his high Tory motives for deploring the anti-monarchical Milton's inappropriately "Turkish" sentiments toward women have long been recognized as both self-serving and, given Johnson's own sexual politics, hypocritical.[3] Yet as Gilbert and Gubar's influential treatment clearly shows, liberal critics have been just as convinced that Milton's new standard of companionate marriage was far more masculinist than feminist. Drawing on well-known facts about Milton's ill-advised marriage to Mary Powell and the legend of his "serviceable" daughters, these critics have concluded that the poet clearly failed to extend his concept of Christian liberty to women. Thus, despite their claim to legalize divorce for the "good of both sexes," his divorce tracts actually continue the battles of the sexes by other means.

Yet this line of argument begs an important question: *either* as his contemporaries believed, Milton's ideals were too advanced for the men of his age (perhaps including himself); *or* they are misogynistic by any standard, contemporary or modern – a point that not even Johnson would have been inclined to defend. Confusion on these key issues has been considerably heightened by the critical tendency to read Milton's portrait of Dalila – the epitome of bad women and bad spouses – as his ultimate exoneration of his divorce tract argument. While not wrong in itself, this conflation too often obscures the fact that both the tragedy and the tracts portray unfit spouses as the products of unfit marriages, which are not made by either partner alone. To emphasize this point, *The Doctrine and Discipline of Divorce* describes the "spontaneous" creation of bad spouses in the genderless language of universal cosmology:[4]

Seeing then there is indeed a twofold Seminary or stock in nature, from whence are deriv'd the issues of love and hatred distinctly flowing through the whole masse of created things, and that Gods doing ever is to bring the due likenesses and harmonies of his work together, except when out of two contraries met to their own destruction, he moulds a third existence, and that it is error, or some evil Angel which either blindly or maliciously hath drawn together in two persons ill imbarkt in wedlock the sleeping discords and enmities of nature lull'd to purpose with some false bait, that they may wake to agony and strife. (*CPW* 2:271)

The only remedy for the "enmities of nature" produced either by natural error or by some other malicious agent is thus to follow God's example and issue a benign "divorcing command" that restores order out of Chaos by "the separating of unmeet consorts" (*CPW* 2:273). Milton himself thought of taking this course with Mary Powell and Samson actually follows it with Dalila, although not without giving their mistaken "third existence" its due. Although he naturally wishes to dismiss the "traitress" in silence, he (or his poet) grants even this most "unmeet consort" every right to exonerate herself, and only ends their marriage once she completely fails to do so. For, by then, it has become plain to both partners that their continued union will only produce even more mutually destructive "third existences."

Samson's willingness to debate the issues involved in his mistaken marriage despite his bitter feelings closely reflects Milton's open admission that a strong "spur of self-concernment" (*CPW* 2:226) motivated his own divorce arguments. Yet the other, idealistic aspect of his motives has been conceded by even his most hostile modern critics, nearly all of whom agree that if he were "merely" self-interested or had simply wanted to change English law so that he could obtain a divorce, he could have argued his case on the grounds of desertion already well established in English Protestant thought.[5] Long before his first marriage, however, Milton had closely followed John Selden's researches into Hebrew marriage and divorce simply because they confirmed his own naturalistic and/or anti-sacramental views on the subject.[6] By further reforming all human relationships on the pattern of civil contracts, he believed that his divorce arguments would perform the function of a Reformed Theseus in defeating the monolithic minotaur, Custom. By providing "the clue that windes out this labyrinth of servitude to such a reasonable and expedient liberty," Milton – and others bold enough to join him – would advance human freedom and household peace so far that he might "be reck'n'd among the publick benefactors of civill and humane life; above the inventors of wine and oyle" (*CPW* 2:240).[7]

Yet this Reformed Theseus also demanded a Reformed Ariadne to help him defeat the monstrous force of Custom. Depicting this monster who constantly strives to "persecute and chase away all truth and solid wisdome out of humane life" as an androgynous amalgam of a female face and a serpentine male trunk, he summons an equally androgynous force to defeat it: "Time the Midwife," who arrives to "church" or legitimate the "father of his young *Minerva*" (*CPW* 2:223–25). Although Milton's critics persist in discussing this strange hybrid as a "masculinist" allegory, its redemptive function is clearly filled not by a traditional father-figure but by a benign mother/midwife who can either "deliver" Truth via male parthogenesis (as here), or bring her to birth from a "womb of teeming" female ideas (*CPW* 2:224–25). While admittedly bizarre, this androgynous creative principle betrays no more real hatred or fear of "effeminacy" than Milton's more successful tributes to maternal creation.[8] Nor did he ever retract his androgynous claim to restore divorce for "*the good of both Sexes*," even when female contemporaries like the infamous Mrs. Attaway and the still unidentified "*Maids at Algate*" took him at his word. He not only held his ground after being bitterly denounced by Presbyterians in Parliament and the anonymous male critic addressed in *Colasterion*, but actually aligned himself with the "maids" whom he claimed had more wit than the scrambled "Servingman at Addlegate" (*Colasterion, CPW* 2:750).

This consistent tilt toward androgyny is ultimately rooted in Milton's monist conviction that God's goodness prevented him from establishing two contradictory "revealed wills grappling in a fraternall warre with one another" (*DDD, CPW* 2:295), and that he rather seeks a harmonious synthesis at every level of his creation. As a result, Milton reasons that the ancient purity of Hebrew divorce is innately consistent with both Christian liberty and natural law, the two consistent principles guiding God's universe. This position causes him to reject the standard Calvinist dichotomy between fallen "female" nature and the "manly" dispensation of grace in favor of a truer Reformation that would reestablish the original "inseparability of body and spirit" ordained in Eden.[9] Unlike those who would "animalize" human nature by separating body from spirit or granting priority to the body, he hoped that his teaching would spiritually *and* physically raise "Many helples Christians" of all sexes "from the depth of sadness and distresse." Thus just as Christ broke the old Sabbath law in order to cure the physical distress suffered by the woman "*whom Satan had bound eighteen years*" (*CPW* 2:335), his spirit of Truth would "set free many daughters of *Israel*" from a similar bodily plight.

Here, as elsewhere, Milton grounds his characteristic anti-legalism in Christ's anti-pharisaical preference for mercy over sacrifice (Matt. 12:3). His final divorce tract, *Colasterion*, thus reiterates the ideals of his first, *The Doctrine and Discipline of Divorce*, by condemning the "fleamy clodd" (*CPW* 2:740) who would prefer ritual observance to Christian liberty *or* charity:

It is not the formal duty of worship, or the sitting still, that keeps the holy rest of Sabbath; but whosoever doth most according to charity, whether hee work, or work not; hee breaks the holy rest of Sabbath least. So Mariage being a civil Ordinance made for man, not man for it; hee who doth that which most accords with charity, first to himself, next to whom hee next ows it, whether in mariage or divorce, hee breaks the Ordinance of marriage least. (*Colasterion, CPW* 2:750)

Here, as throughout his four divorce tracts, Milton reserves his bitterest scorn for Pharisees or "Philistines" who (like his Dalila herself) would forsake Christian liberty in favor of the "Egyptian bondage" of canon law. Like

"Mr. Addlegate," such individuals care more for the physical or "carnal" than the spiritual aspects of both true marriage and worship, which Milton links to their regressively patriarchal attitude toward women. Pushing the Protestant emphasis on companionate marriage to its logical if unlooked-for conclusion, he recasts its prime purpose not as enforced procreation but as a spontaneous, "*individual and intimat conversation, and mutual benevolence*" between man and wife (*CPW* 2:609; italics in the original). Moreover, as *Paradise Lost* clearly shows, in seventeenth-century parlance the words "conversation" and "benevolence" carry strong sexual connotations that Milton also refuses to ignore or demote so long as sexuality serves rather than hinders spiritual and emotional intimacy. If not, divorce may be justified to prevent what cannot be maintained in spirit from becoming an enslaving physical or legal "idol" – the exact opposite of Christian liberty (*CPW* 2:275–78).

Both Milton's seventeenth-century readers and his modern critics have been inclined to dismiss these lofty notions as hypocritical since (as he himself ruefully concedes) their author could have spent little time "conversing" with his first bride before their marriage. Yet both sets of readers tend to ignore Milton's willingness to sacrifice his reputation for these principles, which actually sent him in search of a more suitable partner once Mary's desertion made further conversation impossible. The response of the "witty Miss Davis" to his suit will probably never be known, but even had she agreed, their hopes would have been ruined by the political and social considerations that caused his wife's family to arrange a "surprise" reconciliation. Given Milton's life-long problems with his uncharitable Royalist mother-in-law and with Mary's daughters (whom Mrs. Powell quite probably turned against him), the enforced "benevolence" that thereafter followed was probably no more successful than his own principles would have predicted. These circumstances alone would have soured many an idealist against women, but both the textual evidence of his sonnets (especially Sonnets 9, 10, 14, and 23) and his epic portrait of Eve suggest the reverse. So, too, does *Colasterion*, which idealistically and categorically rejects the traditional Augustinian argument that only men, not women, were created for rational conversation. In contrast to supposedly more "enlightened" contemporaries like Sir Thomas Browne and Michel de Montaigne, he insists that women have the same capacity for "mental fellowship from which . . . classical commentators on friendship disqualify" them. In fact, Gregory Chaplin finds Milton's position so radical that it virtually makes "hierarchical gender difference . . . disappear."[10]

Yet the type of objection raised by the anonymous "Servingman" addressed in *Colasterion* is not limited to contemporary males. Modern feminists like Gilbert and Gubar take essentially the same position when they reject the "liberal" or egalitarian case for equality in favor of late twentieth-century "identity" politics and its separatist ideal of female "embodiment." Thus, like Milton's early opponent, they claim that the classical languages employed by him and other men of his era are deeply inimical to women, for Greek and Latin "not only are . . . the quintessential languages of masculine scholarship (as Virginia Woolf, for instance, never tired of noting), they are also the languages of the Church, of patristic and patriarchal ritual and theology. Imposed upon English, moreover, their periodic sentences, perhaps more than any other stylistic device in *Paradise Lost*, flaunt the poet's divine foreknowledge."[11] This passage alone seems to justify Louis Menand's exasperated remark that "only an English professor would believe" that either Milton or his periodic sentences is chiefly "responsible for the historical subjugation of women."[12] For in forgetting that modern feminism was largely built upon the periodic sentences mastered by Mary Wollestonecraft and her successors in England and America, this historical *reductio ad absurdum* also overlooks Milton's rejection of the paternalistic liturgy of the Anglican church and his consistent use of English in addressing his fellow countrymen and women on national issues like marriage and divorce, freedom of the press, and church reform.[13] Last but hardly least, it overlooks Virginia Woolf's arguments in favor of the female mastery of Greek and Latin in *A Room of One's Own*, which highly praises that "valiant old woman," Eliza Carter, because she "tied a bell to her bedstead in order that she might wake early and learn Greek."[14]

Yet even professional Miltonists often casually assume the poet's complicity with paternalism, as when a recent edition of his works featured the portrait of a guileful Dalila happily "Samsonizing" her sleeping husband beneath Chrysostom's Latin motto, FOEMINA DIABOLO TRIBVS ASSIBUS EST MALA PEIOR, or, "A bad woman is worse than the devil by a small coin." In fact, Milton's *Tetrachordon* not only refutes this traditional proverb but gives it an entirely new, egalitarian twist by remarking that if "a bad wife is a help for the devill, . . . the like may be said of a bad husband" (*CPW* 2:607). Even Milton's Samson freely acknowledges this truism, which, along with other prominent parallels between the divorce tracts and the tragedy, led Northrop Frye to make the now usual connection: although "The Bible does not call Dalila Samson's wife, . . . in Milton she must be a wife to absorb his divorce arguments." Given the drama's strikingly equitable treatment of the common duplicity/complicity of both genders in bad marriages, Frye also influentially separated Samson from his misogynistic chorus, whose inability to "fully understand the meaning of the events they are involved in" is betrayed by their "doggerel" verses. In contrast, he finds Dalila so sympathetically rendered that Frye believes Milton must be "of Dalila's party without knowing it."[15] Yet, if here as elsewhere Milton typically gives strong positions to both antagonists, Frye unfortunately forgets that *Samson Agonistes* actually exonerates *neither* spouse. Like the fallen Adam, Samson at first blames the victim, but as he begins to recover his "calling," ceases to scapegoat his wife so childishly. By at last accepting responsibility for his fall, he then comes to realize that neither human sympathy nor human heroism justifies the genderless weakness of deliberate wickedness. As Frye intuited, this new realization completely invalidates the chorus's masculinist attempt to separate "pardonable" masculine faults from inexcusable feminine failings, while even more significantly *validates* Samson's new understanding that women can only become male "snares" through a mutual indulgence in sexual idolatry. By strutting about like "a petty god" invulnerable to all comers (529), he made an "unfit helpmate" of both his spouse and himself; but by overcoming the angry, vindictive, self-justifying warrior within, he at last becomes a hero fully "fit" to converse with his wife and his God.

A similar dynamic is clearly evident in the divorce tracts, which gradually move beyond Milton's first, awkward attempts to vindicate both "unfit" partners of sin while still wincing from the "self-concernment" of wounded pride. Focusing less on "unmeet" spouses than on unmeet divorce laws that value the physical and sexual "bone" of marriage above its spiritual heart and soul, his third tract radically redefines the bond that makes marriage mates "one flesh" as "a relation much rather then a bone; the nerves and sinews thereof are love and meet help." If well formed, these sinews "seldom break," but they will not "knit . . . every couple that maries" if their "nerves" were "never truly joyn'd" by mutual love and esteem (*Tetrachordon*, CPW 2:604). In that case, these malformed "knots" should be dissolved by the same authority that mistakenly "knit" them: the individual consent of both parties. The unfallen Adam of *Paradise Lost* similarly recognizes the importance of spousal consent when he refuses to command Eve to remain "tied" to his side against her will, even while fully aware that their mutual enemy would be confronted better together than alone. This passage is crucial to understanding Milton's thinking on the subject, for while unlike all subsequent wives Eve is literally Adam's flesh and bone, she too was never meant to be a "lifeless rib" with no independent volition or "conversation."[16] Although Eve's argument for individual self-reliance is usually linked to Milton's position in *Areopagitica* (*CPW* 2:527), Adam's response is even closer to the logic of the divorce tracts: if a husband can "find no contentment from the other, how can he return it from himself, or no acceptance, how can hee mutually accept?" For without free consent, his wife's discontent may become permanent rather than (as with Eve) merely transitory. The need for consent significantly intensifies after the fall, when spouses more frequently find themselves at cross purposes. If this schism proves irreparable, then "What more equal, more pious then to untie an accidental conjunction of this or that man & woman, for the most natural disagreement of meet from unmeet, guilty from guiltless, contrary from contrary?" (*CPW* 2:237). This sentence succinctly recapitulates Milton's historic progression from treating "unmeet," blameworthy, or "guilty" mates, to empathizing with those who are both simply and inexplicably "contrary."

Although like virtually everyone else in his era, Milton grounds his doctrine in the conventional Pauline teaching of "natural" masculine priority, his critics have also generally overlooked his striking modifications of this teaching. Because he believes that the universal principle of Christian liberty is more fundamental than the particular male principle of headship, he accounts it a somewhat mysterious honor that man has been chosen to guide a female partner who was never meant to be a merely serviceable "servant" but rather an innate "part of that empire which God proclaims him to, though not equally, yet largely, as his own image and glory: for it is no small glory to him, *that a creature so like him* should be made subject to him." At the same time, he allows for "particular exceptions" to this subjection, as when the wife "exceed her husband in prudence and dexterity, and he contentedly yeeld" (*CPW* 2:589, emphasis added). Although hardly radical from a modern perspective, this new teaching effectively overturns the conventional system in which intrinsically inferior women are innately subject to men. It not only means that they can no longer be considered legal property (as they remained throughout the nineteenth century), but also that they must be accepted as negotiating partners in a sense that clearly made his male contemporaries quiver at the bone (viz., *Colasterion*). No wonder, when Milton is ready to defend an afflicted woman's right to flee an oppressive husband despite the lack of any "plain" scriptural basis for this right. Again invoking the higher principle of universal natural law, he simply refuses to believe that "the rescript of *Antoninus* in the Civil Law [should] give release to servants flying . . . to change thir cruel Maisters," but that "God who in his law also is good to injur'd servants . . . [should] not consider the wrongs and miseries of a wife which is no servant" (*CPW* 2:626–27).

Dalila, misogyny, and Milton's divorce

Those who level charges of blatant masculinism at Milton's divorce tracts usually place at least some of the blame on his need to maintain a "biblically correct" argument. Yet this excuse actually tends to obscure his implicitly unbiblical definition of marriage as a most *un*despotic "league of love and willingnes," where "if faith bee not willingly kept, it scars is worth the keeping; nor can bee any delight to a generous minde, with whom it is forcibly kept." In contrast to Paul's insistence that both slaves and wives should accept their condition so long as they do not endanger their eternal salvation, *Tetrachordon* universally condemns the unjust "enthrallment" of any human "to one who cannot, or will not bee mutual . . . [as] the ignoblest, and the lowest slavery that a human shape can bee put to" (*CPW* 2:624–26). Although here as elsewhere Milton conventionally casts these beliefs in terms of the neutral "he," he also leaves no doubt that this pronoun embraces the "afflictions of a wife . . . which is no servant" (*CPW* 2:626–27). Given his absolute clarity on these points, one must question whether much of the animus of modern critics is really aimed at Paul's teachings on headship, especially when their charges prove startlingly counter-factual. Thus when Mary Nyquist insists that Milton everywhere makes "use of plural forms potentially inclusive of both sexes only to come to rest with a nongenerically masculine *he*," or when James G. Turner claims that the "woman alone is obliged to be mutual," as Chaplin notes, we must be careful to ascertain that their charges do not represent a deliberate conflation of "Milton's tactical response to his opponent's claim" with his own far less conservative position.[17]

An extreme example of this strategy can be found in Shari Zimmerman's support of the Nyquist/Turner charge that the duty of being "mutual" belongs only to wives. In the passage in question, Milton states that the marriage covenant "differs from personal duties," for if these

> be not truly don, the fault is in our selves; but mariage to be a true and pious mariage is *not in the single power of any person*; the essence whereof, as of all other Covenants is in *relation to another, the making and maintaining causes thereof are all mutual*, and must be a communion of spiritual and temporal comforts. *If then either of them cannot, or obstinately will not be answerable in these duties*, so as that the other can have no peaceful living, or enduring the want of what he justly seeks, and sees no hope, *then strait from that dwelling love, which is the soul of wedloc, takes his flight, leaving only some cold performances of civil and common respects*, but *the true bond of mariage, if there were ever any there, is already burst like a rott'n thred.* Then follows dissimulation, suspicion, fals colours, fals pretences, and wors then these, disturbance, annoyance, vexation, sorrow, temtation eevn in the faultles person. (*CPW* 2:630–31; my emphasis).

Quoted whole, Milton's stress on the mutual obligations of "either party" makes his use of the generic "he" obvious: the needs and sympathies of his female audience are not dismissed in silence any more than "unmeet" wives should be. Yet Zimmerman argues that this passage does silence them by warning that "cold performances" toward their husbands will justify suspicions of their "inward rottenness." As a result, she concludes that Milton denies *all* women the freedom he grants even to "traitresses" like Dalila: the privileges of "ranging freely, disobeying her husband's commands, or presenting to public view any cause for suspicion," all of which supposedly provide grounds for "silent dismission."[18] Yet in both his divorce tracts and in his tragedy, Milton actually attributes "cold performances" to cold *marriages*, not wives, and thus to both partners.[19]

Clarifying these points also helps to show that the eighteenth-century confinement of bourgeois women to the private sphere did not actually begin during the late revolutionary period or even the Restoration.[20] As many recent studies of revolutionary women have shown, their freedom actually increased throughout this period. In its earlier phases, Milton himself heaped praise on Parliament for accepting the public petitions of "women, . . . and that sometimes in a lesse humble guise then for petitioners, [who] . . . have gone with confidence, that . . . neither . . . would [they] be rejected, nor their simplicity contemn'd, nor their urgency distasted either by the dignity, wisdome, or moderation of that supreme Senate; nor did they depart unsatisfi'd" (*Apology against a Pamphlet, CPW* 1:926 [1642]). Afterward, their public role was ably defended by important early feminists like Aphra Behn, Bathsua Makin, and Margaret Fell.[21] The fact that Milton later continued to support their cause is most fully confirmed by his treatment of Dalila, who, in accordance with his revolutionary principles, is neither "silenced" nor considered unfit on the basis of any external sexual or physical criteria, not even her lack of chastity. Of course, as a Nazarite, Samson at first agrees with the chorus's traditional complaint that both Dalila's Philistine uncleanness and her "unchaste" collusion with her people's priests and public officers contaminated and finally castrated him (or at least his "eyes"). Yet, ironically, his final marital conversation with her finally releases him from the paternalistic assumptions condemned both in the divorce tracts and by his own bad example.

The autobiographical resonances of the tragedy suggest that Milton himself may have experienced a similar marital progress, if not with Mary, then with later wives. Like the young Milton, Samson confesses that he initially mistook Dalila's "virgin veil, / Soft, modest, meek, demure" (1035–36) for personal and "conversational" virtues that she actually lacked. He thus sees himself erring in much the same way that *The Doctrine and Discipline of Divorce* argues that "best govern'd men . . . lest practiz'd in these affairs" (*CPW* 2:249) are liable to err. Yet, since Samson admits never having been one of the "wisest men and best" (1034), either by nature or past experience with the woman of Timna, from the very first he accepts more responsibility than Milton earlier allowed to inexperienced bachelors. This first, modest step toward accepting his share of the blame ends with his freely accepting Dalila's "bitter reproach, but true," that he set the precedent for her transgression when "I to myself was false ere thou to me" (*SA* 820, 823). Yet, as noted above, he accordingly grants her only "such pardon therefore as I give my folly" and weakness (824–25). Critics who consider this concession uncharitable typically forget that Samson is taking the divorce tracts' most holistic approach to marital failure by rooting both male "mistake" and female "perverseness" in the passive lack of self-awareness and active pursuit of self-deception common to both genders. Both males and females rightfully desire love, honor, and personal validation, but these desires are only ethically valid when they transcend mere selfishness or pseudo-heroism. Female pandering to male lust or pride is thus no more truly honorific than a male spoils system which swaps power, gold, and social status for sexual trophies (836–37), for both barter away the intellectual and emotional mutuality essential to "true" marriages.

Of course, Samson is initially no more aware of this higher marital ideal than Dalila herself. Discovering it through an unexpected and unpleasant confrontation that finally reveals their mutual inability to converse, he only gradually realizes the extent to which both were fully complicit in her treachery. By encouraging her exploitation of weaknesses falsely identified as strengths, he "justly" found himself "enslav'd / With dotage, and his sense deprav'd" (1040–41) by his enemies as well as himself. Even so, Samson cannot be justified in divorcing Dalila until she flatly refuses to accept her share of guilt and responsibly to converse in the more honest terms he now demands, a fact that can only be established through their heated but nonetheless beneficial debate.[22] However, in true Greek tragic style, the unfallen potential implicit in this debate is concealed both from Samson and from an audience who is initially "ensnared" along with him and his chorus. Dalila's entry is thus conspicuously seductive as she "demurely" floats in equipped with all the traditional physical "gear" of feminine sexuality. Yet even here, she does not appear as a mere "image of earth and fleam" (*CPW* 2:254), but as an ambiguous, amphibious

> thing of Sea or Land?
> Female of sex it seems,
> That so bedeckt, ornate, and gay,
> Comes this way sailing
> Like a stately Ship
> Of *Tarsus*, bound for th' Isles
> Of *Javan* or *Gadire*
> With all her bravery on, and tackle trim,
> Sails fill'd, and streamers waving,
> Courted by all the winds that hold them play,
> An Amber scent of odorous perfume
> Her harbinger, a damsel train behind.
>
> (*SA* 710–21)

Like Cleopatra on her barge, Dalila first appears as a classical temptress made even more sinister through her association with the satanic sea powers of Tyre and Tarshish (cf. *Tarsus*, *PL* 1:200). This description links her both to the Satan/leviathan of *Paradise Lost* and to the "fishy" Philistine idol, Dagon, whose Semitic name means "fish" but in this connection also suggests a sea-monster. Nevertheless, just as Eve's unwanted presence fruitfully traps Adam into understanding that only fallen men blame women for their falls, Samson ultimately learns that the reappearance of this "rich *Philistine* matron" (722) functions precisely like "the noted fish" of *Tetrachordon*: to "ensnare" him into realizing his own Philistinism. According to the Yale edition of Milton's prose, this "'noted Fish' is probably the squid, which, in the medieval bestiaries, escapes by surrounding itself with a cloud of ink" (*CPW* 2:242). Yet *Tetrachordon* argues that even Christ rightly used such "fishy" tactics in confronting the Pharisees' questions on remarriage, for "The manner of these men comming to our Saviour, not to learne, but to tempt him, may give us to expect that their answer will bee such as is fittest for them, not so much a teaching, as an intangling" (*CPW* 2:642). In *Surprised by Sin*, Stanley Fish (who appears to be playing on his own name here) famously proposed that *Paradise Lost* uses this "reader-response" trick to trap its audience into its initial sympathy with the devil.[23] Yet these tactics are even more appropriate in presenting an ambiguous woman like Dalila than an insidious supernatural foe like Satan, especially since this trick "classically" helps Milton to entangle both the self-pitying Samson and his surprised audience into fruitfully debating murky questions of religious, domestic, and civil liberty – the three-pronged subject of both his prose tracts and his tragedy (*CPW* 4.1:624).[24]

Milton's prefatory remarks on classical tragedy strongly hint that the answers to these debates will only surface in the drama's inky Euripidean climax, and this point is confirmed as Dalila's veil turns out *not* to disguise the "accomplisht snare" (*SA* 230) whose "unlivelines & naturall sloth . . . is really unfit for conversation" (*CPW* 2: 249).[25] While Samson and Dalila will in fact need to separate due to irreconcilable differences, their conversation soon teaches the audience that their incompatibility is neither innate nor acquired but the natural by-product of their inability to agree on the nature of human good and natural liberty. Of course, the outcome of this public debate is partly overdetermined by the Hebrew/Philistine or male/female poles of the debate, but its actual openness is indicated by the continuing critical debate over its outcome. The poles themselves are relatively clear: as in Sonnet 23, a second wife is offered ritual purification exceeding any available under the "old Law," but unlike Milton's "espoused saint," Dalila rejects it in favor of the old idols of tribal law and feminine bondage.[26] However, the fact that hers is a *human* failure, not any uniquely "feminine" inability to comprehend higher things, is underscored both by the Alcestis-like heroine of the sonnet and by the subsequent entrance of the Philistine "giant," Harapha. Far more than Dalila herself, Harapha represents the limitations of the tribal mentality: the lack of any independent verbal, intellectual, or moral resilience outside of his customary authoritarian sphere. Since both Samson and Dalila gain this resilience from their common "feminine" understanding of suffering, Harapha's appearance ironically invalidates Dalila's disingenuous self-defense due to "natural" female inferiority. Besides this truly weak excuse, she summons the whole misogynistic catalogue of traditional feminine defects to her aid: the curiosity, fickleness, garrulity, and jealousy "incident to all our sex" (*SA* 774). Yet these defects also fail to exonerate her since they are so obviously shared by both Harapha and Samson, and since her husband's renewed strength so obviously stems from his simultaneous admission and repentance of them. In contrast, her hypocritical excuses not only convict Dalila as charged, but confirm Samson's mature belief that weakness is not a feminine quality of any kind, but rather the last refuge of scoundrels of both sexes (834).

Dalila defines herself as just such a scoundrel when she finally admits that her true motive for betraying her husband was not feminine weakness but misconceived strength and overweening pride: she aimed at becoming a Philistine version of Jael – the Hebrew woman who single-handedly smote the powerful Sisera (976, 982–84) – without considering the justice of her cause. For while Jael slew a pompous general who presumed upon her feminine weakness, as Samson rightly complains, Dalila betrayed her own husband in defiance of both tribal and universal law:[27]

> Being once a wife, for me thou wast to leave
> Parents and country; nor was I their subject,
> Nor under their protection but my own,
> Thou mine, not theirs; if aught against my life
> Thy country sought of thee, it sought unjustly,
> Against the law of nature, law of nations.
>
> (885–90)

Dalila's response to these objections is almost as insulting as Sisera's presumption upon Jael's weakness. Ignoring Samson's attempt at rational redress, she now suggests that sexual congress with her was and will be well worth the price of a betrayal she asks him simply to "forget," since "That what by me thou hast lost thou least shalt miss" (927) – his eyes. This unsubtle sexual innuendo not only proves that Dalila conceives of marriage as a power struggle in which the men officially on top can be secretly controlled by the women below in return for sexual favors; it also illustrates her self-indulgent inability to realize how much her own behavior has already "opened" Samson's formerly blinded eyes. Since drinking from her "fair enchanted cup" (934) has led him into a humiliating political captivity mirroring his sexual captivity, their relationship can only be resumed by mutually accepting the more egalitarian ethic that Samson now upholds. For only then can they both work toward the universal standard of well-being that the divorce tracts regard as "the great and almost only commandment of the Gospel [:] . . . to command nothing against the good of man, and much more no civil command, against his civil good" (*CPW* 2:638–39).[28]

Dalila's final rejection of this universal law in favor of a "blind" provincialism that falsely promises to make her one of "the famousest / Of Women, sung at solemn festivals, / Living and dead" (*SA* 976, 982–84) thus invalidates her supposedly "enlightened" feminist ideals. By opting for the patriarchalism of a Spinoza – someone who would deny women (like children and the insane) the ethical responsibility that Samson holds out to her – Dalila condemns both herself and the mores of her culture. As a result, her crime actually consists not in choosing a public role but in choosing the wrong public. By violating the universal "law of nature, law of nations" (890), she lends support to gods who, through this very violation, declare themselves to be morally and spiritually empty idols. Nor is Samson's "law of nations" a legal fiction either then or now, since spouses cannot be legally coerced into harming or testifying against one another to this day. By voluntarily abrogating this code and colluding to deprive her husband of his own "freedom by his naturall birth-right" (*CPW* 2:589–90; cf. 2:273–74),

Dalila forfeits both their collective human rights and her feminine liberty to "Magistrates / And Princes" (*SA* 850–51), priests and "wisest men" of "grave authority" who "took full possession" of her "Virtue . . . truth, duty" (857, 867–70). By defending their superior right to these dear possessions, she additionally invalidates her claim to have acted as a loving spouse (790–99). Instead of providing "meete help," she has ignored the "superior and more naturall law . . . that the wiser should govern [and cherish] the lesse wise, whether male or female" (*CPW* 2:589).[29] Since by his own admission Samson was the less wise ("Immeasurable strength they might behold / In me, of wisdom nothing more than mean," *SA* 206–7), her repeated refusal to contribute either to her husband's or to their common marital good has violated all the fundamental laws of love (905–6).

At the same time, Samson's innate weaknesses do not explain much less justify his delegation of moral responsibility to her, as he slowly realizes (373–419, 448–59, 488–501, 532–40). Gradually considering his own culpability as a cause rather than an effect of Dalila's sins against him, Samson engages in a "trial but what is contrary" which at last reveals that he too had worshipped God as an idol or tyrant rather than as a merciful proponent of human growth through failure and correction. This realization is crucially important, since it alone legitimates Samson's demand that Dalila choose between an arbitrary tribal god and a God whose universal laws support human liberty rather than servility to idolatrous priests who cannot "acquit themselves and prosecute their foes / But by ungodly deeds" (896–900). In this context, Dalila's rejection of this offer is not merely a refusal of Samson, his God, or his people, but of the cardinal libertarian principles that Milton believed were commonly upheld by natural, Hebrew, classical, and Christian law. As in the divorce tracts, these principles have been too often ignored by readers who assign beliefs he opposes to Milton himself. Here, they include the chorus's tribal belief that Samson's "unmanly despair" is inherently rooted in a "false, effeminate creation" like Dalila. From that perspective, she is indeed not just as a "manifest Serpent" in the end, but a Levitically impure thing of "Sea or Land" from the beginning—a "Traitress," "sorceress," "Hyena," a "thorn intestine," and all the other accusations that the angry Samson initially levels at her and his chorus never rises above (725, 819, 748, 1037–38).[30] Yet this view of the tragedy completely fails to account for Samson's gradual recognition of the mutually fallacious values shared by Dalila, himself, and his people, which are not simply the work of his "fallacious bride" but of all the worldly "Idolists, and Atheists" whom his Nazaritic pride has aided and abetted (532–33, 452–56). Leaving his chorus to wallow in their own objectifying mythos of female duplicity, depravity, and castrating desire, Samson now perceives that the "sting" of male engulfment is eternally "engendered" in the combined masculine/feminine roots of narcissistic, incestuous pride (cf. *PL* 2.752–814). As an antidote, he adopts his author's belief in an interpersonal rather than a paternalistic model of marriage that places the spousal contract of Christian liberty above everything except the divine and natural laws supporting it.

Unlike conventional Protestant Reformers such as Bullinger, Paraeus, Dod and Cleaver, Ames or Perkins, or even humanists like Erasmus, Milton did not continue to regard marriage as a "kind of contract which has a special supernatural binding force . . . not to be judged according to the usual principles of human contracts."[31] In replacing the chorus's Levitical or unilateral conception of the marriage contract with Milton's bilateral, conversational model, Samson must thus reject his former association of "effeminacy" with the violation of sexual, ritual taboos and "seals" (*SA* 49), and accept the female principle within. Fish accurately identifies this feminine principle with Samson's "womanish vulnerability to the power of words," but accepts the chorus's "masculinist" assessment of it as an "Oedipal" punishment inflicted by his failure to secure his "vessel" and maintain his "seal." Having incontinently spilt his secrets, Samson loses all manhood and honor along with his sight: symbolically and all but literally castrated, he effectively "becomes a woman."[32] Yet this resolutely unredemptive, masculinist reading not only overlooks Milton's relentless critique of the male heroic ethic both here and in *Paradise Lost*, but also forgets the positive signs of Samson's "feminine" spiritual renewal growing with his hair.

Milton's rejection of the traditional heroic ethic in *Paradise Lost* is well known: the "long and tedious havoc [of] fabl'd Knights / In Battles feign'd" leaves "the better fortitude / Of Patience and Heroic Martyrdom / Unsung" (*PL* 9.30–34). Yet readers too often forget that *Samson Agonistes* continues this critique not just in the person of Harapha but also in the values that both Manoa and the chorus share with their failed hero (*SA* 130–38, 1119–55). These pseudo-values not only lead to the misogynistic scapegoating of Dalila – for them, the *only* cause of Samson's unheroic fall from the "top of wondrous glory, / . . . To lowest pitch of abject fortune" (167, 169) – but also to the false belief that she has forever "cut him off" from his calling. The end result is an unwavering justification of traditional male dominance. Since throughout history "wisest Men / Have err'd, and by bad Women been deceiv'd" (210–11), and since few have ever maintained a manly continence so perfect as to keep their "weaker vessel" permanently in thrall, "What

Pilot so expert but needs must wreck / Embark'd with such a Steersmate at the Helm?" (1044–45). Hence the chorus upholds only one "universal Law" – the law of absolute female submission denied by Milton's divorce tracts, his Adam, and his Samson. For this law

> Gave to the man despotic power
> Over his female in due awe,
> Not from that right to part an hour,
> Smile she or lour:
> So shall he least confusion draw
> On his whole life, not sway'd
> By female usurpation, nor dismay'd.
> (1053–59)

Since this absolute "Law" is so intimately tied to the Danite chorus's fatalistic conception of their deity as a merciless tyrant who damns all "saints" for the slightest stumbling and/or failing to "persevere" (667–709), Samson renounces its teaching along with the riddles and other "snares" of the heroic ethic that eventually ensnared him in the same toils as his enemies.[33] In reevaluating a heroic career devoted to taunts, boasts, rage, mutual retaliation, and deception, he thus begins to understand that these tactics only derailed him from his divine mission by fostering his vanity and vulnerability to flattering women. Having "degenerately serv'd" (419) these idols, "Soft'n'd with pleasure and voluptuous life," he was soon "fit" only to be shorn "like a tame Wether" (534, 538). Yet by renouncing this ethic and turning toward the truly transsexual power of Christian liberty, he can at last rupture the domestic, civil, and religious bondage that caused him to misunderstand not just his Nazarite vows, his election, and his actual intemperance, but also the true will of his God:

> But what avail'd this temperance, not complete
> Against another object more enticing?
> What boots it at one gate to make defense,
> And at another to let in the foe,
> Effeminately vanquish't? by which means,
> Now blind, disheart'n'd, sham'd, dishonor'd, quell'd,
> To what can I be useful, wherein serve
> My Nation, and the work from Heav'n impos'd,
> But to sit idle on the household hearth
> A burdenous drone. (558–67)

In beginning to pose these questions, Samson first begins to identify both his father's and Dalila's hearth as "effeminate" idols worse than any physical intemperance or Nazarite infraction, an effort that ends in his "open" or public demonstration of God's anti-hierarchical will above *any* tribal "hearth" or "*Ebrew . . . Law*" (1319–20).

The availability of this Christian liberty to women as well as to men, to saints like either Samson or the Alcestis of Sonnet 23, is stressed by the succession of bird images that end the drama. The chorus first sees the renewed hero as a warlike masculine eagle, then as a feminine dragon or redeemed "type" of Dalila (977), and finally as an androgynous phoenix, "that self-begott'n bird" who "revives, reflourishes . . . From out her ashy womb" (1699, 1703–4).[34] Manoa unwittingly reinforces this androgynous imagery when he envisions both youths and maidens congregating at Samson's memorial tomb to rehearse his painful self-discovery through marriage and his sad recovery through divorce. Because this renewal is contingent upon the synthesis of opposing forces – male and female, love and hate, creation and destruction – Gilbert and Gubar were actually more right than they realized in remarking that the manly poet's need of "*being ministered to* hints that his powers are not quite absolute, that in fact he has been reduced to a state of dependence upon his female descendents [*sic*]" or daughters. Yet they were also wrong in failing to see that the process remains reversible: just as Samson is dependent upon Dalila, so Milton's daughters are dependent upon him. For in creating the most powerfully intelligent and ethically self-determining female character of his era, he also drafts the first literary portrait of a woman who commits wrongs *not* truly "incident to all our sex," but to fallen humanity as a whole.[35]

NOTES

1. Sandra M. Gilbert and Susan Gubar, *The Madwoman in the Attic: The Woman Writer and the Nineteenth-Century Literary Imagination*, 2nd. edn. (New Haven: Yale University Press, 1984), 187–221; see especially 187–88, 210–11, 212–15. The reference to Milton's "bogey" is taken from Virginia Woolf in *A Room of One's Own* (San Diego: Harcourt Brace Jovanovich, 1929) 118.
2. Johnson makes the case both for Milton's misogyny and for the "missing middle" of his tragedy in his famous *Lives of the English Poets* (London: Oxford University Press, 1912), 109, 131. Twentieth-century defenders of Dalila and/or the Philistines include William Empson, *Milton's God* (London: Chatto & Windus, 1965), 211–28; Irene Samuel, "*Samson Agonistes* as Tragedy," in *Calm of Mind*, ed. Joseph Anthony Wittreich, Jr. (Cleveland: Case Western Reserve University Press, 1971), 235–57; Virginia R. Mollenkott, "Relativism in *Samson Agonistes*," *Studies in Philology* (*SP*) 67 (1970): 89–102; Jackie DiSalvo, "Intestine Thorn: Samson's Struggle with the Woman Within," in *Milton and the Idea of Woman*, ed. Julia M. Walker (Urbana: University of Illinois Press, 1988) 211–12; and

John C. Ulreich, "'Incident to All Our Sex': The Tragedy of Dalila," in *Milton and the Idea of Woman*, 185–210. In the present volume, Achsah Guibbory picks up the Johnsonian theme by linking Milton's reputed antifemininism to his anti-Hebraicism, but Joseph Wittreich regards both as integral to his critique of fallen male heroism; see Wittreich, *Interpreting "Samson Agonistes"* (Princeton: Princeton University Press, 1986) and *Shifting Contexts: Reinterpreting "Samson Agonistes"* (Pittsburgh: Duquesne University Press, 2002).

3. For an early exploration of Johnson's political motives, see William Haller, "'Hail Wedded Love,'" *ELH* 13 (1946): 79–97. Earlier feminists like Anna Brownwell Jameson even more stringently objected to his attempt "to degrade . . . , disfigure . . . , and darken" England's "great and sacred poet"; see *Memoirs of the Loves of the Poets: Biographical Sketches of Women Celebrated in Ancient and Modern Poetry* (1829; Boston: Ticknor and Fields, 1863), 251–53.

4. Commenting on this passage, John Halkett only slightly exaggerates when he says that Milton's emphasis on "the human measure of all law" is seen most forcefully here: "By giving the theory of elemental magnetism – of unity through love and chaos through hatred – psychological equivalents in matrimony, . . . the whole issue of fitness becomes . . . profoundly ethical" in a naturalistic and universal sense. See *Milton and the Idea of Matrimony: A Study in the Divorce Tracts and" Paradise Lost"* (New Haven: Yale University Press, 1970), 53–54.

5. Gregory Chaplin, "'One Flesh, One Heart, One Soul': Renaissance Friendship and Miltonic Marriage," *MP* 99.2 (2001): 266–92; 271. Halkett arrives at the same conclusion in his more extensive study of *Milton and the Idea of Matrimony*.

6. In considering Milton's use of John Selden's research on Hebrew marriage, Matthew Biberman proposes that Milton tacitly accepted a woman's independent right to divorce on the grounds of incompatibility even though it never existed in Hebrew law. See "Milton, Marriage, and a Woman's Right to Divorce," *Studies in English Literature 1500–1900 (SEL)* 39 (1999): 131–53.

7. As the historian Perez Zagorin observes, Milton's powerful "contempt of custom" similarly caused him to justify regicide and the abolition of monarchy via the law of nature. See *Milton: Aristocrat & Rebel. The Poet and His Politics* (New York: DS. Brewer, 1992), 83.

8. See John Rumrich, "The Art of Generation" (chapter 5), in his *Milton Unbound* (Cambridge: Cambridge University Press, 1996).

9. Stephen Fallon, "The Metaphysics of Milton's Divorce Tracts," in *Politics, Poetics, and Hermeneutics in Milton's Prose*, ed. David Loewenstein and James Grantham Turner (Cambridge: Cambridge University Press, 1990), 69–83, cited 73. For the standard account of Milton's view of Christian liberty, see Arthur Barker, *Milton and the Puritan Dilemma, 1641–1660* (Toronto: University of Toronto Press, 1942), 223, 258–59. As Barker shows, this concept strongly differs from the Antinomians' claim that the Elect could no longer sin at all.

10. Chaplin, "'One Flesh, One Heart, One Soul,'" 282; see also 287.

11. Gilbert and Gubar, *The Madwoman in the Attic*, 211.

12. Louis Menand, "Illiberalisms," *The New Yorker*, May 20, 1991, 106. Menand is cited in Joseph Wittreich's instructive essay on "Milton's Transgressive Maneuvers: Reception (Then and Now) and the Sexual Politics of *Paradise Lost*," in *Milton and Heresy*, ed. Stephen B. Dobranski and John P. Rumrich (Cambridge: Cambridge University Press, 1998), 244–66.
13. Elizabeth Cady Stanton also adopted "male" periodic sentences in basing her declaration of the rights of women on the model of Jefferson's Declaration of Independence.
14. Woolf, *A Room of One's Own*, 69.
15. Northrop Frye, "Agon and Logos: Revolution and Revelation," in *The Prison and the Pinnacle*, ed. Balachandra Rajan (Toronto: University of Toronto Press, 1973), 154, 159–60.
16. For a strong feminist reading of Eve's right to garden on her own, see Diana Benet, "Abdiel and the Son in the Separation Scene," *Milton Studies* 18, ed. James D. Simmonds (1983): 129–43.
17. Chaplin, "One Flesh," 289. Alarmingly few commentators have heeded Halkett's similar warning in *Milton and the Idea of Matrimony* (27–29) against confusing the local strategies of Milton's divorce arguments with his overall views on women and/or sexuality. For very different views of the divorce tracts from Chaplin's or mine, see James Grantham Turner, *One Flesh: Paradisal Marriage and Sexual Relations in the Age of Milton* (Oxford: Clarendon Press, 1987), and Mary Nyquist, "The Genesis of Gendered Subjectivity in the Divorce Tracts and in *Paradise Lost*," in *Re-membering Milton: Essays on the Texts and Traditions*, ed. Mary Nyquist and Margaret W. Ferguson (London: Metheun, 1987), 99–127. Nyquist does not consider Dalila, but her belief that Milton relegates the female to "lightsome conversation" only (112) is contradicted by both Eve and Dalila.
18. Shari A. Zimmerman, "Disaffection, Dissimulation, and the Uncertain Ground of Silent Dismission: Juxtaposing John Milton and Elizabeth Cary," *ELH* 66 (1999): 553–89, cited 563. On 565, Zimmerman cites Nyquist's "Gynesis, Genesis, Exegesis, and the Formation of Milton's Eve" 177) in *Cannibals, Witches, and Divorce: Estranging the Renaissance*, ed. Marjorie Garber (Baltimore: Johns Hopkins University Press, 1987); and Turner's *One Flesh*, 221, on 566.
19. Halkett shows that Milton clearly differs from Bucer in attributing marital failure to the innate personalities, not the active will of either party; *Milton and the Idea of Matrimony*, 29–30.
20. In "The Father's House: *Samson Agonistes* in its Historical Moment," John Giullory argues that Samson's recuperation is the "*return* of election, the return of being chosen rather than choosing" (*Re-membering Milton*, 156), but in Milton's view, a "fit society" (*CPW* 2:310) must always be based on voluntary, revocable covenants.
21. See the author's Introduction and Elizabeth M. Sauer in this volume.
22. For related approaches to the difference between Eve and Dalila, see Mary Ann Radzinowicz, "Eve and Dalila: Renovation and the Hardening of the

Heart," in *Reason and the Imagination: Studies in the History of Ideas 1600–1800*, ed. Joseph A. Mazzeo (New York: Columbia University Press, 1962), and also *Toward "Samson Agonistes": The Growth of Milton's Mind* (Princeton: Princeton University Press, 1978); Dayton Haskin, "Divorce as a Path to Union with God in *Samson Agonistes*," *ELH* 38 (1971): 358–73; and Arnold Stein, *Heroic Knowledge: An Interpretation of "Paradise Regained" and "Samson Agonistes"* (Hamden, CT.: Archon Books, 1965).

23. See Stanley E. Fish, *Surprised by Sin: The Reader in "Paradise Lost"* 2nd. edn. (Cambridge, MA: Harvard University Press, 1998).

24. For a general discussion of the relevance of Milton's views on "religious, domestic, and civil liberty" to the tragedy, see Martin, "The Phoenix and the Crocodile: Milton's Natural Law Debate with Hobbes Retried in the Tragic Forum of *Samson Agonistes*," in *The English Civil Wars in the Literary Imagination*, ed. Claude Summers and Ted Pebworth (Columbia, MD: University of Missouri Press, 1999), 242–70.

25. On the drama's Euripidean background, see Stella Revard, "Dalila as Euripidean Heroine," *Papers on Language and Literature* 23 (Summer, 1987): 291–302, and Wittreich, *Shifting Contexts*.

26. Samson can thus be seen as a type of Hercules and/or Christ, who rescues Alcestis in Sonnet 23. On Samson as a type of Christ, see F. Michael Krouse, *Milton's Samson and the Christian Tradition* (Princeton: Princeton University Press, 1949), and Frye, "Agon and Logos: Revolution and Revelation." For a refutation of this view, see Wittreich, *Interpreting "Samson Agonistes"* and *Shifting Contexts*; and for links between Sonnet 23 and the divorce tracts, see B. J. Sokol, "Euripides *Alcestis* and the 'Saint' of Milton's Reparative Sonnet," *SEL* 33. 1 (1993): 131–49.

27. Frank Cross shows in *Canaanite Myth and Hebrew Epic: Essays in the History of the Religion of Israel* (Cambridge, MA: Harvard University Press, 1973), and Milton knew through John Selden, that the Jews and Canaanites shared many sacred laws, texts, and customs.

28. Milton derived these universal law principles from both Cicero and Aquinas; see R. S. White, *Natural Law in English Renaissance Literature* (Cambridge: Cambridge University Press, 1996), 26–27, 34–35, 216–42, and Martin, "The Phoenix and the Crocodile."

29. Of course, as Turner observes in *One Flesh*, this powerful passage in *Tetrachordon* does not absolve the divorce treatises of all "masculinist" bias. In the same place Milton refers to woman as an "inferiour sexe" purposely made for man, who is alone "the portraiture of God." *Paradise Lost* is also notoriously ambivalent on the subject; see Martin, *The Ruins of Allegory: "Paradise Lost" and the Metamorphosis of Epic Convention* (Durham, NC: Duke University Press, 1998) chapter 6.

30. Joan S. Bennett influentially discusses the fallen chorus's inability to follow Samson's self-liberation from the old law in *Reviving Liberty: Radical Christian Humanism in Milton's Great Poems* (Cambridge, MA: Harvard University Press, 1989), 119–60. As Laura Lunger Knoppers shows, Milton reworks both Proverbs

and the book of Judges "to demonstrate [that] the need for male discipline, not of the transgressive female, but of the self," is the only "solution to the threat of foolishness and harlotry – both of male and female, Samson and Dalila." See "'Sung and Proverb'd for a Fool': *Samson Agonistes* and Solomon's Harlot," *Milton Studies* 26 (1990): 249.
31. Halkett, *Milton and the Idea of Matrimony*, 9, 12.
32. Stanley Fish, "Spectacle and Evidence in *Samson Agonistes*," *Critical Inquiry* 15 (1989): 556–86; cited 382.
33. As Wittreich shows, Milton not only opposed the Calvinist doctrine of the "perseverance of the saints," but, in *Samson Agonistes*, uses its defects to trace the causes of revolutionary failure. See *Shifting Contexts*, 121, 131–46.
34. Dayton Haskin discusses the Phoenix image in roughly parallel terms in "Divorce as a Path to Union with God in *Samson Agonistes*," 373.
35. Wittreich finds convincing evidence that at least some seventeenth-century women understood Milton's Dalila in just this way. Bidding "Milton to join his voice to hers," Jane Lead "repeatedly analogizes herself with Delilah" since his neutralization of "her character in *Samson Agonistes*" allows her to imagine a "new, chaste, faithful Delilah" who fosters rather than "Samsonizes" her husband: *Shifting Contexts*, 142–43.

PART II

The gendered subjects of Milton's major poems

CHAPTER 4

The profession of virginity in A Maske Presented at Ludlow Castle

William Shullenberger

It is hard to calculate the genre-shock and gender-shock of Milton's Ludlow *Maske*. Its staging of Alice Egerton's passage into womanhood reconfigures the totemic magic of the masque genre by making the figure of the virgin, rather than the king, the emblem and human center of the moral and regenerative energies of the world. In her profession of virginity (*Maske* 779–99), the Lady articulates an ethical and aesthetic self-recognition which signals not only her invulnerability to Comus, but her prophetic arrival at moral and sexual maturity. The Lady's virginity, as she exercises it and represents it in poetry, song, and ultimately in dance, discloses itself as the point where the temporal realities of bodily existence intersect with the spiritual possibilities of the eternal. If the mythic subtexts of her ordeal threaten her with dismemberment and dispersal, virginity is the outward and visible sign of continuity, integration, and unity.[1] It is not the fugitive and cloistered virtue valorized in patristic and medieval doctrines of celibacy, but the source of an activist, expressive, world-challenging magic consonant with Reformation social theology and complementary to its sexual ethic of companionate marriage. It makes her rhetorically and politically stronger, rather than more vulnerable.[2]

So the Lady's high-minded, austere rebuke to Comus is not a recycling of medieval notions of celibacy. It advocates virginity as a preemptive defense of and preparation for a chaste life of "redeemed sexuality":[3]

> Shall I go on?
> Or have I said enough? to him that dares
> Arm his profane tongue with contemptuous words
> Against the Sun-clad power of Chastity
> Fain would I something say, yet to what end?
> Thou hast nor Ear nor Soul to apprehend
> The sublime notion and high mystery
> That must be utter'd to unfold the sage
> And serious doctrine of Virginity,

> And thou art worthy that thou shouldst not know
> More happiness than this thy present lot.
> Enjoy your dear Wit and gay Rhetoric
> That hath so well been taught her dazzling fence,
> Thou art not fit to hear thyself convinc't;
> Yet should I try, the uncontrolled worth
> Of this pure cause would kindle my rapt spirits
> To such a flame of sacred vehemence,
> That dumb things would be mov'd to sympathize,
> And the brute Earth would lend her nerves, and shake,
> Till all thy magic structures rear'd so high,
> Were shatter'd into heaps o'er thy false head. (779–99)

The Lady's questions here are odd rhetorical markers. To whom are they addressed? Clearly she is not asking Comus, her dramatic adversary, for permission or assessment. She seems, rather, to be pausing to check in with herself, to be taking a deep breath to muster her energies for the vehement outburst to follow. Her hesitations highlight the crucial nature of the passage, which was added to the performance script for the first publication of the *Maske* in 1637, and subsequently included in the 1645 *Poems*.[4] This visionary addendum widens the performed *Maske*'s field of vision and of rhetoric. It elaborates the conditions of the mind's freedom, and indicates the kerygmatic power of words spoken from the place of that freedom.[5]

For the unmarried Lady, the textual co-ordination of chastity and virginity which vexes some of Milton's critics is not a disjuncture but a continuity. In her amplified speech, "the sage / And serious doctrine of Virginity" (786–7) appears as the third term in the doctrinal register of virtues that includes the "holy dictate of spare Temperance" (767) and "the Sun-clad power of Chastity" (782). Syntactic parallelism and continuity create a bridge from the performance text into the new material of the published text and create ambiguity about the relation of terms. Looked at one way, "the Sun-clad power of Chastity" seems virtually equivalent to and interchangeable with the "sage / And serious doctrine of Virginity": the Lady uses different yet parallel phrases to talk about the same condition. Yet the sequencing of the virtues also seems to position "Chastity" as a prior term in an ethical and spiritual series which climaxes in "Virginity." In this sense, chastity is a necessary prolegomenon to a unique and untranslatable order of being, virginity. This doctrinal trinity echoes the Lady's previous fortifying vision of "pure-ey'd Faith, white-handed Hope," and "unblemish't form of Chastity" (213–15). In the earlier soliloquy, finding herself alone "in single darkness" (204), the Lady invented iconographical markers for Faith, Hope, and Chastity, which invested them with the attributes – pure eyes, white hands, unblemished form – of her own virginity. In her defensive rebuttal of Comus, she now dogmatizes them as a way of stiffening their conceptual resistance to the corrosively equivocating "dazzling fence" (791) of Comus's rhetoric. Chastity, as she articulates it, is the dispositional armor of virginity. It is virginity made conscious of itself by the trial of passions within and pleasures round about (*Areopagitica*, 733), and made articulate in its own self-defense.

Angus Fletcher suggests that the mystique of virginity is greatest when a young woman like Alice Egerton approaches sexual maturity: "one can go on being chaste as long as one likes, but virginity (in its ideal essence, which is not to be confused with its merely physical aspect) suffers from entropy. Virginity at fifteen is more perfect than virginity at fifty."[6] This provocative insight strikes one of Fletcher's rare false notes. How could virginity "in its ideal essence" suffer from entropy, when it is the virginal body, "its merely physical aspect," that grows old and withers, as libertine poets like Comus always like to remind their virgin prey? One could argue that under the Protestant dispensation, "virginity at fifteen is more perfect than virginity at fifty," because the sexual destiny preferred and proferred by the All-Giver of the reformers is chaste companionate marriage. Yet Fletcher doesn't seem to intend this political point. Rather, he inadvertently betrays that he shares with Comus a common male assumption about the superior desirability of young and undefiled women. His misprision is valuable for its cultural implication: the symbolic and social value of virginity comes into focus at that time when the young woman discovers her erotic vitality. As a social value, virginity "guarantees to the female her value within the social system of reciprocity."[7] Construed this way, virginity is a marketable value which tends not to empower the girl for herself, but simultaneously renders her newly vulnerable to masculine attention and redefines her subjection to her father's sense of family interests. At the same time that the girl debuts in the general social estimation as potential erotic object, conjugal partner, and bearer of children, her sexual purity becomes the dangerous focal point of male fantasy, desire, and competition.

Yet Milton dramatizes how the social vulnerability of a young woman can be countered by the potential strength that she discovers in the discipline of desire. Virginity is a virtue which cannot typically defend itself by physical might; its strength rests in its concentration of physical poise with psychological and rhetorical force. Crossing through puberty to womanhood, the virgin discovers herself to be not just an object of others' desire, but capable herself of desiring, and thus an active source and center of desire. Her ethical recognition and orchestration of her own desire, rather than its repudiation, becomes the key to her charisma. Spenser's Britomart, wayfaring and warfaring in quest of her beloved Artegall, is the great model of this mobilizing transformation of desire. The strength of the virgin's resistance to sexual demand is increased by the strength with which she feels touched by the demand. Her virginity, that is, paradoxically discovers its strength in relation to the strength of the desire which it calls into being. Desire makes virginity consciously shape itself in the form of an idealized and hope-directed form of self-knowledge.

Reviewing the careers of Spenser's "dazzling Apollonian androgynes," Belphoebe and Britomart, Camille Paglia describes chastity as "a self-armouring of personality": "Every detail and edge is deeply incised, because Spenserian personality must be forcibly carved out of obdurate nature and defended against the erosion and lassitude of fatigue and hedonism."[8] The same can be said of their literary godchild, Milton's Lady, whose own charismatic desire defines itself in resistance to Comus's enervating appeal. If, as Jacques Lacan claims, "desire finds its meaning in the desire of the other," influenced by and reflective of a previous, more powerful and inclusive desire, the impenetrable and radiant self-certainty of chaste desire establishes its originary priority in the circulation of desire around it.[9] It orders according to its own design the desire which discovers it.

A desire both activated and chastened by virginal self-recognition is the source of a power which the various characters of the *Maske* testify to as magical. The sources of this virgin magic disclose themselves if we consider the power discovered by the Lady in relation to the magic exercised by Prospero in *The Tempest*, from which Milton drew poetic resources for his *Maske*.[10] *The Tempest* is a drama entailing magic which circles around the crisis of female maturation in a world of male struggles for power. Miranda in *The Tempest* prefigures Milton's Lady as a girl entering sexual maturity and being tested and prepared for chaste marriage. Unlike the Lady, Miranda experiences no stage of familial separation or liminal self-examination in her drama. She has been her Daddy's girl, and remains a good one, with limited opportunity to show the spunk and improvisatory genius of Shakespeare's comparable romantic heroines, Rosalind, Viola, and Perdita. Miranda's emerging charisma and value as virgin remain at the disposal of and under the tutelary control of her father. Prospero is the virtual god of power in Shakespeare's romance, yet his magic does not come from nowhere. Its intellectual sources are in his books, but its energy source is suggestively linked to his relationship with his daughter. Prospero's magic can be interpreted psychologically as the creative resolution of the conflict he feels in regard to his daughter's sexual maturation. Miranda, like the Lady, is passing through puberty to womanhood, and the question of her sexuality, first raised in the attempted rape by Caliban, takes on urgency with the shipwreck of Prospero's enemies. Miranda is the only woman on the island, and her relation to her father, who has nurtured, protected, and tutored her, is necessarily intimate and intense. Her virgin sexuality, at Prospero's disposal yet respected and protected by him, provides the energy source of his magic.

His sustained renunciation of desire for her, figured forth in the tense master-slave relation to Caliban, returns to him in the sublimated form of Ariel, his eager and dynamic spiritual intimate. Caliban images forth to Prospero the specter of his own sexual anxieties, and Prospero's persecutory harshness toward Caliban evidences an uneasy self-mastery. The aerial omnipotence of his magic is a sign of desire perfectly sublimated and serviceable. Prospero's testing of Ferdinand by setting him in Caliban's place as log man, by instructing him in the mastery of lust, completes the civilizing task which he had abandoned with Caliban. In effect, he so chastens and structures Ferdinand's desire as to teach Ferdinand to master the Caliban in himself, a project about which Prospero is constantly vigilant in his own life. Prospero's preparation of his daughter for chaste marriage must break the charmed circle of their relationship. In orchestrating her courtship with Ferdinand, he prepares himself to abandon his magic and depart from the fantasy island where he has exercised it.[11]

The story of desire in *The Tempest*, then, is the story of Prospero's desire, yet his magic can not be interpreted without noticing its coincidence with his daughter's virginity, and with a curious straitening of her role as a Shakespearean romantic ingenue. We might say that Milton constructs the dramatic experiment of his *Maske* out of the question of what might have happened to Miranda if her father were not around to protect and supervise her passage from childhood to womanhood. The problem of desire is principally the Lady's, not her father's, to struggle with, and so the promise of desire will be hers to enjoy. Ritual release from paternal oversight frees the Lady for the liminal ordeal that opens to her the power implicit in her virginity, rather than mystifying and deferring it in the service of her father. The *Maske* thus dramatizes the transformation of Lady Alice's virginity from an unblemished physical condition, paternally sheltered, to an autonomous structure of ethical self-defense and source of visionary poetic energy. The Lady prepares to become in effect a mage for herself, a dramatic development that strikingly marginalizes Lord Brackley, both as

Lady Alice's father and as the king's representative, and thereby dispells the patriarchal absolutism which typifies magic in the masque genre.[12]

By extending her self-defense with her profession of virginity, the Lady sharpens the focus of her differences with Comus by making them explicitly sexual. One might think that this is playing into his hands by talking about the one thing about which he keeps beating around the bush. Oddly enough, this in fact inverts the terms of their difference: her idealistic sexual frankness exposes him, with his grandiloquent indirection, as the coy one. She introduces a mode of erotic self-determination that is, she announces, beyond his comprehension. At the same time, she makes explicit a co-ordinate theme that is fundamental both to her differences with him and to her self-determination: language. She triply reiterates the point that she won't walk the walk or talk the talk of Comus: "Thou hast nor Ear nor Soul to Apprehend . . . thou art worthy that thou shouldst not know . . . Thou art not fit to hear thyself convinc't" (784, 788, 792). Her speech is, indeed, less an account of the physical condition of virginity or an exposition of its "sage / And serious doctrine" (786–87) than a demonstration of the rhetorical and poetic power it authorizes and inspires. In fact, she does not say what she would like to say. She refers in the subjunctive to the speech which Comus does not deserve to hear: "Fain *would I something say*, yet to what end? / . . . Yet *should I try*, the uncontrolled worth / Of this pure cause *would kindle* my rapt spirits" (783, 793–94; my emphasis). Strangely without content, her encomium is a *tour de force* of implication.

In praising virginity while refusing to explicate it, the Lady deploys a strategy which is similar to the traditional topos of inexpressibility, yet structured and nuanced differently. The topos of inexpressibility we know most famously from the *Divine Comedy*: what the poet or his character experiences is beyond the poor powers of even the most inspired human speech.[13] Perhaps because of his prophetic confidence in the providentially inspired Word, Milton resorts to this topos rarely and briefly, particularly in the ambiguous epithet "unexpressive" (Nativity Ode, 115; *Lycidas*, 176). Even in the most sublime passages of *Paradise Lost*, the angelic messenger Raphael expresses confidence in the powers of analogy and "process of speech" to accommodate divine and spiritual activity to human understanding (5.563–75; 7.176–79). The Lady also implies the compatibility of her concept and experience with language. It is not that what she has in mind could not be said. It is just that she will not say it, for certain good reasons, under the conditions where she finds herself. If she were to say it, Comus and everything about him would be blown away: "the brute Earth would lend her nerves, and shake, / Till all thy magic structures rear'd so high, / Were shatter'd into heaps o'er thy false head" (797–99).

You go, girl! William Kerrigan rightly notices the co-ordination of her rhetorical stance with her ethical position: "Her doctrine of virginity remains undivulged, itself virginal, as if speech this intimate would be equivalent to the sexuality her virtue forbids: the exhibition of the self to the other."[14] Kerrigan, however, implies an outcome to the possible divulging of the doctrine that is at odds with the Lady's own claim. The Lady does not imply that her doctrine or her sexuality would be defiled by her revelation of it to Comus. She implies that it would destroy him.

Perhaps we can call the Lady's rhetorical strategy the figure of reserved expressibility: in a highly charged dramatic situation, the indefinite figure of what *might* be said authorizes the performative force of what *is* said.[15] Paradoxically, the actual words spoken invest in those yet to be spoken a power that most auditors will prefer not to question. We can recognize it in a pragmatic common ploy of parental discipline. Who among us has not quavered under the threat, "Just wait until I tell your father"? In terms of its production of anxiety and guilt and remorse, could the telling itself ever measure up to the *threat* of telling?[16] As Kerrigan implies, the Lady's rhetoric functions in regard to the language it deploys as her virginity functions in regard to her sexuality: it gathers its power from what it withholds. Like virginity itself, a condition of self-presence that gains its authority from what it reserves to itself and God, this rhetoric reserves a pure "doctrine" from ears that are not fit to hear it. The power of the Lady's actual, audible speech comes from its implication and deferral of a higher order of speech that is never heard because it can only be fully present to itself. The power of this reserved Word depends upon its not being spoken. Kathleen Wall refers appropriately to "the armor of Logos" as the source of the Lady's strength.[17] Yet it is the word *not* spoken, a transcendental yet internalized Logos which corresponds to her virginal self-presence, that generates the strength of her outward verbal armor. This internalized Logos is a full Word represented as a force that is imminent and yet unexpressed. The full Word makes itself felt as a phantom presence authorizing and empowering the empty word of actual speech, which acknowledges its own comparatively limited expressive and performative power.[18] Yet if the full Word is an implication of actual speech, could it also be really an effect of actual speech, a mystification of the power of language by a language that seems to confess its own apparent insufficiency? Must Father really come home in order for the threat to have already accomplished what it intends?

This deconstructive conundrum does not present itself to the Lady, who so fully believes in what she implies that she does not have to say it explicitly. Lacan writes, "It is proper to the Word to cause to be understood what it does not say":[19] the Lady's skillful use of the figure of reserved expressibility makes Comus a believer too. So she gains the upper hand, rhetorically disarming and unmanning him. Comus flinches:

> She fables not, I feel that I do fear
> Her words set off by some superior power;
> And though not mortal, yet a cold shudd'ring dew
> Dips me all o'er, as when the wrath of *Jove*
> Speaks thunder and the chains of *Erebus*
> To some of *Saturn's* crew.   (800–5)

Comus gets the cold sweats here, a contrast to those seminal "gums of glutinous heat" (917) from which the Lady will have to be purified and released. The cold sweats are a symptom of dread before the epiphany of "superior power." The analogy associates this power with the punitive judgment of a wrathful divine Father. Not by what she *does* say, but by the power of what she claims she *could* say, the Lady convinces Comus that divine justice stands for her and behind her. Yet Comus's analogy also blurs the difference between its comparative terms: the Lady has spoken thunder in just the way that Jove speaks thunder. The full Word of divine Logos coincides with the implied Word of virginity's self-announcement, and "sets off" her spoken words as instruments of reserved power. The Lady thus turns the conditions of her vulnerability here – her femininity, her captivity, her constrained speech – into sources of divinely authorized verbal power.

Circe's best boy, devotee of Venus and "vow'd Priest" of Cotytto and Hecate (124–38), Comus speaks for the mythic Mother Goddess in her most copious, engrossing, and sinister forms. Here he acknowledges that the Lady speaks for the Father, and the Father speaks – or would speak – for and through the Lady. This is not a claim that the Lady makes explicitly for herself, but Comus's own testimony. If there is a phallic contest in this fencing match between an innocent girl and Comus, whose progenitor Bacchus is the god referred to by George Sandys as "the father of generation," Comus himself acknowledges that the Lady has won.[20] As Lacan interprets the phallus of Freudian theory, the phallus is a signifier of power and of a desire that is synonymous with power.[21] The Lady demonstrates that the symbolic power of the phallus is not the biological or the cultural property of men. The power of the phallus, as of the Logos, lies in its spectral displacement from the moment and site of speaking, and its identification with an authority both remote and incontestable, incontestable because it is remote. The Lady gains authority over Comus by mastering the differential logic of the Symbolic order, the regime of language which underwrites the order of culture. Lacan calls the authorizing term of the Symbolic order "le nom du Pére."[22] The English translation, "The name of the Father," obscures the crucial French pun, "le *nom/non* du Pére," "the *name/no* of the Father," but it is a pun that the Lady understands, even though she herself has fortunately never read Lacan. She speaks the paternal "no" to Comus's desire in such a way as to convince Comus that he believes he hears the Father himself speak it.

Comus's fear and trembling fulfill the Elder Brother's confident prediction of virgin chastity's power over her adversaries:

> What was that snaky-headed *Gorgon* shield
> That wise *Minerva* wore, unconquer'd Virgin,
> Wherewith she freez'd her foes to congeal'd stone,
> But rigid looks of Chaste austerity
> And noble grace that dash't brute violence
> With sudden adoration and blank awe? (447–52)

Elder Brother's emblematic representation of chastity, prior to the Lady's debate with Comus, anticipates and complements the Lady's articulation and achievement of chastity. Elder Brother's comparatively naive reproduction of conventional icons of militant chastity exposes some mythological and psychological complexity in its formation and expression that a more sophisticated account of the virtue might knowingly repress or refine.[23] Such is the case with the complex image of Minerva and the Gorgon shield, which flashes up out of an Ovidian repository that forms the tragic subtext of the Lady's ordeal. "Rigid looks of Chaste austerity" indicate the double power of chastity over the predatory eye. The archetypal virgin, Minerva, goddess of wisdom and militant chastity, petrifies her foes both with her looking and with how she looks. She arrests and intimidates the gaze of the potential voyeur with an impenetrably rigid and keen gaze of her own, as well as with an armored body-image resistant to violence of thought or action. Her petrifying power results from her appropriation of and merger with Medusa, her opposite. In Elder Brother's iconography, Minerva *wears* rather than *carries* the Gorgon shield, suggesting in the figure a coincidence of female opposites.

George Sandys notes this strange coincidence in his observation that Minerva was "called *Gorgon* by the Cyrenians; a name agreeing with her war-like disposition."[24] Sandys reads Perseus's slaying of Medusa as an allegory that neatly parallels the Lady's victory over the temptation of the Circean Comus:

> Perseus is also taken for the reasonable soule; the *Graeae* [two sisters whose shared single eye provides Perseus direction toward the sleeping Medusa], for that knowledge and wisdom which is acquired by experience; without whose eye or conduction, *Medusa*, lust and the inchantments of bodily beauty, which stupifies our senses, make us altogether unusefull, and convert us as it were into marble, cannot be subdued . . . Thus provided, *Perseus* kills *Medusa*, reason corporall pleasure: yet lookes not on her, but only sees her deformity in the shield of *Pallas* (as we view without prejudice to our sight the eclyps of the sun in the water) since it is not safe to behold what our hearts are so prone to consent too.[25]

Elder Brother parallels Sandys by declaring chastity dominant over "lust and the inchantments of bodily beauty." However, his superimposition of the two figures exceeds Sandys by implying that chastity exercises power over others by merging with its opposite, the spectral image of lust. Minerva, the apotheosis and sponsor of chaste character, wears a sign of her overmastery of desire, not only the desire of others, but of the desire which motivates her. The strength which the chaste woman obtains from the mastery of desire in herself becomes available to her as a defensive shield against the potential aggression she excites. If we compare Elder Brother's use of the Medusa myth to that of Sandys, and to that of Ben Jonson in *The Masque of Queens* – "When Virtue cut off Terror, he gat Fame"[26] – we notice that in Elder Brother's elaboration, Minerva has reclaimed her shield from Perseus. In effect she recovers this cephalic trophy as a sign of female, rather than male, mastery over whatever is symbolized in Medusa's stonifying power.

Chastity's power thus comes as a triumph of female sublimation. With its Renaissance spiritual and alchemical resonances, "sublimation" is also the psychoanalytic term for the process whereby erotic energies are released from their primary sexual motivations and objects, and committed toward culturally sanctioned and supported forms of self-satisfaction and social activity. In psychoanalytic theory, sublimation "de-sexualizes" libidinal energies by way of a provisional narcissism: "The transformation of a sexual activity into a sublimated one (assuming both are directed towards external, independent objects) is now said to require an intermediate period during which the libido is withdrawn on to the ego so that desexualisation may become possible."[27] So it is that the Lady's ordeal traces the path of desire's sublimation through an intermediate narcissism. In her ritual isolation in the forest of desire haunted by Comus, her resilient response to "calling shapes and beck'ning shadows dire, / And airy tongues that syllable men's names" (207–8), and her crystallization of her own awakened desire as the idealized form of a self resistant to erotic subjection, she goes through an episode of solipsistic self-reckoning which prepares her for a reawakened and other-directed encounter with the world beyond herself.

The virginal self exemplified by the Lady thus emerges as the first achievement and initiatory act of a career of mature sublimation. When virginity becomes conscious of itself and chooses itself in this way, it becomes a positive translation of the narcissism evoked in the Lady's sublime song to Echo (230–43). An idealized and coherent image of self becomes the project of desire and the commanding image to be displayed to the world.[28] Maturing ego and virginal body image coincide: the body becomes the perfect form and expression of the self in its nascent self-consciousness. Although the Lady's body-self is cathected in the critical moment of her recognition of desire, it is not cathected as an object to be captivated by desire, but as an idea to be preserved, nourished, defended by desire. It emerges as a state of self-presence and self-dignification, without lapsing into the self-absorption or self-consumption that determine the fates of Echo and Narcissus, whose pathetic destinies the Lady has "translated" (242) in her song.

Yet the figure of the Medusa's head, decapitated, fixed, framed, displayed on Minerva's shield, as the primary feature of her petrifying look unsettles the neatness of this psychoanalytic alchemy. In a suggestive little essay, Freud links the terror of the Medusa to the child's dread sight of the mother's genitals, and the fear of castration that it engenders:

> This symbol of horror is worn upon her dress by the virgin goddess Athena. And rightly so, for thus she becomes a woman who is unapproachable and repels all sexual desires – since she displays the terrifying genitals of the Mother. Since the Greeks were in the main strongly homosexual, it was inevitable that we should find among them a representation of a woman as a being who frightens and repels because she is castrated.[29]

Freud's analysis is compatible with Sandys's Renaissance explanation insofar as both interpret the Medusa figure as a mythologization of the fear and the threat associated with woman. In Sandys's account, Medusa stands for "lust and the inchantments of bodily beauty";[30] in Freud's account, she represents the fate of castration that waits upon the child who does not renounce his mother as primary sexual object. Yet although Freud detects the theme of female sexuality in the tale, and links it to the practice of virginity, he composes a male-directed narrative of the Medusa's head as a monitory parable of castration. His sketchy account represses certain narrative elements and tries to finesse several contradictions.

The ambiguity of the Medusa's head as sexual signifier remains implicit yet unaccounted for (perhaps deliberately) in Freud's account: does he read it as a phallic symbol or as a symbol of the lack of the phallus? Freud suggests that the power of the image lies in what it does not show, the phallus which has been stricken from the Mother, "the absence of which is the cause of the horror." Yet Athena paradoxically deploys it as a phallic emblem, a fetish implement of paralyzing power. Freud seems to support a phallic reading when he interprets the snaky hair of Medusa literally as the mother's genital hair, but symbolically as "a multiplication of penis symbols."[31] At the same time, he interprets the image as a whole as a terrifying sign of female lack. The figure is deployed in such a way as to suggest a recovery, however, either what Freud might call the return of the repressed, the missing phallus of the mother, or something perhaps even more terrible to patriarchally fashioned consciousness: what Julia Kristeva calls the *chora*, the maternal nest, the black hole of generation wreathed with phallic serpents, sign of all natural origin and end.[32] Finally, Freud overlooks certain elements of the Medusa tale which ambiguate his explanation of "woman as a being who *frightens and repels* because she is castrated" (my emphasis). The terror of Medusa is inextricably bound up with a beauty that draws men to her. If she were only repulsive to look upon, why would men be lured to search her out, and risk their lives for a glance? So Freud understands the virgin as "a woman who is unapproachable and repels all sexual desires," without accounting for the ambivalence she inspires by awaking the very desires she is able to repel, transforming the violence of lust, in Elder Brother's formulation, to "sudden adoration and blank awe" (452).

In *The Metamorphoses*, Medusa's beauty inflames Neptune to rape her in the shrine of Minerva. The offended goddess, in typical Ovidian fashion, blames the victim and transforms her hair to serpents. Yet in a further irony typical of Ovid, Medusa's makeover is not only punitive but preservative. Henceforth Medusa will be protected by her serpentine corona from the threat of violation. Beware, beware, her flashing eyes, her floating hair: a beauty powerful enough to solicit the desire of a god is set off as taboo, a thing of dread and awe, not to be beheld without sacrifice. From object of desire to image of dread to sacrificial icon: Medusa undergoes a sacrificial transformation that reverses the terms of her suffering. Ritually violated, marked, shunned, decapitated, preserved as monitory emblem, she is a scapegoat of desire whose negative image is a paralyzing charm against the desire she provokes.

Perseus is able to decapitate her, but only with the periscopic device of the shield supplied by Minerva. Sandys stresses the importance of the shield, implying that it figures as the power of undistorted Reason in his allegory. The method of indirect and abstracted perception is crucial to his insight. We could consider it as a mode of reflective consciousness, the gift of Minerva, apotheosis and muse of cunning intelligence. Since Perseus holds it as a mirror up to the nature of Medusa, we might furthermore associate it with the abstracting and framing nature of art. The shield as mirror is a blade which severs subject from object; the blade is a shutter which severs object from image; the shield that fixes the image is a frame that preserves it, uncannily lifelike, eternally and indifferently cold, chilling to behold. The shield of Pallas is a prophylaxis against the exposure to the Medusa that it represents, in the same way that the framing devices of tragedy are prophylactic against the powers of Dionysus which they represent.[33] Medusa, looking within the frame, sees herself first, and fatally: freeze-framed by her own terrifying beauty, she suffers the fate of Narcissus, only drastically, instantaneously foreshortened. Perseus, looking at her by means of the mirror-shield's indirect representation, can behold her beauty without perishing, as, Sandys notes, "we view without prejudice to our sight the eclyps of the sun in the water."[34]

Medusa's story, then, is one of the *Maske*'s several embedded parables of translation. She is ravished by a god, a common fate for the nymphs and women of Ovid's desire-driven myth, a virtual fate in which Milton's Lady subliminally participates through her confrontation with Comus. In a single metamorphic stroke, Medusa's beauty is transformed to horror: a counterpoint to the tale of Philomela's ravishing, also evoked in the *Maske* (234–35, 566), which transforms the horror of her mutilation and revenge into beauty. Medusa suffers an abbreviation of the fate of Narcissus, yet she does not re-enter, as he does, the vegetative cycle of nature. She is removed from the life cycle to serve as an instance of a particularly powerful mode of representation. Her image is fixed on the mirroring shield that has destroyed her, turning it from a reflective frame to a representational icon, a performative work of totemic art that defends chastity. Although Perseus continues to use the shield as his ultimate weapon, it is on loan and in trust from the virgin goddess Minerva. In Milton's tale, Elder Brother restores it to the goddess and, metonymically, to his sister, endowing her with the attributes and resources of unconquerable virginity.

As a series of tales of threatened virgins provide the tragic subtext for the Lady's ritual sublimation of beauty into strength, the figure of Medusa beheaded becomes the iconographic key to the paradox of that sublimation. Medusa's head: a seal on the maidenhead, and its uncanny double; a DO NOT ENTER sign on the virgin portal. Like the proliferation of snakes that wreathe it, the figure is multiple, ambiguous, and indeterminate in its significations, which only amplify its power. Freud suggests that it is the impossible, lost maternal phallus which, in Elder Brother's account of it, returns to haunt those who would defile daughters and devotees of chastity. It is at the same time the sign of that loss, a warning of castration to befall the violater of the paternal taboo. Exceeding both positions in the phallic system of psychic representation, it mystifies female sexuality as an enigma incalculable by the economics of patriarchal symbolization. It is the iconic transformation of the collective fate of ravished women, displayed as visual horror and put to the retrospective task of paralyzing any assaults on chastity. It is an uncanny coincidence of female opposites: archaic, chthonian fetish brandished by transcendent, serene virginity.[35]

The image of Medusa's head thus bears the same mutually constitutive relation to the "look" of the Lady's Minervan beauty that the implied Word of the "sage / And serious doctrine of Virginity" (785–86) bears to the Lady's spoken words. If her speech indicates her access to the symbolizing power associated with the phallus of the Father, her look evidences her association with the incalculable genital mysteries of the Mother. The terror of her look, like the terror of her speech, depends upon its implication of a power in potential, and all the more powerful in its ghostly imminence. Deploying the phallic verbal authority of the Father and the specular, genital dread of the Mother, the Lady effectively rebuffs Comus in both the verbal and the visual, the Symbolic and the Imaginary fields of their confrontation. Doubly phallic, the Lady seems invulnerable. One might be led to wonder, "This is quite a girl. Can she play tennis, too?" The point, though, of her concentration of sublimated energies, is that the phallus is itself a metaphor, a figuration of desire and of power.[36] The virginal body, intact, untraversed and unwounded by sexual intrusion, impenetrably protecting interior mysteries, is itself an energy-charged outward and visible sign of this desire and this power. The Lady's power expresses itself rhetorically and represents itself through images. It is consequently the source of a poetry of prophetic force.

If the Lady realizes and expresses such prophetic force in her confrontation scene with Comus, however, her apparently passive silent role in subsequent movements of the *Maske* seems puzzling. It is in keeping with Milton's sense of the contingency of human virtue to set limits in the *Maske* to what the Lady can do for herself. A type of the heroic Jesus of *Paradise Regained*, whose virgin rigor is a trope for his ethical strength, the Lady can endure, resist, and rebuff the adversary whose testing clarifies and concentrates her moral strength, but she does not deliver herself. This is where Sabrina comes in. A minister of grace and the Lady's fairy godmother, Sabrina baptizes the Lady into the active life of chaste female desire, releasing and mobilizing the charity implicit and potential in chastity's necessary self-defense. Furthermore, as the Lady's profession of virginity has located her sense of power in the unspoken, so her silence in the final movements of the *Maske* is entirely consonant with her transformed condition and her highly charged symbolic status. Her silence speaks her profession of virginity as loudly as her words. It is a sign of power poised and ready, of imagination so full of itself that it need not overflow in speech, so already in touch with its future that the need to speak of it, or the possibility of speaking of it, is laid to rest. Although the *Maske* decorously reattunes itself to the political occasion of Lord Brackley's investiture, and nominally restores the Lady with her brothers to the security and the authority of their father, it makes its concluding investiture of poetic magic in the Lady. For the moment she is blessed, everything she looks upon is blessed. Her final actions as she dances in the revels are a sublime miming, a gestural allegory that implies the more removed mysteries of the soul's bliss.[37] The *Maske* in its final movements speaks for her, which is very different from saying that it silences her.

NOTES

1. On the threatened Lady as a figure of the endangered Orphic poet, see Michael Lieb, *Milton and the Culture of Violence* (Ithaca: Cornell University Press, 1994).
2. Critics who treat the radical political implications of the encomium to virginity include John Rogers, "The Enclosure of Virginity: The Poetics of Sexual Abstinence in the English Revolution," in *Enclosure Acts: Sexuality, Property, and Culture in Early Modern England*, ed. Richard Burt and John Michael Archer (Ithaca: Cornell University Press, 1994), 229–50; Maureen Quilligan, *Milton's Spenser and the Politics of Reading* (Ithaca: Cornell University Press, 1983); and Richard Halpern, "Puritanism and Maenadism in *A Mask*," in *Rewriting the Renaissance: The Discourses of Sexual Difference in Early Modern Europe*, ed. Margaret W. Ferguson, Maureen Quilligan, and Nancy J. Vickers (Chicago: University of Chicago Press, 1986), 88–105. More recently, Kathryn Schwarz argues that, as a form of "empowered self-restraint," the chastity demonstrated by the Lady provides evidence of ethical agency "in which women not only verify their own virtue but determine its meanings and effects." See Schwarz, "Chastity, Militant and Married: Cavendish's Romance, Milton's Masque," *PMLA* 118.2 (March 2003): 271–72.
3. B. J. Sokol, "'Tilted Lees,' Dragons, *Haemony*, Menarche, Spirit, and Matter in *Comus*," *RES* new series 16 (1990): 309–24.

4. A convenient review of the textual history and variations of the *Maske* appears in *A Variorum Commentary on the Poems of John Milton*, vol. 2: *The Minor English Poems*, ed. A. S. P. Woodhouse and Douglas Bush (New York: Columbia University Press, 1972), 736–40, 952. See also John Shawcross's detailed "Certain Relationships of the Manuscripts of *Comus*," *PBSA* 54 (1960): 38–56.
5. "By adding this peroration, Milton develops the range of his fable and framework. For while in this fable virginity assumes chastity, chastity does not require virginity. Virgin being transcends the chaste. In his final reworking of the text Milton suddenly throws the whole of the *Maske* into relief by clarifying this transcendence": Angus Fletcher, *The Transcendental Masque: An Essay on Milton's "Comus"* (Ithaca: Cornell University Press, 1971), 212. For arguments about the apparent tension between marital chastity and militant virginity created by Milton's addition of the passage, see Arthur E. Barker, *Milton and the Puritan Dilemma, 1641–60* (Toronto: University of Toronto Press, 1942), 339, and John Rogers, "The Enclosure of Virginity," 233.
6. Fletcher, *The Transcendental Masque*, 212.
7. *Ibid.*, 239.
8. Camille Paglia, *Sexual Personae: Art and Decadence from Nefertiti to Emily Dickinson* (New York: Random House, 1991), 182, 176, 179.
9. Jacques Lacan, *The Language of the Self: The Function of Language in Psychoanalysis*, trans. Anthony Wilden (New York: Dell, 1968), 31.
10. See Mary Loeffelholz, "Two Masques of Ceres and Proserpine: *Comus* and *The Tempest*," in *Re-membering Milton: Essays on the Texts and Traditions*, ed. Mary Nyquist and Margaret W. Ferguson (New York: Methuen, 1987), 25–42: Christopher Kendrick, "Milton and Sexuality: a Symptomatic Reading of *Comus*," in *Re-membering Milton*, 43–73; John Guillory, *Poetic Authority: Spenser, Milton, and Literary History* (New York: Columbia University Press, 1983), 73–93.
11. This argument about intersubjectivity and the sources of Prospero's magic was presented in Shullenberger, "Prospero's Potent Art," at the Forum on Shakespeare and Gender, MLA Convention (New York, December 30, 1986).
12. "Surely Milton," Christopher Kendrick observes in "Milton and Sexuality," "is denying the king's power its just representational weight" (59).
13. Ernest Robert Curtius, *European Literature and the Latin Middle Ages*, trans. Willard R. Trask (New York: Harper & Row, 1963), 159–62.
14. William Kerrigan, *The Sacred Complex: On the Psychogenesis of "Paradise Lost"* (Cambridge, MA: Harvard University Press, 1983), 30.
15. Jean E. Graham identifies the Lady's rhetorical figure as "*praeteritio*, an ironic refusal to speak," as denominated by Henry Peacham; or the parallel structure of "*paralepsis*, or the passager," defined by Puttenham. Neither these figures nor *occupatio* seem to me to define the Lady's strategy, since, in each of these figures, an apparent gesture of refusal to speak ironically leads to a disclosure of what was to be withheld. See Graham, "Virgin Ears: Silence, Deafness, and Chastity in Milton's *Masque*," *Milton Studies* 36 (1998): 5.

16. Donne deploys the figure of reserved expressibility as a threat to his mistress in his cruelly brilliant amorous lyric, "The Apparition."
17. Kathleen Wall, "*A Mask Presented at Ludlow Castle*: The Armor of Logos," in *Milton and the Idea of Woman*, ed. Julia M. Walker (Urbana: University of Illinois Press, 1988), 52–63.
18. This account of the Lady's strategy is informed by Lacan's rumination of "full Word [*parole plein*]" and the "empty Word [*parole vide*]" in *The Language of the Self*, especially 9–29, 55–61.
19. *Ibid.*, 58.
20. George Sandys, *Ovid's Metamorphoses English'd, Mythologized, and Represented in Figures*, ed. Karl K. Hulley and Stanley T. Vandershall (Lincoln: University of Nebraska Press, 1970), 196.
21. On the role of the phallus as a signifier in the formation of the subject, see especially Jacques Lacan, "On a Question Preliminary to any Possible Treatment of Psychosis," in *Ecrits*, trans. Alan Sheridan (New York: W. W. Norton, 1977), 179–225. See also Anthony Wilden's commentary, "Lacan and the Discourse of the Other," in *The Language of the Self*, especially 161–66, 185–88. See also Fredric Jameson, "The Imaginary and the Symbolic in Lacan: Marxism, Psychoanalytic Criticism, and the Problem of the Self," *Yale French Studies* 55–56 (1977): 338–95; and Joseph H. Smith, *Arguing with Lacan: Ego Psychology and Language* (New Haven: Yale University Press, 1991), 95–106, 119–22.
22. Lacan, *Ecrits*, 198–99.
23. Several recent studies have examined what they take to be either Milton's or the Elder Brother's misreading of Ovid's account of the Medusa myth. See Julia M. Walker, "The Poetics of Antitext and the Politics of Milton's Allusions," *SEL* 37 (1997): 160–61; John Leonard, "'Thus They Relate, Erring': Milton's Inaccurate Allusions," *Milton Studies* 38 (2000): 113–17. I do not find anything in Elder Brother's idealizing misprision that exceeds the ingenious and flexible practices of Renaissance allegorization.
24. Sandys, *Ovid's Metamorphoses*, 247.
25. *Ibid.*, 220.
26. Ben Jonson, *The Masque of Queens*, 351, in *Ben Jonson: Selected Masques*, ed. Stephen Orgel (New Haven: Yale University Press, 1970), 93.
27. L. Laplanche and J.-B. Pontalis, "Sublimation," in *The Language of Psychoanalysis*, trans. Donald Nicholson-Smith (New York: W. W. Norton, 1973), 433.
28. Laplanche and Pontalis, "Narcissism," in *The Language of Psychoanalysis*, 255–57.
29. Sigmund Freud, "The Medusa's Head," in *Sexuality and Psychology of Love*, trans. Philip Rieff (New York: Collier Books, 1963), 212–13.
30. Sandys, *Ovid's Metamorphoses*, 220.
31. Freud, "The Medusa's Head," 212.
32. Julia Kristeva, *Powers of Horror: An Essay on Abjection*, trans. Leon Roudiez (New York: Columbia University Press, 1982), 13–14.

33. My colleague Michael Davis at Sarah Lawrence College has taught me a lot about tragedy's relation to its sponsoring deity. See Friedrich Nietzsche, *The Birth of Tragedy and the Case of Wagner*, trans. Walter Kaufman (New York: Random House, 1967).
34. Sandys, *Ovid's Metamorphoses*, 220.
35. Paglia, *Sexual Personae*, 83.
36. Katharine Eisaman Maus analyzes the signifying potentialities of the Lady's body for Milton in *Inwardness and Theater in the English Renaissance* (Chicago: University of Chicago Press, 1995), 200–9.
37. "More remov'd mysteries" is a phrase drawn from Ben Jonson's defense of the written text as the soul of the masque, in his preface to *Hymenaei*, ll. 16–17. See *Selected Masques*, 48.

CHAPTER 5

The genders of God and the redemption of the flesh in Paradise Lost

Marshall Grossman

Why are there essents rather than nothing? . . . The range of this question finds its limit only in nothing, in that which simply is not and never was. Everything that is not nothing is covered by this question, and ultimately even nothing itself; not because it is *something*, since after all we speak of it, but because it is *nothing*. Our question reaches out so far that we can never go any further.[1]

I placed a jar in Tennessee . . .[2]

WHAT DOES GOD WANT?

In the beginning "God is All in All," yet, when Satan crosses the abyss at the end of the second book of *Paradise Lost*, he encounters Chaos and Old Night, subsisting as gendered entities:

> the throne
> Of Chaos, and his dark pavilion spread
> Wide on the wasteful deep; with him enthroned
> Sat sable-vested Night, eldest of things,
> The consort of his reign.[3] (*PL* 2.959–63)

Apart from a cautious dubiety about the veracity of Satan's experience, a reader is entitled to register surprise at the quasi-allegorical ontology of these characters, to be curious about the import of their genders and to be confused about the notion that Night is "eldest of things," in view of the invocation to light that opens book 3:

> Hail holy Light, offspring of Heav'n first-born,
> Or of th' Eternal co-eternal beam
> May I express thee unblamed? Since God is light,
> And never but in unapproached light
> Dwelt from eternity, dwelt then in thee,
> Bright effluence of bright essence increate.
> (*PL* 3.1–6)

If from eternity, "God is light," then darkness must be an equally original absence, existing wherever God's effluent essence has not yet flowed. Yet it is not clear where that effluence exists, since we are told by God the Father himself that he fills "infinitude" but that he also withdraws his goodness from time to time (*PL* 7.167–73). Both Chaos and its recent encroachment by divine creation may thus be explained by the actions of an infinite God, who fills and thereby prevents the vacuity of space, but also withdraws or extends his informing "goodness" according to his will, leaving variable pockets of material "space" undefined or un-informed. When Satan speaks to "the Anarch old" he offers to restore to Night "her original darkness . . . / . . . And once more erect the standard there of ancient Night" (*PL* 2.985–86).[4] Still, it is one thing for darkness to precede the advent of light, another for that *original darkness* to occupy space, and to comprise the realm of an independently subsisting female monarch at that. One can make the case logically that before creation there were two possible states, *something*, the eternal being of God, and *nothing*, which would be all else.

But neither *something* nor *nothing* can be conceptualized independently of the other. If darkness is – originally – the *absence* of light, then darkness before light is unimaginable. The words *absence* (*ab+esse*, literally: "to be away") and *nothing* (no thing) both imply a privation of some necessarily thought thing. Milton's cosmogony, then, imagines a prior *something*, derived from God, *pro se*, which fills space, but which may be deformed into Chaos. Apparently Milton's effluent deity both ebbs and flows, establishing his eternal presence and the temporally and locally contingent absence of his "goodness," as the primal differential dividing not something from nothing, but creation from chaos.

To appreciate the importance of this arrangement to the theodicy of *Paradise Lost*, we might ask how Milton's cosmogony confronts the constraints underlying a more orthodox construction. Augustine, who knew first hand the allure of Manichaean dualism, understood and made explicit the importance of understanding the *nothing* that stands against the *ens* of God as the absence of something and not as a substance in itself. For Augustine *nothing* is not *a thing* in the sense of a negative substance; it is the privation of substance.[5] The terms in which gender is distinguished, fe-*male* and wo-*man*, similarly derive meaning from the supplemental absence of the gendered other inscribed in their roots – not as a belated "after-thought" but integrally. Each gender is substantively defined by its other, as in the bawdy puns seventeenth-century English usage recognizes when distinguishing between *thing* and *no thing*. By reducing sexual difference to a function of the presence or absence of the phallic thing, these puns inscribe in little what Milton's epic performs cosmologically.[6] Genesis begins with a binary: there is "darkness and void" and the movement of the "spirit of God." This movement produces a proliferating series of oppositions: heaven and earth, darkness and light, firmament and earth, water and dry land, until, at 1:27, "God created man in his own image, in the image of God he created him; male and female he created them" (AV).[7] The dissonance between "created him" and "created them" recapitulates – as the generation of gender – the initial doubling implicit in God's creation of his own image. For reasons unstated, God creates an other of himself, but somehow also divides this *man* into *man* and *woman*; in this way Genesis 1:27 at once continues and arrests that process of differentiation with which creation begins. It retains man and God within the unity of a single image, and man and woman within the unity *man*, who is that image. Of course this procedure is almost immediately revised by Genesis 2:21–23. In this putatively earlier (J-text) version the dialectic of difference within identity plays out in more homely and concrete terms. Adam becomes man when the *woman* is physically taken out of him in the form of a rib ("she shall be called Woman because she was taken out of man"; 2:23).[8] Paradoxically, he is marked with the phallus precisely by surrendering a bone to the woman, who, although she receives the thing henceforth missing from Adam, will always signify not that (phallic) thing but its absence. She appears before him not as the thing itself, which he has surrendered to and for her, but rather as the embodiment of its lack. Henceforth, men will not be created by the hand of God but rather will emerge headfirst from the nothing between her legs. Having gone through this rather complicated procedure to break the universe into creator and creature and then to break the creature into male and female embodiments of the same divine image, God immediately begins to reverse the process: "She shall be called Woman, because she was taken out of Man. Therefore shall a man leave his father and mother, and shall cleave unto his wife; and they shall be one flesh" (1:23–24).[9] Surely this tale is as strange as it is familiar. I believe it bears heavily on the question of God's will, which I propose to understand paradoxically as that (thing) which God wants; but first, I want to return to the general question generated by God's wanting. I prefaced this essay with Heidegger's paraphrase of Liebniz's great question: why is there something rather than nothing? Why would God want to reflect himself in creatures he then sets out to reabsorb?

Heidegger's revision of Milton's contemporary, Leibniz, reaches back to Milton in ways that are fascinating but also well beyond the scope of this chapter. Suffice it to say that Liebniz's answer to the question (as to all other questions) is the principle of sufficient reason: all things have a cause and there is a reason for every cause. Therefore, things exist for a reason, and the reason is God. Heidegger perceives in Leibniz's formulation a circularity that continues the historical-linguistic tendency to render *logos* as *ratio* and thus subsume Being in a purely formal notion. Referring again to the translations of *logos*, we might say that the word of God is cut off from the saying so that the cause passes over into its effect. Thus *logos*, which included God as the ground of Being, is reduced to logic, or what Heidegger calls *Grundsätze*. Milton's tarrying with Chaos may be seen as an attempt to be mindful of Being by attempting to represent the *Abgrund* of *Grund*, the abyss of reason as the repository of Being without form.[10]

As a heuristically nominalized, non-substance, *nothing* could not have attributes like darkness, territorial coherence, and, most outlandishly, gender. In a poet other than Milton or a poem other than *Paradise Lost*, one might assume that the ascription of accidents of gender, color, and shape to *nothing* is metaphoric, a convenience of poetic expression not to be puzzled over. It might indeed be comforting to say that, as surely as Keats knew urns do not talk, Milton knew that pre-existence had no shape, color, or gender, and that to question the figures of Chaos and Night would be a naive failure to grasp the conventions of language. Working against this comforting supposition, however, is the fact that Milton's metaphors characteristically trail ontological residues. Moreover, the personification of Night is not an isolated moment in *Paradise Lost*, but is rather, as we shall see, an integral element in the poem's theodicy, which requires the subsistence of an innocent pre-existing matter.[11]

Augustine's theodicy, which depends on the argument that evil is the privation of good, with no positive subsistence of its own, evades the question of the subsistence of matter before creation first by positing, *mirabile dictu*, that God creates out of nothing, but also by asserting a primal division between corruptible and incorruptible substances:

Summum bonum quo superius non est, Deus est: ac per hoc incommutabile bonum est; ideo vere aeternum, et vere imortale. Caetera omnia bona non nisi ab illo sunt, sed non de illo. De illo enim quod est, hoc quod ipse est: ab illo autem quae facta sunt, non sunt quod ipse. Ac per hoc si solus ipse incommutabilis, omnia quae fecit, quia ex nihilo fecit, mutabilia sunt. Tam enim omnipotens est, ut possit etiam de nihilo, id est, ex eo quod omnio non est, bona facere, et magna et parva, et coelestia et terrena, et spiritualia et corporalia. Quia vero et justus est, ei quod se genuit, ea quae de nihilo fecit, non aequavit.

[The highest good, than which there is no higher, is God, and consequently He is unchangeable good, hence truly eternal and truly immortal. All other good things are only from Him, not of Him. For what is of Him, is Himself. And consequently if He alone is unchangeable, all things that He has made, because He has made them out of nothing, are changeable. For He is so omnipotent, that even out of nothing, that out of what is absolutely non-existent, He is able to make good things both great and small, both celestial and terrestrial, both spiritual and corporeal. But because He is also just, He has not put those things that He has made out of nothing on an equality with that which He *begat* out of Himself.][12]

According to Augustine, then, some entities may be generated *ex nihilo*, others *pro se*. Such a theodicy by division runs contrary to Milton's characteristic and highly reflexive monism, which imagines a universe far more dynamic than that envisaged by Augustinian dualism.[13] Whatever controversy may remain about Milton's monism, the juxtaposition of Raphael's description of divine generation in *Paradise Lost* and Augustine's in *De Natura Boni contra Manichaeos* establishes a clearly pointed difference:[14]

> O Adam, one Almighty is, from whom
> All things proceed, and up to him return,
> If not depraved from good, created all
> Such to perfection, one first matter all,
> Endued with various forms, various degrees
> Of substance, and in things that live, of life;
> But more refined, more spiritous, and pure
> As nearer to him placed or nearer tending
> Each in their active spheres assigned,
> Till body up to spirit work, in bounds
> Proportioned to each kind.   (5.469–79)

Where Augustine is at pains to separate corruptible nature from the incorruptible subsistence of God, Milton's archangel asserts the homogeneity of all matter. For example, in the discussion of angelic digestion in *Paradise Lost* 5.404–43, just prior to the quoted lines, Milton's narrator famously draws attention to his heterodox materialism with the otherwise gratuitous aside:

> So down they sat,
> And to their viands fell, nor seemingly
> The angel, nor in mist, the common gloss
> Of theologians, but with keen dispatch
> Of real hunger, and concoctive heat
> To transubstantiate.   (5.433–38)

The "one first matter all" exists in more or less created states, dynamically changing as it responds to the rarefying influence of God. Following Raphael's example, Fallon finds the process of transformation subsumed under the paradigms of digestion and motion.[15] This transubstantiating process unfolds in time ("till body up to spirit work") and can be proportionally expressed in space as distance: "As nearer to him placed or nearer tending." Distance over time is motion. Milton's Chaos too, though un- or not-as-yet- "created," is in motion, but the motion, being random, makes no progress toward getting anywhere:

> A dark
> Illimitable Ocean without bound,
> Without dimension, where length, breadth, and highth,
> And time and place are lost; where eldest Night
> And Chaos, ancestors of Nature, hold
> Eternal anarchy, amidst the noise
> Of endless wars, and by confusion stand.
> For Hot, Cold, Moist, and Dry, four champions fierce
> Strive here for mast'ry, and to the battle bring
> Their embryon atoms.   (2.891–900)

Catherine Gimelli Martin has shown in detail why the materiality Milton accords to Chaos and Night before creation, if not seriously confronted and resolved, would undermine the core issue of his theodicy: "without a fully formless plasticity governing both the primordial and the emergent level of material history, "logically" God or good would have to be at least indirectly responsible for Satan or evil."[16] The crucial functionality of Augustine's disposition of creation into two immutably separate categories, *ab deo* and *pro se*, becomes apparent in the comparison. By emptying nature of pre-existing substance and walling off that part sharing in the substance of God, Augustine places the origin of evil in a reversion to an original absence. Milton has no such recourse. As Fallon has shown, his universe is not only material but animist – like its daughter Eve, it has, in some sense, a will of its own.[17]

John Rumrich notes that "For the materialist Milton . . . the realm of potential creation preceding actual creation possesses a shadowy existence of its own. In a realm that exists before creation, any ontological deficiency conveyed by Miltonic allegory signifies only – to indulge in an instructive tautology – that the matter has not yet undergone creation."[18] I suggest that the conflation of motion and substance, along with the distinction between random and ordered motion, considerably refines Milton's notion of pre-existing matter. One analogy that comes to mind is magnetism. The motion of atoms in a metal is more or less random until a magnetic field is applied. Magnetism imparted to a metal is the effect of lining the atoms up and constraining their motions in a single direction. Although Milton could not have understood magnetism at this atomic level, he would have had reason and precedent to conceive of God as the lodestone of the universe. William Gilbert, in his great treatise *De Magnete*, published in 1600, had extrapolated from experimental data the conclusion that "The magnetic force is animate, or imitates a soul; in many respects it surpasses the human soul while that is united to an organic body."[19]

Matter's will is more *or* less a will toward God: more for matter moving along the line of progress "up to God," less for matter following the random and contradictory motions of its "embryon atoms." From one point of view, in fact the point of view made available at the beginning of book 3 when "th' almighty Father from above, / From the pure empyrean where he sits / High throned above all highth, bent down his eye, / His own works and their works at once to view" (56–59), the impelling force organizing the upward motion of nature is the will of God. Yet reflected into matter as the will toward God, God's will in the creature works against the resistance not only of evil consequent to its postlapsarian corruption, but also the resistance of its own material nature, the somatic motions of its as yet undigested, not yet magnetized stuff. Creation, then, imparts the will of God to the pre-existing material (which is itself the matter of God). This will of God returns to him as a will toward God. In the case of "man," the image of God returns the image of God's will as a will toward God – a desire to rejoin the undifferentiated immediacy of his being. Apparently, then, what God wants is himself: he desires, that is, to encounter himself – his desire – in the will of a willful other. This other is effected by his word – as the spoken self of his speaking.[20]

In taking seriously the gendered and original subsistence of Chaos and Old Night, we depend so far on the shaky ground of satanic discovery for our knowledge of the beginning of *things* and the "original darkness" that preceded it. No less authority, however, than (Milton's) God, the father, informs us of the end of things:

> The world shall burn, and from her ashes spring
> New heav'n and earth, wherein the just shall dwell,
> And after all their tribulations long
> See golden days, fruitful of golden deeds,
> With joy and love triumphing, and fair truth.
> Then thou thy regal sceptre shalt lay by,
> For regal sceptre then no more shall need,
> God shall be All in All.   (3.334–41)

The question of the gendered subsistence of Chaos and Old Night now subsumes the theodicy of creation itself and poses what Heidegger called the fundamental question of metaphysics: "Why is there something rather than nothing?" What is the point of Milton's God's timeless self-division into temporal and gendered creatures destined – in the end – to return to unity within him? What are the implications of Milton's use of images of sexual reproduction to represent this iterative process? If creation begins with God's differentiation of his own substance into heaven and earth and the created things therein and ends with the reabsorption of all things, so that "God shall be All in All," one may legitimately ask what is accomplished – from God's atemporal point of view – by the motile digestive and procreative processes of created matter, "the race of time / Till time stand fixed beyond [which] is all abyss" (*PL* 12.554–55)? Milton's narrative reaches back to the already belated, gendered entities of Chaos and Dark Night and continues until "the race of time" terminates with the image of the phoenix, rising asexually from its own ashes. In question, then, is nothing less than the causelessness of God's "will," because, according to God's self-description, it is impossible for Milton's God to want – that is, to lack – anything:

> Boundless the deep, because I am who fill
> Infinitude, nor vacuous the space.
> Though I uncircumscribed myself retire,
> And put not forth my goodness, which is free
> To act or not; Necessity and Chance
> Approach not me, and what I will is Fate.
> (7.168–73)

As bounded, historically situated, and mortal creatures, we generally *want* what we lack. This condition of the human will is apparent in Milton's Adam, whose first acts of will are to inquire who he is "or where or from what cause" (*PL* 8.270), and then to ask God to supply the "partaker" he finds missing from his survey of Eden's creatures. Because Milton frequently represents the immense processes of creation and history in terms suggesting mammalian conception, gestation, and parturition, it seems a natural extension of Adam's healthy curiosity to ask not only "What does God want?" but also, "What is the nature of his wanting?" Is God's *will* his desire or something else entirely? If God's will is fate, what could it mean for God to want? To make sense of the notion of God's will, it is necessary to impute to matter a certain recalcitrance, a counter-will comprising a resistance to fate. This resistance, which is consistently figured as feminine, is, for Milton's texts, the hard kernel of Christian liberty. Because matter must be possessed of itself in order to mediate God to himself, he must give himself away so that this alienated self may offer itself back to him. Thus the detour of God's will through the living material bodies he creates returns to him a kind of knowledge: the experiences of boundedness, finitude, and resistance that distinguish will from fate so as to open the dimensions of time and motion. The most concentrated figures of this exchange are, of course, the incarnation and passion, which is, for Milton's God, explicitly a two-way street: "thy humiliation shall exalt / With thee thy manhood also to this throne; / *Here* shalt thou sit *incarnate*, here shalt reign / Both God and man, Son both of God and man" (*PL* 3.313–16, my emphasis). Redemption is both of and in the flesh. The interplay of self-surrender and self-possession that underlies God's will may seem less strange or opaque when compared with the progenerative activities of God's adversary and his image.

Images of insemination and parturition are numerous in *Paradise Lost*. One might suspect that Milton institutes the paradigm of sexual procreation to figure the creation of the universe, but only in ways determined to stretch and finally exceed the metaphor's limits until the attentive reader is led to a state of reflexive confusion. The classical muses are feminine and the invocation at the beginning of Milton's epic certainly alludes to classical precedent. When the "heavenly Muse" is further identified as the "Spirit," both traditional English usage and the grammatical gender of classical precedents *(anima)* reinforce the identification of the Spirit as feminine. Yet the Spirit that broods birdlike over the abyss also impregnates it, and it is in "this wild abyss, / The womb of Nature and perhaps her grave" (*PL* 2.910–11) that beginning and ending appear destined to meet.

These curious images of the brooding Spirit and the uterine abyss are elaborated or glossed by the much more elaborate representation of sexual generation that intervenes between the images of the impregnating Spirit and pregnant abyss of book 1, and the womb/grave of nature in book 2. With Satan standing at the breech of hell – the gate between the newly created world of the lost and nowhere at all – we hear an operatic recasting of the birth of Athena in the story of the cephalic delivery of Sin. Springing from Lucifer's head, Sin is an idea without pre-existing material, a concept without material cause:

> All on a sudden miserable pain
> Surprised thee, dim thine eyes, and dizzy swum
> In darkness, while thy head flames thick and fast
> Threw forth, till on the left side op'ning wide,
> Likest to thee in shape and count'nance bright,
> Then shining Heav'nly fair, a goddess armed
> Out of thy head I sprung. (2.752–58)

As the material excrescence of Lucifer's rebellious thought, and so an idealized fragment of him, Sin appeals to his narcissistic desire: "Thyself in me thy perfect image viewing / Becam'st enamoured, and such joy thou took'st / With me in secret, that my womb conceived / A growing burden" (2.764–7).[21] Because we know that God will soon create man in his image, Sin's account of Satan's "amour" amounts to a distorted prolepsis of the divine creation to be represented in book 7. After Lucifer, enamored of his own thought, engenders Death in her, Sin gives birth, delivering her burden, proleptically again, in pain and suffering:

> Pensive here I sat
> Alone, but long I sat not, till my womb
> Pregnant by thee, and now excessive grown
> Prodigious motion felt and rueful throes.
> At last this odious offspring whom thou seest
> Thine own begotten, breaking violent way
> Tore through my entrails, that with fear and pain
> Distorted, all my nether shape thus grew
> Transformed.   (2.777–85)

Although the parodic structure of the trinity in Satan, Sin, and Death is often observed, I do not know that the precise temporal inversion of the order of generation has been noted. The originary event in the narrative plot of *Paradise Lost* is the mysterious generation of the Son: "This day I have *begot* whom I declare / My only Son" (5.603–4, my emphasis). The difficulty presented by these lines is attested by the energy and persistence with which scholarship has tried to make it go away.[22] Following the sequence, however, God announces that he has begotten, declared, and anointed the Son (whatever, for the moment, that all might actually mean). Creation in the flesh, and all the baggage of somatic sexuality that follows from it, is the necessary alternative to the satanic model of cerebral conception: the Son, begotten mysteriously by God, includes God's will that he be surrendered to the flesh of Mary's sealed womb – born again, as a human child. Through the efficacy of the Son ("And thou my Word, begotten Son, by thee / This I perform" [7.163–64]), God first repeats the pregnant abyss trick, to create in the abyss our distinctly fecund "world":

> darkness profound
> Covered th'abyss: but on the wat'ry calm
> His *brooding* wings the spirit of God outspread,
> And vital virtue infused, and vital warmth
> Throughout the fluid mass   (7.233–37)[23]

The genders of God

Like Sin, Eve, too, begins as a thought, but unlike Lucifer, for whom thought is all, and the Father, whose begetting collapses temporal order, Adam goes to God for help in realizing his conception. Taking Adam's thought ("your desire"), God creates Eve out of the substance of Adam's body – Adam's rib is, then, the material kernel or pre-existing matter that combines with Adam's idea of a mate to form Eve as an independent creation. The process is described as a masculine birth in which God delivers Eve from Adam's side:

> Mine eyes he closed, but open left the cell
> Of Fancy my internal sight, by which
> Abstract as in a trance methought I saw,
> Though sleeping, where I lay, and saw the shape
> Still glorious before whom awake I stood,
> Who stooping opened my left side, and took
> From thence a rib, with cordial spirits warm,
> And life-blood streaming fresh; wide was the wound,
> But suddenly with flesh filled up and healed:
> The rib he formed and fashioned with his hands;
> Under his forming hands a creature grew,
> Manlike, but different sex. (8.460–71)

Eve takes form from Adam's wish and the matter of life represented by his bleeding rib. The material from which she is fashioned is contributed by Adam, but, like all material in Milton's universe, it originates with, in fact as, God.

After death the living form decays – the soul returns to God and the body returns to the disorganized state of Chaos – where it is available to embody some different form. Left to themselves, things revert to less organized states over time. Take away the energetic processes Milton calls "concoction" in *Paradise Lost* 5 – processes that continue to transform original matter from one form to another in the direction of greater and greater rarefaction ("the grosser feeds the purer") – and the body returns to the simpler elements from which it was made. As Martin indicates, Milton's description is consistent with the modern idea of entropy. In positing a dynamic interaction between two drives, however, one entropic, seeking disintegration, and one unifying, seeking to regain the oneness of a universe in which God is All in All, Milton also rather closely anticipates Freud's late division of libido into the opposing drives toward death and life.[24] Adam and Eve are "one flesh," but when she first sees him, she runs away, preferring, however briefly, her image in the water, and, in book 9, she wants to garden on her own for a while. One flesh, or at least one rib, becomes two wills which will to join but also to separate. If chaos is a storehouse of raw materials and nature is what emerges from those materials when they are informed and energized by God – then chaos is indeed the womb of nature. Yet if God were to withdraw his inspiration, nature would lapse back to its unformed condition and chaos would be its grave. Against this background we may refine our question of God's "will": what, if anything, is altered by creation and its end? Why would God design a system in which his goodness divides and confronts itself as the positive attraction of divine love and the resistance of a material drive toward death and dissolution?

"WITH ME I SEE NOT WHO PARTAKES" OR, WHY NOT TAKE ALL OF ME?

Eve, Chaos, matter are specifically endowed with positive subsistence and a will in varying degrees independent of God's will. Their substance, alienated from God according to his will, becomes independent of him, as Eve is independent of, yet made from, Adam. Sin, on the other hand, is not. As the image not of Satan but of Satan's thought, his conceptions in her consume her, as one thought cancels and supersedes another. Since, unlike the mediated motivations of his composite creatures, God's will is identical to himself ("and what I will is fate"), in the deity, the division of self and image can only work if the image proves to be another self – not simply a simulacrum but an other that comes to know itself by acknowledging its own desires. Yet Adam and Eve, God and creation, matter and form strive to become each other; that is, they strive to heal the self-division that the imaging process is designed to represent.[25] So, I submit, what God wants is himself: but not his whole self – which would collapse immediately into unity with its original – but rather, himself, as sufficiently different to be his other (self). This want and the will that represents it need some explanation. Thus I propose to approach the difficult question of divine will indirectly through a more easily posed question, "what does Adam want?"

In book 8 Adam's account of himself to Raphael tells how, finding himself alive, he wandered about seeking his creator until sleep overtook him, and he dreamed of Eden and a "shape divine." When he awakes, God appears to him: "before mine eyes all real, as the dream / Had lively shadowed" (*PL* 8.310–11):

> Up hither, from among the trees appeared
> Presence divine. Rejoicing, but with awe
> In adoration at his feet I fell
> Submiss: he reared me, and Whom thou soughts't I am,
> Said mildly, Author of all this thou seest,
> Above, or round about thee or beneath.   (8.313–18)

After granting Adam the garden and advising him of the single prohibition, God gives him dominion over the creatures, "in sign whereof each bird and beast . . . After their kinds" is brought before Adam to be named and to "pay their fealty / with low subjection" (8.342–45). The beasts come before Adam two by two, and "endued" by God with "sudden aprehension" (*PL* 8.353–4), Adam understands their nature. This apprehension also allows Adam to tell God what he wants, for the first time. Having reviewed the creatures, Adam reports "but in these / I found not what methought I wanted still" (*PL* 8.354–55). The ensuing colloquy does much to reveal the nature of wanting in *Paradise Lost*.

"I found not what methought I wanted still" (*PL* 8.355); as I have argued elsewhere, a close reading of this sentence not only indicates Adam's dialectical dependence on Eve, but also the general economy of desire in Milton's epic. If the aim or the effect of Christian regeneration is, as the Lord's Prayer indicates, to do the will of God "on earth as it is in heaven," then in order to participate as an agent (rather than an object) of divine providence, the individual Christian must strive to discover and to want (or will) what God wants. He or she must desire the desire of God. Adam's observation of what he does not see in Eden sets in motion a chain of rhetorical discoveries involving this proverbial cross coupling of "my will and thine." "I . . . me[thought] . . . I." Adam's negative, declarative sentence deploys three first person pronouns in an eight-word clause (the complete sentence includes the prepositional phrase, "but in these"). In raising the question of what might be called rhetorical discovery, I am concerned precisely with the sort of issue undergraduates sometimes raise: what is the difference between writing "I found not what methought I wanted still" and something more straightforward like "I did not find what I wanted," or, to conserve meaning better, "I did not find what I thought I wanted"? In short, I want to examine the textual performances set in motion by the scheme of chiasmus that makes an accusative first person pronoun the pivot between two nominative first person pronouns: "I . . . me . . . I."

A speaking subject is, first of all, the subject of a verb (I *speak*). Adam's locution posits also a temporal sequence; the first "I" having found, the second "I" wants. Between having found and wanting still, Adam's *methought* articulates the specific moment of a mediating reflection. By becoming the subject and object of his thought, Adam comes to recognize himself as *wanting*. In modern English *me thought* is a syntax error, using the accusative case in a nominative phrase. Of course, we recognize the usage as archaic not wrong. It probably would have been recognized as archaic in 1667 as well, and the history of the word bears on the representation in which it appears. *Methinks* is the sole surviving form of OE *þync(e)an*, a verb used impersonally without an expressed subject, and always with a dative pronoun to mean "It *seems* to *me*." In OE the forms of this verb and of *þenc(e)an*, "conceive in the mind, exercise the mind" remained distinct, but "owing to the fact that both *þync-* and *þenc-* gave ME. *þink-*, and both *þoght-* and *þuht-* appeared in ME. as *þought*, *thought*, they became confused and finally fell together."[26] Bearing this history, about which Milton may or may not have known, Adam's "methought" serves to give his sentence a middle voice; neither passive nor active, but rather reflexive, it brings together the ideas of *appearing to (or for)* oneself and of conceiving of oneself in one's own mind and sets them in a temporal and causal sequence: Eve first occurs to Adam as an absence, when, naming the animals, he comes upon (in rhetorical terms, *he invents*), and suddenly apprehends, the category of *mate*. From that moment, and only from that moment, he is alone. Encountering himself as the object of that solitude, he becomes at once the subject and the object of (his own) desire: "in solitude / What happiness, who can enjoy alone, / Or enjoying all, what contentment find?" (*PL* 8.364–66).

If Adam's moment of wanting as a chiasmic encounter with the idea of himself – with himself as the object of his contemplation – gives rise to the fantasy of Eve, a mate who will be like himself, yet with whom he will converse and engender, how does his situation differ from that of Satan, who encounters his idea of rebellion as the fantasy of Sin? The answer, of course, is that Adam seeks and secures the intervention of God in the fulfillment of his desire to see his image in another, while Satan's desire is to be God, which is realized in the inverted form of rebellion as the desire that God not be. To return briefly to Heidegger's ontological question of *the Being of beings*, we might consider that at this point Adam's request for Eve is the result of an ontological meditation, in so far as he appeals to God as the ground of Being for the "*essent*," Eve, while Satan's doctrine of self-begetting regresses to a merely *ontic* experience of being without positing a Being of being. From a theological point of view the difference between Adam's appeal to God for a procreative mate and Satan's auto-parturition of Sin is that between a creative interaction with the divine and a solipsistic misprision of fantasy as material reality. From a phenomenological point of view Milton's paralleled creations add the depth of careful observation to the moralized distinction between a good, intersubjective trajectory of desire of another like the self, and its narcissistic collapse into a desire for the self.[27] In yet another register, the distinction between Satan's desire and Adam's parallels that between Freud's primary and secondary processes. For the former, which respond only to the "pleasure principle," there is no perceived distinction between the material and hallucinatory satisfaction of desire. The latter, responsible to the "reality principle," discerns threats to the life of the organism, over-riding immediate pleasure with concerns for safety. Thus, in primary processes – for example, a dream – wishes are fulfilled in fantasy that would be too costly to act out in waking life. It is of interest to the present argument that the Freudian *Ich* mediates between the appetites of primary process and access to control of the voluntary muscles (not normally available in sleep for example), so that in the secondary process, satisfaction is mediated by work and the resistance of the material world. Beside the intervention of God, the salient difference between the creation of Sin and that of Eve is the incorporation of material – Adam's "Rib, with cordial spirits warm, / And life-blood streaming fresh" (*PL* 8.466–67) – into Eve, as opposed to the *nothing* of Satanic negation from which Sin appears. One might say that Adam's fantasy is the formal cause of Eve, and his taken body part, her material cause. God is her efficient cause through his labor of "fashioning" her from Adam's rib but also her final cause, in that he knew "it was not good for man to be alone." Sin admits of no such analysis, no such collaborative creation.[28] As the thought of negation joined to the absence of material, she is the phenomenal appearance of nothing – the reified form of the negative – a generation from Satan's thought exemplifying the *creatio ex nihilo* Milton otherwise seems at such odd pains to reject.

I began this discussion by trying to notice and account for the various scenes of generation instanced in *Paradise Lost*. Two of these – the generation of Sin and the creation of Eve – may now be juxtaposed with a third scene of pre- rather than pro-creative activity: the Father's off-stage "begetting" of his only Son. Completing a detour through these three scenes will return us finally to the questions of what Milton's God wants and why Chaos and Old Night are gendered.

> This day I have begot whom I declare
> My only Son, and on this holy hill
> Him have anointed, whom ye now behold

> At my right hand; your head I him appoint;
> And by myself have sworn to him shall bow
> All knees in Heav'n, and shall confess him Lord:
> Under his great vicegerent reign abide
> United as one individual soul
> For ever happy.   (5.603–11)

I have already adverted to the difficulty posed by this narrative; the difficulty, that is, of knowing just what sort of process is denoted by the verb *to beget* in this context and what relation begetting has to the subsequent anointing. It seems, however, that whether or not the Son exists prior to his begetting, he is on "this day" created *as the Son* and anointed vicegerent of his Father's Kingdom. Yet what does it mean to be the Son of God? Using the procedures by which we analyzed the creations of Sin and Eve, we might approach this question in terms of Aristotelian causes. Our answer will be incomplete because Milton tells us nothing of how the Son was *fashioned*, but he does tell us something – though equivocally – about the material from which he is made, the form he is given, and the purpose for which he is begotten. In the invocation to holy light that begins book 3, Milton ascribes a predicate to God and extends it also to his Son. "God is light" and his Son is the material effluence of his "bright essence increate." Milton's cautious words are, in turn, a verbal representation of that "bright effluence." Although Milton's trajectory from divine *lux* to visible *lumen* employs a commonplace, it is, in the universe of *Paradise Lost*, emphatically not a metaphor. Light is, indeed, their material substance and the *begetting* of the Son represents a material transformation of that substance.[29]

A similar transformation of a common metaphor to a literal assertion occurs in Raphael's comparison of knowledge and food, which begins "knowledge is *as* food" but joins with other and stronger identifications (most notably, "the fruit . . . whose mortal taste / Brought death into the world" [*PL* 1.2–3]) to assert an ontological continuity between physiological and intellectual digestive processes. This continuity undermines the semantic impertinence necessary to mark the statement as figurative, so that knowledge becomes, in fact, not like food, but rather, a kind of food (*PL* 7.126–30).[30] This rhetorical hovering between analogy and ontology performs within the text the movement of self-alienation and recuperation ascribed to God's *creatio pro se* beyond the text, conferring on the text a (feminine) subjectivity distinct from Milton's in the same way that a creature's subjectivity is distinct from God's. This eccentric textual subject, the womb of meaning that exceeds the masculine will of its author so that he may enjoy and regain himself, constitutes, as it were, the free will of the text.

NOTES

1. Martin Heidegger, *An Introduction to Metaphysics*, trans. Ralph Manheim (New Haven and London: Yale University Press, 1959), 1–2. *Essents* is Manheim's coinage from *essens essentis*, a non-existent present participle of *sum* distinct from simple *ens*, used to translate, in this instance, Heidegger's *die Seienden* (translator's note, ix). In the quoted sentence it may be taken as "things that are"; Heidegger's "fundamental question" recapitulates that of Milton's contemporary, Leibniz: "Why is there something, rather than nothing?"
2. Wallace Stevens, "Anecdote of the Jar," in *Poems*, ed. Samuel French Morse (New York: Vintage, 1959), 21.
3. All citations of Milton's poetry refer to *John Milton: The Complete Poems*, ed. John Leonard (New York and London: Penguin Books, 1998).
4. The notion that vacuity must be actively prevented lest darkness regain dominion appears again when Uriel describes the mechanics of earth and moon in 3.724–32, and in Raphael's hypothetical description of "other suns perhaps / With their attendant moons . . . / Communicating male and female light, / Which two great sexes animate the world" (7.148–51).
5. See, for example, *Concerning the Nature of Good, Against the Manicheans* (*de Natura Boni Contra Manichaeos*) in *Patrologiae, Series Latina Prior*, ed. J.-P. Migne (Paris, 1861), esp. chapters 1, 24, and 26.
6. I derive the outlines of my argument from Lacan's late "mathemics" of sexuation. See Jacques Lacan, *Encore: On Feminine Sexuality, The Limits of Love and Knowledge: 1972–1973. The Seminar of Jacques Lacan*, Book 20, ed. Jacques-Alain Miller, trans. Bruce Fink (New York: Norton, 1998), 78–81. See also Lacan's discussion of the phrase, "There's such a thing as One *[Y a d'Un]*," 66–71.
7. See Mieke Bal's brilliant reading of the Priestly-text (Gen. 1:26–27) account of creation in "Sexuality, Sin and Sorrow: The Emergence of the Female Character," in *Lethal Love: Feminist Literary Readings of Biblical Love Stories* (Bloomington and Indianapolis: Indiana University Press, 1987), 104–30, esp. 112–19.
8. The Geneva Bible (1560) adds as commentary: "Or, Mannes, because she commeth of man: for in Ebrewe Ish, is man, and Ishah the woman."
9. Historical criticism drastically reduces the difficulty, complexity, and explanatory suppleness of these texts by dividing them into earlier and later versions. For Milton, the scripture's apparent contradictions would necessarily be resolved by higher (more synthetic) understanding.
10. For further discussion, see Renato Cristin, *Heidegger and Leibniz: Reason and the Path*, trans. Gerald Parks (Dodrecht, Boston, and London: Kluwer Academic Publishers), esp. 3–22.

11. On the ontological force of metaphorical redescriptions in general, see Paul Ricoeur, *The Rule of Metaphor: Multi-Disciplinary Studies of the Creation of Meaning in Language*, trans. Robert Czerny, Kathleen McLaughlin, and John Costello (Toronto: University of Toronto Press, 1977), 303–13.
12. *De Natura Boni Contra Manichaeos*, 42, cols. 551–52; *Concerning the Nature of Good, Against the Manichan*, trans. Albert H. Newman, in *A Select Library of the Nicene and Post-Nicene Fathers* (Grand Rapids, MI: Wm. B. Eerdmans, 1956), 4. 351. I have added the emphasis on *se genuit* "*begat* out of himself" to draw attention to the presence of the birth image that is, at least, latent in Augustine's Latin text and as counterpoint to Satan's claim, in *PL* 5.860–1, to have been "self-begot, self-raised / By our own quickening power."
13. Regina Schwartz remarks that "Milton's uncompromising monism leads him to suspect latent dualism even here, to wonder if Augustine has not merely substituted 'nothing' for evil as a second principle": "Milton's Hostile Chaos: '. . . And the Sea Was No More,'" *ELH* 52 (1985): 338. Given the specific requirements of Milton's monistic theodicy, his suspicions were well founded. For the literary historical contexts of Milton's monism, see Grossman, "Subsequent Precedence: Milton's Materialist Reading of Ficino and Tasso," *Surfaces* 6 (1996), electronic publication: http://pum12.pum.umontreal.ca/revues/surfaces/vol6/grossman.html. On the dynamism of Milton's universe, see Stephen Fallon, *Milton among the Philosophers* (Ithaca: Cornell University Press, 1991) 103.
14. On the development over time of Milton's monistic materialism, see *ibid*. 78–110, and John Rumrich, "Milton's Arianism and Why it Matters," in *Milton and Heresy*, ed. Stephen B. Dobranski and John P. Rumrich (Cambridge: Cambridge University Press, 1998), 75–92.
15. *Milton Among the Philosophers*, 103–4.
16. Catherine Gimelli Martin, "Fire, Ice, and Epic Entropy: The Physics and Metaphysics of Milton's Reformed Chaos," *Milton Studies* 35, ed. Albert C. Labriola (Pittsburgh: University of Pittsburgh Press, 1997), 77. See also Rumrich, *Milton Unbound*, 141–45.
17. Fallon, *Milton among the Philosphers*, 107: "For Milton, soul, and the life, which springs from it, are not anomalies in a dead material world; instead, life is the usual condition of matter." See also John Rogers, *The Matter of Revolution: Science, Poetry and Politics in the Age of Milton* (Ithaca: Cornell University Press, 1996), esp. 112–22.
18. John Rumrich, *Milton Unbound* (Cambridge: Cambridge University Press, 1996), 129.
19. William Gilbert, *De Magnete* (London, 1600). Book V chapter XII is especially suggestive. See *De Magnete*, trans. P. Fleury Mottelay (New York: Dover, 1958), 308–12. Joseph Wittreich discusses Milton's awareness of the "new science" and how he exploits the contradictions between old and new to enhance his narrative: "Milton deploys a theory of science to gloss the Creation story of religion, even to subtend the poem's Christocentric theology, and to mediate, at the same time, another problem of the 'modern' world, the relationship

between the sexes". Joseph Wittreich, "'Inspir'd with Contradiction': Mapping Gender Differences in *Paradise Lost*," in *Literary Milton: Text, Pretext, and Context*, ed. Diana Treveno Benet and Michael Lieb (Pittsburgh: Duquesne, 1994), 142, 45.

20. Cf. Jacques Lacan, "The Subversion of the Subject and the Dialectic of Desire in the Freudian Unconscious," in *Ecrits: A Selection*, trans. Alan Sheridan (New York: Norton, 1977): "Being of non-being, that is how *I* as subject comes on the scene, conjugated with the double aporia of a true survival that is abolished by knowledge of itself, and by a discourse in which it is death that sustains existence" (300).

21. On Milton's use of Hesiod's version of the birth of Athena, see Philip J. Gallagher, "'Real or Allegoric': The Ontology of Sin and Death in *Paradise Lost*," *English Literary Renaissance* 6 (1976): 317–35; esp. 332–34. On Sin and Death as meta-allegory see: Maureen Quilligan, *Milton's Spenser: The Politics of Reading* (Ithaca: Cornell University Press, 1983), 85–92; Herman Rapaport, *Milton and the Postmodern* (Lincoln, NE: University of Nebraska Press, 1983), 168–207; R. A. Shoaf, *Milton, Poet of Duality: A Study of Semiosis in the Poetry and Prose* (New Haven: Yale University Press, 1985), 23–24; Marshall Grossman, *"Authors to themselves": Milton and the Revelation of History* (Cambridge: Cambridge University Press, 1987), 44–47; and Gordon Teskey, *Allegory and Violence* (Ithaca: Cornell University Press, 1996), 42–43.

22. See, for example, the opening sentence of Alastair Fowler's lengthy gloss: "These lines are among the most controversial in the poem; and quite unnecessarily so." Citing the obvious sources in Ps. ii and Heb. 1:5, Fowler confidently asserts that "begot" must be taken to mean "declare" rather than what it obviously means in Genesis, and more pointedly, just 240 lines further into the text, when Satan suggests that the angels may have been "self-begot, self-raised / By our own *quickening* power" (5.860–61, my emphasis), lines for which Fowler deems no explanatory note necessary: *The Poems of John Milton*, ed. John Carey and Alastair Fowler (London: Longman, 1980).

23. See John Rogers's discussion of *PL* 7.233–42. Rogers notes in this passage a concatenation of insemination and digestion, which he calls "perhaps the most troubling natural philosophic event in the poem" and "the key to the puzzling political science of *Paradise Lost*." For Rogers "the tartareous dregs of creation introduce into the otherwise monistic world of the poem a residual trace of dualism" (132–34). After tracing the natural history of the passage through a number of contemporary sources, Rogers attributes this return of a so-carefully repressed dualism to Milton's disillusion with the "popular sovereignty" he had earlier anticipated (141).

24. Martin, "Fire, Ice, and Epic Entropy: The Physics and Metaphysics of Milton's Reformed Chaos"; see Sigmund Freud, *Beyond the Pleasure Principle* (1920), esp. chapter 6, and *Psychoanalysis Terminable and Interminable*, section 7, in *The Standard Edition of the Complete Psychological Works of Sigmund Freud*, trans. James and Alex Strachey, 24 vols. (London: Hogarth, 1953–73), vols. 18 and 23.

25. Cf. Rumrich, *Milton Unbound*, 141–45.
26. *OED*, sv. † "think," $v.^1$, $v.^2$ and "methinks."
27. On the phenomenology of sin in *Paradise Lost*, see Grossman, *"Authors to themselves": Milton and the Revelation of History* (Cambridge: Cambridge University Press, 1987).
28. On the importance of collaboration in *Paradise Lost*, see Amy Dunham Stackhouse, "Disseminating the Author: Milton and the Trope of Collaboration," unpublished dissertation, University of Maryland, 1998.
29. Cf. William Kerrigan, *The Sacred Complex: On the Psychogenesis of "Paradise Lost"* (Cambridge, MA: Harvard University Press, 1983), 144–50.
30. See *ibid.*, 237–38.

CHAPTER 6

Transported touch: the fruit of marriage in Paradise Lost

John Rogers

Milton's unfinished, posthumously published theological treatise, *De Doctrina Christiana*, includes in its first book a chapter on "The Special Government of Man before the Fall: Dealing Also with the Sabbath and Marriage." In what seems at times a catch-all for discussions that must not have fit anywhere else, Milton, or the compositor of this Miltonic treatise, sutures together in chapter 10 a consideration of the Edenic problem of the forbidden fruit, which naturally does belong in a chapter on the government of man before the fall, with considerations of the problems of divorce and polygamy, institutions that are only really relevant to the government of man after the fall. In the first two manuscript pages of this chapter in the *De Doctrina*, Milton forwards his most thoroughgoing theorization of God's commandment not to eat the fruit of the tree of knowledge. In eighteen subsequent manuscript pages, Milton confronts the possibility (a possibility taken seriously by many of his contemporaries) that God before the fall had issued another commandment, a marriage commandment that explicitly instituted the practice of marriage and implicitly prohibited the practices of divorce and polygamy, two institutions whose legality Milton had championed in the polemical divorce pamphlets of the previous decade.

When taken as a single unit of theological argument, this chapter makes little sense. Milton takes little care to connect the problems of the prohibition of the fruit with the complications of marriage law: the prohibition of the fruit was presumably to be obeyed without questioning, while the marriage commandment admitted, he argues at length, of numerous contingencies and escape clauses. The seeming logical muddle that results from this peculiar conjunction of topics has largely, and understandably, been ignored by the scholars of Milton's theology, surfacing as a matter of interest only in the last ten years as critics have revisited the topic of his authorship of the *De Doctrina*. Yet whatever the conceptual asymmetry between the Edenic prohibition of the fruit of the tree of knowledge and the divine institution of marriage, it must nonetheless be said that this chapter of the treatise does manage to tackle those matters, however disparate, most seriously at issue in the story of the fall of Adam and Eve related in *Paradise Lost*. I would like to begin this chapter by proposing the idea that the uncertain coherence of Milton's theological argument exposes his struggle not only to make the best theological sense he can of that ultimately inexplicable event, the fall, but to emplot that scriptural event within a plausible literary narrative.

In one brief passage in the *De Doctrina*, Milton sets forth his only theoretical articulation of the slender tie that binds the topic of marriage to that of the forbidden fruit:

Man was made in the image of God, and the whole law of nature was so implanted and innate in him that he was in need of no command. It follows, then, that if he received any additional commands, whether about the tree of knowledge or about marriage, these had nothing to do with the law of nature, which is itself sufficient to teach whatever is in accord with right reason (i.e., whatever is intrinsically good). These commands, then, were simply a matter of what is called positive right. Positive right comes into play when God, or anyone else invested with lawful power [*iusta poteste*], commands or forbids things which, if he had not commanded or forbidden them, would in themselves have been neither good nor bad, and would therefore have put no one under any obligation.[1]

In attempting to justify God's exercise of arbitrary power, Milton brings the obviously unlike phenomena of fruit and marriage into a meaningful structural alignment by focusing on their common relation to the issue of authority. Like God's institution of marriage, the divine law against the fruit is not the product of a natural or a moral law, discoverable by the inward power of human reason; it is an arbitrary, or what Milton calls a "positive," law, a law decreed more or less at whim by God, or, as Milton notes, by "anyone else invested with lawful power."

In the case of the prohibition on eating the fruit of the tree of knowledge, Milton insists that the commandment had to be an arbitrary, positive, one, because man's obedience could not have been made evident if the prohibition of the fruit had been a simple consequence of the law of nature, or an innately discernible moral law: "For man was by nature good and holy, and was naturally disposed to do right, so it was certainly not necessary to bind him by the requirements of any covenant to something which he would do of his own accord." Had the prohibition of the fruit not been issued as an arbitrary commandment, had it been the consequence of a natural, rather than a positive, divine law, man would never have been in a position to demonstrate his obedience to God: "he would not have shown obedience at all by performing good works, since he was in fact drawn to these by his own natural impulses, without being commanded" (*CPW* 6:352). Instinctively, naturally good, man could never have proven his obedience without the arbitrary commandment; but, too, he would never have sinned, since a transgression of a law of nature would have so violated his own natural impulses.[2]

What, though, of the suggestion that the marriage commandment was no less a product of arbitrary law than the prohibition of the fruit? The surprising juxtaposition of God's prohibition of the fruit and his commandment to marry does little to forward Milton's specific discussion of Edenic law in the theological treatise. Yet in the connection Milton forges in his treatise between fruit and marriage, we can discern a clue to the relation laid forth in *Paradise Lost* between the contradictory representations of the great prohibition and the untenable social formation that is Adam and Eve's marriage. We can discern further, I submit, an explanation of the fall that exceeds in explanatory value anything that Milton would be able to contain within the more constrictive parameters of abstract theological argument. What follows, here, is an admittedly speculative reading of the fall in *Paradise Lost*: the reading prompted, perhaps even necessitated, by the passage in chapter 10 of *De Doctrina* treating the fundamental arbitrariness of the commandments regarding both fruit and marriage.

When Milton comes to tackle the problem of the forbidden fruit in his theological treatise, he supplies the orthodox Augustinian understanding of its status as an empty signifier, "a pledge or memorial of obedience" (6:352). With precisely the same argument, in *Paradise Lost*, Milton has Adam explain to Eve that this one rule constitutes the "only sign of our obedience" (4:428). Nevertheless, the poem cannot be said to represent the great commandment with any great consistency. As William Empson was the first to note, the fruit functions in the poem, as in the treatise, as an arbitrary sign in Milton's theological universe; but it also has a life as a complex natural entity within the unusually precise scientific world of Milton's vitalist cosmos. Although the characters noisily insist that that fruit was proscribed completely arbitrarily, Milton's narrator, after the fall, suggests the possibility that there had been mysterious organic powers lurking in the fruit all along: "the force of that fallacious Fruit, / That with exhilarating vapor bland / About thir spirits had play'd, and inmost powers / Made err" (9.1046–49). The effect of the eating may have been less a matter of God's choice to judge and punish his creatures for the violation of a decree than a more straightforward matter of physiological cause and effect.[3]

The narrator thereby admits into a poem otherwise committed to the orthodox position that the eating of the fruit was an act "in itself neither good nor evil" (*CPW* 6:352) the possibility that the law against the fruit was in fact a reasonable one, a law issued not as an arbitrary edict, but as a natural consequence of the rationally discernible law of nature. This alternative, naturalistic understanding of the prohibition was the theory pursued with great literalism by Milton's older contemporary, the natural philosopher Jean Baptiste van Helmont, who suggested in his 1648 *Ortus Medicinae* that the law against the fruit was simply a friendly admonition, the Father's perfectly reasonable warning to the first couple not to be so foolish as to eat the only fruit in the garden whose ingestion brings mortality. When Milton, in book 9, suggests that in eating the fruit Adam and Eve had been "eating Death" (9.792) he seems almost to allude to van Helmont, for whom Adam did "eat his own and posterities Death . . . because that Death was placed in the Apple, but not in the opposition of eating: And therefore that Death from the eating of the Apple was natural, being admonished of, but not a curse threatend by a law."[4] If Milton's narrator is right to suggest that the fruit contained within itself a physical force of fallenness, then it is not entirely unreasonable to think that it was not the commandment itself, but the possibly false aura of arbitrariness surrounding the commandment, that ultimately produced the conditions that made the fall possible. For Milton in *Areopagitica*, Adam would have been incapable of demonstrating his virtue if the commandment had not been arbitrary, and if that arbitrariness had not in some sense functioned as a provocation: "We ourselves esteem not of that obedience, or love, or gift, which is of force: God therefore left him free, set before him a provoking object, ever almost in his eyes; herein consisted his merit, herein the right of his reward, the praise of his abstinence." The provoking object Milton establishes in *Paradise Lost* was less the fruit itself than its arbitrary prohibition, which appears to have the effect, despite all of the poem's protestations of the free choice of its characters, of provoking, perhaps even necessitating, the fall into disobedience.[5]

When Milton discusses the arbitrary marriage commandment in *De Doctrina Christiana*, he appears to be referring to God's decree in Genesis 2:18, "It is not good for man to be alone: let us make him a help like unto himself." This commandment establishes the central rule of marriage in Eden, which, he goes on to explain, "consisted in the mutual love, delight, help and society of husband and wife" (*CPW* 6:355). These are the idealized ends of marriage with which we are familiar from many passages both in *Paradise Lost* and in the divorce pamphlets. In *Tetrachordon*, Milton had also insisted on the importance of the divine arbitrariness of that commandment, its distance from the realm of nature and natural law: "though mariage be most agreeable to holines, to purity and justice, yet is it not a naturall, but a civill and ordain'd relation" (*CPW* 2:601). Why, Milton asks in the divorce pamphlet, would God have commanded marriage at all, if, as a part of the law of nature, it were something that man would have come to instinctively: "were it meerly naturall why was it heer ordain'd more than the rest of morall law to man in his originall rectitude, in whose brest all that was naturall or morall was engrav'n without externall constitutions and edicts" (*CPW* 2:602).

The answer to that question, which appears in both *Tetrachordon* and *Paradise Lost*, involves an insistent distinction between two aspects of marriage. Marriage does, he avers in both of those works, have a foundation in nature, the naturally loving drive for companionship and intimacy that moves most men and women. This lesser, predominantly corporeal, aspect of marriage man would have come to regardless of a divine commandment, and it finds its scriptural foundation in the words Adam utters in Genesis 2:23–24: "And Adam said this is now bone of my bones, and flesh of my flesh" and "Therefore shall a man leav his father and his mother, and shall cleav unto his wife; and they shall be one flesh." However, the other, more important aspect of marriage, that which arises as a consequence of a divine decree, involves not the natural physical union, but the social and domestic harmony established in the fit marriage: "Mariage is a divine institution joyning man and woman in a love fitly dispos'd to the helps and comforts of domestic life" (*CPW* 2:612).

Milton is careful to distinguish between the natural and the divinely instituted social aspects of marriage because, he argues, divorce would be unthinkable if marriage had its foundation exclusively in natural law: "For if it were in nature, no law or crime could disanull it, to make a wife, or husband, otherwise then still a wife or husband, but only death" (*CPW* 2:601). Committed to his belief that God permits divorce, Milton obliges himself to disqualify Genesis 2:23 (Adam's "flesh of my flesh") and Genesis 2:24 ("they shall be one flesh") as part of the superior, because arbitrary, divine marriage commandment. These figures of an indissoluble fleshly union of man and woman are thus not to be understood as prescriptive, but as merely descriptive of the perfect harmony of the first couple's union. Of the suggestion in Genesis 2:24 that "they shall be one flesh," Milton insists in the *De Doctrina Christiana* that "This is neither a law nor a commandment, but an effect or natural consequence of that very intimate relationship which would have existed between Adam and Eve in man's unfallen state. Nothing is being discussed in the passage except the origin of families" (*CPW* 6:355). For Milton, an elemental natural law, like that which brings a man and a woman together for the simple purpose of procreation, seems almost structurally to be inviolable. However, a divine law, such as God's ordination of the "fit disposition" of love "to the helps and comforts of domestic life and solace," admits of so many contingencies (what if the love, for example, no longer be fitly disposed?) that the social contract drawn up in accordance with it seems to Milton's perhaps self-serving reason to be eminently dissoluble: "No Ordinance therefore givn particularly to the good both spiritual and temporal of man, can bee urg'd upon him to his mischeif" (*CPW* 2:624).

Convinced in *Paradise Lost* that the fleshly union of Adam and Eve is a lesser aspect of their marriage, Milton carefully follows Genesis in ascribing exclusively to Adam the understanding of marriage as a connection of flesh. It is thus Adam, and not Raphael or the narrator, who declares, with no small degree of self-interest: "I now see / Bone of my Bone, Flesh of my Flesh, my Self / Before me." (8.494–96). That Milton feels Adam's personal declaration of their physical connection the inferior part of marriage is evidenced by Adam's false appeal to natural law to justify his fall: "I feel / The Link of Nature draw me: Flesh of Flesh, / Bone of my Bone thou art" (9.913–15). When the relation of husband and wife is exclusively figured, as Adam figures it here, as a "Link of Nature," the virtuous choice of divorce becomes unimaginable. Feeling the natural, rather than the divinely ordained, aspect of marriage to be dominant, Adam finds it impossible to separate himself from Eve, an action permissible in the contingent world of a divinely ordained marriage, and the only action that would have enabled him to remain obedient both to the spirit of the divine marriage commandment and to the divine interdiction of the fruit.

In *Tetrachordon*, as we have seen, the distinction between the natural and the divine foundation of marriage pointed, in the main, to the difference between the physical and the social aspects of married life. It was not Milton's concern in that treatise, as many critics have noted, to focus on the phenomenon of sexual inequality; if anything, *Tetrachordon*, which explicitly permits a wife to divorce a husband, pointed to the implicit equality of man and woman.[6] The helpmeet God commands for the first husband in Genesis 2:18 is viewed there as a reflection or replica of Adam: "another self, a second self, a very self it self" (*CPW* 2:600). But in the chapter on "The Special Government of Man before the Fall" in *De Doctrina Christiana*, Milton adds something new to the understanding of the social compact between husband and wife ordained by God in Genesis 2:18. It is God's arbitrary dictum, and not the law of nature, that establishes the fact of sexual hierarchy in marriage, as is made clear by the full quotation of the passage cited above only in part: "Marriage also, if it was not commanded, was at any rate instituted, and consisted in the mutual love, delight, help and society of husband and wife, *though with the husband having greater authority [iure licet viri potiore]*" (my italics). Milton goes on to add what we know to be the case in the Bible: "The husband's authority became still greater after the fall" (*CPW* 6:355). However, this hermeneutic commonplace, founded on Genesis 3:16, is only mentioned after Milton has established that the husband's *initial* authority, before the fall, was grounded not in nature, but in an arbitrary decree issued after their creation.

In identifying marriage as an institution whose hierarchical structure is grounded not on the ontological makeup of the first man and the first woman, but on a revelation issued at a specific moment in time after the creation, Milton is speaking to, and modifying, a long tradition in the politically inflected understanding of Genesis. In his reading of Genesis, Luther had already established the opposing position of Adam and Eve's ontological inequality and social equality. Arguing that "the woman certainly differs from man, for she is weaker in body and intellect," Luther suggested further, on the basis of Genesis 2:18, that, despite her natural inferiority, Eve was, before the fall, to enjoy an absolute social equality: "Had the woman not been deceived by the serpent, she would have been equal to Adam in all things."[7] In his *Laws of Ecclesiastical Polity*, Richard Hooker had followed Luther in formulating his own unequivocal derivation of sexual inequality from nature. Woman's "subalternation" to man for Luther "is naturally grounded upon inequality": "woman therefore was even in her first estate framed by nature not only after in time but inferior in excellency also unto man." For Hooker, the natural foundation of sexual inequality was essential both for social harmony ("because things equal in every respect are never willingly directed one by another") and, more important, for the preservation of the mystery of "that kind of love which is the perfectest ground of wedlock."[8]

In opposing the Lutheran naturalization of sexual inequality in his *Commentary on Genesis*, Calvin had anticipated Milton's belief that Eve was ontologically equal but divinely ordained to be socially inferior.[9] In his 1641 *History of the Creation* the Calvinist George Walker would go even further than Calvin in his argument for the ontological equality of Adam and Eve:

that they both were created in the image of God; and that the difference of their sexes, and the creation of the Woman after the Man, of a Rib taken out of mans side, doe not make any *difference of their nature, and kind*; but both are of one kind, and both made in the image of God and after his likenesse: And Women as well as Men are capable of the same grace, and fit to bee heires of the same glory in Heaven, where there is *no difference of male and female*.[10]

Milton, I believe it can be shown, attends closely to the Calvinist understanding of a natural equality on which is superimposed an arbitrary distinction between male superiority and female inferiority.

As is the case with all the instances of "special government" enumerated in *De Doctrina Christiana*, including the prohibition of the fruit and God's precept sanctifying the Sabbath, the divine dicta must be revealed to man, as they are never discernible by natural reason.[11] The importance of the arbitrary marriage commandment (as well as its distinction from the aspects of marriage that flow from nature) finds careful articulation in *Paradise Lost*, despite the poem's official insistence that the prohibition of the fruit was the *only* arbitrary command given Adam and Eve (5.551–52). In his naturalization of marital inequality, Richard Hooker had insisted on its immediate perceptibility by rational beings; the inferior female was framed by nature, and "in so due and sweet proportion as being presented before our eyes, might be sooner perceived than defined."[12] Yet despite Milton's general commitment to the Hookerian conviction in the primacy of natural law and human reason, he counters Hooker by reaching back to the arbitrary God of Calvin when sketching the delicate contours of marriage. Some of the most striking moments of Milton's epic emerge in contexts in which he makes it clear that marriage is not simply, to cite *De Doctrina Christiana*, the "natural consequence of that very intimate relationship which would have existed between Adam and Eve in man's unfallen state" (*CPW* 6:355). Even when using their presumably perfect, rational faculties, neither Adam nor Eve is able to intuit anything like the hierarchical constitution of their relationship. Legal ordination rather than ontological facts, all distinctions of authority and superiority must be revealed to them by divine instruction. Eve, to cite just the most striking example, describes hearing the prescript of the warning voice (was that the marriage commandment?) wake her from her poolside reverie and inform her of her indebtedness to the man she must henceforth consider her guide and head; until she was authoritatively instructed otherwise, Adam appeared to Eve decidedly inferior, "less fair, / Less winning soft, less amiablie mild" than the image she saw of herself (4.479–80).

Eve's instinctive, natural understanding of their union seems to have been supplemented by additional marital prescripts from God: Adam tells Raphael of his meeting with Eve, "on she came, / Led by her heavenly maker, though unseen, / And guided by his voice, nor uninformed / Of nuptial sanctity and marriage rites" (8.487). This divine initiation into marriage seems, in this last instance, to involve the sacred mystery of Miltonic sex. Elsewhere, however, Eve explains the nature of the marriage commandment in terms of the origins of sexual hierarchy that Milton theorizes in *De Doctrina Christiana*. "My Author and Disposer," Eve says to Adam, "what thou bidst / Unargu'd I obey; so God ordains, / God is thy Law, thou mine" (4.635–37). Rather than a natural consequence of an unequal creation, Eve suggests, her obligation to obey Adam arises from a divine, presumably arbitrary, ordination issued, we have to assume, *after* her creation: "So God ordains." Scrupulously careful to distinguish the egalitarianism founded in nature from the inequality imposed by a subsequent legal decree, Milton at moments such as these takes pains to remove the hierarchical structure of earthly marriage from any rationally discernible foundation in natural law. Woman's subordination to man must be taken on faith.

There are moments, it must be said, in which the poem is less clear in its identification of sexual hierarchy as the product of an arbitrary decree. We have seen how the related phenomenon of the prohibition of the fruit seems at times in *Paradise Lost* to be variously derivable from either the revealed law of God or the rationally discernible law of nature. So, too, is the law of sexual subordination, which seems in the main to be an arbitrary legal decree, but which also finds justification in the poem as the physiological consequence of Eve's ontological indebtedness to Adam. The reader, in fact, is never given authoritative instruction in the relative status of Adam and Eve, who initially appear in the poem to be equally majestic and lordly:

> Two of far nobler shape erect and tall,
> Godlike erect, with native Honour clad
> In naked Majestie seemd Lords of all,
> And worthie seemd, for in thir looks Divine
> The image of thir glorious Maker shone,
> Truth, Wisdom, Sanctitude severe and pure,
> Severe but in true filial freedom plac't;
> Whence true autoritie in men.
>
> (*PL* 4.288–95)

The narrator, at this juncture, hastens to correct any sense of their equality that may have been suggested by their physical appearance, their seemingly equal ability to reflect "in thir looks Divine / The image of thir glorious

Maker" (4.291–92). Countering the impression that the "true autoritie" embodied by Adam and Eve is equal authority, the narrator moves on to explain their inequality:

> though both
> Not equal, as thir sex not equal seemd;
> For contemplation hee and valour formd,
> For softness shee and sweet attractive Grace,
> Hee for God only, shee for God in him:
> His fair large Front and Eye sublime declar'd
> Absolute rule; and Hyacinthin Locks
> Round from his parted forelock manly hung
> Clustring, but not beneath his shoulders broad:
> Shee as a vail down to the slender waste
> Her unadorned golden tresses wore
> Disheveld, but in wanton ringlets wav'd
> As the Vine curles her tendrils, which impli'd
> Subjection.   (4.295–308)

In this correction of our presumably mistaken first impression that Adam and Eve might be equal, the narrator does not, as we might expect, shift the ground of our judgment from the ontological realm of nature to the legal realm of divine commandment; he makes no attempt to explain God's legal appointment of Adam as Eve's authoritative head. He proceeds instead to maintain his natural perspective and evince their hierarchical differentiation by their appearance ("thir sex not equal *seemd*" [my italics]), attributing their difference in status not to the law of God but the law of nature. The narrator initially adduces their difference in status ("Hee for God only, shee for God in him") by a focus on the presumably perceivable difference in musculature: Adam's body was formed for valor and contemplation, Eve's for softness and grace. While valor and softness could conceivably be identified with male and female body types, the way in which male contemplation and female grace could be made visibly manifest in bodily form is left unexplained. Given the already skewed and unexpected turn the narrator has taken, we should perhaps not be surprised that the ontological appeal to nature ultimately fails to demonstrate the inequality the narrator has asserted. Ignoring, as John Guillory has noted, any obvious, because inalterable, biological marker of sexual distinction, such as genital difference, the narrator grounds the hierarchy of the sexes on the exceedingly fragile evidence of the length of their hair: "Shee as a vail down to the slender waste / Her unadorned golden tresses wore . . . / . . . which impli'd / Subjection." Yet it is a law of man and not a law of nature that identifies women with long hair. Eve's long hair may "imply subjection" under some culturally determined conditions, but the cultural use of hair length to mark sexual difference is obviously as arbitrary as any commandment decreed by God.[13] The poem's half-hearted attempt to ground sexual hierarchy in nature gives way to its dominant conviction that Eve's subordination to her husband was arbitrarily ordained by God after their creation.

To be sure, the fact of sexual inequality remains, regardless of the foundation invoked to justify it. One might of course be tempted to suggest that the opposition of an inequality founded on ontology and an inequality founded on decree is a distinction without a difference. Milton, however, was incalculably sensitive to the tension between natural and positive law, between facts grounded in the inherent reasonableness of nature and those emanating from the arbitrary fiat of absolute power, be that power human or divine. Committed, throughout all of the mature works to the foundation of humanity, society, and even divinity in the regularity of reason and the law of nature, he could only have countered his own rationalist instincts with the utmost care and precision. If, as I am suggesting, *Paradise Lost* presents what is ultimately a conflicted picture of the origin of marriage and the difference between the sexes, we are obliged to speculate about motive. Why does Milton's poem seem so committed to having it both ways?

The energy of the account of paradise, and the account later of the fall, derives from Milton's compellingly contradictory derivation of Edenic politics. Eden is naturally egalitarian, its inhabitants entirely free and self-determining; but, at the same time, the special government of Eden is structured as an inflexible aristocratic hierarchy, in which the male class, which may not have any significant natural advantages over its female counterpart, nonetheless enjoys the privileges that come with a sanctioned seal of social superiority. The situation, in other words, is untenable; the contradictory social formation of paradise, inherently unstable. Why would Milton so structure his poem and its earthly polity?

Milton has grounded his unfallen society on such a shaky foundation, despite his best theological instincts, despite his persistently earnest drive to create a coherent picture of a coherently organized, just universe – he has planted his paradise on such shifting sands *in order to justify the fact of the fall in a perfect world*. Eve, we know from her soliloquy after her fall, had brought to the temptation the burden of her arbitrary subordination to Adam; there she makes clear that the arbitrary marriage commandment helped produce the conditions that made her disobedience possible. Wondering whether to share the fruit with Adam, Eve asks if she should

> keep the odds of Knowledge in my power
> Without Copartner? So to add what wants
> In Femal Sex, the more to draw his Love,
> And render me more equal, and perhaps,
> A thing not undesirable, sometime
> Superior; for inferior who is free?   (9.820–25)

Milton had argued in *Tetrachordon* that the marriage commandment had to have been arbitrary, else "no law or crime could disanull it," and divorce would have been impossible. A different but related argument charges the pages of *Paradise Lost*. Here the inequality dictated by the marriage commandment has to be seen as arbitrary, else the Fall would have been impossible.

Milton, it should be pointed out, need not be thought surreptitiously committed in *Paradise Lost* to establishing the true equality of husband and wife. His concern lies rather with his strong theodicial determination to understand how the fall can occur in a perfect world. The only way that John Milton, the great critic of arbitrary magistracy, can imagine a perfectly good person willfully choosing to do a perfectly bad thing is to imagine that person negotiating the contradictory derivations of authority in an overwhelmingly arbitrary political structure. This is of course the same set of negotiations Satan confronted in the overwhelmingly arbitrary political universe of Milton's heaven. A heavenly being presumably believed to be a fellow angel, the Son, whom God will belatedly represent as having been genuinely worthier than his compeers ("By Merit more then Birthright Son of God" [3.309]), is presented most explicitly by God as having been arbitrarily exalted above Satan and the other angels ("This day I have begot whom I declare / My only Son, and on this holy Hill / Him have anointed, whom ye now behold / At my right hand" [5.603–606]). Like the fruit of the tree of the knowledge of good and evil, whose inherent qualities both do and do not justify its prohibition, and like Adam, whose nature may or may not justify God's appointment of him as Eve's head and guide, the Son's intrinsic merit may or may not have merited God's proclamation to the angels: "your Head I him appoint" (5.606). These three provoking objects, at the root of the poem's chief acts of rebellion, may have been provocative because the decrees they embodied were arbitrary. It is just as likely, however, that the real provocation in each of those cases was the maddening uncertainty about whether the laws being issued were arbitrary or not. "Mysterious Law!" exclaims the narrator in book 4, as he interrupts his narrative to hymn the beauty of wedded love (4.750). The mystery of the law of marriage is from one perspective the source of its divine perfection; but it is at the same time the mystery clouding all the poem's divine edicts, whether regarding marriage, the fruit, or angelic hierarchy, that lies at the foundation of the fall. God's commandments, especially the marriage commandment, appear in this structuralist light almost to have necessitated Eve's tragic eating of the fruit. The fruit of marriage is the fall.

In *Paradise Lost*, the arbitrary prohibition of the fruit and the arbitrary institution of sexual hierarchy in marriage do not receive the theoretical statement of their connection that Milton sets forth, however briefly, in that sentence from *De Doctrina Christiana*. But Milton does in his poem – for the sake of *narrative* justifiability – bring these two aspects of the special government of Eden before the fall in to some type of intimate verbal relation. He does this, I would like to propose, with a word he takes from his source in Genesis: "touch." The word "touch" had been for centuries a flashpoint for students of the intricacies of the biblical account of the fall. In Genesis 2:17, God tells Adam, "but of the tree of the knowledge of good and evil, thou shalt not eat of it: for in that day that thou eatest thereof thou shalt surely die." But when the serpent begins discussing this prohibition with Eve, she embellishes that initial decree with something new: "God hath said, 'Ye shall not eat of it, neither shall ye touch it, lest ye die'" (Gen. 3:3). As Michael Lieb has noted, biblical exegetes, both Jewish and Christian, had long focused on Eve's anomalous verb "touch," some of them suggesting that she just made this "up at the time of the temptation."[14] In *Paradise Lost*, Milton attentively reproduces this anomaly, having Eve tell Satan not just once but twice that she and Adam had been forbidden not only to taste but also to *touch* the fruit (9.651, 9.663).

The Jahwist's Eve will always be inscrutable, her motives beyond the scope of this chapter. Why, though, does *Milton's* Eve pile onto the original commandment an additional restriction nowhere sanctioned by God? An answer might be found in the poem's previous book. In book 8, the category of "touch" had asserted itself in one of the most troubling issues discussed in the colloquy between Adam and Raphael. Adam explained to the archangel that most of the sensory experiences he enjoys in paradise "work in the mind no change": "these delicacies / I mean of taste, sight, smell." "But here," he says, speaking of his intimacy with Eve, "Far otherwise, transported I behold, / Transported touch" (8.525–27). Transported by touch, Adam confesses, he cannot see Eve's ordained inferiority: "so absolute she seems, / And in her self complete, so well to know / Her own, that what she wills to do or say, / Seems wisest, virtuousest, discreetest, best" (8.547–50). Alarmed by this litany of superlatives, Raphael chides Adam for this succumbing to the power of touch, a sense, he notes coarsely, that was equally "vouchsafed / To cattle and each beast" (8.579–82). It is possible that Raphael cautions tactile moderation from nothing more than a concern that sexual passion can overwhelm the faculties of judgment and reason. Yet far more than a simple precipitant to a heightened state of unreason, touch is that sensation that compels Adam to forget the divine marriage commandment, the arbitrary decree by which he was appointed Eve's superior. When Adam touches Eve, a natural gesture for which he appears to have needed no instruction or decree, something like a natural state of equality, or, worse, a hierarchical inversion, makes itself felt. Raphael institutes his partial ban on touch in book 8, with his famously contracted brow, as a practical measure to keep from dissolution the sexual hierarchy ordained by God after the Creation.

Milton can be seen, as early as the divorce pamphlets, to have been thinking of "touch" as a principle opposed to the divine institution of marriage. In *Tetrachordon* Milton derived the inferior, natural aspects of marriage not only from Adam's claim that Eve was bone of his bone and flesh of his flesh, but from the priestly description of God's creation of Adam and Eve in Genesis 1: "male and female created he them" (Gen. 1:27). Like Adam's "flesh of my flesh," the mention of God's creation of humanity as "male and female" can only point to the lesser, sexual component of marriage: the simple "end of matching man and woman . . . and lawfulness of the mariage bed" (*CPW* 2:592). Even the "triviall glosses" of this scriptural passage in Genesis 1, however, acknowledge the inferiority of the naturally authorized aspect of marriage: "they confesse," Milton writes, "that what here concerns mariage is but a brief touch, only preparative to the institution which follows more expressely in the next Chapter," the second chapter of Genesis in which God establishes marriage on the hierarchically firmer ground of the characterization of wife as help meet. By "brief touch," the casual phrase Milton uses to describe scripture's natural derivation of marriage, he means, surely, a passing reference or hint (*OED*, "touch" *n.*, 16a). Milton's strange mention of the Bible's "touch" as a description of the sexual union within marriage, however, seems to draw us closely to Eve's transported "touch" just a few verses later in Genesis 3:3.

At the temptation, Eve, in adding to God's commandment an additional prohibition against touching, has intuited the structural logic of appointed hierarchy with which Milton's epic is everywhere concerned. She has touched on the secret structural alliance throughout the poem between the state of obedience instituted by the arbitrary prohibition of the fruit and the state of sexual subjection instituted by what seems to be the arbitrary appointment of one sex over the other. Raphael had interdicted

Adam's excessive devotion to the touch of Eve that transported him from his proper sense of his own superior status. Extravagantly dutiful, excessively responsible, Eve transports this domestic interdiction, which touches her so near, into that other, more abstract, interdiction, which lies at the theological center of the story; she transports the "touch" from book 8 to book 9, from the arbitrary world of unequal domestic relations to the possibly arbitrary world of man's definitely unequal relation with God. A needless prohibition that she has simply made up, Eve intensifies the arbitrariness of the original prohibition by adding a prohibition so arbitrary that its only sanction is in Eve herself. Her hand "seis'd" by Adam at the moment she acceded to his appointment as her superior (4.489–91), she appropriates that tactile transgression and transfers it to the scene of temptation: "her rash hand . . . / . . . reaching to the Fruit, she pluck'd" (9.780–81).

Eve's response to the structural incoherence of the special government of Eden before the fall naturally proves her undoing. Thus the structural analysis of the fall occasioned by Milton's structural alignment of the exercises of arbitrary authority in both the domestic and the religious spheres compels us to ask that question about which the poem is understandably so nervous. Did Eve really have a choice? Well, the Father, addressing the assembled angels after the Fall, attempts to wash his own hands of any responsibility for the original sin. He declares that there had been "no decree of mine / Concurring to necessitate his fall, / Or touch with lightest moment of impulse / His free will." (10.43–46).

Theoretically, of course, the Father is right: there is technically no point in the story in which the Father can be said to have intervened in the world of nature and tipped the scales of human action, "touch[ing] with lightest moment of impulse / [man's] free will." But the Father, in this final moment of self-justification, employs that most weighted and pressing of verbs, "touch". And while he is right to insist that he did not touch the free wills of Adam and Eve with a decree to fall, this verb reminds us of the deeper structural reason for which he did not need to intervene in order to have the story turn out as it did. There did not need to be an additional decree to fall, because the two arbitrary decrees suggested by the word "touch" – the prohibition of the fruit and the subordination of Eve – created a government sufficiently unstable that it was perfectly able to fall apart of its own accord.

Satan, of course, understood all of this. Having experienced the disintegration of heaven that resulted, as if inevitably, from the Father's arbitrary appointment of the Son as the head of the other angels, Satan knows all about God's "special governments." This is why he is able, in a matter of moments, to put his finger on one of the poem's deepest truths. Upon overhearing the first conversation between Adam and Eve, Milton's Satan has heard enough to know how it is he will destroy their innocence. He has heard of God's arbitrary interdiction of the fruit; he has witnessed God's arbitrary authorization of one sex over the other. In both of these instances of the arbitrary exercise of authority, Satan sees an inherent, structural contradiction that he knows will be easy to exploit. It is here that Satan declares his arrival at his scheme of their destruction: "O fair foundation laid whereon to build / Their ruin" (4.521–22). Milton doesn't seem eager to establish the validity of Satan's claim of God's injustice. He tries very hard, in fact, to disprove it, charging the poem with its massive and compelling celebration of a creaturely freedom that could never be constrained by structural necessity. Yet Milton, driven to explain Eve's transgression even at the expense of his conviction of her absolute freedom, is nonetheless willing to expose the intrinsically unstable foundation of Eden's hierarchical society. Thus in presenting a picture of unfallen paradise so riven by conflicting derivations of legal authority, Milton lays the foundation for our understanding of how and why the story turns out as it does.

NOTES

1. *Complete Prose Works of John Milton*, vol. 6, ed. Maurice Kelley, trans. John Carey (New Haven: Yale University Press, 1973), 353. All quotations in English from Milton's *De doctrina Christiana* are from John Carey's translation in this edition, which will be hereafter noted as *CPW* parenthetically in the text. The original Latin text is cited from *The Works of John Milton*, ed. Frank Allen Patterson (New York: Columbia University Press, 1933), vol. 15.
2. The best discussion of the importance of the command's arbitrariness is Michael Lieb's, in *The Poetics of the Holy: A Reading of "Paradise Lost"* (Chapel Hill: University of North Carolina Press, 1981), 89–118.
3. William Empson, *Milton's God* (London: Chatto and Windus, 1965), 188. See also William Kerrigan, *The Sacred Complex: On the Psychogenesis of Paradise Lost* (Cambridge, MA: Harvard University Press, 1983), 252, and John Rogers, *The Matter of Revolution: Science, Poetry, and Politics in the Age of Milton* (Ithaca: Cornell University Press, 1996), 155–56.
4. Jean Baptiste van Helmont, *Ortus Medicinae* (1648); English translation, *Oriatrike, or Physic Refined* (London, 1662), 653. James Turner discusses van Helmont's treatment of the prohibition in *One Flesh: Paradisal Marriage and Sexual Relations in the Age of Milton* (Oxford: Clarendon, 1987), 150. See also the discussion in Rogers, *Matter of Revolution*, 155–56.
5. Though my perspective differs from his, I am indebted to W. Gardner Campbell, whose paper, "Milton's Provoking God," was presented at the Modern Language Association meeting, San Francisco, December, 1998.

6. The law of nature to which Milton appeals in *Tetrachordon* concerns the natural right of the wise to govern the less wise, regardless of sex. Natural superiority and inferiority seem in this famous example to be equally distributed among men and women: "Not but that particular exceptions may have place, if she exceed her husband in prudence and dexterity, and he contentedly yeeld, for then a superior and more naturall law comes in, that the wise should govern the lesse wise, whether male or female" *(CPW* 2:589).
7. Martin Luther, *Luther's Commentary on Genesis*, vol. 1, trans. J. Theodore Mueller (Grand Rapids, MI: Zondervan Publishing House, 1958), 34, 55.
8. Richard Hooker, *Of the Laws of Ecclesiastical Polity*, 2 vols. (London: Dent, 1907), 2:391 (book 5, section LXXIII).
9. Calvin, in *A commentarie of John Caluine, vpon the first booke of Moses called Genesis*, trans. Thomas Tymme (London, 1578), 72, writes of the social implications of Genesis 2:18: "Some think, that by this speech, the difference which is betweene both sexes is noted, and that so it is shewed, how much more excellent the man is, then the woman. But I like better of another interpretation, which differeth somewhat, though it be not altogether contrarie: namely, that when in the person of man, mankinde was created, the common worthiness of the whole nature, was with one title generally adorned, where it is said, *Let vs make* man: and that it was not needful to be repeated in the creating of the woman, which was nothing else but the addition & furniture of the man." Teaching the natural equality of all human beings, Genesis, for Calvin, attributes the social inequality of men and women to God's arbitrary appointment, or assignment, of a distinction between Adam and Eve: "Now seeing God assigneth the woman to be an helpe fo the man, he doth not only prescribe vnto women a rule of their calling, that they may the better do their dutie: but also pronounceth that matrimonie shalbe in verie deed vnto men a notable stay & helpe of life" (72). See John Witte, Jr., *From Sacrament to Contract: Marriage, Religion, and Law in the Western Tradition* (Louisville, Kentucky: Westminster John Knox Press, 1997), 96.
10. George Walker, *History of the Creation* (London, 1641), 174–75. For Walker, however, Eve's social inferiority was not a product of divine decree, but the logical consequence of Adam's prior creation, which gives "a kinde of *power and authority over the Woman* in outward things, which concerne *Ecclesiasticall and Civill order*" (176).
11. All of God's arbitrary commandments are undiscoverable by natural reason, in part because they were all issued after the creation. The belatedness of all God's arbitrary commandments is emphasized in the *De Doctrina*, though Milton deliberates at great length on whether Adam was ever informed about the commandment regarding the Sabbath: "But it is not known, because there is nothing about it in scripture, whether this was ever disclosed to Adam or whether any commandment about the observance of the Sabbath existed before the giving of the law on Mount Sinai, let alone before the fall of man" (*CPW* 6:353).
12. Hooker, *Laws*, 2:391.

13. See John Guillory, "From the Superfluous to the Supernumerary: Reading Gender into *Paradise Lost*," in *Soliciting Interpretation: Literary Theory and Seventeenth-Century English Poetry*, ed. Elizabeth D. Harvey and Katharine Eisaman Maus (Chicago: University of Chicago Press, 1990), 87n. The length of a woman's hair was of course not universally acknowledged to be a sign of subjection. Ignoring the Pauline association of female subjection with the veil, the early sixteenth-century Cornelius Agrippa had argued, to the contrary, that a woman's long hair, and her natural protection from male-pattern baldness, suggested her superiority: "But besides this charming Excellency [female beauty], which not only invites, but commands our admiration; Woman is endowed with another natural Ornament not vouchsaft to Men; her Hair growing to that becoming length, as to veil those more reserved parts, whereof Modesty commands concealment . . . Now in men, that noble member the Head, is often by Age or other Infirmity plundered of Hair, its native Ornament, and grows defored with a despicable Baldness, from which misfortune Women by an extraordinary priviledge of Nature are exempt" (*Declamatio de nobilitate et praecellentia foeminei sexus*; translated as *Female Pre-eminence* [London, 1670], 21–22).
14. Lieb, *Poetics of the Holy*, 98.

CHAPTER 7

The experience of defeat: Milton and some female contemporaries

Elizabeth M. Sauer

This chapter situates Milton's "experience of defeat" in relation to that of sectarians, particularly female visionaries who in the 1650s and '60s contributed to a literature of suffering. In the early modern period, England subsumed the history of ancient Israel into its national providential narrative, which for dissenters and millenarians was to culminate in a temporal *regnum Christi*. Male and female prophetic writers originally subscribed to this notion of England's chosen or "peculiar" status, but already in the 1650s went on to lament the nation's failure to live up to its early promise. The concept of election in fact demanded constant adjusting in the face of shifting personal and national events, including the "experience of defeat," which Christopher Hill and Marxist historians of early modern England identify with the failure of the Good Old Cause.

In his influential study of the response of Milton and male radicals to the aftermath of the revolution, Hill admits: "I was disappointed not to be able to find any woman who left adequate evidence of her experience of defeat." Since women were valued members of the religious sects, Hill attributes the lack of records about women's testimonies, including those on personal and political defeat, to the general dearth of information about women in the period. He nevertheless canvasses a number of possible female candidates, among them Margaret Fell, Mary Cary, Anna Trapnel, and Aphra Behn, who might have participated in the development of such a tradition. Yet the role call almost as quickly ends with dismissal: Fell contributed "in the sphere of Quaker organization rather than of ideas," while Trapnel, like Cary, fell silent after defeat; and Behn "was not visibly a radical before 1660."[1] In light of Hill's observations, one might in fact rephrase Joan Kelly's famous question "Did women have a Renaissance?" and Margaret W. Ferguson's follow-up discussion about whether women had a Reformation to ask instead whether seventeenth-century women had a revolution.[2]

If women did experience a revolution, how does it compare with that of the male revolutionaries like John Milton, whose state of political disillusion

Hill and Marxist critics and historians describe in detail? In this chapter, I demonstrate that the experience of defeat that Hill and others have gendered male was in various ways *recognizably* part of the history of female dissenters before, as well as after, 1660. The record of women's personal and political disaffection, including that triggered by the failure of God's national cause, constitutes a significant part of the literary tradition of women radicals and prophets. Patricia Crawford recently argued that while the revolution "did not alter any of the fundamental constraints on women's lives," it did offer greater opportunities for personal and collective expression justified and authorized through claims to spiritual equality.[3] Sectarians, like Mary Cary, Anna Trapnel, Margaret Fell, and Anne Wentworth, on whom I concentrate, relied heavily on the printed word not only to spread political and dissenting opinions but also to produce a literature of suffering.[4]

Michael Walzer reminds us that "oppressed individuals rarely experience their oppression as individuals. Their suffering is shared, and they come to know one another in a special way."[5] In recounting their trials, female dissenters, like their male counterparts, not only appealed to readerships and imagined communities of supporters but also developed genealogies which often linked their suffering to that of the ancient Israelites, a people poised between election and dejection. The dissenting literature of the seventeenth century is in fact replete with references to the Hebrew scriptures, which served as the ur-texts for the "Great Books of Sufferings."[6] Invoking the popular England-as-Israel commonplace, John Rogers associates his compatriots with Old Testament Jews, who, in the age of prophecy, often received "experiences."[7] At the same time, the typical portrayal of the Jews is double-edged: Puritans and sectarians read Israelite history as fundamentally tragic, since, despite the Jews' peculiar status, their unrepentant apostasy was followed by rejection. Judged in relation to this context, Margaret Fell's identification of Quaker history with the Jews' sufferings in ancient and early modern times reveals a level of tolerance rarely exhibited by any of her male contemporaries.

The documented female experience of defeat has something to teach us about Milton's exploration of tragedy, loss, and dispossession in *Paradise Lost*, a "Great Book of Sufferings," which uses the Genesis account and the tribulations of the Hebrews as etiologies for his post-Restoration epic. From the start, "all our woe" (*PL* 1.3) becomes Milton's refrain, echoing throughout the poem, particularly and predictably in the descriptions of hell and the postlapsarian world, which are connected by the prophecy of the "warning voice": "*Woe to the inhabitants on earth*" (*PL* 4.5). "Woe" is not gendered female in *Paradise Lost*; nor does it originate exclusively with Eve. Rather, it is part of the shared experience of Adam and Eve and their heirs, including the faithful who face "heavy persecution" and "suffer[]" for Truth's sake" (*PL* 12.531, 569). An examination of Milton's accounts of suffering provides insight into his tempered apocalypticism, his reassessment of English election, and his consequent embrace of a feminized notion of consolation and heroism through which the seeds of revolution are newly sown.

This is not a study of influence – direct or indirect. My position on Milton's association with the dissenters is best articulated by David Loewenstein, who claims that Milton's radical religious politics resembled that of dissenters from whom he nevertheless maintained a "polemical and authorial independence."[8] Loewenstein is, however, one of several eminent literary critics and historians, including Christopher Hill, Michael Wilding, Sharon Achinstein, and Kristen Poole, who focuses primarily on Milton's male contemporaries in examining the poet's relationship to the radical tradition.[9] This chapter is intended to broaden the context for Milton's work by exploring the discursive exchanges between canonical and popular literature, especially the dialogue between women's writing and their more canonical male contemporaries.

The practice of recording the experiences of defeat and persecution was an integral part of the Protestant tradition long before George Fox first instructed Quakers to document their trials in what would be known as the "Great Book of Sufferings." The confessions of conversion experience, as Nigel Smith identifies them, were in fact a mode of spiritual expression required for entry into the community of the gathered church,[10] John Bunyan's *Grace Abounding* serving as the culmination of this form. These testimonies enabling spiritual regeneration were sometimes accompanied by prophesying and vice versa, prophecy being induced by a traumatic process of coming to grace. As the climax of confession, the dream or vision also served as a form of witnessing for the gathered church or community of believers. Documented accounts of prophets' lives likewise publicized these experiences, though they were not always recorded by the prophets featured in them. Independently produced "confessions of faith" by women included Jane Turner's *Choice Experiences of the Kind dealings of God before, in, and after Conversion* (1653), though better known were the accounts by women and men compiled in John Rogers's *Ohel or Beth-shemesh. A Tabernacle for the Sun* (1653), Samuel Petto's *The Voice of the Spirit* (1654), and Henry Walker's edition of *Spirituall Experiences, Of sundry Beleevers* (1653).

The dissenters best known for registering their acts of suffering and experiences of confession were the Friends, or Quakers as they were called by their detractors. In 1657 Fox encouraged Quakers to present their sufferings to judges of assize, and in 1658 he organized a system of recording sufferings which would be incorporated by Ellis Hookes into the "Great Book of Sufferings".[11] Female dissenters, however, did not wait for an official decree before documenting their trials. Margaret Fell did so before 1657, and she was joined in this endeavor by other female dissenters and Puritans. In the same way, Milton's exploration of his experience of defeat was not the impetus for his contemporaries to record theirs. Nor should his trials be used as a benchmark for interpreting the accounts of sufferings produced by his contemporaries – male or female. For this reason, I examine the female dissenters' literature of suffering as constituting a distinct tradition as well as an instructive model for reinterpreting Milton's experience of defeat.

I wish to develop Sharon Achinstein's persuasive discussion of the relationship between *Samson Agonistes* and the Restoration persecution of dissenters by concentrating on the communities imagined by the literature of suffering, and by considering as well some women participants in the "dramas of dissent."[12] Women indeed comprised a significant proportion of a number of the sects. B. S. Capp observes, for example, that in Fifth Monarchist church lists, women outnumbered men. In the preface to the reader in *These several Papers was sent to the Parliament*, Mary Forster recognizes that "It may seem strange to some that women should appear in so publick a manner, in a matter of so great concernment as this of Tithes"; but the petition includes about 7,000 signatures from Quaker women, headed by Margaret Fell's name.[13] In light of this evidence, Hilary Hinds cautions us "to think of women not as an adjunct to the radical sects, but as centrally formative of all aspects of the sectarian phenomenon: their congregational composition, the writings and prophecies produced from within their ranks, and the ways in which they were perceived by others."[14] The focus on women in this study, then, is not intended merely to complement the current literary and cultural interest in gender studies, but to do justice to the accounts and experiences of early modern dissenters who included women in their acts and monuments, their great books of sufferings, and their dramas of dissent.

To identify the civil war and Interregnum with a period of suffering is not to deny that a revolution took place, but to indicate that it was experienced differently by women, who were deprived of the means and the opportunities for engaging in political activity. If women experienced a revolution, it was a "revolution in print." Certainly, however, this revolution was also double-edged: though their output doubled during the mid-century, it still constituted only about 1 percent of all revolutionary writings. Of the material that was produced, much dealt with religious issues and personal struggle.[15]

When Hill chooses not to include women in his study of the *Experience of Defeat*, he does so in part because he associates the revolution with a time of radical change and identifies the Restoration as the moment when hope dissolves into disappointment and disillusion. Hill also explains that the female radicals to whom he alludes wrote either before or after 1660 and not both (with the exception of Margaret Fell), thus frustrating the effort to chart the experience of defeat. It is important, however, to recognize that the millenarian expectation which inspired hope in the revolutionary cause developed in the first place in response to the experience of defeat, including crises of faith in the authority of church and state.

Earlier apocalyptic ideas had been given their greatest impetus by the publication of John Foxe's *Acts and Monuments*, which exposed the Pope as Antichrist and anticipated the fall of the Pope and Turks. Seventeenth-century Puritans and other dissenters used Foxe's prophecies as a lens for interpreting contemporary history. Sectarians in particular relied heavily on Foxe's work, while also generating their own accounts of suffering, culminating for Quakers in Joseph Besse's *Collection of the Sufferings of the Quakers* (1753). In observing that Archbishop Laud refused to license a new edition of Foxe in 1637, Milton stated in *Animadversions* that the martyrs were "so hatefull to the *Prelates*, that their story was almost come to be a prohibited book" (*CPW* 1:678–79). Parliament, the persecuted and imperial instrument of God which would overthrow the episcopacy, would fulfill the millennial promise to raise a New Jerusalem by using a holy war to meet its ends. Yet the tremendous faith Puritans and dissenters developed in the prospect of social and national reform soon waned, the establishment of the Rump in 1649 being the first in a series of betrayals. The millenarian, Daniel Border, editor of the *Faithful Scout*, wrote about the Rump in 1652: "Ye have promised Haulcion dayes; but I fear a monstrous Age."[16] The emergence in the late 1640s and early 1650s of radical sects like the Fifth Monarchists should thus be regarded as "a reaction to fading, not rising expectations."[17]

Identified by Christopher Hill as "one of the most interesting and least studied of the Fifth Monarchists,"[18] Mary Cary was an active participant in shaping the sect's program in the 1650s. The prefatory sections of Cary's major work, *Little Horns Doom & Downfall*, include a series of epistles from major religious figures who endorsed her work: Hugh Peter, Henry

Jessey, and Christopher Feake (a–a7v). Peter and Jessey supported the cause of Jewish readmission, and the latter in fact communicated the English millenarian fascination with the Jews to Rabbi Menasseh Ben Israel, a fascination Cary certainly shared and promoted.[19] Her treatise is also replete with references to the persecuted saints, who now expectantly (a5) await the end of their trials and the coming of the kingdom. Cary assigns Parliament the task of advancing the divine plan and restoring justice: "For it is here evident, that as the afflicted condition of the Church for twelve hundred yeeres and more under the Pope, was long ago prophesied of; so this Parliament which were to be the instruments of the Churches deliverance in their measure, were also long ago prophesied of" (42). In *A New and More Exact Mappe*, Cary invests the people of her day with prophetic powers. Her definition of the "people," moreover, was more inclusive and her notion of "prophesy" less restrictive than Milton's (cf. *Areopagitica*, *CPW* 2:556) when she declares that: "all Saints have in a measure a spirit of Prophesie" (106) and "all might prophesy, that is (in the lowest sense) be able to speak to edification, exhortation and comfort."[20] Yet the apocalypticism that characterized Cary's prophecies and the literature of dissent generally during the civil war years was frustrated by the experience of defeat, provoked by the failure of the Rump to implement the reforms desired by the radicals. Cary's last published work, *Twelve Humble Proposals* (1653), an appeal to Cromwell, acknowledges with regret: "there were many good men, (though too many bad also) who brought in a blessed change (though not such a reformation as was expected)" (1).[21]

One year after Cary's *Twelve Humble Proposals* appeared, the Fifth Monarchist, Anna Trapnel, was tried for sedition, witchcraft, madness, and prophesying. Trapnel's dramatic entry into the political arena the following year saw the publication of four tracts after the Barebones Parliament was dissolved, including *The Cry of a Stone* in which Trapnel identifies the Lord Protector with Gideon – an iconoclast-cum-traitor.[22] *The Cry of a Stone*, a transcription of the prophetic verses and prayers Trapnel spoke while in a trance at Whitehall, describes both her afflictions and "*Jacobs* trouble" (22). Jacob refers here to the people of Israel and now the Fifth Monarchists who struggled to prepare for Christ's arrival. The second coming, which had seemed imminent ("they looked for a birth"), was in fact distant ("it is yet in travel" [or travail/labor]) (22), owing to Cromwell's betrayal of the cause. The political prophecies in *The Cry* would feature centrally in her 1654 trial following her arrest in Cornwall. The details of her prophetic mission to the South-west, her hearing in Plymouth, and her imprisonment are laid out in *Anna Trapnel's Report and Plea*. Appealing to a wide readership of "all sorts of people, high and low," the tract addresses a cross-section of sympathetic readers who make up an imagined community of spectators, judges, and converts to the testimony of the persecuted prophet. Trapnel's courtroom drama is intended to vie with "the worlds stage of Reports, and Rumors" which transformed her into "a Monster or some ill-shaped Creature."[23] In reenacting the drama of justice, she presents marked exchanges between herself and the authorities who interrogated her about the authorship of *The Cry of a Stone*. When she "*denies the book*" after it is presented to her, Judge Lobb orders a public reading of her apocalyptic, political vision of the horns, where Cromwell as the little horn of the Beast replaces Cary's allegorization of Charles I in like terms several years beforehand (*Report*, 25; Cary, *Doom*, 42). The question is then put to Trapnel again, but once more she responds evasively, referring in the passive voice to "*what was spoken . . . at* White-Hall."[24] Recorded by a male "relator," who acknowledges that he transcribed only as much as he could with his "very slow and unready hand,"[25] *The Cry of a Stone* is at several removes from the speaker and from the speech community which received the prophecy first-hand. The "rude multitude," Trapnel announces in *Report and Plea*, is eventually persuaded by her testimony and performance: "*Sure this woman is no witch, for she speaks many good words, which the witches could not*. And thus the Lord made the rude rabble to justifie his appearance" (28).

Notorious in their formational years for political activism and opposition to secular authority, the Friends encouraged males and females of the sect to engage in literary production and record in particular their "experiences" of trial.[26] The Friends regarded their own sufferings as the last and greatest in a long series extending from Genesis to Revelation.[27] They resolved to commit their history to print in order to relieve themselves of indignation, develop a communal identity, provide evidence of divine judgment and favor, and to encourage the restoration of justice. Their testimonies of suffering served to witness to the truth and confirm their salvation, in light of II Timothy 2:12 which Mary Howgill invokes in denouncing Cromwell for persecuting the saints: "*them who suffer with him shall reign with him*."[28]

Mary Howgill, who was jailed in Kendal in 1653 and later again in Exeter for her public assertion of Quaker doctrine, was one of many sectarian women subject to persecution or imprisonment in the pre- or early Restoration years. In his *Collection of Sufferings*, Besse, after recording the imprisonment of Priscilla Cotton and Margaret Cole, lists among those who were gaoled in Exeter in 1655 not only Mary Howgill but also Elizabeth Cutland, Jane Bland, Lucy Field, Mary Erbery, Anne Harrison, Katharine Evans, and Jane Ingram who, he notes, died as a result of the unbearable conditions of the prison (1:149). Among the many female sectarians who documented their experiences of suffering were Elinor Channel, Anna Trapnel, Anne Jefferies, Anne Audland, Margaret Vivers, Sarah Tims, Dorothy Waugh, Hester Biddle, Priscilla Cotton and Mary Cole, Katharine Evans and Sarah Chevers, Elizabeth Hooton, and Margaret Fell.

The most prominent female dissenter, Margaret Fell, made significant contributions to the Quaker literature of personal and communal suffering. Her first published work, *False Prophets, Antichrists, Deceivers, which are in the World* (1655), exposes the hypocrisy of English Protestants who allegedly aided their fellows on the continent while persecuting Quakers at home. As her text and the Quaker literature of suffering indicated, the Friends' sense of community was reinforced by their connection with Christ's suffering, with that of the early Christians, Foxe's Marian martyrs, and also with the suffering Jews – ancient and contemporary.[29] Though they were in fact excluded from the Whitehall Conference on the Jewish readmission, Quakers were among those who attributed to the Jews an important role in the final days. Fell's identification with the Jews' tribulations and their messianic expectations provides a context for her history of Quaker sufferings. In the same year that she produced *For Manasseth-Ben-Israel: The Call of the Jews out of Babylon* (1656), Fell characterized the persecuted Quakers as "a *suffering people*, under every *Power & Change*, and under *every profession of Religion* that hath been . . . since we were a People."[30] *A Declaration and an Information* accuses the government of persecution and was personally presented by Fell to the king on April 22, 1660. Concerned to persuade the authorities of the truthfulness of her testimony and to counter "false informations" about her community, Fell concludes with a list of witnesses, many of whom actively contributed to the development of the Quaker literature of suffering.[31]

If Hill overlooks the connection between Milton and the female prophets, Joseph Wittreich elides the Interregnum and Restoration experience of prophecy by reminding us that "at the time *Paradise Lost* was being brought to completion the Quakers were awarding women equality with men and crediting both sexes with the capacity of prophesying."[32] In fact, a less egalitarian concept of the Quaker community emerged under the Clarendon Code (1661–65), which began with the Quaker Act and the Act of Uniformity (1662) and later led to the 1670 Coventicle Act which further endorsed the persecution of dissenters. Under such circumstances, Quakers introduced self-censorship and curtailed the public actions of women in particular.[33] For that reason Fell felt compelled to write *Womens Speaking Justified* and defend the role of the prophetic women in the church. Even so, her tract is "careful and conservative" in its claims.[34] Using scriptural evidence to construct a visionary company of female prophets, Fell justifies women's prophesying, which is needed now more than ever in the face of persecution. Her image of the final battle features Christ as conqueror accompanied by his wife, the church, the heavenly New Jerusalem, who defeats the "false Speaker."[35] Ten years later in *The Daughter of Sion Awakened* (1677), Fell locates the tribulations of the ancient Hebrews in terms of the ongoing battle between the "cursed seed" and the "good Seed" (4), terms derived from the sentence passed on the serpent in Genesis. Fell by extension links the struggles of the Hebrews and the first Christians to those of the Quakers who uphold the model of the primitive church in her day (12).

The authority of the writer to engage religious or spiritual matters conventionally depended on her affiliation with godly communities;[36] and indeed, visionaries of the period generally belonged to particular religious congregations. Yet what shape does the narrative of someone outside the gathered church or someone dismissed by the community assume? The autobiographical treatises written in the Restoration period by the Baptist and millenarian, Anne Wentworth, provide a partial answer. Accused by fellow Baptists of being "*a proud, passionate revengeful discontented*, and *mad woman . . . that has unduly published things to the prejudice and scandal of my husband, and that hath wickedly left him*,"[37] Wentworth was intent on setting the record straight by obeying the "command of God to publish the things which concern the *peace of my own soul* and *of the whole nation.*" Adopting the model of the conversion narrative, Wentworth recounts the eighteen years of abuse to which she was subjected by her husband, years she spent in "a wilderness of affliction."[38] She repeats the number eighteen to emphasize its symbolic significance: Israel was persecuted by the Philistines and the Ammonites for eighteen years (Judges 10:8); and, according to Luke 13:10–17, "a daughter of Abraham" was held in Satan's bondage for this length of time before being freed by Christ on the Sabbath. For Wentworth, deliverance from oppression involves her release from domestic and community ties; it involves as well a separation from the physical self and a "full communion between Christ and my soul, the love knot, the comely bands of marriage." Having circumvented secular authority, including that held by a husband over his wife, Wentworth in an act of defiance and submission gives birth to the Word – a prolonged, laborious process which she resisted "for eleven months together." She thus defends the prophet's call to a public ministry and anticipates her/Israel's liberation from captivity. Though the treatise ends, as does her *The Revelation of Jesus Christ*, with her resignation to patient waiting, Wentworth's writing of the self and her reading of historical occurrences have at once a private/spiritual significance as well as a public/political one. Indeed God reveals to Wentworth that her "*oppressions* and *deliverance* had a *public ministry* and *meaning* wrapped up in them."[39]

The account of Wentworth's personal struggle in *The Revelation of Jesus Christ* (1679) – one that she was preparing while writing the *Vindication* – repeats many of the themes of the earlier text. Isolated and stripped of her "good Name" by her community, Wentworth emerges as a new Zion; the conclusion of the treatise describes her final revelation and judgment as a warning to an unrepentant nation of Babylon. As the true bridegroom, God refurbishes the house allegedly stripped of its goods by Wentworth's husband, and Wentworth then prepares her visions for publication. While waiting for God's intervention, Wentworth hears him declare:

> From Heaven will I the Lord come to appear,
> For to make them all my own voice to hear:
> And all those, that long to see this thing done,
> Must patiently wait till I the Lord do come.[40]

The experience of waiting for the Lord of which Cary spoke in her apocalyptic *Little Horns Doom* (163) is now personalized and depoliticized in Wentworth's prophetic Restoration lament.

A considerably more poised and formal account of personal affliction and patient waiting is offered in Milton's Sonnet XIX (*c.* 1652?) in which the blind poet undertakes to justify the ways of God to himself. Invoking Matthew 25:26, as Cary herself had done one year beforehand,[41] Milton cites the example of the slothful servant who was punished by his master for failing to use or invest the talent he received. Ten years earlier, Milton invoked the parable in justifying his intrusion into matters of ecclesiastical politics: should he fail to apply "those few talents which God at that present had lent [him]" to assist the church in a time of trial and oppression, an inner voice would reproach him for being "brutish," "slothfull," infantile (*CPW* 1:804–5). Now in the sonnet, the poet himself is the victim of suffering; "one Talent which is death to hide," he laments, is "Lodg'd with me useless,"[42] though the desire to serve the master has only increased. In an astute analysis of Milton's talent for suffering, Jeffrey Shoulson describes this sonnet as "perhaps one of the fullest and most personal investigations into the value of suffering Milton ever wrote."[43] Yet the transition from the octave to the sestet is marked by a shift from the first to the third person, as well as by a change of voice and a movement toward a resolution, which locates the poet's private struggle in relation to the divine plan. An internal voice declares the value of patient waiting and paradoxically grants the blind poet insight: "'God doth not need / Either man's work or his own gifts; who best / Bear his mild yoke, they serve him best . . . / . . . / They also serve who only stand and wait'" (9–11, 14). Milton is expectant, though this sense of anticipation is decidedly different from that of his earlier days. The talent to which he refers is not buried nor strictly associated with standing and waiting, but identified instead with faith, persistence, and insight. Personal suffering becomes part of the genealogy and history of "all our woe."

National expectancy was the order of the day in the early 1640s and '50s. Not unlike his millenarian male and female contemporaries, Milton initially combined the language of apocalypse with the idea of English election. The fiery apocalyptic vision *Of Reformation* imagines a chosen nation, a "*Britannick Empire* [built up] to a glorious and enviable heighth" – a "great and Warlike Nation" awaiting the imminent Second Coming (*CPW* 1:614, 616). Yet throughout the treatise, Milton reads English history as evidence that God's providential favors had not been fully acknowledged by England, which therefore suffered cyclical declines. *Areopagitica*'s representation of the holy nation, which was "chos'n before any other" to sound "the trumpet of Reformation to all *Europ*" (*CPW* 2:552), speaks optimistically and prophetically about the coming of the kingdom. Only a few years later, the nation's declining revolutionary aspirations set the stage for Milton's shifting positions on the question of England's election. *Eikonoklastes* laments England's choosing the path back to monarchy by rejecting the Bible's preference for judges and prophets. Milton thereafter restricts his designation of the "elect" to the fit though few (*CPW* 3:339–40) as his faith in the English becomes shaken by what he later describes as the backsliding of the English like "the *Jews* . . . to *Egypt*" (*The Readie & Easie Way*, *CPW* 7:387).

Like the early church evangelists who were forced to reassess their theology of an imminent Second Coming, Milton, along with seventeenth-century dissenters, conceded in the Restoration years that Christ's kingdom would not materialize. Yet in his experience of defeat, Milton nevertheless retained a "religious commitment to political process" and to the collectivity as evidenced in his poetry.[44] At the same time, the collective is now reduced to "an invisible public of like-minded readers."[45] Milton's lofty style and heavy reliance on the classics may also complicate David Loewenstein's suggestion that Milton's "fit though few" refers to dissenting readers (i.e. religious radicals).[46] Yet certainly there are links between Milton and the radicals, particularly the common emphasis on the inner light or the paradise within, as Loewenstein demonstrated in reference to *Paradise Regained*,[47] as Achinstein observed in her study of *Samson Agonistes*, and as Kristen Poole maintained in analyzing *Paradise Lost*, in which Milton "rejects the radical hopes for reentering the past Eden but ends with an affirmation of the Quaker emphasis on the light within."[48] Other connections to the radical tradition also emerge, particularly if we recall the writings of Milton's female contemporaries. Their example can teach us first that Milton's experience of defeat reaches beyond the political realm to the personal and the social. Like female dissenters, Milton developed a genealogy of suffering leading back to the ancient Hebrews; highlighted the inclusiveness and communal nature of suffering; struggled to justify the ways of God; identified personal trial as a sign of grace; and attributed to Eve as the first woman a key role in the foretold redemption. *Paradise Lost* becomes Milton's "Great Book of Sufferings" in which he links personal and national tragedy and develops a narrative of loss and consolation experienced by males and females alike.

When Milton informs us that "Woman is her name of man extracted" (*PL* 8.496), he underscores the historical, physical, and linguistic connection between "woman" and "man." "Woman" is derived from the Old English *wif*, meaning "female," and *mann*, that is, "human being." "Woman" thus has no etymological link with "woe," nor does Milton take advantage of phonetic associations between the terms, even though radicals indulged in this practice.[49] Milton also steers away from the tradition of charging Eve alone for "Mans First disobedience" (*PL* 1.1) by taking great pains to ensure that both Adam and Eve appear equally culpable for their disobedience. In book 9, the aftermath of Eve's fall into temptation is presented in terms of the disruption of natural order: "Earth felt the wound, and Nature from her seat / Sighing through all her Works gave signs of woe, / That all was lost" (9.782–84). When Adam announces his intention to die with Eve, saying "from thy State / Mine never shall be parted, bliss or woe" (9:915–16), the shared experience of sinfulness is conveyed by the repeated account of Nature's fall:

> Earth trembl'd from her entrails, as again
> In pangs, and Nature gave a second groan,
> Sky low'r'd, and muttering Thunder, some sad drops
> Wept at completing of the mortal Sin/Original.
> (9.1000–4)

Adam thus becomes complicit in the original act of disobedience.

The scene of judgment in book 10 offers more evidence of the "apparent guilt" (10.112) of both Adam and Eve. After calling on the couple to testify, the Son passes his sentence first on the serpent, "instrument / Of mischief" (10.166–67), then on Eve, and finally on Adam. Though the fallen pair remains oblivious to this fact, the Son's sentence mixes punishment with promise in accordance with Genesis 3:15 as messianic prophecy (10.175–80). Milton had explained in *De Doctrina* that "in pronouncing the punishment upon the serpent, at a time when man had only grudgingly confessed his guilt, God promised that he would raise up from the seed of the woman a man who would bruise the serpent's head, Gen. iii, 15. This was before he got as far as passing sentence on man. Thus he prefaced man's condemnation with a free redemption" (*CPW* 6:416). While this exegesis of Genesis 3:15 corresponds with that of other early modern anti-Calvinist apologists, it was popular among visionaries generally as Margaret Fell's description of the age-old contest between the "cursed seed" and the "good Seed," reminds us.[50] Fell here again highlights the role of women in the final battle against the serpent, as the Holy City, the New Jerusalem, takes her place beside Christ, her bridegroom. Given this promissory preface, Eve's curse of bringing children "in sorrow forth" and of submitting to her husband, whether in Genesis, Fell, or Milton (*PL* 10.193–96), should seem less devastating. The sentencing of Adam to a *laborious* existence (10.201–2) should also appear less severe. Milton's first couple, however, resorts to mutual accusation, giving way to Adam's anti-feminist diatribe. Eventually, Eve, in utter despair, proposes a truce, momentarily coming closer to atonement and repentance than her husband. Her heroic gesture, involving an identification with the suffering Adam, is an attempt at "restor[ing] the shattered human community, searching past guilt, self-assertion and self-justification, and terror to a restored interdependence with Adam."[51]

After Eve assumes responsibility for the fall, Adam converts her self-referential phrase "sole cause to thee of all this woe" (10.935) to "our share of woe" as he reflects on "how we may light'n / Each other's burden in our share of woe" (10.960–61). His recollection of the judgment, "thy Seed shall bruise / The Serpent's head" (10.1031), carries the weight of prophecy, which is feminized, as was the case in Anna Trapnel's prophecy of the coming of the kingdom as a postponed birth that was "yet in travel" or travail/labour.[52] Sentenced to hard labor, Eve's suffering will ultimately be rewarded, Adam recalls: "to thee / Pains only in Child-bearing were foretold, / And bringing forth, soon recompens't with joy, / Fruit of thy Womb" (10.1050–53; Luke 1:42). Milton then replaces the image of the weeping, suppliant Eve who first approaches Adam for forgiveness (10.914ff.) with the portrait of the weeping couple, offering to God an unmediated prayer of confession (10.1086–92). Barbara Kiefer Lewalski observes that, like Samson, Adam and Eve "now repent, struggle to understand God's prophecies, learn to endure suffering with patience, and prepare to wait with faith and hope for the working out of God's providential design."[53]

In the prophetic books of the epic, where reprobate Israelites are featured as descendants of a fallen Adam and Eve, Milton advances the tragic narrative of the original sin and act of suffering, a practice that female dissenters themselves applied in order to anchor their personal and communal struggles in the history of the chosen race. The descendants of the first couple inherit an empty garden and also find themselves continually dispossessed in the biblical, Miltonic, and prophetic texts of the persecuted or estranged. As Adam and Eve are banished from Eden, so is entitlement to the promised land now denied to a diaspora people. In *De Doctrina*, Milton comments on the lesson derived from the example of the Jews who are dispersed: "not only to make them pay the penalty of their sins but much rather to give the whole world a perpetual, living proof of the existence of God and the truth of his scriptures" (*CPW* 6:132). Onto the Jews' history and literature of suffering, Christian writers, both male and female, inscribed their own pilgrim's progress.

The way to the promised land is now "Through the wild Desert, not the readiest way" (*PL* 12.215), Michael warns Adam. In recounting the tragic Hebraic-Christian narrative of postlapsarian history, a few antiheroes emerge who will "amaze / Thir proudest persecutors" (12.496–47). John R. Knott compares these exemplary figures to the Marian exiles: "the idea of 'suffering for Truths sake' that Adam articulates looks chiefly to the future experience of members of the true church. As witnesses to God's truth among the enemies of truth, Abdiel, Enoch, and Noah illustrate both the vehemence that Milton admired and a constancy that in difficult circumstances would make martyrs."[54] The catalogue of sufferers extends beyond those who are directly or indirectly named in *Paradise Lost* to include all the faithful: "heavy persecution shall arise / On all who in the worship persevere / Of Spirit and Truth" (12.531–33). The trials of faith here recall chapter 11 of the Epistle to the Hebrews, which begins with the example of Abel and concludes with accounts of affliction experienced by the nameless Israelites:

Women received their dead raised to life again: and others were tortured, not accepting deliverance; that they might obtain a better resurrection: And others had trial of *cruel* mockings and scourgings, yea, moreover of bonds and imprisonment: They were stoned, they were sawn asunder, were tempted, were slain with the sword . . . they wandered in deserts, and *in* mountains, and *in* dens and caves of the earth

– a passage that also serves as a gloss for interpreting trials of the Waldensians about whose massacre Milton wrote in the Interregnum.[55]

As it unfolds in the final books of *Paradise Lost*, human history looks like an unending series of defeats, Christopher Hill observes; yet properly understood, he continues, history is actually "a series of examples which challenge us in the present. Some time we must break out of the cycle of failure and defeat."[56] Breaking out now involves looking within, as Adam and Eve gradually recognize, and as the female dissenters demonstrated in their responses to disillusionment and loss. The original sentence of suffering contains the promise of redemption as truth is born(e) out of suffering and the cycle is broken and history incarnated. Knowing good by evil, Adam and Eve realize that from the woman's seed will spring the chosen one of Israel, the "great deliverer, who shall bruise / The Serpent's head" (12.149–50). Every occurrence of the word "woman" in the final books of *Paradise Lost* is associated with the promised seed, the seed of revolution. Reading Milton in dialogue with his radical female contemporaries sensitizes us to the identification of the fallen penitent woman as the medium through whom the language of sorrow and redemption is articulated. Milton's representation of the bearing of truth involves both conceptually and physically a new kind of *travail* and experience of "temper[ing] joy with fear / And pious sorrow" (*PL* 11.361–62). Giving poetic expression to "SEEING WITH SORROW" (*CPW* 6:466; Psalm 38),[57] Eve announces in her closing sonnet in *Paradise Lost* that

> God is also in sleep, and Dreams advise,
> Which he hath sent propitious, some great good
> Presaging, since with sorrow and heart's distress
> Wearied I fell asleep.   (12.611–14)

The news of deliverance is offered in a vision, countering the satanically induced dream of falling which Eve experienced in book 5. Here in Eve's sonnet (*PL* 12.609–23), Milton's earlier Sonnet XIX, with its resolution to patient waiting in the face of trial, finds a new context and speaker. Eve's revelation is, appropriately, double-edged:

> This further consolation yet secure
> I carry hence; though all by mee is lost,
> Such favor I unworthy am voutsaf't,
> By mee the Promis'd Seed shall all restore.
> (12:620–23)

Her talent, like that of her historical female counterparts, is insight into her destined role of service in carrying out the divine plan. The final image in the poem is of the shared experience of Adam and Eve wandering together "in sorrow forth": "They hand in hand with wand'ring steps and slow, / Through *Eden* took thir solitary way" (12.648–69). The reference is to Psalm 107, which describes the faithful elect who "wandered in the wilderness in a solitary way" (Psalm 107:4), assured "in their trouble" of their deliverance by God (107:6).

Milton's sisters and daughters, God's English*women*, and the Eves of the postlapsarian world have a talent for suffering, forbearance, and insight,[58] enabling this visionary company to develop a language of prophecy rooted in scriptural authority. Their common identification with the Hebraic tradition – an act of personal and national self-fashioning – frames their experience of suffering, lending it a historical and communal context. In turn, the literature of suffering "for Truth's sake," as we have seen, both allows and complicates the justification of God's ways for men and women. Moreover, it unsettles conventional responses to Milton as prophet-poet and demands a reconception of epic prophecy. No longer "realized wholly within the limits of the absolute past" where "it does not touch the reader and his real time,"[59] epic prophecy becomes historicized, grounded, and even feminized in *Paradise Lost*. Prophecy now entails "seeing with sorrow," a shared experience of triumph and defeat in which Eve and early modern female radicals participate alongside Adam and John Milton.

NOTES

1. Christopher Hill, *The Experience of Defeat: Milton and Some Contemporaries* (New York: Viking, 1984), 21.
2. Joan Kelly, "Did Women Have a Renaissance?" in *Women, History and Theory: The Essays of Joan Kelly* (Chicago: University of Chicago Press, 1984) 19–50; Margaret W. Ferguson, "Moderation and its Discontents: Recent Work on Renaissance Women," *Feminist Studies* 20.2 (1994): 332.
3. Patricia Crawford, "The Challenges to Patriarchalism: How did the Revolution Affect Women?" in *Revolution and Restoration: England in the 1650s*, ed. John Morrill (London: Collins and Brown, 1992) 113. Also see Lois G. Schwoerer, "Women's Public Political Voice in England: 1640–1740," in *Women Writers*

and the Early Modern British Political Tradition, ed. Hilda L. Smith (Cambridge: Cambridge University Press, 1998), 56–74.
4. I am applying this expression not only to Quaker persecution literature (see Joseph Besse, *Collection of the Sufferings of the People Called Quakers* [London, 1753]) but to the testimonies of hardship and trial produced by seventeenth-century sectarians generally. On the experience of defeat of a non-sectarian who nevertheless used her writings as "radical protest," see Sidney Gottlieb, "An Collins and the Experience of Defeat," in *Representing Women in Renaissance England*, ed. Claude J. Summers and Ted-Larry Pebworth (Columbia: University of Missouri Press, 1997), 216–26.
5. Michael Walzer, *Obligations: Essays on Disobedience, War, and Citizenship* (Cambridge, MA: Harvard University Press, 1970), 51.
6. "Great Books of Suffering" refers specifically to the work of the Quaker Ellis Hookes, but in this chapter to the literature of suffering by dissenters generally. On the Hebraic literature of suffering, see Jeffrey S. Shoulson, *Milton and the Rabbis: Hebraism, Hellenism, & Christianity* (New York: Columbia University Press, 2001).
7. John Rogers, *Ohel or Beth-shemesh. A Tabernacle for the Sun* (1653), qtd in Nigel Smith, *Perfection Proclaimed: Language and Literature in English Radical Religion 1640–1660* (Oxford: Clarendon Press, 1989), 45.
8. David Loewenstein, *Representing Revolution in Milton and his Contemporaries: Religion, Politics, and Polemics in Radical Puritanism* (Cambridge: Cambridge University Press, 2001), 11.
9. Christopher Hill, *Milton and the English Revolution* (London: Faber and Faber, 1977); Michael Wilding, *Dragon's Teeth: Literature in the English Revolution* (Oxford: Clarendon, 1987); Loewenstein, *Representing Revolution*; Sharon Achinstein, *Milton and the Revolutionary Reader* (Princeton: Princeton University Press, 1994). Achinstein's *Literature and Dissent in Milton's England* (Cambridge: Cambridge University Press, 2003) includes discussions of Mary Mollineux and Elizabeth Singer Rowe but concentrates on Milton's male contemporaries and Restoration successors. Also see Kristen Poole, *Radical Religion from Shakespeare to Milton: Figures of Nonconformity in Early Modern England* (Cambridge: Cambridge University Press, 2000).
10. Smith, *Perfection Proclaimed*, 5. Also see chapter of his volume "Prophecy, Experience, and the Presentation of the Self" (23–72).
11. Eventually George Fox's own experiences would be compiled in *A Journal or Historical Account of the Life, Travels, Sufferings, Christian Experiences . . . of . . . George Fox* (London, 1694), for which Margaret Fell Fox produced an introduction, entitled: "The Testimony of Margaret Fox Concerning her Late Husband George Fox; Together with a brief Account of some of his *Travels, Sufferings* and *Hardships* endured for the *Truth's* sake."
12. Sharon Achinstein, "*Samson Agonistes* and the Drama of Dissent," *Milton Studies* 33 (1996): 133–57.
13. B. S. Capp, *The Fifth Monarchy Men: A Study in Seventeenth-Century English Millenarianism* (London: Faber and Faber, 1972), 82; *These several Papers*

was sent to the Parliament (London, 1659), For the list of signatures, see 7–72.
14. Hilary Hinds, *God's Englishwomen: Seventeenth-Century Radical Sectarian Writing and Feminist Criticism* (Manchester: Manchester University Press, 1996), xxxi.
15. This statistic is taken from Patricia Crawford, "Women's Published Writings 1600–1700," in *Women in English Society, 1500–1800*, ed. Mary Prior (New York: Methuen, 1985), 266; qtd in Hilda L. Smith and Susan Cardinale, "Introduction," in *Women and the Literature of the Seventeenth-Century: An Annotated Bibliography based on Wing's Short-title Catalogue*, comp. Hilda L. Smith and Susan Cardinal (New York: Greenwood Press, 1990), xii. On the female literature of suffering, see Helen Ostovich and Elizabeth M. Sauer, "Religion, Prophecy, and Persecution," in *Reading Early Modern Women: An Anthology of Manuscripts and Texts in Print, 1550–1700*, ed. Ostovich and Sauer (New York: Routledge, 2004), chapter 4.
16. Daniel Border, *Faithful Scout* 95 (Nov. 5–13, 1652), 743.
17. Capp, *The Fifth Monarchy Men*, 58.
18. Christopher Hill, *The English Bible and the Seventeenth-Century Revolution* (London: Allen Lane, 1993), 308.
19. David S. Katz, *Philo-Semitism and the Readmission of the Jews to England 1603–1655* (Oxford: Clarendon Press, 1982), 104; M. Cary, *Little Horns Doom & Downfall... A New and More Exact Mappe; or, Description of "New Jerusalems" Glory* (London, 1651), esp. 139–60. *Little Horns Doom* deals with Daniel's visions of the four kingdoms, while *A New and More Exact Mappe* promotes a specific political agenda.
20. Cary, *Little Horns Doom*, 237. See Jane Baston, "History, Prophecy, and Interpretation: Mary Cary and Fifth Monarchism," *Prose Studies* 21.3 (1998): 7. Anna Trapnel refers simply to "Oh Prophets all" (*The Cry of a Stone; Or a Relation of Something Spoken in Whitehall "etc."* [London, 1645], 33).
21. By 1654 sectaries had lost all confidence in the army and Cromwell, Christopher Hill observes in *The World Turned Upside Down: Radical Ideas during the English Revolution* (London: Temple Smith, 1972), 70.
22. Trapnel, *The Cry*. On Gideon, see *"The Cry of a Stone" by Anna Trapnel*, ed. and intro. Hilary Hinds (Tempe: Arizona Center for Medieval and Renaissance Studies, 2000), xxxi–xxxv.
23. Anna Trapnel, *Anna Trapnel's Report and Plea, or a Narrative of Her Journey from "London" into "Cornwal"* (London, 1654), A4, 49.
24. Ibid., 25.
25. *The Cry*, a2v.
26. Geoffrey F. Nuttall, *Record and Testimony: Quaker Persecution Literature 1650–1700* (1970s transcript, housed at the Library of the Society of Friends, London), 15. See George Fox, *A Collection of Many Select and Christian Epistles*, 2 vols. (Philadelphia, 1831), 1:134–36 (epistles CXL, CXLI, 1657).
27. See [A. Hutchins *et al.*], *Caines Bloudy Race know by their Fruits* (London, 1657).

28. *A Remarkable Letter of Mary Howgill to Oliver Cromwell, Called Protector* (London, 1656), 2. II Timothy 2:12 is also featured on the title page of George Foxe's *A Journal or Historical Account of the Life, Sufferings, Christian Experiences and Labour of Loves of... George Fox.*
29. See Bonnelyn Young Kunze, *Margaret Fell and the Rise of Quakerism* (Stanford: Stanford University Press, 1994), and Judith Kegan Gardiner, "Margaret Fell and Feminist Literary History: A 'Mother in Israel' Calls to the Jews," in *The Emergence of Quaker Writing*, ed. Thomas Corns and David Loewenstein (London: Frank Cass, 1995), 42–56.
30. Margaret Fell, *For Manasseth-Ben-Israel: The Call of the Jews out of Babylon* (London, 1656); *A Brief Collection of Remarkable Passages and Occurrences Relating to . . . Margaret Fell, but by her second Marriage M. Fox* (London: J. Sowle, 1712), 105.
31. M. F., *A Declaration and an Information From us the People of God called Quakers* (London, 1660), 8.
32. Joseph Anthony Wittreich, *Feminist Milton* (Ithaca: Cornell University Press, 1987), 108.
33. Within two years, the London Yearly Meeting of Friends would recommend to the ministry that Quakers be required to "avoid all imagined, unseasonable and untimely prophesyings; which tend not only to stir up persecution, but also to the begetting of airy and uncertain expectations" (A. R. Barclay, *Letters, & c. of Early Friends* [London, 1641], 332).
34. Elaine Hobby, "Handmaids of the Lord and Mothers in Israel: Early Vindication of Quaker Women's Prophecy," in *The Emergence of Quaker Writing*, 89.
35. Smith, *Perfection Proclaimed*, 51.
36. M. F., *Womens Speaking Justified, Proved and Allowed by the Scriptures* (London, 1667), 17; Fell, *The Daughter of Sion Awakened* (1677), in *A Brief Collection*, 526.
37. Anne Wentworth, *A Vindication of Anne Wentworth . . . preparing . . . all people for Her Larger Testimony* (1677), in *Her own Life: Autobiographical Writings by Seventeenth-Century Englishwomen*, ed. Elspeth Graham Hilary Hinds, Elaine Hobby, and Helen Wilcox (New York: Routledge, 1989), 185. On the symbolic significance of 18, see *A true Account of Anne Wentworths being cruelly . . . dealt with by . . . Anabaptists* ([London], 1676), 15.
38. *Vindication*, 188, 189.
39. *Ibid.*, 193, 188, 193.
40. Anne Wentworth, *The Revelation of Jesus Christ* ([London], 1679), 10.
41. For Cary's use of the parable of the talents, see *Doom*, a4.
42. Milton, Sonnet XIX, lines 3–4.
43. *Milton and the Rabbis*, 192.
44. Linda Gregerson, "Milton's Post-Modernity: Community after the Commonwealth," Sixth International Milton Symposium (University of York, UK, July 1999).
45. Leah S. Marcus, *Unediting the Renaissance: Shakespeare, Marlowe, Milton* (New York: Routledge, 1996), 211.

46. Also see N. H. Keeble, "Milton and Puritanism," in *A Companion to Milton*, ed. Thomas N. Corns (Oxford: Blackwell, 2001), 131.
47. Loewenstein, *Representing Revolution*, 247ff.
48. Christopher Hill concludes: "There is no evidence that Milton ever adopted the post-1661 Quaker position of pacifism and abstention from politics" (*Experience*, 315). Also see Loewenstein, *Representing, Revolution*, 202–41; Poole, *Radical Religion*, 181.
49. Priscilla Cotton and Mary Cole make "woman" synonymous with "weakness" but indicate that "woman or weakness" resides in the male and female (*To the Priests and People of England* [1655], 7). Also see Edward Burrough, *An Alarm to All Flesh With an Invitation to the True Seeker* (London, 1660), 7–8.
50. *The Daughter of Sion Awakened*, 4.
51. William Shullenberger, "Wrestling with the Angel: *Paradise Lost* and Feminist Criticism," *Milton Quarterly* 20 (1986): 79. Also see Margo Swiss, "Repairing Androgyny: Eve's Tears in *Paradise Lost*," in *Speaking Grief in English Literary Culture: Shakespeare to Milton*, ed. Margo Swiss and David A. Kent (Pittsburgh: Duquesne University Press, 2002), 281–82.
52. Trapnel, *The Cry*.
53. Barbara Kiefer Lewalski, *"Paradise Lost" and the Rhetoric of Literary Forms* (Princeton: Princeton University Press, 1985), 230.
54. John R. Knott, "'Suffering for Truths sake': Milton and Martyrdom," in *Politics, Poetics, and Hermeneutics in Milton's Prose*, ed. David Loewenstein and James Grantham Turner (Cambridge: Cambridge University Press, 1990), 165.
55. See Milton, Sonnet XVIII. J. B. Stouppe, *A Collection of the Several Papers* (1655), and Samuel Morland, *The History of the Evangelical Churches* (1658), are "Great Book[s] of Sufferings" of the period which feature accounts of female and male victims of the massacre.
56. *Experience*, 313.
57. In *Feminist Milton*, Joseph Wittreich uses Mary Cary's works as a gloss for reinterpreting Eve's concluding speech in *Paradise Lost*, in which the "onceimminent apocalypse is still impending" (p. 109). Also see his largely sympathetic portrait of a prophetic Eve in Books 11 and 12 in "'John, John, I blush for thee!': Mapping Gender Discourses in *Paradise Lost*," in *Out of Bounds: Male Writers and Gender(ed) Criticism*, ed. Laura Claridge and Elizabeth Langland (Amherst: University of Massachusetts Press, 1990), 22–54.
58. See Eva Figes's *The Tree of Knowledge* (London: Sinclair-Stevenson, 1990) and Kevin Pask's chapter on "Milton's Daughters," in his *The Emergence of the English Author: Scripting the Life of the Poet in Early Modern England* (Cambridge: Cambridge University Press, 1996), 141–70.
59. M. M. Bakhtin, *The Dialogic Imagination: Four Essays*, ed. Michael Holquist, trans. Caryl Emerson and Michael Holquist (Austin: University of Texas Press, 1981), 31.

CHAPTER 8

Samson and surrogacy

Amy Boesky

Surrogate L. *surrogatus*, pp. of *surrogare* to choose in place of another, substitute. **A**: to appoint as successor, deputy, or substitute for oneself **B**: substitute

For Milton's Samson, the most painful aspect of captivity is produced by the dilemma of surrogacy. *To be* for Samson is to subject himself to a will he cannot entirely know or understand. The urgently repeated question of the poem – for whom is Samson an instrument? – deflects attention away from the fact that Samson is *always* an instrument, whether for the Hebrews, the Philistines, or for God, his body used to fulfill purposes which are not his own. In his captivity Samson is continually reminded by the characters around him that his labors are being used by the Philistines against his own people. Even his rest from labor is not his own. More disturbingly, Samson's desires are construed as separate from him, divinely ordained. "Motions" that move within him suggest that while desire is experienced as bodily, it is in fact a propulsion that he can gauge but that he did not himself produce. What made him long for the bride at Timnah, and then for Dalila? As Samson explains to the Chorus, his first marriage was not the fulfillment of his own desire, but rather the beginning of his "divine labor": "what I motion'd was of God; I knew / From intimate impulse, and therefore urg'd / the Marriage on" (*SA* 222–3). His marriage to Dalila he construed as "lawful from my former act." His "motions" can be interpreted heroically to the extent that they are understood not as his own, but as God's. His triumph, for those who read the poem as regenerative, is as much an act of laboring for or under as is his grinding at the Philistine mill. Samson does not shed subjection in the poem so much as transpose it.

Samson's surrogacy has found itself replicated in the poem's reception, wherein *Samson Agonistes* has been presumed to be *really* a story other than the story it narrates. Readers have substituted for Samson's stories interpretations which revise and reappropriate his sacrifice. These interpretative substitutions are closely tied to issues concerning the poem's representation of the body. Does surrogacy render the body defective? If so, are there aspects of Samson's own corporeality that cannot be taken away from him, however much readers have wanted to do so?

Since the influential study by F. Michael Krouse in 1949, the question for most readers of *Samson Agonistes* has not been whether to read the poem typologically, but how to do so. Is Samson a defective Hebrew or a Christian hero? The unstated assumption lines up Christianity and heroism on one side of the interpretative camp and Hebraism and defectiveness on the other. For Krouse did not merely urge that the poem be Christianized, but suggested that the poem's brilliance lay in the challenge required by the poem to effect this: the transmutation of the "bare biblical character" Milton found in Judges, "to a modern reader almost brutal in its violence, into a tragic hero of great spiritual stature."[1] Milton "greatly humanized" Samson, Krouse maintained, by proving him to be in essence a Christian, a task all the more laudable given the paucity of Milton's vexing source: "Surely no passage of the Old Testament – with the possible exception of the Book of Esther – is more fraught with the hard vindictiveness of ancient Hebraism than the chapters of the Book of Judges which recount the story of Samson" (12). It is not this unappealing Old Testament Samson that Krouse claims is the real source for Milton's poem, but instead the Samson of Hebrews who rises to the rank of saint, praised as one who manages to remain victorious despite his trials through faith in God. The praise for Samson here "marks a divergence," Krouse explains, "at the very beginning of the Christian era, between the Hebraic and the Christian conceptions of Samson. [The author of Hebrews] wrote with the purpose of reminding them that Judaism had been superseded by a higher form of religion, in which everything that had gone before was caught up, absorbed, and transmuted" (p. 30). Not only must Samson be read typologically, Krouse concludes, but the poem must be read "in the light of Christian tradition" in order for it to cohere with Milton's master plan to "justifie the wayes of God to man" (p. 133).

In the generations since Krouse's study was published, a consensus has developed among Miltonists that *Samson Agonistes*, published along with *Paradise Regained* in 1671, is intended to be read together with that poem, their meanings complementary;[2] that Christian typology is instrumental in understanding Samson as a Miltonic hero;[3] that *Samson* is a Christian tragedy;[4] and that in the comparison between Samson and the Son, Samson is inadequate.[5] The poem, in other words, has come to be read as a Hebrew poem in a particular and troubling way – that is, as a poem about the inferiority of the Hebraic in light of Christian heroism. "Hebrew" in such readings is always a comparison. These readings emphasize the positive value Samson's representation has for Milton's (larger) project – the glorification of the Son in *Paradise Regained* – without considering how that project is secured at the cost of rendering abject and defective the body of the Hebraic hero.[6]

The conjunction between the Hebraic and the "defective" has rich resonances in critical literature beyond Milton scholarship. Consider, for instance, Elaine Scarry's reading of the Hebrew Bible in her influential study, *The Body in Pain* (1985).[7] For Scarry, the primacy of scenes of wounding in the Old Testament are deeply implicated in what she construes to be a "problem that arises within the structure of belief."[8] Scenes of wounding "recur so frequently" in the Old Testament that they necessarily trouble readers, "Jewish or Christian." Scarry goes on to describe God's manifestation to the Hebrews in terms that recall her earlier chapters on political torture in the first part of *The Body in Pain*:

God's invisible presence is asserted, made visible, in the perceivable alterations He brings about in the human body; in the necessity of human labor and the pains of childbirth, in a flood that drowns, in a plague that descends on a house, in the brimstone and fire falling down on a city, in the transformation of a woman into a pillar of salt, in the leprous sores and rows of boils that alter the surface of the skin, in an invasion of insects and reptiles into the homes of a population, in a massacre of babies, in a ghastly hunger that causes a people to so glut themselves on quail that meat comes out of their nostrils, in a mauling by bears, in an agonizing disease of the bowels, and so on, on and on.[9]

Though Scarry hastens to admit that there are many moments in the Old Testament when God refrains from wounding, "and above all, the largest framing act of the narrative – the creation and growth of a people and their rescue from their human oppressors – establishes the benevolent context in which these other, themselves terrifying, scenes occur" – she raises numerous concerns. The New Testament "radically revises" the Old for Scarry as it sheds the former's "discrepancy in embodiedness." For Scarry, the New Testament is at once a radical revision and a "supplement"[10] to the Hebraic scriptures. In the New Testament, witnessing – "the bodily alteration of sensory apprehension" (seeing, hearing, touching) – replaces the Hebrew Testament's "bodily alteration of pain." In the New Testament a "scene of wounding" becomes "instead a rhythmic return to a scene of healing."[11] Jesus replaces the weapon, and while "the human body is in each case the site for the analogical verification of the existence and authority of God ... the alterations are almost always now in the direction of recovery."[12]

Scarry often conjoins "Judeo-Christians" or describes Christian and Jewish readers jointly and severally reading the Hebrew Testaments, but she also maintains that the Christian scriptures are a radical revision, a retelling of the Old Testament "from the point of view of sentience." What she imagines in the transition between the Old Testament and the New is no less than "a change in the very structure of belief, a change in the nature of religious imagination."[13] While in the New Testament the moral distance between man and God "is as great as in the Old Testament [it] no longer depends on a discrepancy in embodiedness."[14] Feeling, interiority, witnessing, and recovery replace wounding. Scarry's continued use of the word "problem" in her readings of the Old Testament underscores the extent to which she reads these narratives as defective: "It is crucial that these two be said together: the problematic knowledge is not that man has a body; the problematic knowledge is not that God has no body; the problematic knowledge is that man has a body and God has no body – that is, that the unfathomable difference in power between them in part depends on this difference in embodiedness."[15] In the New Testament for Scarry this "problematic knowledge" is resolved by the fact that the Christian God is embodied: "the fact of Christ having a body is so central a premise of the narratives that it is unnecessary to follow its elaborations at any length here"; "To have a body is, finally, to permit oneself to be described."[16] In the shift from the Hebraic to the Christian, which for Scarry is positive and progressive, a shift is secured from "believing" to "making": "in this shift, weapon becomes tool, sentience becomes active, pain is replaced by the willed capacity for self-transformation and recreation, and the structure of belief or sustained imagining is modified into the realization of belief in material making."[17]

Scarry's reading of the two testaments as connected, like two parts of a vast literary work, enables her to argue that the Hebrew scriptures present a "frail but persistent theme" that only "becomes dominant once God in the Christian scriptures enters the body directly."[18] Her use of the words "frail" and "dominant" in a text so attentive to the discourses of power and its abuses underscores her sense of the implicit failure of Hebraic representation. In the Hebrew Testament the knowledge of God, she maintains, is achieved only through "the bodily alteration of pain."[19] The plight of Milton's Samson as it is so often represented in Milton scholarship is troublingly consistent with this widely held idea; for the Hebrew hero, knowledge of God is achieved in the recognition of the self as defective; the wound that can only be healed in the Christian surrogate providential history will supply.

The problem of the Hebraic, then, is one lens through which we see Samson's corporeality. The other, also problematic, is the poem's idea of the maternal. These two ideas – the corporeal and the maternal – act as surrogates for each other and for the idea of the "defect" in Milton's poem. Of all Milton's poems, *Samson Agonistes* is the one that most evocatively describes the body and its susceptibilities. Despite his constant attempts to tame or to reject it, Samson lives in and through his body. He senses God's presence in every pore, his strength diffused "No less through all my sinews, joints, and bones." Samson's is the body subjected, captive, in "brazen fetters," grinding at the enemy's mill. The poem charts the sensitivity of the body to pain: to darkness, to exhaustion, to torment. The poem brilliantly navigates sensory loss – the disjointing of words, the refusal of touch, and the opacity of blindness. Yet at the same time it captures the body's openness to sensation: the tactile experience of moving from sunlight to shade as light dissipates on the skin; the moisture of dank air inside a prison; the sensation of allaying thirst with sweet water. Interiority and exteriority have been inverted as the poem opens, so that when Samson struggles, inwardly stung, it is always against another exterior: a sepulcher, a shell, a wall of darkness. The vulnerability of the body's interior – the "tender" ball of the eye, the smooth layers of intestinal tissue – are juxtaposed to their painful penetration by exteriorized objects: hornets that are "armed," visitors who sting like scorpions or serpents.

For all the prominence of bodily imagery in the poem, in much of *Samson Agonistes* the body is explained away, made other than itself. Samson's is the abject body, the body that must be renounced, and the body that despite renunciation betrays, with all its appetites and susceptibilities. Samson's degradation is represented as a bodily sinking down and spreading out; "inferior to the vilest now become / Of man or worm" (73–74), he "lies at random, carelesly diffus'd / With languish't head unpropt" (117–18). The darkness and filth that occlude him further suggest degradation. Samson's body is dangerous, violent, unclean.

This emphasis on the body cannot be read in isolation from the related emphasis on Samson as Hebraic; that he is Hebrew is always expressed alongside (and as an aspect of) the problem of having and being a body. As Sander Gilman observes, "the very analysis of the nature of the Jewish body, in the broader culture or within the culture of medicine, has always been linked to establishing the difference (and dangerousness) of the Jew."[20] Samson's strength and his great size make him grotesque; he is a kind of hyper-Hebrew, larger than life, hugely marked as other by both his hair and his circumcision. The mark of his chosenness is also the primary site of woundedness or defect. Pinioned in his body, Samson's desire for escape and for death are continually figured as the desire not to be seen, not to be a "scorn" and a "gaze," not to be entrapped in a body that continually betrays him. Again, in Gilman's terms, "the desire for invisibility . . . lies at the center of the Jew's flight from his or her own body"; for it is in visibility that the body betrays itself as foreign, repulsive, unclean.[21] Gilman points out that "the vocabulary of difference" that informs the representation of the Jew as body (and as Other) can be traced to the "earliest Christian texts, including . . . the Gospels."[22] The Jew experiences his own body as alien, as different, and this difference is summed up in Samson's degraded condition – "O change beyond report" (118); "O miserable change!" (340). For all of those who see him, visibility confers on Samson the status of difference. Different in his glory, when he towered over and crushed all enemies, Samson is now different in defeat, soiled, blinded, in "low dejected state" (339).[23]

If the body can be made less bodily, it can be more generalized, less Hebraic – and hence stronger. The abject body must be decorporealized. This is why metaphor in the poem so often works to make Samson's body something other than a body. Samson's body is seen always from the outside, even by Samson himself. Two strands of metaphor work to denaturalize Samson: images of containment and images of weaponry. The capacity to contain is one of the poem's favored metaphors for bodily experience. Such metaphors suggest the possibility of something held or hidden within these containing devices, but this inwardness is never glimpsed. Even the "tender ball" of the eye is a container for sight which Samson laments was "confin'd" there (95). Why could not sight like feeling be "diffus'd" through every pore (96)? The image of the body that had the capacity to see through every one of its pores is countered by the poem's presentation of discrete, isolated spots of the body that can be penetrated or injured. Within every box or prison there is a smaller box or prison. The body is a "moving grave," a "dungeon," a sepulcher; silence is a "fort," the heart – in a moment of susceptibility – can be "unlock'd," and hence destroyed. Each such container promises the divulging of an interior but delivers instead another exterior, another "prison within prison."

The inside that cannot be seen or described is heightened in the poem's reiterated descriptions of extraordinary strength. Strength, unlike sight, is diffused for Samson throughout every part of his body, as he tells Harapha: "diffus'd / No less through all my sinews, joints, and bones." Yet despite this diffusion, strength (which is always externalized) makes the body less sentient. To have a body is to become a weapon: hornets as they swarm inward are "armed," Dalila approaches like a "stately ship" and leaves like a Serpent "discover'd" by her sting. In his strength Samson is unarmed – "and weaponless himself / Made arms ridiculous" – in part because his extraordinary strength makes the brassy artillery of the Philistines seem trivial, and in part because Samson's entire body functions as God's weapon. Samson's own weapons augment but denaturalize his body. Unlike the Philistine "spear and shield," the forgery of "brazen shield and spear, the hammer'd Cuirass, Chalybean temper'd steel, and frock of mail," the "plated backs" and "crested helmets" that clang and clash throughout the scenes of Philistine armies, Samson relies on "the jaw of a dead ass, his sword of bone." Samson's weapons, bone and wood, seem to grow out of his body like natural projections, rendering his body almost grotesque. Samson's hand is instrumental in this regard. It is Samson's hand that "tore the lion, as the lion tears the kid"; Samson's hand that broke the two cords as if they were "threads / Touched with the flame." Samson's hand – which Dalila tries to touch, sparking Samson's furious threat to tear her apart "joint by joint" – appears to be allied with God's. His exceptional strength is always allied with danger. "Safest he who stood aloof," the chorus remembers in their first lengthy description of his previous power (136). In the grim metonymy by which bodies are reduced to parts, Samson's strength wreaks havoc: "old Warriors turn'd / Thir plated backs under his heel"; "a thousand foreskins fell" (144). Each recollection of past strength is documented by its victim or victims: "and with a trivial weapon fell'd / Their choicest youth; they only lived who fled" (264–65). The desire to approach Samson, variously described by the Chorus, Manoah, Dalila, and Harapha, is partly an effect of this tremendous power; like a detonated weapon, Samson is fascinating now that he can be touched. The proximity of a human hand makes him recoil with rage: he threatens to tear Dalila to pieces, and to Harapha declares that he will, with only an oaken staff, beat him to death in spite of his "gorgeous arms." Hands, which imply sentience, are always allied for Samson with arms, that part of the human body whose very name is synonymous with weaponry. The constant ellision between Samson's body and adjacent weapons dehumanizes Samson, who is seen through it to be God's instrument rather than his own agent. According to Scarry, the gulf between God and man is determined by the Old Testament's "discrepancy in embodiedness" – God and humanity are positioned at two vertical ends of the instrument, God all voice, humanity all body (212). To read Samson in this way is to read the Samson narrative against its typological surrogate.

SURROGATE LABOR

Of the many puzzles surrounding Milton's treatment of the Samson story, one – the representation of Samson's mother – has garnered little attention. In the King James translation of Judges, Samson's mother is important to the narrative, though never named. It is Samson's mother who seeks out the divining voice that assures her that she will have a child despite her barrenness, and it is Samson's mother who receives instruction for Samson's upbringing as a Nazarite. In Judges, motherhood is made more prominent by the fact that it is deferred; Samson is created only after God's intervention and his mother's bodily purification (she must abstain from wine and unclean food to produce a child, and the child's hair must remain uncut as both sign and insurance of his special strength). The peculiarities of Samson's birth – the experience of longing, sacrifice, and divine intervention through embodied generation – are important to Milton's poem; Samson tells the history of his own birth twice, both to revise it and to underscore its significance (23–36; 633–638).

While readers have argued heatedly over many aspects of Milton's *Samson*, the representation (or suppression) of the maternal figure in the poem has elicited little comment. *Samson Agonistes* is understood to be a poem about fathers.[24] In *Paradise Regained* Milton has been seen to give surprising weight to the educative role of Mary;[25] in contrast, Milton's *Samson* has been seen as characteristically patriarchal, its primary work to engage a mortal son with his divine father. Here again Milton's most Hebraic poem is seen as partial or insufficient, a kind of "not yet" to its companion in the 1671 volume. Samson's mother, as Roy Flannagan remarks in his recent edition of Milton's poem, is significant to the poem only to the extent that she is not in it.[26]

However, the terms "absent" and "present" are less helpful to considerations of the maternal figure in Samson than is the study of the problematic nature of generation itself and its relation to the poem's more explicit subjects of servitude, deliverance, and vengeance. The figure of the maternal gets represented in the poem through surrogate tropes of opening, straining, and release, and, as such, is importantly involved with the poem's representation both of the Hebraic and of labor.

At the heart of the Samson story as it gets told in Judges, the maternal is first experienced as a defect. As Scarry observes, "to be barren [in the Hebrew scriptures] is not just to be without child but to be unalterable, unable to change from the state of without child to with child: barrenness is absolute because it means 'unalterable' except by the most radical means, unalterable except by divine intervention."[27] A child is longed for; the mother is barren. Bodily insufficiency necessitates a turning (or a returning) to God for assistance. After prayer, sacrifice, and abnegation, Samson's parents are given a son, but the child (whose body must also be marked and restricted) is neither wholly of them nor for them. Generation – here, the making of a child – is a central story in the Old Testament in part because it is an embodied story. The dread of the unalterable body in the biblical maternal narrative resonates importantly with *Samson Agonistes*; this, after all, is Samson's deepest anxiety – that he will be unyielding, unalterable, useless to God and to himself.

In two ways the maternal figure is importantly affiliated with Samson, not in spite of her shadowy role but precisely because of it: first, in this centrality of the body, in its capacity for pain, alteration, and generation; and second, in the combination of embodiment and surrogacy. The body borrowed – the body overtaken by another and used for its purposes, defined by a production it can neither own nor name – these terms conjoin the figure of the maternal body with that of the bondsman or slave. Writing on Hegel, Judith Butler describes the self-erasure of the bondsman in this way:

In the experience of giving up what he has made, the bondsman understands two issues: first, that what he is is embodied or signified in what he makes, and second, that what he makes is made under the compulsion to give it up. Hence, if the object defines him, reflects back what he is, is the signatory text by which he acquires a sense of who he is, and if those objects are relentlessly sacrificed, then he is a relentlessly self-sacrificing being. He can recognize his own signature only as what is constantly being erased, as a persistent site of vanishing. He has no control over what he puts his name to or over the purposes to which he seeks to fasten his name. His signature is an act of self-erasure; he reads that his signature is his, that his own existence appears to be irreducibly his own, that what is irreducibly his own is his own vanishing, and that this vanishing is effected by another – that is, that this is a socially compelled form of self-erasure.[28]

The surrender and self-erasure of the bondsman – first subjected by the external Lord, then by the internalization of that figure in the emergence of his own unhappy conscience – is suggestive of the relationship posited between desire, sacrifice, and denial in Old Testament representations of maternal creation. Maternal productions, like the labors of the unhappy bondsman, happen both through and for another. In Butler's reading of Hegel, an important point is elucidated: the enslavement that produces subjectivity is not the enslavement by the Lord, but rather the internalized self-enslavement which it produces:

The bondsman takes the place of the lord by recognizing his own formative capacity, but once the lord is displaced, the bondsman becomes lord over himself, more specifically, lord over his own body; this form of reflexivity signals the passage from bondage to unhappy consciousness. It involves splitting the psyche into two parts, a lordship and a bondage internal to a single consciousness, whereby the body is again dissimulated as an alterity, but where this alterity is now interior to the psyche itself. No longer subjected as an external instrument of labor, the body is still split off from consciousness. Reconstituted as an interior alien, the body is sustained through its disavowal as what consciousness must continue to disavow.[29]

SURROGATE BIRTH

One of Scarry's most illuminating readings of the Old Testament can be found in the connection she draws between scenes of wounding and scenes of generation. Both, Scarry argues, are signs of God's presence. The wounded body is the body that has become all interior, its sentience magnified. Scarry notes that this bodily turning-inside-out is importantly allied with belief. If disobedience or disbelief is habitually described in the scriptures as a stiffening or bodily withholding, woundedness (like generation) suggests that the body can be permeated by God. Samson's turning inside-out (his corporeal and spiritual punishment) converges with a growing sense of being acted on or acted through. When Samson hurts, his pain registers internally. Dalila's betrayal works in him like a "thorn / Intestine," a remarkable metonym in which she becomes weapon and he becomes entirely interior. Despite the abjection of such woundedness, it offers a description of the body not as an outside, but as an inside.

At the end of the poem, Manoa turns from the semi-chorus's description of the Phoenix back to the subject that has preoccupied him throughout: his son's body – where it is, what state it is in, how to house and protect it. "Let us go find the body where it lies / Soak't in his enemies blood." That body has been the site of all converging interests in Samson, whether Hebrew or Philistine, from Dalila's desire for touch to Harapha's curiosity over the source of his strength to the chorus's ruminations over the nature of his temptations. Paradoxically, it is only in its final reduction to "clotted gore" that Samson's body ceases to be seen by his father as incapacitated. Instead, this "clotted gore" confirms for Manoa God's presence in (and through) his son's body. It is finally by his capacity to wound and to be wounded that Samson confirms for his father that he was truly God's, "favoring and assisting to the end." In this final act of wounding and being wounded, Manoa knows at last what and who Samson is, expressed ineffably in tautology: "Samson hath quit himself / Like Samson" (1709–10).

If Manoa is able truly to know his son only as he dies, it is in part because that death is figured in several ways as a birth. When Samson recounted his own birth early in the poem, he had allied it both with sacrifice and with the presence of God.

> O wherefore was my birth from heaven foretold
> Twice by an Angel, who at last in sight
> Of both my Parents all in flames ascended
> From off the altar, where an Offering burned
> As in a fiery column charioting
> His Godlike presence, and from some great act
> Of benefit revealed to Abraham's race? (23–29)

Samson recollects his history as preceded by divine edict. The simultaneity of his narration suggests that the foretelling of his birth – his breeding "order'd and prescrib'd" (30) – coincided with the act of his sacrifice. Samson's temporal compression brilliantly elides lament ("O wherefore") and proclamation, past sacrifice and present. For if Samson's birth is recalled as an ordering and prescription, the image of the angel rising in a fiery column complements that vision with its own. The sacrifice gives birth to the angel – or at least to its embodiment. This is inverted in Manoa's grieving acceptance of his son, for it is as Samson is disembodied – as he becomes a name, a narrative – that he apparently becomes most real to his father. Perhaps, given the associations the poem has established between wounding and the act of generation, it is not surprising that the most explicit references to childbirth in *Samson Agonistes* should come not at the beginning of the poem, but at its close. When Manoa learns from the Messenger that his son is dead he reverts to a vocabulary of stillbirth:

> What windy joy this day had I conceived
> Hopeful of his delivery which now proves
> Abortive as the first-born bloom of spring
> Nipped with the lagging rear of winter's frost.
>   (1574–77)

It is Samson's death which "begets" the vocabulary of conception, delivery, abortion, and the firstborn killed. In the Messenger's narrative of Samson's death, Samson's role as "great deliverer" is repeatedly emphasized as the spectacle at the temple becomes a recapitulation of childbirth. Samson strains between the two pillars as a child struggles to be born:

> This uttered, straining all his nerves he bowed
> As with the force of winds and water pent,
> When mountains tremble, those two massy pillars
> With horrible convulsion to and fro
> He tugged, he shook, till down they came and drew
> The whole roof after them.   (1646–1651)

If Samson is figured as "great deliverer" of the Israelites, he must also be seen here as the great deliverer of himself, dying in a scene that recreates childbirth as a kind of embodied revenge. The recourse to a poetics of childbirth here does not ameliorate the violence at the temple, but further underscores the extent to which wounding and generation are allied. Samson, who has made arms ridiculous, leans on the massy pillars of the temple with "both his arms," feeling the arched roof with "his arms," his head inclined. Critics have long debated whether to read this final scene as an act of verification or of violence, perhaps reluctant to admit the extent to which, in Samson's death, verification and violence coincide. God proves "whose God is God" through Samson's arms. In Scarry's terms: "the two kinds of scene – generation and wounding – have so much in common that it seems possible that the persistent and troubling occurrence of human hurt is the result of its conflation with generation in the Old Testament habit of mind, a conflation of the sources of pain and creation."[30] If childbirth is a way in which the interior of the body is made visible, this turning inside-out is achieved only through wounding and through pain. Samson's death works as such a turning inside-out. Strikingly, Samson dies "tangled in the fold" of human flesh: in his delivery he is "immixed" with other bodies, "hearts . . . drunk with wine," "fat regorged," a holocaust of gluttonous interiors (1657, 1665, 1669–71).

This first image of delivery is followed almost immediately by the chorus's description of the Phoenix:

> Like that self-begotten bird
> In the Arabian woods embossed,
> That no second knows nor third,
> And lay erstwhile a holocaust,
> From out her ashy womb now teemed,
> Revives, reflourishes, then vigorous most
> When most unactive deemed,
> And though her body die, her fame survives,
> A secular bird ages of lives.   (1699–1707)

In this passage, the longstanding association between the Phoenix and Christ wrenches the image out of the particularity of Samson's story. Here, in the center-most part of the passage, is that bodily interior that the poem had kept hidden: the "ashy womb," the place where mortality is at once born and inverted. The image of the Phoenix's birth recapitulates Samson's story of his own nativity by conjoining sacrifice and ontology, yet turns away from Samson's prior act of delivery. It is a mythic story, not a material one; the Phoenix (bird, and not human) is self-begotten, not indebted to the violence or hurtfulness of human generation. The eulogy Manoa offers ("Samson hath quit himself / Like Samson") is tautological, a refusal to elaborate Samson's story through metaphor or allusion. The chorus elaborates Manoa's eulogy by extending the tautology into conceit: Samson has died *not* like Samson, but instead has died like the Phoenix, who in turn dies like Christ. Here, in this chain of substitutions, is the poem's final (and greatest) act of wounding. The chorus effectively replaces Samson with his paradoxical surrogate, the Samson of Hebrews and not of Judges, suggesting that the value of this death can best be secured through metaphor, displacement, and allusion – through the suggestion that Samson has quit himself not as Samson, but as Christ. In the delivery of this interpretative surrogacy, the chorus creates a legacy that Milton's readers have found difficult to dispel.

NOTES

1. F. Michael Krouse, *Samson and the Christian Tradition* (Princeton: Princeton University Press, 1949), 14.
2. Mary Ann Radzinowicz, *Toward "Samson Agonistes": The Growth of Milton's Mind* (Princeton: Princeton University Press, 1978), 227–28.
3. William G. Madsen, *From Shadowy Types to Truth: Studies in Milton's Symbolism* (New Haven, CT: Yale University Press, 1968), 95.
4. Anthony Low, *The Blaze of Noon: A Reading of "Samson Agonistes"* (New York: Columbia University Press, 1974), 8.
5. Madsen, *Shadowy Types*, 114.
6. The distinction between typology and allegory is discussed in Eric Auerbach's well-known "Figura," in *Scenes from the Drama of European Literature*, trans. R. Mannheim (New York: Meridian, 1959), pp. 11–76. More recent investigations into the distinctions between typology and allegory can be found in Joel Fineman, "The Structure of Allegorical Desire," in *Allegory and Representation*, ed. Stephen Greenblatt (Baltimore: Johns Hopkins University Press, 1981), 26–60. Thomas Luxon takes issue with the distinction between allegory and typology in *Literal Figures: Puritan Allegory and the Renaissance Crisis in Representation* (Chicago: University of Chicago Press, 1995).
7. Elaine Scarry, *The Body in Pain: The Making and Unmaking of the World* (New York: Oxford University Press, 1985).

8. *Ibid.*, 182.
9. *Ibid.*, 183.
10. *Ibid.*, 184, 212.
11. *Ibid.*, 212.
12. *Ibid.*, 213.
13. *Ibid.*, 210.
14. *Ibid.*, 184.
15. *Ibid.*, 209.
16. *Ibid.*, 215, 216.
17. *Ibid.*, 220.
18. *Ibid.*, 233.
19. *Ibid.*, 212.
20. *The Jew's Body* (New York: Routledge, 1991), 39.
21. *Ibid.*, 235, 193.
22. *Ibid.*, 235.
23. The fullest elaboration of Samson and the Hebraic can be found in Jason Rosenblatt's essay, "Samson and the Law," in *Form and Reform in Renaissance England: Essays in Honor of Barbara Kiefer Lewalski*, ed. Amy Boesky and Mary Crane (Newark: University of Delaware Press, 2000), pp. 321–37. Rosenblatt's deeply thoughtful essay takes a very different approach from mine; he argues that the recognition of Samson's adherence to Hebrew law helps to bolster an unironic reading of Samson's regeneracy.
24. See, for example, John Guillory's discussion in "Dalila's House: *Samson Agonistes* and the Sexual Division of Labor," in *Rewriting the Renaissance: The Discourses of Sexual Difference in Early Modern Europe*, ed. Margaret Ferguson, Maureen Quilligan, and Nancy Vickers (Chicago: University of Chicago Press, 1986), 106–22.
25. Dayton Haskin makes this persuasive argument in *Milton's Burden of Interpretation* (Philadelphia: University of Pennsylvania Press, 1994), 123–38.
26. "Like Samson's mother, the Woman of Timnah represents a significant omission from the biblical plot, and another meaningful female absence in the dramatic poem": *The Riverside Milton*, ed. Roy Flannagan (Boston and New York: Houghton Mifflin, 1998), 785.
27. Scarry, *The Body in Pain*, 194.
28. Judith Butler, *The Psychic Life of Power: Theories in Subjection* (Palo Alto: Stanford University Press, 1997), 40.
29. *Ibid.*, 42.
30. *The Body in Pain*, 197.

CHAPTER 9

"*I was his nursling once*": nation, lactation, and the Hebraic in Samson Agonistes

Rachel Trubowitz

At the culmination of his long lament on the "miserable change" inflicted upon him, Samson despairs that "I was his nursling once" (*SA* 634). This chapter takes Samson's painful recollection of his chosen status as God's "nursling" as a point of departure for an investigation of the play's – and its hero's – preoccupations with "purity." To be sure, such preoccupations have been well documented; but surprisingly little attention has been paid to the intimate connections between the question of "purity" in *Samson Agonistes* and Samson's self-definition as God's "nursling." This omission becomes particularly meaningful when we consider the close intersections between Samson's "nursling" identity and his Nazarite election, an election defined by the deity's prohibition against "wine and all delicious drink" (541). For Samson to remain a Nazarite, and, hence, "separate to God," he must assert his purity by drinking only providentially sanctioned fluids, specifically, the "clear milky juice" (551) that anoints him as God's "nursling" and Israel's "great Deliverer" (279). Samson's role as national redeemer is closely tied to special "maternal" forms of nurture. As Manoa observes, "For this did th' Angel twice descend . . . for this / [God] Ordain'd thy nurture holy" (362) and "caus'd a fountain at thy prayer / From the dry ground to spring, thy thirst to allay" (581–82). As these lines suggest, Samson's identity as Israel's champion is rooted in his maternal "nurture holy": in "clear milky juice" and the sacred fount offered by a nursing deity, but, notably, not in mothers' milk itself. *Samson* thus creates a gap between embodied and disembodied forms of motherhood – a space clearing that is crucial not only to the play's staging of Samson as Israel's "great Deliverer" but also to its vision of the reformed Israel.

It is telling that Milton occludes the figure of Samson's mother, who is given a significant role in Judges 13–16. He also conflates Dalila and Manoa as ungodly "mothers" whom Samson ultimately must reject. In their efforts to domesticate Samson, both Dalila and Manoa offer to "nurse" him, but Samson refuses not only Dalila's "nursing diligence" but also Manoa's paternal nurturance. God is the only "mother" from whom Samson can receive "nurture holy" and "pure" identity. "Under his special eye," Samson recalls, "Abstemious I grew up and thriv'd amain" (636–37); and, as the Chorus observes, only God's "secret refreshings" could "repair [Samson's] strength" (666). By rejecting both Dalila and Manoa, Samson reinforces the play's radical division between godly and ungodly, disembodied and embodied, forms of maternal nurture; he also blurs the boundaries between "Philistine" and "Hebrew" identities. The hero thus both breaks up the monism that organizes Hebrew Scripture and undermines Israel's governing self-definition as a godly nation separate from all others. Cut loose from the body and the received character of its national election, Israel is poised for inclusion and reformation within the new universal, spiritual order that is imagined by Milton's drama. Milton's spiritualizing of maternal nurture positions his drama in striking opposition to a wide range of early modern texts, from *The Faerie Queene* to Richard Brathwait's *The English Gentleman and English Gentlewoman*, all of which assign the nursing mother a crucial material role in shaping the national body politic. The discourse on maternal breast-feeding in Puritan didactic literature on "household government" such as William Gouge's oft-reprinted *Of Domesticall Duties* has special relevance in this context, since the space that Gouge and other domestic guidebook authors devote to the nourishment and nurture of infants accords exactly with Milton's own understanding in *Of Education* that the nurture of children "from the cradle" is "worth many considerations." Indeed, Milton maintains that the primacy of nurture is a subject that he himself would have addressed "if brevity had not been my scope" (*CPW* 2:414–15.) Yet while *Of Education* would seem to place Milton in sympathetic dialogue with writers such as Gouge, *Samson Agonistes* shows that the mature Milton's assessment of the social value of maternal nurture differs considerably from the position adopted in the Puritan guidebooks. These guidebooks celebrate the identity-forming power of maternal nurture modeled in Hebraic Scriptural ideals of nursing motherhood, such as Sarah and Jochobed, the mother of Moses. By contrast, Milton's Samson rejects not only Manoa's proffer of "maternal" nurture but also the elect identity or "pure self" constituted by mothers' "milk" – the monist "self" that appears in both the guidebooks and their Hebraic paradigms.

Yet if Milton repudiates the Hebraic/Puritan linkage between maternal nurture and "pure" identity as a key component of character formation, he does not turn to "the paternal" as a proper model of the "pure" national subject. This route is closed off by the poet's repudiation of the abuses of monarchical, papist, and other corrupt institutional forms of "male" power in his prose works. Hence Milton opposes both the Reformers' innovative efforts to make motherhood a central measure of social/national identity and Restoration attempts to renew traditional patriarchal forms of authority and power, and instead endorses a universalist model of identity that echoes the view of Paul in Galatians 3:28: "There is neither Jew nor Greek, there is neither bond nor free, there is neither male nor female, for ye are all one in Christ Jesus."[1] This prescription negates not only the categories of "maternal" and "paternal," "Hebrew" and "Philistine," but "Cromwellian" and "Stuart" as well. Milton's Pauline model of Reformed English identity as at once universal and Protestant, inclusive and elect, lies behind not just his strange conflation of Dalila and Manoa as maternal nourishers, but also his allusions to nursing and his revaluation of the Hebrew Bible's "maternal," monist means of assuring "pure" identity.

The same "exclusive universalism," to borrow Paul Stevens's apt term, informs Milton's seemingly contradictory vision of the Reformed England as both a separatist and universal community.[2] As Linda Gregerson observes, in Milton's writings "we may behold the modern nation in the full force of its conceptual paradox, a politically and ideologically bounded bastion for an inherently universalist and transnational religion."[3] *Samson Agonistes* allows us to add gender to Stevens's and Gregerson's illuminating formulations of the "conceptual paradox" between exclusion and inclusion that informs both Christian evangelism and the ideology of the modern nation. Milton's devaluation of embodied forms of motherhood and the Hebrew Bible's monist models of "pure" maternal nurture allows him to insert his separatist vision of the Reformed England/Israel into his Pauline model of universal Christian community. This formulation of Christian world community reflects a tolerationist vision of global union; but, at the same time, it also excludes and disavows identities such as "the Hebraic" that resist Pauline inclusiveness by insisting upon remaining spiritually and corporeally separate from "Christendome." This is the elect world order that, in *Of Reformation*, Milton foresees as coming into being after the imminent apocalypse, placing a spiritually reformed England at its center.[4] The same double mandate of inclusion and exclusion, toleration and disavowal, shapes Samson's spiritual regeneration as God's "nursling" in the final moments of the drama when Samson returns "Home to his Father's house" (1733) only in spirit, thereby foreclosing on the embodied measures of national belonging upheld by the Hebrew Bible's maternal measures of "pure" selfhood. "Exclusive universalism" thus informs Milton's treatment of maternal nurture, "the Hebraic," and the reformed Israel/England in *Samson Agonistes*. The poet's allusions to nursing and nurture reflect a matrix of wide-ranging but overlapping concerns, including the spiritualization of motherhood, the supersession of Hebraic Scriptural history, and the "conceptual paradox" that gives rise to the modern nation.

The domestic guidebooks of the period particularly illuminate the ways in which early modern England managed its shifting and paradoxical assumptions about national identity by regulating mothers' roles. As Janet Adelman observes, "boundary panic" rules this turbulent historical moment – a moment in which England's cultural and territorial borders underwent rapid and repeated revision during the dynastic shift between the Tudor and Stuart states, early acts of colonization, and, at mid-century, revolution, civil war, and imperial expansion.[5] Domestic guidebooks and affiliated texts helped to stabilize the cultural construction of the English home so that a nation already in a condition of rapid social change and cultural fragmentation could receive a new "anchor" by defining the relations between the maternal body and the maternal body politic. This ideology was related to the role that breast-milk was believed to play in the formation of personal and national identity.

Guidebook defenses of maternal breast-feeding rest this ideology upon overlapping exegetical and empirical strategies. To note but one example, Robert Cleaver and John Dod in *A Godly Form of Household Government* impugn wet-nursing by appealing to Scriptural precedent. They suggest that Sarah's nursing of Isaac in Genesis 21:7 divinely ordains maternal breast-feeding as "natural" for all women regardless of age or class: Sarah (whose name as translated from the Hebrew means "princess") "nursed Isaak, though she were a Princess; and therefore able to have had others to have taken that paines."[6] William Gouge glosses the example of Sarah in similar terms: "*Sarah* gave sucke to Isaak. The example is to be noted especially of the greater sort: as rich men's wives, honourable mens wives, and the like. For *Sarah* was an honourable woman, a princess, a rich man's wife, a beautifull woman, aged and well growne in years, and the mistress of a family."[7] For the guidebook writers, maternal breast-feeding must be separated from class and shown to be a natural and divine imperative pertaining to all women. In this way maternal nurture could shape identity in relation to the (imagined) collective whole, overriding all merely "local" affiliations.

Another Scriptural passage that the guidebooks use to connect maternal nurture with national identity is Exodus 2:7–9, which shows how the search by Pharaoh's daughter and her maid for a Hebrew woman to wet-nurse the infant Moses leads to hiring of Moses' own biological or "natural" mother. Cleaver and Dod read this text as containing a divine mandate for maternal breast-feeding: "So when God chose a nurse for *Moses*, he led the hand-maide of *Pharoas* daughter to his mother: as though God would have none to nurse him but his mother."[8] The wording here refuses to admit any opposition not only between "nurse" and "mother," but also, indirectly, between Pharaoh's royal daughter and Moses' slave-mother. It is not difficult to decode the anti-hierarchical implications of Cleaver and Dod's reading, nor to see that, even as they level the social differences between master and slave, their insistence that "God would have none to nurse [Moses] but his mother" nevertheless keeps the national boundaries between "Egypt" and "Israel" intact, allowing Moses to evolve "naturally" into Israel's great deliverer from Egyptian bondage. This trajectory, as we shall see, differs considerably from Samson's evolution from Philistine slave to Israel's savior in Milton's drama.

Just as they invoke divine mandate, the guidebook writers appeal to natural law to justify the social benefits of maternal breast-feeding. Cleaver and Dod appeal to "experience" and the truth-claims of empiricism as a way to exhort women to nurse their own babies: "We see by experience that every beast and every fowle is nourished and bred of the same that beare it; only some women love to be mothers, but not nurse. As therefore every tree doth cherish and nourish that which it bringeth forth: even so also it becometh *naturall* mothers to nourish their children with their own milke."[9] By describing maternal breast-feeding as a natural law governing all women, regardless of class, guidebook writers root maternal nurture in both maternal nature and "Mother Nature" (nurture here *is* nature), redefining breast-feeding as a manifestation of the natural law of love.

Their scriptural and empirical arguments in support of maternal breast-feeding closely reflect the period's new formulations of maternal and sexual roles – or what Ruth Perry terms the "invention of motherhood."[10] Pushing against the Galenic single-sex, single-flesh model of sex and reproduction, early modern anatomists such as Thomas Vicary helped to establish women's "natural" difference from men. Under the Galenic model, both men and women were thought to have breasts. By focusing on lactation as a defining mark of gender difference, the new anatomies of motherhood disrupted Galenism's mirror-model of sexuality and reproduction. In Vicary's *The Anatomie of the Bodie of Man*, "the generation of milke" categorically distinguishes the female breast from its male counterpart.[11] As Kathryn Schwarz states in her perceptive gloss of Vicary's *Anatomie*, "And even if, as in the Galenic model, women's genitals are imagined to mirror those of men, producing some degree of reproductive mutuality, the maternal breast is an inescapable site of difference."[12] This new model of gender difference facilitated the enclosure of women in private, unworldly, or "pure," domestic spaces, as Perry suggests.[13] This privatizing of motherhood coheres with Milton's own efforts to spiritualize and universalize maternity, as noted above. Yet while the "invention of motherhood" redefined mothers' roles in private and unworldly terms, it also considerably enhanced the social and national value of maternal nurture. While writing women out of the public realm, the guidebooks also write the "naturall" mother into national service by emphasizing the importance of nursing to keeping "Englishness" intact.

In their attempts to rearticulate "the maternal," the guidebooks help to clarify the very specific socio-political connotations that "the natural" begins to acquire in the early modern period. As Stephen Greenblatt observes, the late sixteenth and early seventeenth centuries represent the precise historical moment when "the natural" comes to replace "the sacred" as the conceptual category that governed English efforts to negotiate difference.[14] Guidebook writers celebrate the "natural" nursing mother for protecting her children from moral taint and perversion by transmitting pure and intact identity through her milk. At the same time these writers repudiate the "unnatural" wet nurse for corrupting the English "complexion" (a term that in this period denotes both "character" and "skin color") and encouraging infidelity to family, nation, and God.[15] The personal threat is as great as the national: "Now if the nurse be of an evil complexion," write Cleaver and Dod, "the child suckling of her breast must need take part with her."[16] The depiction of wet-nursing as an external threat to the moral integrity and purity of the family and the nation begins to acquire proto-racialized nuances, strengthened by the widely embraced conception of maternal breast-milk as "white blood": "nothing else but blood whitened," writes James Guillimeau in *The Nursing of Children*.[17] By invoking the threat of degeneracy and situating it outside the "natural" family, the guidebook writers displaced their anxieties about the instability of the family/nation onto the wet nurse, imagined as an "unnatural," morally "dark," and polluting, alien figure.[18]

David Leverenz has established that domestic guidebook literature on breast-feeding was largely penned by Puritans and intended for a mostly Reformist readership.[19] Republican skepticism about birthright and bloodline as customary measures of class status and dynastic power enhanced the appeal that the guidebooks' emphasis on nurture as a fundamental part of nature had for Puritan Reformers like Milton, Reformers eager to upend existing hierarchies and root out the "Roman" magic and mystery in which dynastic power was shrouded. Indeed, a Protestant and republican revaluation of motherhood and maternal nature and nurture appears to shape Milton's formulation of the "Mothers house private" in *Paradise Regained* (4.639). As Janel Mueller points out, the maternal sphere in Milton's "brief epic" opens up new liberatory personal and social spaces as imagined alternatives to the ruling patriarchal structures of the official church and state.[20] However, Mueller also emphasizes that the maternal-centered, private home in *Samson Agonistes* is not the "discrete alternative domain of *Paradise Regained*" but rather an "ensnaring extension" of official rule.

Appearing side by side in *Paradise Regained* and *Samson Agonistes*, Milton's opposing representations of the maternal sphere highlight the ideological battle lines drawn over motherhood in the period. The same shaping power that Puritan writers increasingly accorded to mothers' milk and the nursing breast also occupied a central place in the royalist "imaginary." As Jacqueline T. Miller notes, the nursing breast "was very much a site of contested control and ownership."[21] We thus find that aristocratic women like Elizabeth Clinton in *The Countess of Lincolns Nursery*, published in the same year as Gouge's *Of Domesticall Duties*, not only echo the guidebooks' celebrations of maternal breast-feeding but also offer similar kinds of exegetical justifications for the argument that mothers should nurse their own babies rather than hand them off to wet nurses, still the most common cultural practice: "Now who should deny the own mother's suckling of their own children to be their duty since every godly matron hath walked in these steps before them: Eve, the mother of all the living, Sarah, the mother of all the faithful, Hannah, so graciously heard of God; Mary blessed of among women."[22] More than anything else perhaps, the afore-mentioned assumption that breast-milk was "but blood whitened" energized royalist efforts to claim ownership of the lactating breast. Queen Anne, the wife of James I, draws on the equation between mothers' milk and blood when she endorses maternal breast-feeding in her letters: "Will I let my child, the child of a king, suck the milk of a subject and mingle the royal blood with the blood of a servant?"[23] Not unlike his wife, James I also represents his royal sovereignty through the language of maternal nurture and nursing. Evoking Isaiah 49:23, "And kings shall be thy nursing fathers," James, in *Basilikon Doron*, tells Prince Henry: "it is your fairest styles, to be called a louing nourish-father," who feeds his subjects with his "nourish-milk."[24] In turn, Cromwell's apologists appropriated the Stuart image of nursing kingship to glorify Cromwell's leadership, as when, in the winter of 1650–51, the annalist of the Independent Church at Cockermouth praised Cromwell as the "nursing father of the churches." This tender portrait of Cromwell as a "nursing father" resonates with Cromwell's own tender imagery of maternal succor and undifferentiated maternal love in his parliamentary speeches.[25]

These contestations over the lactating breast offer an intriguing context in which to read Milton's figurations of maternal nurture in *Samson Agonistes*. Just as the guidebooks ground the assumption that maternal nurture shapes "pure" identity in Hebrew models, so Milton associates this belief with Manoa, Samson's "nursing" Hebrew father. Manoa poignantly expresses his conviction that his nurture will restore Samson's lost election as God's champion. Revived by his tender nurturance, his son will sit "in the house ennobl'd / With all those high exploits of him achiev'd" (1491–92), ready for God to "use him further yet in some great service" (1499). But Manoa's "delight"-ful, domestic vision of an "ennobl'd" Samson is greeted by "hideous noise" – the horrific sound of "Blood, death, and deathful deeds" made when Samson pulls down the walls of Dagon's temple, destroying the Philistine lords and himself (1490, 1509, 1514). The surprising parallels between Manoa's and Dalila's profferings of "nursing diligence" further compromise and contest the Puritan/Hebraic linkage between maternal nurture and "pure" identity. Blurring the boundaries between Israel and its idolatrous Philistine overlords, these parallels undermine Israel's sacred difference from all other nations, its most important measure of "pure" identity.[26] Milton implies that while the paternal and maternal belong to opposing categories, they are actually not all that different. Thus, by extension, rather than acting as opposite, enemy nations, Israel and Philistia are, in fact, locked in a deadly embrace. In narrating his tale of how Israel's governors anticipate Dalila by handing Samson over to the Philistine rulership, the hero insists that an Israel self-enthralled by its own vices actually loves Philistine bondage more than freedom. Israel can thus be counted among those "Nations grown corrupt, / And by their vices brought to servitude / . . . [that] love Bondage more than Liberty / Bondage with ease than strenuous liberty" (268–71). Equally relevant here is the point that Milton emphasizes in *Areopagitica*: without "strenuous liberty," the political subject is consigned to a state of "perpetual childhood." If Israel's love affair with Philistine bondage can be regarded as a bad marriage, this marriage has reduced Israel to the form of a helpless child or "female" partner.

Given the domestic terms in which Samson describes political servitude, it is not surprising that Israel's love of "Bondage with ease" is additionally reflected in his marriage to Dalila. Dalila is not only a treacherous wife but also a "pois'nous bosom snake" (764) – an alluring source of fatal succor and, as such, a deadly "maternal" seductress who robs Samson of his manhood and his Nazarite election. Her poison works by tempting Samson to break his Nazarite vows and take her "fair enchanted cup" (934) – a metaphor that unites idol-worship and transgressive erotics with false maternal succor. Equally notable is that Dalila extends the same fatal "cup" once again when she later offers to domesticate Samson through her "nursing diligence" (924). In divorcing Dalila, Samson would therefore seem at once to regain his manhood and Nazarite separateness by reasserting his restored abstinence and his rejection of the prohibited fluids and fluidity that Dalila as a site of "maternal" impurity emblematizes. Yet, in the end, Samson eliminates the Hebraic prohibitions against mixture in addition to the corporeal and maternal measures of separation and purity in which Israel's integrity and holiness are grounded.

In the meantime, however, Dalila's doubly enthralling role as unclean wife and mother is supplemented by her wayward succor, which the play allies with Manoa's tender care "to nurse [his] Son" (1488).[27] Although an expression of paternal love and sacrifice, Manoa's offer of nurture, like Dalila's "nursing diligence," evokes the dangerous allure of the mother-child dyad and the desire to be reabsorbed into the maternal body, which the play continually associates with emasculation, infantilism, abjection, and bondage. If Dalila's "nursing diligence" would render Samson "in most things like a child" (942), compelling him to "live uxorious to [her] will / In perfect thraldom" (945–46), Manoa's "nursing" would preserve Samson comfortably, but equally abjectly in the premature state of old age, or second childhood, to which his blindness has delivered him. As the Chorus says of Manoa, "Sons are wont to nurse their Parents in old age / Thou in old age car'st how to nurse thy son / Made older than thy age through eyesight lost" (1487–89). As the play makes absolutely clear, Samson must reject both "bad" and "good" figurations of the nursing mother, both Dalila and Manoa. Or, put another way, he must divorce not only Dalila but also Manoa, and so separate himself not only from the Philistine "other" but also from his Hebraic "self." This double separation represents a crucial moment in the drama in which both divorces release Samson not only from his Philistine wife but also from his Hebrew father and, more generally, the world of his Hebraic forebears, Judaic law, and the Israel of Hebrew Scripture.

The seemingly opposed forms of "maternal" nurture that Dalila and Manoa individually extend to Samson are thus collapsed into equivalent forms of "Bondage with ease." Finally, Samson's twinned rejections of Dalila and Manoa reaffirm the submerged identity between the seemingly opposed but, in fact, equally "carnal" Philistine and Hebraic nations. Samson is providentially driven not only to evoke but also to reveal this submerged identity as he regains the "true," spiritual purity that anoints him as God's nursling.

In the so-called "missing" middle of the tragedy, Samson comes at last to embrace fully this salvific, new-modeled "purity." This new notion of purity departs from the Hebraic model in dispensing with the dietary prohibitions, the rites of circumcision, and the ideals of nursing motherhood, such as Sarah and the mother of Moses. Inspired by the "rousing motions in me" (1382), Samson comes to see circumcised and uncircumcised, maternal and paternal, Hebrew and Philistine, as more similar than different. In so doing, he cancels Israel's status as different from all other nations and redefines his nation in relation to the exclusive or "higher" Pauline paradigm of universal inclusiveness. Sharon Achinstein notes in her insightful reading of the "missing" middle of Milton's tragedy that "In his move from 'cannot come' to 'will not come,' Samson is growing to acknowledge the full responsibility of his own assent to higher law."[28] I would add that what, in *Samson*, defines the "higher" nature of this "higher law" is its disembodiment or spiritualization of the "lower" corporeal measures of Hebrew "purity" and "election," including (or especially) maternal nurture. Samson assents to "higher law" because he comes to understand its transumption of Judaic law as a translation from carnal to spiritual purity and so as a point of progressive continuity, of sameness with a difference, and not as final rupture. There is no "reversal" at the "missing" middle because Samson does not experience abrupt and radical change, but rather revelation of the imperfect, but evolving nature of Hebrew history and its corporeal constructions of purity. This understanding is articulated in the prophecy that serves as Samson's final sentence in the play. Despite his self-acknowledged transgression of the Law when he agrees to participate in the Dagonalia, he nevertheless proclaims: "of me expect to hear / 'Nothing dishonorable, impure, unworthy / Our God, our Law, my Nation, or myself'" (1423–25).

The synchronicity Samson establishes between these two contradictory assertions – between transgression and obedience – reflects the play's governing (il)logic, which finds a key source in the millenarian thought that informs the theological and political vision asserted by

Milton's drama. One especially notable aspect of seventeenth-century millenarianism is the coterminous relationship it forges between Jewish conversion and restoration. As Michael Ragussis points out, English millenarian discourse "speaks in the same breath of the Jews' restoration and their conversion."[29] The Jews would be restored to "Israel," that is, Israel as re-formed in Reformation England, at the precise moment in which they would renounce their Judaism and embrace Protestant Christianity. This vision of simultaneous Jewish reclamation and denial, return and departure, is summed up perfectly by Milton's Jesus in *Paradise Regained*. Jesus prophesies that God "Remembr'ing *Abraham*, by some wondrous call / May bring [the Jews] back repentant and sincere" (3:434–35). Ragussis aptly notes that "the 'call' . . . that Milton's Christ hesitantly acknowledges is a critical touchstone of a tradition of millenarian thought about the relation between the Jews' history and world history."[30] Samson's prophecy – his obedience through transgression, his transumptive relationship to the Law – might be read as a response to this "wondrous call," one that situates Samson as the "repentant and sincere" Hebrew, who enters world history and the universal, Christian community (as articulated in Galatians 3:28) by erasing and rewriting his own Hebraic past and particularity.

Hence, while inclusive, the Pauline model of Christian community is also exclusive; indeed, it is exclusive because it is inclusive. As Stevens aptly notes, "the very inclusiveness of the Christians' message becomes a mark of their election and the source of their exclusiveness."[31] It is precisely this exclusive inclusiveness, or "exclusive universalism," that Samson envisions when the "rousing motions within him" convert him to "higher law," turning his violent self-destruction into a phoenix-like rebirth and restoring his identity as Israel's "great Deliverer," not only from the Philistines but also from Hebraic tradition and Law as well.

"Exclusive universalism" also inspires Milton's daring intervention in *Samson* in the entangled matrix of ruling and dissenting seventeenth-century political and religious discourses. One very compelling way to read *Samson Agonistes* is as a revolutionary attempt to wrest control of the Pauline ideal of unity in Christ from governing antitolerationist constructions of England as a nation united spiritually through shared participation in the sacraments and to make it serve instead nonconformist models of social and religious inclusiveness. Milton's drama might be said to translate, or convert, a "ceremonialist" paradigm of community into a "puritan" one, to borrow Achsah Guibbory's very useful terms. Milton had already made this kind of revisionist move in *Areopagitica* by strategically deploying the reconstituted temple of Solomon, which, as Guibbory notes, "the Laudian

Church had invoked to support uniformity in ceremonial worship," to represent the unforced gathering of separatist churches as the inclusiveness proclaimed by Galatians 3:28.[32] In this reformed "temple," the Pauline vision of inclusiveness would peacefully unite all configurations of Christian belief and religious practice. Samson elevates this same ideal of inclusive toleration above tribal exclusivity, sealed in the body, unilaterally imposed by an external rather than internal Law. The play thus steals back the Pauline ideal from the "ceremonialist" model and newly deploys it as a "puritan" paradigm for the emancipation of the spirit and liberty of conscience.

What complicates this reading is that, as Elizabeth Sauer argues, Cromwellian ideals of toleration, tested most dramatically by the Readmission Act of 1656 allowing the Jews to return to England, served the expansionist interests of the Protectorate in Ireland, Jamaica, and elsewhere around the globe.[33] The desire to tolerate "brotherly dissimilitudes" at home was paralleled by the global ambition to federate all nations into a universal brotherhood, an ideal of inclusion that as Daniel Boyarin maintains, paradoxically "produces the discourse of conversion, colonialism, the 'white man's burden.'"[34] Those who fail to become brothers become "others," to be cast down like Cain, the "other" brother. In *Samson*, such casting down is performed by Samson's violent destruction not only of the Philistine "other" but also of his Hebrew "self," thus once again obliterating the distinctions between these two categories. At the same time, this obliteration of difference permits the hero to reconstitute his exemplary selfhood as "Samson" in a new "higher" key: "*Samson* [is] with these immixt, inevitably," even as he "quits himself like *Samson*" (1657, 1709–10).

Samson's death and rebirth have communal as well as subjective implications, for in razing the Philistine nation and himself as "Ebrew," Samson "restores" the field of human experience to its *tabula rasa* state, "at the Beginning," before the proliferation of sin and the disintegration of the universal whole into competing constituencies, engaged in civil war. As James Holstun observes, this *tabula rasa* metaphor of purity was integral to Puritan ambitions in both the New World abroad and the old one at home.[35] It helped to license the imposition of new models of social organization upon supposedly "blank" colonial spaces created by ignorance as well as by the forcible displacement of preexisting cultures, whose seeming unruliness required systematic repression and rationalization.

But, the Hebraic nation, so central to the concerns of *Samson Agonistes*, was England's (and Europe's) archetypal displaced population. Just as the ancient Hebrews were forcibly driven from the biblical Israel, so the modern Jews were forced again and again from their adopted European homelands

Nation, lactation, the Hebraic in Samson Agonistes

in Catholic England, Spain, and France. The Readmission Act would seem to reverse such displacements and, as Sauer aptly notes, thereby proclaim, through this most extreme case of toleration, England's difference from, and superiority to, the Catholic monarchies, past and present, that were its rivals. Exclusion, heretofore the preeminent strategy for achieving integral "Englishness," is reinscribed, at least implicitly, in non-monarchical and Protestant terms as a remnant of primitive pre-Reformation history and its "carnal" measures of national election and communal identity. Inclusion, by contrast, becomes the enlightened or reformed means to "ingather" all peoples into Christian federation, to be realized at the imminent apocalypse. Hence, while a testament to – and a testing of – Cromwellian toleration, the liberal ethos that underpins the Readmission was less a corrective to English perceptions of Jews as unintegrable, and hence deportable, than a new translation of such anti-Jewish perceptions. After 1656, assimilation and conversion rather than displacement and exile become the key modes of erasing Jewishness, facilitating England's assertion of originary authority and power and its liberation from the burdens of the Hebraic testament.

These new strategies for containing "the wandering Jew" at home were replicated abroad, especially in the New World. Indeed, the move from deportation to toleration, from Expulsion to Readmission, finds an important counterpart in England's colonial project in the Americas, where native populations were refashioned as Jews and assigned Hebraic origins, which were then effaced and subsumed by conversion to Christianity. The scope of this double conversionary process reached full force at the precise moment in which Jewish Readmission was being fiercely debated and finally adopted as Cromwellian policy.[36] While seemingly unrelated developments, the Judaizing of the New World (especially New England) and the Readmission of the Jews to a tolerant new England at home sustain the same Anglocentric vision. As Holstun notes, this vision foresees "an ultimate (or penultimate) unity of peoples and of history," of a world population descended from the dispersed or lost tribes of Israel, all awaiting conversion and the ingathering of community at the apocalypse.[37] This reunification is authorized by the same Pauline formula of "exclusive universal" community articulated in Galatians 3:28, which, as this chapter has argued, also informs *Samson Agonistes*. England would usher in the global Christian brotherhood of world history's apocalyptic end-point through its tolerationist policies at home and its missionary projects abroad. This "back to the future" movement erases all precursor histories (synthetically understood as "Hebraic") and restores the world to its "pure" originary moment before the advent of time.

In *Samson Agonistes*, this *tabula rasa* fantasy of "pure" origin is reflected in Samson's release from the engulfing "Hebraic" past, associated with the "maternal" body, subsumed and then transumed in the phoenix's "ashy womb," where he once again becomes God's "nursling." In *Paradise Lost*, these same regenerative "ashes" are associated with the "New Heav'n and Earth" to be ushered in at the End of Days: "Meanwhile / The World shall burn, and from her ashes spring / New Heav'n and Earth, wherein the just shall dwell" (3:333–35). This consummation is at once universal and all-inclusive – a world in which "God shall be All in All" – and particular and exclusive, one "wherein [only] the just shall dwell." The gap between the old World and the "New Heav'n and Earth" also revisits the divide between the "carnal Israel" alluded to in 1 Corinthians 10:18 ("Behold Israel according to the flesh") and the spiritual Israel heralded by the gospels and Paul's epistles. For, unlike the "old" Israel, in which identity is rooted in the body and closely associated with maternal nurture, the "new" Israel is a nation of spiritual converts nourished by the spirit and God alone. Through his exemplary role as a repentant and, ultimately, disembodied or "ashy" Hebrew, Samson epitomizes the new, spiritually regenerated Israel.

Daniel Boyarin observes that the cultural politics of post-Pauline Christianity "allegorized the reality of Israel out of corporeal existence," thereby allowing "for a disavowal of sexuality and procreation, of the importance of filiation and genealogy, and of the concrete historical sense of scripture, of, indeed, historical memory itself."[38] The same post-Pauline disavowal allows Milton to release England/Israel from all local, historical, corporeal, and thus all Hebraic measures of identity, including the ideal of nursing motherhood. Separate and universal, the new Israel of *Samson Agonistes* highlights the "conceptual paradox" that, as Gregerson argues, "*produces* the modern nation" (italics in original).[39] Milton's repudiation of the Hebraic/Puritan paradigm of maternal nurture and its monist model of "self" is indissolubly tied to the "exclusive universalism" that lies behind both the poet's "modern" vision of the new Israel and the post-Pauline disavowal upon which that vision depends.

NOTES

1. Scriptural quotations are cited from the American Bible Society edition of the Authorized (King James) Version of 1611.
2. Paul Stevens, "'Leviticus Thinking' and the Rhetoric of Early Modern Colonialism," *Criticism* 35 (1993): 441.

3. Linda Gregerson, "Colonials Write the Nation: Spenser, Milton, and England on the Margins," in *Milton and the Imperial Vision*, ed. Balachandra Rajan and Elizabeth Sauer (Pittsburgh: Duquesne University Press, 1999), 169.
4. In *Of Reformation*, *CPW* 1:525, Milton, alluding to Matthew 5:14, hails England as the first nation to "set up a Standard for the recovery of *lost Truth*, and blow the first *Evangelick Trumpet* to the *Nations*, holding up as from a Hill, the new Lampe of *saving light* to all Christendome."
5. Janet Adelman, *Suffocating Mothers: Fantasies of Maternal Origin in Shakespeare's Plays from "Hamlet" to "The Tempest"* (New York: Routledge, 1992), 29.
6. Robert Cleaver and John Dod, *A Godly Form of Household Government: For the Ordering of Private Families, according to the Direction of God's Word* (London, 1621), sig. P4r.
7. William Gouge, *Of Domesticall Duties. Eight Treatises* (London, 1622), 509.
8. Cleaver and Dod, *A Godly Form of Household Government*, sig. P4r.
9. *Ibid.*, sig. P4r–v.
10. Ruth Perry, "Colonizing the Breast: Sexuality and Maternity in Eighteenth-Century England," *Eighteenth-Century Life* 16 (1992): 185.
11. Thomas Vicary, *The Anatomie of the Bodie of Man*, issue of 1548 as reissued by the Surgeons of St. Bartholomews in 1577, ed. Frederick J. Furnivall and Percy Furnivall (London: Early English Texts Society, 1888), 55. On Galenic theories of sex and reproduction, see Thomas Laqueur, *Making Sex: Body and Gender from the Greeks to Freud* (Cambridge, MA: Harvard University Press, 1990), esp. pp. 25, 37, 38, 171–4.
12. Kathryn Schwarz, "Missing the Breast: Desire, Disease, and the Singular Effect of Amazons," in *The Body in Parts: Fantasies of Corporeality in Early Modern Europe*, ed. David Hillman and Carla Mazzio (New York and London: Routledge, 1992), p. 147.
13. Perry, "Colonizing the Breast," 185.
14. Stephen Greenblatt, "Mutilation and Meaning," in *The Body in Parts*, 230–31.
15. See "complexion," *OED*, entry 4, which dates the term's first reference to "the natural colour, texture, and appearance of the skin, *esp.* of the face" to 1568.
16. Cleaver and Dod, *A Godly Form of Household Government*, sig. P4r.
17. James Guillimeau, *The Nursing of Children. Wherein is set downe, the ordering and gouernment of them, from their birth; affixed to Childbirth, of the Happie Deliverie of Women* (London, 1612), Preface, 1.i.2.
18. See Rachel Trubowitz, "Cross-Dressed Women and Natural Mothers: 'Boundary Panic' in *Hic Mulier*," in *Debating Gender in Early Modern England, 1500–1700*, ed. Christina Malcolmson and Mihoko Suzuki (New York: Palgrave Macmillan, 2002), 185–208.
19. David Leverenz, *The Language of Puritan Feeling: An Exploration in Literature, Psychology, and Social History* (New Brunswick: Rutgers University Press, 1980), 19.

20. Janel Mueller, "Dominion as Domesticity: Milton's Imperial God and the Experience of History," in *Milton and the Imperial Vision*, ed. Rajan and Sauer, 42–45.
21. Jacqueline T. Miller, "Mother Tongues: Language and Lactation in Early Modern Literature," *ELR* 27.2 (1997): 192.
22. Elizabeth Clinton, *The Countess of Lincolns Nursery* (London, 1622), quoted in Marilyn Yalom, *A History of the Breast* (New York: Knopf, 1997), 85. For commentary on Clinton and mothers' advice books, see Valerie Wayne, "Advice For Women From Mothers and Patriarchs," in *Women and Literature in Britain, 1500–1700*, ed. Helen Wilcox (Cambridge: Cambridge University Press, 1996), 56–79.
23. Cited in William Manchester, *A World Lit Only By Fire* (Boston: Little Brown, 1992), 68.
24. *The Political Works of James I* (reprinted from the 1616 edition), ed. Charles Howard McIlwain (Cambridge, MA: Harvard University Press, 1918), 25.
25. Cited in Claire Cross, "The Church in England, 1646–1660," in *The Interregnum: The Quest for Settlement*, ed. G. E. Aylmer (Hamden, CT: Archon – Shoe String Press, 1972), 120.
26. For the "maternal" implications of Charles I's royal image, see Anne Baynes Coiro, "'A ball of strife': Caroline Poetry and Royal Marriage," in *The Royal Image: Representations of Charles I*, ed. Thomas N. Corns (Cambridge: Cambridge University Press, 1999), 26.
27. Readers generally see Manoa as a limited thinker and false redeemer. For two especially interesting readings of Manoa as limited by his desire to simplify the complexities and rationalize the indeterminacies of his son's life, see Dayton Haskin, *Milton's Burden of Interpretation*, 141, and Stanley Fish, "Spectacle and Evidence in *Samson Agonistes*," *Critical Inquiry* 15 (1989): 556–86. By contrast, Jeffrey Shoulson argues that Manoa is a Christ-like figure in *Milton and the Rabbis: Hebraism, Hellenism, and Christianity* (New York: Columbia University Press, 2001), 250.
28. Sharon Achinstein, "*Samson Agonistes* and the Drama of Dissent," *Milton Studies* 33 (1996): 146.
29. Michael Ragussis, *Figures of Conversion: "The Jewish Question" and English National Identity* (Durham: Duke University Press, 1995), 91.
30. *Ibid.*, 91–92.
31. Stevens, "'Leviticus Thinking' and the Rhetoric of Early Modern Colonialism," 442.
32. Achsah Guibbory, *Ceremony and Community from Herbert to Milton: Literature, Religion, and Cultural Conflict in Seventeenth-Century England* (Cambridge: Cambridge University Press, 1998), 6, 181.
33. Elizabeth Sauer, "Religious Toleration and Imperial Intolerance," in *Milton and the Imperial Vision*, ed. Rajan and Sauer, 217–22.
34. Daniel Boyarin, "'This We Know to Be Carnal Israel': Circumcision and the Erotic Life of God and Israel," *Critical Inquiry* 18 (1992): 504–5.

35. James Holstun, *A Rational Millennium: Puritan Utopias of Seventeenth-Century England and America* (New York: Oxford University Press, 1987), 10.
36. See David Katz, *Philo-Semitism and the Readmission of the Jews to England, 1603–1655* (Oxford: Clarendon Press, 1982) chapter 4.
37. Holstun, *A Rational Millennium*, 111–15.
38. Boyarin, *Carnal Israel: Reading Sex in Talmudic Culture* (Berkeley: University of California Press, 1993), 6.
39. Gregerson, "Colonials Write the Nation," 169.

CHAPTER 10

"The Jewish Question" and "The Woman Question" in Samson Agonistes: gender, religion, and nation

Achsah Guibbory

Milton is England's most Hebraic writer and *Samson Agonistes* his most Hebraic work. Published in 1671 when Milton was living in seclusion – a prophet in a nation that had not followed his advice but had embraced the idolatry of monarchy and the Church of England – this closet drama retells the narrative from Judges in Restoration England, using the Hebrew Bible and Jewish history to understand England's recent experience and present moment.

Debates about *Samson Agonistes* have revolved around whether Samson is a hero, and whether or not the poem shows Samson's "regeneration." There has also been interest in the representation of woman and the feminine in *Samson Agonistes*, with some critics attempting to redeem Dalila from the misogynous charges voiced in the poem. I argue that Milton's Hebraism, his use of the Hebrew Bible, is inseparable from the representation of women and gender in the poem and the question of Samson's "heroism." In this drama about an "*Ebrew*" (*SA* 1319) raised to "deliver" "*Israel*" (39),[1] the "Woman question" is embedded in "The Jewish question," as Milton transforms the narrative from Judges in ways that devalue both the Israelites and women. Implying a parallel between Israel and England, Milton presents a "manly," muscular spirituality and an implicitly Christian liberty that are achieved only as Samson separates from the Israelites, Dalila, and what in the poem is marked as feminine, all of which Milton associates with bondage. As Samson distances himself from women, the feminine, and his Hebraic origins, he provides an exemplary model for Englishmen, gradually detaching himself also from the national ideal that had engaged Milton through the revolutionary period but, with its Israelite mythos and its appropriation by royalists, had become suspect in the Restoration.

Like many of the "godly," Milton understood England's contemporary experience in relation to Israelite history. This turn to the Hebrew Bible was encouraged by the Reformation sense that the biblical history of the Jews typologically described the experience of the Christian church, now liberated from the Babylonian captivity of Rome. The idea that the Christian church was the true "Israel," first defined by Paul (Romans 9, Galatians 3–5), held the possibility for both identification with and opposition to Israel "according to the flesh" (the Jews), whose biblical history could be appropriated.[2] For English Protestants, the Bible became a rich source of "experimental knowledge," and the "Old Testament" with its history of God's chosen people led to a complex identification of England with Israel.[3] Shared by royalists and supporters of the Church of England as well as Puritans, the identification of England with Israel involved a wide range of attitudes toward the Jews. Milton's attitudes were themselves ambivalent, complex, and shifting as he appropriated the history of the biblical Jews to understand his and England's experiences and repeatedly reassessed the relevance of Jewish precedent for Christians. For all his sense of connection with Israel's history and his own empathetic identification with the Hebrew prophets, there was, for Milton, no simple, positive equation of the English with the ancient Jews. Indeed, an anti-Judaic stance, grounded in the idea of the Jews as a "backsliding people," was part of Milton's sense of England's Israelite identity, and his parallels between England and ancient Israel were often, and increasingly, negative.[4]

The category of the "Jews" was slippery in early modern England, in part because (as James Shapiro has shown) Christians were worried about "turning Jew," relapsing into a condition from which Christians had supposedly progressed, much as early modern men feared relapsing into an ontologically prior but imperfect condition and becoming womanish.[5] "Jew" was a difficult, slippery category in other ways too. When Paul tried to answer the question, "who is Israel, inheritor of the promises in the Hebrew Bible," he distinguished Christian "Israel" from the Jews (Israel "of the flesh" [Rom. 9:8]), even though he held out hope that some of them would be "grafted in." Paul, that is, separated Israel of the "spirit" (Christians) from the "Jews," who were represented as being slavishly bound to "the law," even when they strayed into idolatry in the wilderness or Canaan, or embraced rabbinic traditions. Yet, despite Paul's distinction, reinforced by centuries of Christian anti-Judaic polemic, the category "Jew" was not nearly as firm as we might think, particularly since the habit of drawing analogies between Christian England and biblical Israel could produce a sense of identification with ancient Jews and erode distinctions between "Israel" and "Jews." In early modern English usage, "Israelites," "Hebrews," and "Jews" were all synonyms (*OED*), albeit with slight differences – "Hebrews" referring to people descended from Abraham, "Israelites" signifying descendants of

Jacob/Israel to whom God had given a special blessing or covenant, and "Jews" emphasizing religious identity, particularly as distinguished from "Christians." Technically, the term "Jew" (from the Hebrew *Yehudi*) referred to those from the tribe of Judah or those in the southern kingdom of Judah, who were taken into Babylon and later returned to Jerusalem. Yet in early modern England (as now) the term was also used broadly and retrospectively to refer to all those (both the biblical "Israelites" and later people) who accepted the covenant of the Mosaic laws. Although Milton uses "Israelites" in speaking of the ancient, biblical people, he also uses "Jews" in this broader sense. Particularly when Milton urges a specifically religious, Christian perspective, the "Israelites" are "Jews" – and this is crucial to our understanding of Milton's invocations of Israelite precedent in his prose, and our interpretation of *Samson Agonistes*.

In his polemical prose during the civil war period, Milton regularly invoked characters and incidents from the Hebrew Bible. His comparisons of Charles and the royalists to Israel's enemies implicitly identified the godly with ancient Israel. Charles was Agag, king of the Amalekite enemies of Israel against whom God declared continual war (*Tenure of Kings and Magistrates*, *CPW* 3:215; cf. I Samuel 15; Ex. 17:16), and also Pharaoh (*Eikonoklastes*, *CPW* 3:509–10, 516, 573; cf. Ex. 1–15).[6] To fight against such a heathenish enemy was noble – and recalled the deeds of Ehud and others from Judges who had killed tyrannical kings with God's approval (*Tenure* 3:312; *Defence of the English People* 4.i:401). England's liberation from the tyranny of Charles and the prelacy was like the deliverance of the Israelites from Egypt (*Eikonoklastes* 3:580; *Tenure* 3:193; *Defence* 4.i:305).

Milton's Israelite parallels during the revolutionary period invest England with the status of God's chosen people, and suggest how important the appropriation of the Hebrew Bible and biblical Jewish history was in the formation of the early modern English nation.[7] With the tyrant dead and the idolatrous prelates ousted, England seemed a chosen nation like Israel, favored by God, the new, spiritual (Christian) Israel standing on the edge of a glorious future, and delivered by heroes raised up by God. Milton's analogies identify the English with the Israelites, newly entered into Canaan and beginning to establish their nation. Yet as the establishment of the godly kingdom receded further from likelihood in the 1650s and the English appeared inclined to servility and monarchy, they seemed to Milton more like those Israelites in Judges who, having entered Canaan, served "other gods" and threw away the opportunities for deliverance accorded by their heroes. Despite the invocation of precedents from the Hebrew Bible and his own strong identification with inspired prophets like Moses, Milton's parallels between England and the Israelites become increasingly negative, particularly after the success of *Eikon Basilike*, the immensely popular "king's book" published in 1649.

Milton echoed the diatribes of the Hebrew prophets against the apostacy of the Israelites in Canaan as he attacked this "ungratefull and pervers generation" (*Eikonoklastes*, *CPW* 3:346), who idolized the dead king. If after their miraculous "deliverance" the English people would seek a king, they would be like the "foolish *Israelites*, who [after their deliverance from Egypt] depos'd God and *Samuel* to set up a King" (3:580). They "would shew themselves to be by nature slaves, and errant beasts," "fit to be led back again into thir old servitude" (3:581). Reading the narrative from Exodus through the books of Samuel (in which the Davidic monarchy is established) as a record of Jewish idolatry, stupidity, and perversity, Milton interprets Israel's request for a king and the establishment of monarchy as a defection from God. His recurrent and growing fear is that the English in their desire for a restored monarchy will repeat the history of the biblical Jews.

From *Eikonoklastes* on, Milton's comparisons between the English and the Israelites are devastating and undermine the patriotic dreams of nationhood evident in Milton's prose of the earlier 1640s.[8] The identification of the English with ancient Israel is fraught with ambivalence, since Milton imagines the Jews (both in biblical times and later) as "naturally" servile and disposed to slavery. A similar view of the English dominates Milton's *History of Britain* (1670), raising the possibility that liberty and slavishness might be innate and ethnic rather than learned or chosen conditions. His first *Defence* (1651) suggests a disposition to slavery in Jews, citing "our most reliable authorities" Aristotle and Cicero who wrote that "the peoples of Asia readily endure slavery, while the Jews and Syrians are born for it" (4.i:343). Milton's identification with the ancient Hebrew prophets also enables his attack on the Jews, since the prophets criticized Israel for backsliding and idolatry, even for being a wayward people "from the womb" (Isaiah 48:8). It was, indeed, the prophets' criticism of Israel's failings that made them so amenable to anti-Jewish uses by Christians. For Milton, English and Christian liberty is defined against the supposed Jewish affinity for bondage.

There were various possible ways to think about the relation of Christians and Jews, of Christianity and Judaism, in seventeenth-century England, and some people – including Milton – could at times emphasize the continuity and shared values rather than discontinuities. Yet Milton's increasing worries about the apostasy of the English found expression in Israelite analogies that marked the Jews as an example to be avoided even as the analogies indicted the English for their moral failure.

The Restoration confirmed Milton's fear that the English were indeed like the Jews. Published on the eve of the Restoration in a last-minute effort to avert the disaster of a restored monarchy, *The Readie and Easie Way* uses a powerful set of analogies. Ready to restore Charles II, the English are like the ancient Jews in Canaan who rejected the rule of God and his judges/prophets and abandoned the dream of a free Commonwealth – "held by wisest men in all ages the noblest, the manliest," the "most agreeable to all due libertie" and "most cherishing to true religion," and thus "enjoind by our Saviour himself to all Christians" (7:424). Alluding also to a later period of Israelite history, Milton's Jeremiad echoes the ancient prophet's attack on those Jews in Babylon who, longing for peace and plenty, wanted to return to Egypt and "burn incense to the queen of heaven" – an idolatrous Egyptian practice of the Jewish "women" indulged by their husbands (Jer. 42:9–22; 44:15–29). To Milton, the English, who "seem now chusing them a captain back for Egypt" (7:463), are like those Jews who, repeating their wilderness apostasy (Exodus 16:1–3; 32), wanted "to return back to Egypt and to the worship of their idol queen" (7:462) the fertility goddess to whom the "wives" of Judah idolatrously "burned incense" so that they would have "plenty" (Jer. 44:17–19).[9] Milton's gendered language makes clear what has been assumed all along but will be foregrounded in *Samson* – that Christians are identified with liberty, wisdom, nobility, and manliness, whereas the Jews are associated with baseness, foolishness, and subjection to women and the feminine. Recalling Jeremiah's warning of the curse that would overtake the apostate Jews, Milton threatens the English that if they "creep back" to the "thraldom of kingship" (7:422), they will lose their status as God's chosen people and their masculine liberty, and share in the Jews' fate.

The heir of a long tradition of Christian hermeneutic that revised the texts of the Jewish prophets to create a Christian church in "*antithetical relation* to an apostate Israel,"[10] Milton reads the Hebrew Bible from a Christian, Pauline perspective, even as he identifies with the prophets and looks to the ancient Jews to understand England's experience. The Hebrew Bible becomes for Milton the record of a "chosen" people who prepared the way for (and thus were connected with) the Christian church, but who also stubbornly rejected Christ as their savior, preferring the Mosaic law which, in Paul's formulation, was a covenant of bondage, from which Christians have been freed (Galatians 4–5.) As a collective, Milton's Jews are always on the verge of becoming like the gentiles, sinking into bondage, slavery, and idolatry. Yet there are those rare, exemplary heroes like Ehud whose instincts and acts of liberty separate them from their fellow Jews. These heroes are, one could say, like the remnant of Israel whom the Hebrew prophets said would eventually be saved, only here they are saved even before the advent of Christ from what Paul called Jewish bondage – thus providing an important precedent for the hero of *Samson Agonistes*.

Women seem to have had no positive role in Milton's imagining of England's liberty. As the Christian liberty England aspires to is noble and "manly," it is defined against the slavishness of the Jews, who in their bondage are implicitly associated with the feminine, in so far as Milton characteristically represents bondage as unmasculine, effeminate, a submission to one's lower, most irrational, appetites. In *Samson Agonistes*, this web of associations is made explicit, as both Samson's bondage and his "reviving libertie" (*Readie* 7:463) are defined in relation to England, the Jews, and women.

Samson's developing heroism requires his gradual rejection of apostate Israel and the Jews as well as women and what Milton represents as the feminine.[11] True to his source in Judges, Milton never uses the term "Jew" in *Samson Agonistes* (the Hebrew equivalent does not appear until the later biblical books). Samson is referred to as an "Ebrew," his fellow countrymen as "Danites" (list of "The Persons"), "Judah" (265), "Israel" (240, 454), and "Ebrews" (1308). Yet, from the Christian perspective that shapes Milton's poem, Samson and those from the tribes of Dan and Judah are "Jews"; they are under Mosaic Law. To dramatize Samson's emerging Christian liberty, Milton makes Samson a different sort of Jew than Manoa and the Chorus. Eventually divested of the feminine as well as the bondage of the Jews and Mosaic Law, Samson can become a fit ancestor for English Christians. Much as Samson progressively separates himself from his fellow Jews, Milton distances himself from Israel and from England, even while identifying himself with a Hebrew prophet or "messenger" of God.

Samson's condition at the beginning of the drama mirrors Israel's servitude to the Philistines. Ensnared by Dalila (230, 931), he has succumbed to his own version of what Judges calls the "snares" of idolatry that have captivated Israel (2:3). Like Israel, Samson is in captivity, and his bitter recognition that he deserves it because of his idolatrous, sinful ways echoes the refrain in Judges that God has delivered the Israelites over to their Canaanite enemies because they have betrayed him and departed from his ways to serve other gods.

Milton criticism has, understandably, viewed Samson as an "Israelite."[12] However, if Samson is like Israel in the opening scene, his challenge is to become *unlike* Israel, to free himself from idolatry and the bondage that attends the apostate nation. In *The Readie and Easie Way*, Milton insisted that if England returned to monarchy, she would permanently fall out of God's favor, but *Samson Agonistes* is a story about second chances. Samson gets the opportunity to repair his mistakes, to conquer the disposition to effeminate idolatry that has landed him in prison. Insofar as Samson is inwardly and outwardly in bondage, he is the mirror of Israel. It is only as he distances himself from Israel's condition of bondage by detaching himself from unfaithful Israel – as he becomes *unlike* Israel – that Samson proves himself a hero of God, an exemplary pattern the English Christians can follow.

Samson in his state of captivity and despair is a symbol of both Israel and England – once God's chosen but now in bondage to the "forein" rule of a king, now that Charles has been imported from France. Milton implicitly identifies Philistine rule with Charles II's monarchy and the worship of Dagon with the reestablished Church of England.[13] Samson's opening speeches voice not only his own but Israel's misery, having fallen from her former glory into shameful servitude, "debas't / Lower than bondslave" (ll. 37–38). His condition is exactly what Milton had predicted would be England's fate if monarchy were restored. The English would show themselves "spiritless and weak" after having "performed so many brave deeds" (*Defence* 4.i:532); they would be "brought into . . . bondage" as "slaves" and exhibit an unprecedented "ignominie" (*Readie* 7:428; cf. *Eikonoklastes* 3:580–81).

Milton's picture of Samson at the beginning of the drama recalls the warning in *The Readie and Easie Way* that England would become "a scorn and derision" to her "enemies" (422) – a warning that had echoed Jeremiah's prophecy that the Jews who returned to Egypt would be "an astonishment" and "a reproach" (Jer. 42:18). It also recalls the Hebrew prophets' descriptions of Jerusalem, conquered by Babylonians in 587 BCE. Samson's figure evokes the devastated city, symbol of Judaea, described in Lamentations: "How doth the city sit solitary, that was full of people! how is she become as a widow! that was great among the nations . . . how is she become tributary" (1:1). Milton's allusion to Lamentations in this opening dialogue – a crucial addition to Judges – turns Samson into a symbol for Israel, fallen into Babylonian captivity, and, implicitly, for Restoration England. As in the Hebrew Bible, captivity is punishment for apostasy from God. In his isolation and mourning, his sense of abandonment, Samson embodies the defeat, captivity, and desolation of biblical Jerusalem and the analogous fate of which Milton had warned England. Samson's lament – "I dark in light expos'd / to daily fraud, contempt, abuse and wrong," (75–76); "my enemies . . . come to stare / At my affliction, and perhaps to insult" (112–13) – recalls Ezekiel's warning that Jerusalem would become "a reproach among the nations" (Ez. 5:14).

Samson is identified with the figure of Israel described by the prophets as a widowed bride who has broken her covenant with God and thus been abandoned. Yet Milton intensifies and complicates Samson's association with the feminine in the early part of *Samson Agonistes* in ways that go well beyond the prophets. In his bondage to the Philistines, Samson is impotent and feminized, though he insists that his "grinding" in the mill is not "so base / as was my former servitude, ignoble, / Unmanly" (415–17). Throughout his polemical prose, Milton regularly associated the condition of bondage with submission to the feminine, either within man or embodied in a woman. *Eikonoklastes* ridiculed the king's uxorious submission to his Catholic wife (3:420–22), a double subjection to popish idolatry and the rule of a woman.[14] For the English to submit to Stuart rule was a loss of manly liberty, an intensification of the power of the feminine in England. Milton's characteristic depiction in his prose of the feminine as further removed from God, and of subjection to women and the feminine as a betrayal of God, is echoed in Samson's bitter lament that he has lost his manhood by divulging his secret to Dalila.

Women have a far more positive role in Judges, even in the Samson story, than in Milton's version. One of the most significant changes Milton makes to the Judges account of Samson is the erasure of Samson's mother. In Judges, though Samson's mother has no name, twice God's messenger appears to her, announcing she will bear a son who will be a Nazarite (13:3–21). The angel tells her she must obey the food and wine prohibitions so that he will be a Nazarite "from the womb," her purity insuring his as he absorbs his identity through her. Milton, however, takes away the special privilege the Hebrew Bible accords Samson's mother. He collapses her into Samson's "Parents" (25), expanding the role of Manoa. Whereas women in Judges have as much access to God as men and are instrumental in the deliverance of Israel, Milton, as Julia Walker puts it, exiles "the women of Israel from the narrative of his Samson."[15] Milton erases the mother from the narrative and genders the bondage of idolatry as feminine and effeminizing.

The Chorus describes Samson as lying "With languish't head unpropt," "In slavish habit" (120, 123) – a striking image of impotency. Seemingly "abandon'd" (121), unsupported by God, he no longer has the masculine erectness and strength that comes from depending on God rather than

Dalila, who has made him weak and womanish. Samson bitterly complains that he could not keep his secret "But weakly to a woman must reveal it, / O'ercome with importunity and tears" (50–51). In the act of betraying God and his godly identity, Samson has become more like a woman. He feels a special shame that recalls Milton's comment in the first *Defence* that for a husband to be ruled by a wife is "the most shameful and unmanly form of slavery" (4.i:471). Echoing Milton's descriptions of woman as "inferior" in the "inward Faculties" (*PL* 7:541–42), as not created to "rule" (*Defence* 4.i:471), Samson sees himself as defective in "wisdom" (*SA* 53–54), as "not made to rule" (56) – in other words, as like a woman. He lacked even a "grain of manhood" (408). His desire for Dalila is his "foul effeminacy" which "held me yok't / Her Bondslave" (410–11). This effeminacy is not just his own. As Samson in his bondage and weakness is representative of the Israelites, his effeminacy is transferred to them.

In order to regain his manly strength and become reconnected to God, Samson must separate himself from the Philistine Dalila and an idolatry marked as feminine; he also must detach himself from Israel and the Jews. To the extent that Israel figures England, Milton is giving up on England, turning from hopes of national deliverance to focus on a personal, individual connection with God demonstrated in revolutionary acts that offer opportunities for deliverance to other individuals who must each enact a similar separation from idolatry.

Samson's first speech recalls the promise that he "Should *Israel* from *Philistian* yoke deliver" (39). He thinks of himself as Israel's "Deliverer" (40) and speaks of Israel as his "Nation" (565). Yet in his discussion with the Chorus, Samson detaches himself from the Israelites, casting them off as unworthy of deliverance, much as the Son does in *Paradise Regained* (3:403–41). When the Chorus says that "*Israel* still serves" (240) despite Samson's efforts to "begin *Israel's* Deliverance" (225), Samson refuses to take "That fault ... on me" (241) but blames "*Israel's* Governors, and Heads of Tribes" (242) who did not take advantage of the "Deliverance offer'd" (246). Samson's criticism of Israel again voices Milton's of England, whose leaders in 1660 failed to take advantage of the glorious acts performed for their deliverance. Samson's comment that "they persisted deaf" (249) specifically echoes Milton's complaint at the end of *The Readie and Easie Way* that he is speaking to the "deaf," "perverse" English (7:463). Samson indicts the English when he speaks of how they "love Bondage more than Liberty" (270).

Samson's words indicting his fellow Israelites do double duty, for, like the negative Israelite analogies in Milton's prose, they indict the English but also specifically mark the Jews as a people deserving of bondage, a people incapable of liberty, unworthy of imitation, a people whose rejection of their deliverers points toward their rejection of Christ. Milton's version of the story from Judges adds a new, Christian emphasis on the Israelites' rejection of their deliverers, absent in the biblical source. Although Hugh MacCallum has suggested that Milton's dramatization of Judges scrupulously avoids including material from later Israelite and Christian history, Milton subtly but insistently presents the story from a distinctly Christian, Pauline perspective.[16] He reads Judges through Paul, through the New Testament, defining the Israelites (and not just the English) as, generally, a people of bondage incapable of recognizing deliverers. Milton's Samson emphasizes the treachery of the "men of *Judah*" (256) in a way that makes it characteristic of the Israelites, who are said to "despise, or envy, or suspect / Whom God hath of his special favor rais'd / As thir Deliverer" (272–74). We witness a slippage between Judah, the Israelites, and the later Jews, for this single incident becomes generalized into a flaw of the Jews, whose rejection of Christ (never mentioned, but alluded to in lines 245–49, 279, 1213–16) is the culmination of a series of episodes in which they reject their saviors and choose bondage over liberty.

Thus if Samson in one sense identifies himself as the deliverer of Israel and an Israelite, in another he separates himself from the Jews. This double relation to the Jews parallels Milton's own, as Milton identifies with the Hebrew prophets even as he castigates the English for being like the Jews. Samson insists to Dalila that when he married her he was not the "subject" of the Philistines (886), even though Israel was under Philistine rule. Speaking to Harapha, he again detaches himself from the servile condition of the Israelites, insisting that he is different, and that he is not responsible for them. When Harapha taunts him, "Is not thy Nation subject to our Lords?" (1182), Samson's reply resonates with Christian and contemporary significance, echoing Milton's comments in his prose as it condemns both the Jews and the Israelitish English: "if their servile minds / Me their Deliverer sent would not receive, / But to thir Masters gave me up for nought, / Th'unworthier they; whence to this day they serve" (1213–16). Samson's growing detachment from the Israelites, even as he proclaims his loyalty to "*Israel's* God" (1150), suggests the doubleness of Milton's attitude toward the Jews – a people of bondage, incapable of Christian liberty, although some of their history and male heroes are recuperable for Christian purposes. Samson's detachment from the Israelites is a necessary step in his "regeneration"; it will make him an exceptional hero and thus exemplary for England in 1671.

His separation is already implicit when Samson rejects his father's offer to bring him "Home to thy country" (518). The Manoa episode, like the visit of Dalila, is Milton's addition to Judges. Manoa offers a false, "carnal" notion of liberty, believing that he can buy Samson's freedom; he also functions as the earthly, corporeal father whom Samson leaves behind for the divine, untying the bonds of Jewish genealogy. When Samson insists he does not want to sit "idle on the household hearth" (565–66), "preferring strenuous liberty" (271), he identifies Manoa's offer with the effeminating "ease" (271) that Milton regularly associates with bondage, and differentiates himself from both the ancient Israelites and the contemporary English. Samson's Jewish father himself is, notably, feminized, through his offer of domestic ease, which is a counterpart to the life of sensuality that Dalila will offer in the next scene.

The rejection of Dalila is crucial to Samson's recovery of his status as God's hero.[17] In the course of *Samson Agonistes*, the Jewish idea of the Nazarite as "separate to God" (31) is transformed to mean separate from the Jews and from women. Samson's fall from his former glory is the result of having betrayed God, having turned to serve his own effeminizing sensuality and Dalila. In order to become reconnected with God and regain his status of God's hero, he must resist her renewed temptation.

Though some modern readers have argued that Dalila is a sympathetic figure, Milton clearly depicts her as a figure of idolatry. Entering the poem, "Bedeckt, ornate, and gay" (712), she evokes the "Whore of Babylon," identified by Protestants with the Church of Rome, and also the seductive, ceremonial "gay shows" (*The Reason of Church Government [RCG]*, 1:766) of the recently restored English church, whose ceremonies were troped as the "garments" or "clothes" of worship (see, e.g., *Of Reformation* 1:557; cf. *RCG* 1:828). With her "Amber scent of odorous perfume" (720), reminiscent of the incense used in the English as well as Roman Church, Dalila is a contemporarily inflected symbol of the "other gods" in Judges who lead "the children of Israel" to forsake God (e.g., Judges 2:3, 11–12). She thus embodies a heathen idolatry that poses an ongoing, seductive threat to Samson, the Israelites, and the English.[18] Yet Milton also identifies that idolatry with the religion of the Jews. Her splendor and sumptuousness recall Milton's description in *The Reason of Church Government* of the "sumptuous things under the [Jewish] law" which contrast with the "inward beauty and splendor of the Christian church" (1:758), "sumptuous things" which have no place in Christian worship. As he explains, "that which was to the Jew but Jewish is to the Christian no better than Canaanitish" (*RCG*, 1:845). The "Jewish" is here identified with Canaanite idolatry; both constitute bondage that the Christian must cast off. In distancing himself from the Israelites and divorcing Dalila, Samson is thus, in Milton's sense, acting like a Christian.

Dalila embodies the twinned seductions of false religion and monarchy. Moving "Like a stately Ship," with a "damsel train" behind her, she is regal. Attractive, "Courted" even by all the winds, Dalila's allure is powerful: she offers Samson a life of sensual "ease" (917) that appeals to his sexual desire even as it speaks to the supposed Israelite and English preference for "peace and slavery with inaction and comfort upon any terms" (*Defence* 4.i:518; cf. *Readie*, 7:462). We should recall that Milton associated the Stuart monarchy with the bondage of feminine rule (*Eikonoklastes* 3:420). Whereas Samson in his earlier intimacy with Dalila subjected himself to "Feminine usurpation," his rejection of Dalila's offer to return "home," his refusal to live "uxorious to thy will / In perfect thraldom" (945–46), corrects his error and asserts his authority. As Dalila embodies and genders the lure of idolatry and monarchy, Samson in vigorously rejecting her temptation and subduing his effeminating desires proves that he is "manly," godly, and free. Samson's divorce from Dalila is the necessary step for his renewed sense of the divine presence, the turning point in his regaining his "manly" identity and liberty.

As Dalila is a Philistine, loyal to Dagon, she is the antithesis of the Jews, signifying the opposition between true religion and idolatry that structures Milton's poem, but she is also a mirror of the Jews. Her treachery recalls the "men of *Judah*" (256) who also betrayed Samson. Dalila herself draws the analogy when in her final speech she compares her heroism to that of Jael, Israel's heroine:

> in my country where I most desire . . .
> I shall be nam'd among the famousest
> Of Women, . . .
> Not less renown'd than in Mount *Ephraim*,
> *Jael*, who with inhospitable guile
> Smote *Sisera* sleeping through the Temples nail'd.
> (980, 982–83, 988–90)

Dalila's speech not only suggests heroism is relative; it also contaminates *Israelite* heroism, associating it with treachery.

Dalila's speech also functions to call into question the idea of devotion to one's nation. The anachronism of Milton's concern with nation in *Samson Agonistes* has not been appreciated. As Milton well knew, Judges records a period when the Israelites were still a group of tribes, though bound by a shared covenant with God. National community, promised in the covenant at Sinai (Ex. 19:5–6), was a promise for a distant future, not fully realized until David's and Solomon's kingdom was established much later in Canaan (2 Samuel, 1 Kings). Milton's repeated references in *Samson* to the "nation" of Israel collapse the time when Israel was under Philistine rule with the "nation" of the later Israelite kingdom. Milton's dangerous implication is that England under the restored Stuart monarchy is like Israel in bondage under the Philistines.

As Dalila voices the patriotic concern with fame that Milton had earlier in his prose, we see Milton backing away from the idea of nation. By 1671, the idea of nation, as it was grounded on identification with Israel, had become largely the property of royalists, who used it to legitimate and celebrate the restoration of monarchy and the church. Poems by Dryden, Waller, Cowley, and others celebrating the Restoration claimed Israelite analogies and providential favor just as the revolutionaries had during the preceding decades. Sermons greeted Charles II's return as a miraculous "deliverance" of God's chosen nation and elaborated on the Israelite parallels.[19] For many royalists, the reunited kingdom of England was another Israel, restored to peace and stability under the king.

This Restoration context, I believe, explains why *Samson Agonistes* seems wary of the idea of England as nation. As nation is linked with Israel, Philistia, Jael, and Dalila, it is tainted by its association with women, idolatry, and Jews. Yet the dream of nation seems hard for Samson to give up, as it apparently was for Milton. Near the end of the poem, Samson again refers to "my Nation" (1205) and "my Country" (1212). He now, however, understands himself not primarily as Israel's "Deliverer" (1214) but as the "Champion" (1152) of "*Israel's* God" (1150). This is an important shift. In his exchange with Harapha, he asserts his connection with God – "my trust is in the living God" (1140). The language is Hebraic, but as Samson has detached himself from his people, his father, and his wife, his sentiment actually echoes Christ's teaching that "If any man come to me, and hate not his father, and mother, and wife, and children, and brethren, and sisters, yea, and his own life also, he cannot be my disciple" (Luke 14:26). Reflecting as well Milton's disillusion with the English, Samson's focus, increasingly centered on God, shifts from the liberation of others and of his "nation" to his personal, individual relation with God and his public defense of God, no matter what the consequences.

By the end of the poem, Samson has attained a liberty and spirituality that in Milton's thinking is manly, un-Jewish, and implicitly Christian. It is Paul, and especially Galatians 4–5:1, that illuminates Milton's transformation of the Hebrew Samson into an example fit for individual English Christians – and helps us understand why that transformation is grounded on the double, linked rejection of Jewish identity and the feminine. We might see an analogy between Milton's Samson and Saul/Paul, who was moved by God to embrace a new spiritual liberty that set him at a distance from his fellow Jews. As an apostle of Christ attacking the insufficiency of the Mosaic Law yet acknowledging that he, too, is an "Israelite," a "Hebrew" (2 Cor. 11:22; Romans 11:1) who had been circumcised (Philippians 3:5), Paul's relation to Judaism and the Jews is complex.[20] Yet the Pauline texts formulated an influential opposition between Christian liberty (identitified with grace and spirit) and the "bondage" of the Mosaic Law and Judaic practices (identified with works and the flesh). Addressed to recent pagan converts to Christianity, the epistle to Galatians insisted that one did not need to accept Judaism to be a Christian. Though historically Paul's concern was to differentiate between two competing models of Christianity and to welcome gentile converts, the effect was to promote a Christianity more firmly separated from its Jewish roots.

Milton turned to this epistle in *The Reason of Church Government* to explain why the English church must separate from "Judaick law" (1:764) if it wished to avoid falling into "deadly apostacy" (1:766). Recalling Paul's identification of the Jewish with the carnal and the feminine, Milton remarked how the "carnall" "ministery" (1:766) of the Mosaic Law, with its "pompe and glory of the flesh" (1:766), "engendered to bondage the sons of *Agar*" (1:765). The reference is to Galatians 4:24 – 5:1, which formulates the relation between Christians and their Jewish ancestry in gendered terms relevant to *Samson Agonistes*.[21]

In this epistle, Paul addresses the Galatians, who were being urged by some Jewish Christians to be circumcised. Seeking to convince the Christian Galatians they need not adopt Jewish ritual practices, Paul contrasts the "children" of Israel, "in bondage" (Gal. 4:3) under the Law, with those redeemed by Christ, who have become "sons" of God (Gal. 4:5–7), a sign of their manly maturity. Not only is the Galatians' desire to embrace the Mosaic Law seen as a reversion to their former pagan mentality, but the Law is identified with the feminine, cast off to produce a specifically masculine Christian liberty. The "law" is the "woman," the mother, from whom Christ frees people (in Paul's logic) by having himself been born of a woman: "when the fulness of the time was come, God sent forth his Son, made of a woman, made under the law, To redeem them that were under the law, that we might receive the adoption of sons" (Gal. 4:4–5). With Christ, we become "son[s]," "heir[s] of God" (Gal. 4:7). To dissuade the Galatians who want to return to the Law, Paul retells the story of Abraham's two sons and reinterprets Hebrew Scripture so as to condemn the Jewish covenant as a femininely marked bondage.

Paul contrasts Ishmael, son of "a bondwoman" and "born after the flesh," with Isaac, son of the "freewoman," born "by promise." The two sons, with their mothers, become an "allegory" for the "old" and "new" covenants: "the one from the mount Sinai, which gendereth to bondage, which is Agar. For this Agar is mount Sinai in Arabia, and answereth to Jerusalem which now is, and is in bondage with her children. But Jerusalem which is above is free, which is the mother of all . . . Now we, brethren, as Isaac was, are the children of promise" (Gal. 4:22–26, 28). In the Hebrew Bible, Isaac, the son of Sarah, inherited the covenant, while Ishmael was cast out into the desert. In Paul's reworking, which Milton follows, the Christians are the chosen (Isaac), displacing the Jews from their elect position. Though the "children" of "Agar" are those Christians who believe that they need to follow the Law to be redeemed, they are also the Jews, who believe that following the Law is enough, who reject salvation through Christ. The covenant of Sinai, identified with "Agar," is associated with both bondage and the woman, the mother. Sarah, Isaac's mother, disappears for the Christian "children of the promise," replaced by an invisible, spiritual mother, Jerusalem "above," which also replaces the material Jerusalem, center of the Jewish nation, captured and desecrated by the Romans in 70 CE. This passage from Galatians, cited repeatedly in chapter 26 of *De Doctrina Christiana* on Christian liberty (*CPW* 6:522, 525–27, 530), lies behind Milton's argument that to continue the "carnal ministry" of the Law in church worship and government is to return to a feminized, Jewish bondage. Paul's strategy in Galatians 4 also anticipates precisely Milton's erasure of Samson's mother and the movement away from "nation" as well as the identification of the feminine, the Jewish, and bondage in *Samson Agonistes*.

Paul speaks of his own conversion from Judaism as a separation from the maternal womb – "when it pleased God, who separated me from my mother's womb, and called me by his grace" (Gal. 1:13). Paul separates from his mother, linking her with the Law and his Jewish origin as he renounces his former Jewish identity. In *Samson Agonistes*, with its rejection of the feminine and its identification of women with bondage, Milton looks back to Paul, whose spirit inhabits Milton's Hebraic (but not philo-Judaic) poem and shapes the finally masculine spirituality of Samson.

Samson Agonistes, for all its debts to Greek tragedy, is Hebraic, but its Hebraism is distinctly Christian. The Hebrew Bible, like Samson, is converted. Seen from the vantage of Paul, whose formulation of the relation of Jewish and Christian identities stands behind the tropes and structure of Milton's poem, the nature of Samson's heroism becomes clearer. As Paul said, "if ye be led of the Spirit, ye are not under the law" (Gal. 5:18; cited also in *Christian Doctrine*, *CPW* 6:527, 531). The Hebrew prophets, too, had emphasized the importance of the spirit, but Paul's opposition of the spirit of grace to the fleshly works of the Law revised the prophets, who envisioned the integration of the law and spirit in the utopian end-times (e.g., Isaiah 56:7, 66; Ezekiel 40–48; Zechariah 14). Where the Hebrew prophets spoke of the "remnant" of Israel who would be saved (Isaiah 10:20–22; Micah 5:7–8; Jeremiah 31:7–11), Paul made it clear that that "remnant" (Rom. 11:5) would only be those Jews who move beyond the Law, who embrace Christ by faith. Samson is an "Ebrew" who moves beyond the Law to become a Christian before the fact, and thus someone who can serve as a model of spirituality for seventeenth-century Christian Englishmen living in a country where an idolatrous church, grounded in "dead Judaisms," has been restored along with a monarchy, whose supposedly Jewish foundation masks its "gentile" roots. In such a situation, Milton implies, the only appropriate act of worship may be violent, apocalyptic iconoclasm.[22]

Some revisionist readers (notably Joseph Wittreich) have felt that Samson's violence at the end of Milton's closet drama marks him as irremediably Jewish, as un- or even anti-Christian, as still bound to a "carnal" religion. For Derek Wood, Samson exemplifies human life under the Old Testament "Law" – unregenerate, deprived of the light of the gospel and Christ. Yet I think Milton's reworking of Judges makes it clear that, by the end of the poem, the liberty Samson comes to represent is Christian liberty, even if it is never named as Christian.[23] Rejecting the "children of Israel" as incapable of freedom, the turn at the end of *Samson Agonistes* is to the (implicitly Christian) "sons" of Israel, with whom Samson now associates himself in defense of his God (1176) – sons (separated from the Jewish mother, as in Paul) for whom there may still be hope.

Samson has already shown his detachment from Mosaic Law in marrying outside of his "Tribe" (217) and "Nation" (218). Discussing these marriages, the Chorus's remark about how God sometimes suspends his laws (307–21) anticipates Samson's final transcendence of the Law. As Samson deliberates about whether to comply with the Philistine request to appear at their temple, his first thought that it would be "unclean" and a "sin" (1354–62) gives way to the idea that God "may dispense with me or thee / . . . For some important cause" (1377, 1379). The "dispense[ing]" turns out to be the dispensation of the Law, as Samson, feeling "rousing motions" (1382), comes to recognize that he can violate what seems "Our Law" (1386) without doing anything "impure" (1424). His departing words – "of me expect to hear / Nothing dishonorable, impure, unworthy / Our God, our Law, my

Nation, or myself" (1423–25) – reassure the Chorus while also suggesting that, in interpreting "our Law" according to the higher principle of the inward spirit, he is not breaking but fulfilling it (cf. *De Doctrina, CPW* 6:531). Samson's sudden change of mind shows he is no longer bound to the "carnal" Law but to a God who is invisible but communicates within.

The messenger who reports Samson's heroic death can only see him from the outside: "With . . . / . . . eyes fast fixt he stood, as one who pray'd, / Or some great matter in his mind revolv'd" (1636–38). Whereas the Hebrew Bible clearly says Samson prays to God, Milton's Israelite observer – like the Jews who Paul said could not see the spiritual truth – cannot see behind the veil (2 Corinthians 3:13–18), or apprehend Samson's inward, spiritual communion with God. The messenger, Manoa, the Danite Chorus – all at the end of the play reveal the limitations of their understanding even as they embrace Samson's heroism as offering an opportunity for deliverance and recognize that it is now up to "*Israel*" (1714) to "lay hold on this occasion" for liberty (1716). Manoa is still obsessed with worldly honor and shame, wanting to build a material "Monument" to his son (1734). The Chorus expresses a fatalism closer to Greek tragedy than to Jewish providentialism as they speak of Samson "tangl'd in the fold / Of dire necessity" (1664–65). Though they are not treacherous like the other Danites, neither are they regenerate. Rather they stand in a liminal place of possibility. They can only say that it is now up to "*Israel*" (1714) – and the masculinely gendered godly "remnant" of the English – to "lay hold on this occasion" for liberty (1716). Samson's violence in the name of religion is, surely, troubling to us. Yet the indirection of Milton's presentation of Samson's relation with God does not, I think, suggest uncertainty on Milton's part about whether Samson really is a hero of God.[24] Rather it signifies the gulf between, on the one hand, a liberated manly Samson and those few Englishmen who, retaining the seeds of Christian liberty, still might bring down the idolatrous temple and, on the other, the feminized Jews and their seventeenth-century English descendants, who in Milton's view are complicit in their bondage, disbarred from full vision of the truth, and probably incapable of freedom.

NOTES

1. I am indebted to Dayton Haskin, Paul Stevens, and Jason Rosenblatt for their comments on an earlier version of this chapter.
2. On the Pauline and patristic distinction between Israel "according to the flesh" and Israel according to the "spirit" (1 Corinthians 10:18), see Daniel Boyarin,

Carnal Israel: Reading Sex in Talmudic Culture (Berkeley: University of California Press, 1993) esp. chapter 1, 31–60.
3. On the sense of God's special covenant with England, see Christopher Hill, *The English Bible and the Seventeenth-Century Revolution* (London: Penguin, 1993) 264–83; Michael Fixler, *Milton and the Kingdoms of God* (London: Faber and Faber, 1964) 38–45, 76–106; and William Haller, *Foxe's Book of Martyrs and the Elect Nation* (London: Jonathan Cape, 1963). On "experimental reading," see Dayton Haskin, *Milton's Burden of Interpretation* (Philadelphia: University of Pennsylvania Press, 1994).
4. Christopher Hill, *Milton and the English Revolution* (New York: Viking Press, 1977), finds the analogy of Egyptian bondage a "favourite" with Milton and "a Puritan cliché" (206), but does not attend to the anti-Jewish implications of Milton's English/Israelite analogy. On Milton's negative parallels, see Achsah Guibbory, *Ceremony and Community from Herbert to Milton: Literature, Religion, and Cultural Conflict in Seventeenth-century England* (Cambridge: Cambridge University Press, 1998) 183–86. See Jason Rosenblatt, *Torah and Law in "Paradise Lost"* (Princeton: Princeton University Press, 1994), on tension between Hebraic and Pauline impulses in Milton's thinking.
5. James Shapiro, *Shakespeare and the Jews* (New York: Columbia University Press, 1996), esp. chapter 1, pp. 13–42. Thomas Laqueur, *Making Sex: Body and Gender from the Greeks to Freud* (Cambridge, MA: Harvard University Press, 1990), links the fear that men could "regress" into "effeminacy" (7) to the "one-sex model" dominant until the end of the seventeenth century.
6. Paul Stevens, "Milton's Janus-faced Nationalism: Soliloquy, Subject, and the Modern Nation State," *Journal of English and Germanic Philology* (*JEGP*) 100 (April, 2001): 268, observes that Milton represents "the perceived opponents" of England in "biblically derived terms of ethnic hatred."
7. See Stevens's "Milton's Janus-faced Nationalism," and "'Leviticus Thinking' and the Rhetoric of Early Modern Colonialism," *Criticism* 35 (1993): 441–61. On the place of the Jews in the formation of early modern English identity, see also Christopher Hill, "Till the Conversion of the Jews," in *The Collected Essays of Christopher Hill*, vol. 2 (Amherst: University of Massachusetts Press, 1986) 269–300; David S. Katz, *Philo-Semitism and the Readmission of the Jews to England 1603–1655* (Oxford: Clarendon, 1982); Rosenblatt, *Torah and Law*; Shapiro, *Shakespeare and the Jews*.
8. On Milton's patriotism, see Stevens, "Milton's Janus-faced Nationalism."
9. Laura Lunger Knoppers, "Milton's *The Readie and Easie Way* and the English jeremiad," in *Politics, Poetics, and Hermeneutics in Milton's Prose*, ed. David Loewenstein and James Grantham Turner (Cambridge: Cambridge University Press, 1990) 213–25, discusses the importance of Jeremiah and the frame of Jewish history to this tract.
10. Rosemary Radford Ruether, *Faith and Fratricide: The Theological Roots of Anti-Semitism* (1974; rpt. New York: Seabury Press, 1979) chapter 2 (64–116), and esp. 85–86.

11. Rachel Trubowitz, chapter 9 in this volume, finds that *Samson* critiques Hebraism's maternal and "carnal" measures of "purity" in order to assert a "Pauline construction of spiritual purity" (233).
12. See, e.g, Sharon Achinstein, "*Samson Agonistes* and the Drama of Dissent," *Milton Studies* 33 (1996): 133–58, who argues that his personal regeneration is inseparable from his "reunification" with the Israelite community (150–51); and Elizabeth M. Sauer, "Religious Toleration and Imperial Intolerance," in *Milton and the Imperial Vision*, ed. Balachandra Rajan and Elizabeth Sauer (Pittsburgh: Duquesne University Press, 1999), who argues that in his final scene, "Samson as an Israelite severs himself from Philistine bonds and the race of the unclean" (229).
13. Hill, *Milton and the English Revolution*, 428–48, identifies Samson with England and as a symbol for the revolutionary cause. Nicholas Jose, *Ideas of the Restoration in English Literature, 1660–71* (Cambridge, MA: Harvard University Press, 1984), shows Milton's allusions link the Philistines with the Restoration state (155–63).
14. See Mary Nyquist, "'Profuse, proud Cleopatra': 'Barbarism' and Female Rule in Early Modern English Republicanism," *Women's Studies* 24 (1994): 85–130, on Milton's view of "female rule" as "barbarous," an enemy to republican liberty (118, 93).
15. Julia M. Walker, "Only the Phoenix has a Womb: Samson and the Homeless Women of Israel," in *Altering Eyes: New Perspectives on "Samson Agonistes*," ed. Mark R. Kelley and Joseph Wittreich (Newark: University of Delaware Press, 2002) 54–71; quotation p. 68.
16. Hugh MacCallum, "*Samson Agonistes*: The Deliverer as Judge," *Milton Studies* 23 (1988): 259–90, esp. 264–67. Derek N. C. Woods, *"Exiled from the Light": Divine Law, Morality, and Violence in Milton's "Samson Agonistes"* (Toronto: University of Toronto Press, 2001), argues that Milton's tragedy presents a Pauline view of the Jews under the law.
17. See Jackie di Salvo, "'Intestine Thorn': Samson's Struggle with the Woman Within," in *Milton and the Idea of Woman*, ed. Julia M. Walker (Urbana: University of Illinois Press, 1988) 211–29, and "'Spirituall Contagion': Male Psychology and the Culture of Idolatry in *Samson Agonistes*," in *Altering Eyes*, 253–80. Scholars who see Samson's feminine connections in a positive light include Mary Beth Rose, "'Vigorous Most / When Most Unactive Deemed': Gender and the Heroics of Endurance in Milton's *Samson Agonistes*, Aphra Behn's *Oroonoko*, and Mary Astell's *Some Reflections Upon Marriage*," *Milton Studies* 33 (1996): 83–110; Amy Boesky, chapter 8 in this volume; and Paula Loscocco, "'Not less renown'd than Jael': Heroic Chastity in *Samson Agonistes*," *Milton Studies* 40 (2002): 181–200. Wood, "*Exiled from the Light*," 99–117, finds Dalila Samson's "moral superior" (115) and accuses Samson of lacking Christian "charity."
18. Guibbory, *Ceremony and Community*, 219–27.
19. See, e.g., Francis Gregory's *David's Returne from His Banishment*, May 27, 1660; Henry Newcome's *Usurpation Defeated, and David Restored: Being an*

Exact Parallel between David and our Most Gracious Soveraign King Charls II, May 24, 1660.
20. See Daniel Boyarin's *A Radical Jew: Paul and the Politics of Identity* (Berkeley: University of California Press, 1994), whose title suggests Paul's Jewish connection.
21. Boyarin in *A Radical Jew* suggests the "Jewish question" and the "Woman question" are related in Paul "historically and typologically" (156–57).
22. See David Loewenstein's discussion of Samson's iconoclasm in *Milton and the Drama of History: Historical Vision, Iconoclasm, and the Literary Imagination* (Cambridge: Cambridge University Press, 1990), and of Samson as representing the impulse of the apocalyptic spirit of Restoration radicals, in "The Revenge of the Saint: Radical Religion and Politics in *Samson Agonistes*," *Milton Studies* 33 (1996): 159–80. For Michael Lieb, "'Our Living Dread': The God of *Samson Agonistes*," *Milton Studies* 33 (1996): 3–25, Samson embodies a primitive Hebraic concept of the godhead.
23. Joseph Wittreich's *Interpreting "Samson Agonistes"* (Princeton: Princeton University Press, 1986); Wittreich and Kelley's introduction to *Altering Eyes*, 11–29; and Wood, *"Exiled from the Light."* Mary Ann Radzinowicz, *Toward "Samson Agonistes": The Growth of Milton's Mind* (Princeton: Princeton University Press, 1978), finds Samson "prefigure[s] the gift of Christian liberty" (261); Joan S. Bennett, *Reviving Liberty: Radical Christian Humanism in Milton's Great Poems* (Cambridge, MA: Harvard University Press, 1989), believes Samson achieves it. Long ago, Arthur E. Barker, "Structural and Doctrinal Pattern in Milton's Later Poems," in *Essays in English Literature from the Renaissance to the Victorian Age, Presented to A. S. P. Woodhouse*, ed. Millar MacLure and F. W. Watt (Toronto: University of Toronto Press, 1964), 169–94, insisted the late poems are "about" Christian liberty, even though the term does not appear in them (172).
24. Stanley Fish insists we cannot be sure that Samson's "rousing motions" "correspond to some communication . . . between him and God" ("Spectacle and Evidence in *Samson Agonistes*," *Critical Inquiry* 15 [1989]: 571). Dennis Kezar argues for Milton's "interpretive and evaluative disengagement from the play" in "Samson's Death by Theater and Milton's Art of Dying," *ELH* 66 (1999): 295–336; 323. For an example of how recent terrorism has changed the way we read Milton's poem, see John Carey, "A Work in Praise of Terrorism: September 11 and *Samson Agonistes*," in *Times Literary Supplement*, Sept. 6, 2002, 15–16.

PART III

*Gendered subjectivity in Milton's
literary history*

CHAPTER II

George Eliot as a "Miltonist": marriage and Milton in Middlemarch

Dayton Haskin

"The best history of a writer is contained in his writings – these are his chief actions." This opinion is registered in a letter that George Eliot wrote in 1879, in response to a query whether there was to be a biography of her companion, George Henry Lewes, who had died the year before. "Biographies generally," Eliot went on to remark, "are a disease of English literature." In her book *The Real Life of Mary Ann Evans*, Rosemarie Bodenheimer has made these remarks a watchword for studying how Eliot's own writings reveal the inner structure of her life, one of the dynamics of which was a recurring "resistance" to indulging "requests for biographical information about herself."[1] These remarks also shed light upon the vexed subject of how George Eliot read another author who, although he resisted writing an autobiography, wrote a good deal about himself. By the mid nineteenth century John Milton was thoroughly entangled in a network of biographical speculation, and his name was likely to bring to mind popular narratives about a great poet's domestic experience. For her part, Eliot took an interest in the biographical implications of what Milton wrote and published. At times she also sought to disentangle those implications from stories that substituted fanciful speculation about his relations with women for first-hand encounters with his writing.

In more recent times the project of exploring the intertextual relations between Eliot and Milton has been inhibited by other entanglements; for instance, by the assumption that in *Middlemarch* Edward Casaubon represents Milton and provides an apt illustration of what Virginia Woolf denominated "Milton's bogey"[2]; by the claim that the interest in Milton shown in the novel is an aspect of Eliot's self-loathing and accounts for an "authorial vengeance" that she takes on Dorothea Brooke "in the service of female submission"[3]; and by the idea (which Eliot pointedly rejected) that the arguments Milton advanced in favor of divorce are deeply flawed by their patriarchal assumptions about marriage and were in any event a cover for his own self-interest.[4] The ways in which Eliot's writing actually engages Milton show that from early to late in her career she understood that one of the chief actions of Milton's life was his courageous decision to make public his views on the nature of marriage and the grounds on which divorce ought to be made legally permissible. Her sustained interest in Milton's divorce tracts also reveals a good deal about how she thought about one of the most profound actions of her own life, her decision to live with a married man.

The ways in which we can think about Eliot's own entanglement with Milton have recently been reinvigorated by Anna Nardo's major re-evaluation of the subject. In *George Eliot's Dialogue with John Milton* she has reconstructed what Victorian readers generally thought they knew about Milton, showing that their knowledge derived largely from biographical writings, including fiction-filled accounts of his first marriage and popular stories about his treatment of his daughters. She also shows that, in the Victorian period, pictures of Milton as a "domestic tyrant" were made to stand in sharp contrast to a cult of Milton as a lover. She explores the relevance in particular to *Romola* of two contradictory eighteenth-century traditions about Milton – that he was an exponent of modern companionate marriage and that he was a bookish radical who displayed, in Samuel Johnson's words, "a Turkish contempt of females, as subordinate and inferior beings." Suggesting that Milton lurks in the narrative as "the unacknowledged father," Nardo thus proposes that in writing this novel George Eliot was re-enacting the struggles of Milton himself. That is, Eliot was emulating Milton's chief actions and Romola, who upholds Savonarola's own ideals in the very act of opposing him, is the signature of a writer who is determined to hold her author to his own principles.[5]

The degree to which "Milton" had become a screen onto which the Victorians projected their own cultural contradictions is well illustrated in Nardo's careful tracing of the cult of the poet from Keats's sonnet on a lock of Milton's hair through popular representations of Milton – in poems, plays, novels, and paintings – as a kind of Protestant saint. She argues that *Middlemarch* "exposes the excesses" of this cult: by providing hard-won insights into the work required to make marriage satisfying to both partners, Eliot's novel criticizes the ethereal love that devotees like Anna Jameson, who found in Milton's Latin poems addressed to Leonora Baroni evidence of his romantic charm, had infused into their surmise that the poet must have been an ideal lover.[6] More than any previous writer on Eliot, Nardo has made sense of the fact that, during the period when

George Eliot was composing *Middlemarch*, she and Lewes were reading *Paradise Lost* together.

In what follows I want first to illustrate that George Eliot's interest in Milton as an authority on love and marriage dates, significantly, to the period when she began living with Lewes, and then to trace some ways in which *Middlemarch* enables us to think in historically precise terms about the recent claim that, in the history of representing love in English poetry, Milton contributed substantially to inventing "a new kind of intense, private, mutual relationship, which excluded the social and institutional worlds." In *Paradise Lost*, Anthony Low has argued, Milton projected a "little world of privacy and of magical transcendence, and . . . separated married love from its classical connections with civic virtue and from its Christian connections with the Church . . . and society." Low's proposal that Milton helped to define "mutual conjugal love" as "a shelter from the working world" and "a cure for alienation" has a peculiarly Victorian ring to it.[7] In an attempt to discern when and under what conditions Milton was made to do the sort of cultural work that Low ascribes to him, I want to explore what George Eliot, who understood quite well that men's idealistic projection of married life into a separate and allegedly sacred sphere functioned to disempower women, found in Milton's writings on divorce.

From early on in her writing career, even before she took the name George Eliot, Mary Ann Evans had become a "Miltonist" in the precise sense of the term that dates to the Commonwealth, "a follower of Milton in his views on divorce," i.e., of his effort to effect a liberalizing of the legislation governing marriage. In the second half of 1855, not long after she had begun living with Lewes, Mary Ann Evans published two reviews of a new book about Milton by Thomas Keightley. The first appeared anonymously in *The Leader*, which Lewes had founded with his friend Thorton Hunt. Although Keightley's book was called *An Account of the Life, Opinions, and Writings of John Milton. With an Introduction to "Paradise Lost"*,[8] the review largely ignored Milton's epic and allotted nearly half its space to a discussion of *The Doctrine and Discipline of Divorce*. The reviewer quoted extensively from excerpts printed by Keightley and urged their relevance to the parliamentary debates about divorce that were taking place in the mid-1850s. These debates would culminate with the passage of the most significant change in England's legislation governing marriage and divorce since the publication of Milton's divorce tracts in the 1640s: the Divorce and Matrimonial Causes Act of 1857. In particular, the reviewer defended Milton against the long-standing charge that self-interest vitiated his arguments: "Milton," she wrote,

was pleading his own cause as well as urging a general argument, just as, two centuries later, Mrs. Norton . . . is doing in her *Letter to the Queen*. There is much unreasonable prejudice against this blending of personal interest with a general protest. If we waited for the impulse of abstract benevolence or justice, we fear that most reforms would be postponed to the Greek Kalends . . . The Athenians, so far from sharing this ultra-delicate notion of ours, that a man is not to appear in a cause for the very reason that he has an interest in it, would allow no man to bring a case of litigation into court unless he had a personal concern in that case: they distrusted all disinterested officiousness as much as we should distrust a man who set up shop purely for the good of the community. The personal interest may lead to exaggeration, and may be unwisely thrust into prominence, but in itself it is assuredly not a ground for silence but for speech, until we have reached that stage in which the work of this world will be all done vicariously, everybody acting for some one else, and nobody for himself.[9]

It is not known what Hunt, who was still working for *The Leader* and was living openly with Lewes's wife, made of this review. He knew that the reviewer also had a personal interest in reforming the legislation governing marriage, and he might have recognized what is especially striking in retrospect: that she was engaging in the very practices for which she praised Milton. For his part, Lewes must have recognized in the review not only the writer's self-interest but the challenge that her emulation of Milton and her siding with Mrs. Norton posed to views that he had expressed five years earlier. In an unsigned review of Charlotte Brontë's *Shirley*, Lewes had puzzled over the question whether women, by virtue of the experience of menstruation and of an aptness for maternity, could ever achieve equality with men "in respect of intellect." "They have had," he wrote (as if no woman who would read his words could be thought to count), "no Shakespeare, no Bacon, no Newton, no Milton, no Raphael, no Mozart." "The grand function of woman," he went on, "is, and ever must be, Maternity."

[F]or twenty years of the best years of their lives – those very years in which men either rear the grand fabric or lay the solid foundations of their fame and fortune – women are mainly occupied by the cares, the duties, the enjoyments and the sufferings of maternity. During large parts of these years, too, their bodily health is generally so broken and precarious as to incapacitate them for any strenuous exertion; and, health apart, the greater portion of their time, thoughts, interests, and anxieties ought to be, and generally are, centered in the care and the training of their children. But how could such occupations consort with the intense and unremitting studies which seared the eyeballs of Milton, and for a time unsettled even the powerful brain of Newton?[10]

Mary Ann Evans, whom he met not long after he had published these views, had by 1855 begun to unsettle the presuppositions on which Lewes raised the question of women's intellectual equality with men. In the years ahead, as George Eliot, she would unsettle as well the condescension with which Lewes praised a handful of women writers, including Mrs. Norton, who "are second only to the first-rate men of their day."[11]

Before taking up Mary Ann Evans's other review of Keightley's book, it is worth dwelling on the relevance of the celebrated case of Caroline Sheridan Norton. Lewes was unable to obtain a divorce from his wife, Agnes, who for some years had been bearing children to Hunt. This private state of affairs lay behind the interest in the *Leader* review in a public controversy, which had been set in motion when a Royal Commission was appointed in 1850 to examine existing legislation on marriage and divorce. Originally, the idea was to remove matrimonial matters from the jurisdiction of ecclesiastical courts, or Doctors' Commons, as they were generally known. Proponents of reform envisaged the establishment of a special new court composed of the Chancellor and other leading legal dignitaries, which would exercise full power to grant or to deny divorces, either divorce *a vinculo matrimonii* ("from the bond of marriage") or separation *a mensa et thoro* ("from bed and board"). In 1854, some months before the Chancellor, Lord Cranworth, brought his proposed reform bill before the Lords, Caroline Norton had printed privately, at her own expense, a pamphlet entitled *English Laws for Women of the Nineteenth Century*. In it she detailed how, after being married to a lawyer who had for many years abused her, denied her custody of their children, and appropriated her earnings as an author, she had learned "piecemeal" what the English laws were and how they were made to work. Taking as her text Dickens's "It won't do to have Truth and Justice on our side: we must have Law and Lawyers," she argued that she was not merely seeking sympathy for having been "insulted, defrauded, and libelled" by her husband.[12] She was giving publicity to her own case because it was representative of the condition of many women, who were precisely made non-existent in and by English law, since the current legislation touching on marriage assumed that the interests of husbands and wives were necessarily the same and that, according to the common-law principle of coverture, a woman's interests were "covered" by provisions that protected the interests of her husband. In all of English history only a handful of women had successfully petitioned Parliament for divorce *a vinculo*.

The proposed reforms in Lord Cranworth's bill did not envisage a remedy for the plight of women, however. The reformers' concern was the prohibitive expense of divorce for men. The man's dilemma is dramatized in Dickens's novel of 1854, *Hard Times*, when Stephen Blackpool approaches his employer, Josiah Bounderby, for advice about what to do given that he is tied by marriage to a "drunken creature . . . so foul to look at, in her tatters, stains and splashes, but so much fouler than that in her moral infamy."[13] "Why, you'd have to go to Doctors' Commons with a suit," Bounderby tells Stephen,

and you'd have to go to a court of Common Law with a suit, and you'd have to go to the House of Lords with a suit, and you'd have to get an Act of Parliament to enable you to marry again, and it would cost you (if it was a case of very plain sailing), I suppose from a thousand to fifteen hundred pound . . . Perhaps twice the money.[14]

Like Dickens, the parliamentary reformers of the 1850s were concerned about inequities of class among men seeking divorce. Whether they were seeking precisely to exclude the possibility that divorce proceedings would be initiated by an aggrieved woman or not, their proposals did nothing to remedy the anomaly by which married women were non-persons in the eyes of the law. If Mrs. Norton's privately printed pamphlet of 1854 caused a stir, her *Letter to the Queen on Lord Cranworth's Marriage and Divorce Bill*, which was copyrighted and published and sold by Longman, Brown, Green, and Longmans in 1855, brought the injustice of a married woman's plight to a much wider readership. The relevance of this letter to Mary Ann Evans's review of Keightley is that Mrs. Norton justified speaking up in the face of her husband's unjust treatment by arguing that she had a sacred vocation to write in the cause of justice. (Although the reviewer does not remark on it, we should note that Keightley printed the autobiographical passage from *The Reason of Church Government* in which Milton tells of having been "church-outed by the prelates" and seeks to justify his presumption in speaking out publicly by presenting his writing as a fulfillment of the biblical injunction to make use of his talents.) The terms and categories that Caroline Norton enlists recall Milton's famous justification in his antiprelatical pamphlets of deferring his poetic career in order to intervene in debates of national import:

My husband has taught me, by subpœnaing my publishers to account for my earnings, that my gift of writing was not meant for the purposes to which I have hitherto applied it. It was not intended that I should . . . prove my literary ability by publishing melodies and songs for young girls and women to sing in happier homes than mine, or poetry and prose for them to read in leisure hours, or even please myself by better and more serious attempts to advocate the rights of the people or the education and interests of the poor.

He has made me dream that it was meant for a higher and stronger purpose, that gift which came not from man, but from God! It was meant to enable me to rouse the hearts of others to examine into all the gross injustice of these laws.[15]

The climax of this self-presentation proclaims the cause of justice for "all the women of England." It also makes explicit something that Milton, in the divorce tracts, dared to acknowledge only indirectly when he asked (in a passage reproduced by Keightley and cited in the *Leader* review) that some "tender pity" might be extended to "those who have unwarily, in a thing they never practised before, made themselves the bondmen of a luckless and helpless matrimony."[16] Like Milton, Caroline Norton believed that both her personal sufferings and rhetorical abilities qualified her to take on established authority. She resolved to speak up for "many hundreds" of other women, she explains, and to "comment on and explain the cause of that wrong, which few women are able to do."

For this I believe God gave me the power of writing. To this I devote that power. I abjure all other writing till I see these laws altered. I care not what ridicule or abuse may be the result of that declaration. They who cannot bear ridicule and abuse are unfit and unable to advance any cause; and once more I deny that this is my personal cause – it is the cause of all the women of England . . . Meanwhile my husband has a legal lien on the copyright of my works. Let him claim the copyright of this![17]

In her review for *The Leader* Mary Ann Evans did not acknowledge her own self-interest in the current parliamentary debates about divorce. Yet she explicitly praised Mrs. Norton for having published an account that revealed the personal basis for her claims. Urging a parallel between the action taken by Milton and that taken by a contemporary who wrote as one woman speaking for others, she endorsed a kind of courage that the conventions of anonymous reviewing did not permit her to exercise herself.

Mary Ann Evans's other review of Keightley's book appeared in *The Westminster Review*, the journal which, although her name was not publicly connected with it, she was virtually running. It began by announcing that Keightley had succeeded in "vindicat[ing] Milton from the charge of ill-conduct towards his children," and then turned to noticing the "admirable" work the author had done in representing Milton's prose writings. This review focused principally on *Of Education* and its odd relation to its author's actual practice as a school-master. The anonymous reviewer congratulated Milton for having failed to live up to his stated ideal of placing "first-rate authors into the hands of boys" and remarked that the "ordinary effect" of introducing "the finest products of genius" to young persons is a "vulgarizing... by premature familiarity."[18] This observation, articulated by a woman who would compose what Virginia Woolf memorably referred to as one of the few English novels actually written for grown-ups, is consistent with the ironic perspective adopted by the narrator in *Middlemarch*, who reports that the youthful Dorothea had come to imagine that she would be happy marrying "the judicious Hooker" or Milton in his blindness.[19] What is significant about these remarks here is that they clarify a position taken in the *Leader* review, where Mary Ann Evans drew inspiration from Milton's elevation of personal experience over scholastic learning in affairs of the heart. The *Leader* review makes no attempt to evaluate the validity of Milton's interpretations of scripture. It proposes to value Milton as a writer because he dared on moral grounds to oppose the established ecclesiastical and civil authorities.

The *Leader* review shows, then, on what basis Mary Ann Evans invested authority in Milton. It also constitutes relevant background for George Eliot's mature understanding of a literary predecessor who was in the business of writing "home epic," for which the narrator in *Middlemarch* insists the starting point is marriage, as it had been for Adam and Eve (Finale, 832). Before Mary Ann Evans took Keightley's volume in hand, she had become intimately acquainted with the case of a man who had suffered many wrongs within his marriage. Moreover, as someone with a personal interest in the laws governing divorce, she had meditated on the *Letter to the Queen*, in which a wife who had suffered extensively at the hands of a noted aristocrat showed that she could "identify . . . injustices because she had personally endured them." As Mary Poovey observes, Caroline Norton was able to expose injustices in "explicitly political terms" by "transforming herself from the silent sufferer of private wrongs into an articulate spokesperson in the public sphere."[20] What Mary Ann Evans astutely recognized when she read Keightley's extracts from *The Doctrine and Discipline of Divorce*, then, was that Milton's political status at the time he wrote his tract had also been marginal. She admired the extraordinary courage with which he had made his address to Parliament and put his name to the pamphlet. Sympathetic to Milton because his "plea for divorce . . . drew down on him plenty of Presbyterian vituperation," and knowing that his proposals for reform had failed for more than 200 years, she teased out of his elaborate argument the autobiographical self-revelations of a person whose own vituperations only barely masked the deep hurts that had qualified him to speak up. The climactic work of the review was to present Milton not as the author of *Paradise Lost*, but as a stand-in for Lewes, whose personal situation the reviewer was not about to publicize. "For want of a more modern pendant to Mrs. Norton's plea," Milton's case was made to show that men, too, could be victims of the nation's unjust marriage laws and that even a man might need to take risks in negotiating the fearful passage from silence to speech.[21]

When we consider what had interested Mary Ann Evans in Keightley's book and then turn to *Middlemarch*, we can see that it is not the ineffectual Casaubon whom George Eliot has made truly reminiscent of Milton. Casaubon is radically unlike the historic poet. Eliot depicts him as a man who is unfit for intimate conversation: he has no interest in politics and "only cares about Church questions" (ch. 6, p. 53). In religion, strikingly unlike Milton, he practices a "wise conformity" (ch. 3, p. 25). Moreover, he never publishes his master-work because of his fear of self-exposure.

It is true that several conspicuous aspects of the portrait of Casaubon are compatible with the idea, which descends from Johnson, of Milton's "bogey": the father-figure, steeped in classical learning, using up his eyesight working on a project of epic proportions, desirous to have a talented reader, convinced that he is dedicated to truth but misunderstood by his contemporaries. When, however, in chapter 29 the narrator attempts to revolt against the recurring tendency to present Dorothea's "point of view [as] the only possible one with regard to ... marriage" and seeks to reveal the "intense consciousness within" Casaubon (ch. 29, p. 278), the reader finds in this man's interior life only a parody of Milton. Casaubon has been thinking of marriage, we learn, not in the Miltonic terms of a "meet conversation" between "fit" partners, but as "an outward requirement," a duty "like religion and erudition, nay, like authorship itself," which he was obliged to fulfill (ch. 29, p. 280). Having been desirous of a "helpmate" to "enable him to dispense with a hired secretary," he believed that in Dorothea "Providence ... had supplied him with the wife he needed. A wife, a modest young lady, with the purely appreciative, unambitious abilities of her sex, is sure to think her husband's mind powerful." Tellingly, however, the narrator is unable to sustain Casaubon's point of view. "Whether Providence had taken equal care of Miss Brooke in presenting her with Mr Casaubon was an idea" that is certain to occur to the reader, though it "could hardly occur" to the character whose consciousness is being articulated here (ch. 29, p. 279). The narrative is thus trained back on the heroine's disillusionment: "Dorothea had thought that she could have been patient with John Milton, but she had never imagined him" to be as her husband turned out to be, "stupidly undiscerning and odiously unjust" (ch. 29, p. 282). In short, the portrait of Casaubon exposes the degree to which Dorothea had been deluded and victimized by popular ideas about Milton as a lover.

Casaubon is no John Milton, not even the "Milton" of Johnson's remark about "Turkish contempt." It is a defining aspect of his character that one thing he knows about the historic poet concerns the domestic history that was routinely rehearsed out of Johnson in popular historical fiction (ch. 7, p. 64). Still, at some moments the narrator represents him as thinking of himself in quasi-Miltonic terms, as when he "imagined that his long studious bachelorhood had stored up for him a compound interest of enjoyment" (ch. 10, p. 85). Certainly Casaubon thought he could recommend himself in terms clean opposite to those in which respectable Victorian men of letters often presented the lives of lesser writers, such as, say, Doctor Donne, whose erotic poetry was increasingly being read as evidence that the hero of the well-known *Life* by Izaak Walton had spent his youth sowing wild oats:[22] "I can at least offer you," Casaubon writes to Dorothea in his marriage proposal, "an affection hitherto unwasted, and the faithful consecration of a life which, however short in the sequel, has no backward pages whereon, if you choose to turn them, you will find records such as might justly cause you either bitterness or shame" (ch. 5, p. 44). While Dorothea may have considered herself above the foolishness that credited the picture of young Milton as a romantic gallant, she can hardly have found this self-recommendation attractive.

While Eliot represents Casaubon as a man "unfit" (to invoke Milton's category) for Dorothea, in her portrait of the marriage of Lydgate and Rosamond Vincy she negotiates the risks entailed in dramatizing a possibility to which the author of the divorce tracts had given more conspicuous play: that a woman might in fact prove deficient as a wife. This is to say that *Middlemarch* also prompts readers to imagine the consequences of a coupling of persons "unfit" for one another on grounds similar to those said in Victorian biographies to have separated Milton and Mary Powell. Keightley, for instance, rehearsed the information from John Aubrey that Mary had been "brought up and bred where there was a great deal of company and merriment, as dancing," and added from Edward Phillips that "the quiet and seclusion of her husband's abode were not agreeable to one who had been used to . . . merriment and joviality."[23] More importantly, Eliot represents Rosamond in terms consistent with the dubious implication in Milton's divorce tracts that a marriage will fail if the wife proves unfit for "all the more estimable and superior purposes of matrimony." At the same time, Eliot gives Lydgate something of Milton's reforming zeal, but she represents him as far more timid than Milton in applying it in what he regards as the lowly domestic sphere. When experience shows how little his wife shares of his intellectual aspirations, Lydgate attempts to hide from himself his "profound mistake," though it remains "at work in him," the narrator observes, "like a recognized chronic disease, . . . enfeebling every thought" (ch. 58, p. 591). Lydgate keeps his wife in ignorance of his sufferings and then blames her for failing to understand and support him. Perversely echoing his despair, Rosamond feels "it was no use to say anything" to him (ch. 75, p. 759). While the story is set some quarter of a century before the parliamentary debates about Lord Cranworth's bill, thereby muting the possibility that the characters will imagine divorce as a "remedy," Eliot herself draws strength from Milton's conviction, memorably expressed in *A Second Defence of the English People* (*CPW*4.1:622–25), that domestic liberty is of a piece with civil liberty and that the public and private spheres powerfully intersect. Eliot assigns this insight above all to the mature Dorothea.

Even more than Lydgate, Dorothea is represented in terms reminiscent of Milton as George Eliot found him in the prose tracts he wrote in the cause of ecclesiastical, domestic, and civil liberty. As Milton's youthful resolve to write an epic doctrinal to a nation was suspended during the period of civil strife, when he wrote (as it were) only with his left hand, Dorothea's "spiritual grandeur" was "ill-matched with the meanness of opportunity," and she does not find the "epic life" for which she yearns (Prelude, p. 3). In the event, she enters marriage thinking she can be "useful" to her new husband by learning "to read Latin and Greek aloud . . . , as Milton's daughters did" (ch. 7, p. 63). Nonetheless, she emerges as the heroine of Eliot's "home epic," as she actively resists the "dead hand" of her husband, especially the codicil in his will that expressly forbids her to marry Will Ladislaw upon pain of forfeiting her inheritance. If for a time Dorothea profoundly mistook Casaubon for an "affable archangel" (ch. 29, p. 283), this error associates her with the youthful pamphleteer, who confided in passages quoted in the *Leader* review how in his idealism he had betrayed himself into the "bondage" of "a luckless and helpless matrimony" with an "image of earth and phlegm." Dorothea naively strives to be the obverse of Milton's portrait of the unfit mate, who – as the "nameless answerer" of *The Doctrine and Discipline* pointed out – he depicted as wholly disadvantaged in conversation unless she were able to "speak Hebrew, Greek, Latine, & French, and dispute against the Canon law as well as you."[24] For Dorothea, who (the narrator has earlier informed us) has "very childlike ideas" on the subject, "the really delightful marriage must be that where your husband was a sort of father, and could teach you even Hebrew, if you wished it" (ch. 1, p. 10). Like Milton, who as much as acknowledged (in another passage quoted in the *Leader* review) that his imagination had projected liveliness and companionable sympathy onto "the bashful muteness of a virgin," Dorothea is said to have "supplied all that Mr Casaubon's words seemed to leave unsaid" (ch. 5, p. 50).

Later, as Dorothea acknowledges her love for Ladislaw and enters into her second marriage, her defiance of the codicil recalls another well-known episode in Milton's marital history. When Keightley included the story of how Milton, "regarding his union with Miss Powell as terminated by her obstinate desertion of him," courted "the daughter of a Dr. Davis," he retold it with a difference. Whereas Milton's nephew Edward Phillips had said that Miss Davis was averse to his suit, and another biography of 1804 had claimed that the decisive reason the marriage did not come about was that, after the Battle of Naseby, the Powells needed Milton's connection to the parliamentary side and so worked out a reconciliation, Keightley sought to account for Miss Davis's reluctance on grounds that spoke more directly to Victorian readers: any offspring of the marriage, he observed, "would be held to be illegitimate" and Miss Davis would have found herself "quite excluded from the society of her own sex – a thing few virtuous women can patiently endure."[25]

The latter observation touched Mary Ann Evans deeply. It throws some light, I think, on the two visits to Rosamond made by Dorothea in the last book of *Middlemarch*. When Dorothea first resolves to uphold Lydgate's innocence of implication in the bribery scandal, she seems to be motivated largely, though not exclusively, by having witnessed for two years the injustices that gossip and innuendo have done to Ladislaw. Her first visit fails in its purpose to make Rosamond aware of her husband's innocence and thus to renew the bond between husband and wife; and Dorothea's inference that what she had seen upon entering the Lydgates' house was Will making verbal love to Rosamond robs her of some of the indignation she has felt on Will's behalf. It also reveals to her a possibly self-interested basis of her desire to reunite Rosamond and Lydgate. Nonetheless, Dorothea's unconscious attraction to Will, which Rosamond has rightly recognized as the basis for Casaubon's cruel act in making the codicil, suggests that in seeking this intimacy with Rosamond more is at stake than vindicating a good man in the eyes of his wife: Dorothea seeks society with her own sex on the assumption that the two women have in common their love for men who are unjustly misunderstood, and also partly because she understands that her feelings for Will do not endear her to other women. If, as I am suggesting, Eliot's narrator allows us to divine an admixture of impure motives in Dorothea, who may be seeking unconsciously to shore up Rosamond's commitment to Lydgate in order to keep Rosamond and Will apart, it is precisely here that Mary Ann Evans's praise for Milton in the *Leader* review is most pertinent. As the novel moves to its climax, Dorothea commits another of "those determining acts of her life," and with a "mixed result" (Finale, 838). At the end of the narrative we may be no nearer to the Greek Kalends of "abstract benevolence." Yet, as readers, we have been brought closer to acknowledging that personal interests may have a valid place in moral action. Dorothea finally discovers in her personal interest, even after it has seemed to be lost to her, "not a ground for silence but for speech." Unlike the Bulstrodes, whose sufferings are compounded by their inability to talk with one another about what is central to their lives, she overcomes every inhibition that makes her hesitant to speak up.

The more disinterested component of the action taken by Dorothea to bring Lydgate and Rosamond together is indirectly given a name earlier in the novel, and that name is "Milton." The chapter-motto for the episode (Chapter 52) in which Farebrother generously holds his own aspirations for marriage in abeyance and woos Mary Garth for his rival adapts the final words of Wordsworth's address to Milton in the "London, 1802" sonnet: "His heart / The lowliest duties on itself did lay." In relation to the biographical traditions in which Milton was entangled, this was the most ambiguous feature of Wordsworth's claim that Milton should be living in the nineteenth century, for England again had need of him. What were those "lowly duties" that the exemplary Milton had willingly embraced? The work of a schoolmaster? Drudging for the Commonwealth? What I am proposing finally about *Middlemarch* is that George Eliot – averse as she was to the self-exposure entailed in the life of a publishing writer – interpreted the bottom line in Wordsworth's sonnet by way of the divorce tracts. Like Farebrother's willingness to swallow his pride and hold his ambitions in check, Milton's willingness to embrace the humiliating task of developing a socially constructive argument about the nature of marriage from his own individual experience cost him a great deal. Eliot recognized that in his divorce tracts Milton had laid himself open to public scrutiny. Yet he had rendered his anger as well as his suffering potentially useful to others.[26]

What then is to be concluded about the widespread notion that Milton was for women writers not just a father-figure but, in Harold Bloom's words, "the great Inhibitor, the Sphinx who strangles even strong imaginations in their cradles"?[27] To continue to subscribe to this dogma would require us to forgo the opportunity to appreciate how, at her particular moment in history, George Eliot read Milton from a position of strength and independence. She looked upon Milton in his divorce tracts the way a mother might regard the anger and frustration of her son: with admiration for his demand for justice and for his energy, with patience and yet with a willingness to criticize him, and ultimately with a disposition to join forces with him to produce a socially useful outcome from his experience. While other Victorian readers may have been made marble by thinking of Milton as a massy twin pillar of English literature, the author of *Middlemarch* had long since been drawing strength from his independent spirit, recognizing that, after having been humiliated by his wife's desertion of him and at a moment when he had no particular political standing, Milton had taken action. He had made a name for himself – and had gained public ignominy – by speaking up against a pervasive domestic injustice. For more than 200 years his arguments had been disregarded. Yet the publishing of his divorce tracts had been one of the chief actions of Milton's whole life. In the mid nineteenth century the writings on marriage that he forged out of his own experiences – including the home epic aspects of *Paradise Lost* – could at last be recognized for their enduring value, even for their timeliness. In a world in which the time when everyone acts for someone else and nobody for himself has been deferred indefinitely, Milton's writings repeatedly reopen the possibility of speaking about kinds of suffering that are worsened when we remain silent.

NOTES

1. Rosemarie Bodenheimer, *The Real Life of Mary Ann Evans: George Eliot, Her Letters and Fiction* (Ithaca: Cornell University Press, 1994) xiii. Eliot's letter is cited as the first sentence of the book.
2. This assumption seems to have become widespread after the publication of Sandra M. Gilbert's essay, "Patriarchal Poetry and Women Readers: Reflections on Milton's Bogey," *PMLA* 93 (1978): 368–82, and its reincarnation in Gilbert's and Susan Gubar's book, *The Madwoman in the Attic: The Woman Writer and the Nineteenth-Century Literary Imagination* (New Haven: Yale University Press, 1979). Even so discerning a reader as Elsie Michie seems to be under the spell of Gilbert when she proposes that Eliot's heroine "is devoted to Casaubon because he embodies an ideal of 'high' culture"; see *Outside the Pale: Cultural Exclusion, Gender Difference, and the Victorian Woman Writer* (Ithaca: Cornell University Press, 1993) 163.
3. Gilbert and Gubar, *The Madwoman in the Attic*, 484. For a valuable although only inchoate critique of the views of Gilbert and Gubar, see Diana Postlethwaite, "When George Eliot Reads Milton: The Muse in a Different Voice," *ELH* 57 (1990): 197–221.

4. Annabel Patterson, in the shrewdest of readings of *The Doctrine and Discipline of Divorce* as a "concealed autobiographical novel," dwells rather heavily on "By-ends." See "No meer amatorious novel?" in *Politics, Poetics, and Hermeneutics in Milton's Prose*, ed. David Loewenstein and James Grantham Turner (Cambridge: Cambridge University Press, 1990) 85–101. For a fine study of Milton's personal interest in liberalized marriage legislation, see Stephen M. Fallon, "The Spur of Self-concernment: Milton in his Divorce Tracts," *Milton Studies*, 38: *John Milton: The Writer in his Works*, ed. Albert C. Labriola and Michael Lieb (Pittsburgh, PA: University of Pittsburgh Press, 2000) 22–42; cf. also Matthew Biberman, "Milton, Marriage, and a Woman's Right to Divorce," *SEL* 39 (1999): 131–53.
5. Anna Nardo, *George Eliot's Dialogue with John Milton* (Columbia: University of Missouri Press, 2003), Part 1, 66–82. For the context of Johnson's remark, see *Lives of the English Poets*, ed. George Birkbeck Hill, 3 vols. (Oxford: Clarendon Press, 1905), vol. 1, 157.
6. See Nardo, *George Eliot's Dialogue with Milton*, 103, and (more generally) chapters 2 and 4; cf. [Anna Brownwell (Murphy)] Jameson, "Milton and Leonora Baroni," in *Memoirs of the Loves of the Poets: Biographical Sketches of Women Celebrated in Ancient and Modern Poetry* (1829; New York: Harper; Boston: Russell, Odiorne, 1833), chapter 19.
7. Anthony Low, *The Reinvention of Love: Poetry, Politics and Culture from Sidney to Milton* (Cambridge: Cambridge University Press, 1993) 195, 201, 205.
8. Thomas Keightley, *An Account of the Life, Opinions, and Writings of John Milton. With an Introduction to "Paradise Lost"* (London: Chapman and Hall, 1855). Keightley reminded readers that Milton's unsuccessful "efforts to have a change made in the law of marriage and divorce" had nonetheless yielded "some proselytes, on whom the title of Miltonists was bestowed" (37).
9. The review from *The Leader* (6 [August, 1855]: 750) is reprinted under the title "Life and Opinions of Milton" in *Essays of George Eliot*, ed. Thomas Pinney (New York: Columbia University Press; London: Routledge and Kegan Paul, 1963) 154–57; cited here from 156.
10. [G. H. Lewes], unsigned review in the *Edinburgh Review* 91 (Jan., 1850); reprinted in *The Brontës: The Critical Heritage*, ed. Miriam Allott (London: Routledge and Kegan Paul, 1974) 160–61. In *Outside the Pale*, Michie offers illuminating commentary on other aspects of this passage: 144–47.
11. Lewes in *The Brontës*, 162.
12. Quoted in the account by Jane Gray Perkins, *The Life of the Honourable Mrs. Norton* (New York: Henry Holt, 1909) 239–40.
13. Charles Dickens, *Hard Times for These Times* (Oxford: Oxford University Press, 1955), Book 1, chapter 10, p. 67.
14. *Ibid.*, I, 11, p. 75. On some ways in which, in the version of the novel published in *Household Words*, Dickens connected Stephen's case specifically with Mrs. Norton's, see Margaret Simpson, *The Companion to "Hard Times"* (Westport, CT: Greenwood, 1997) 131–32.
15. See Perkins, *The Life of the Honourable Mrs. Norton*, 246–47.

16. See Pinney, *Essays of George Eliot*, 156–57.
17. See Perkins,*The Life of the Honourable Mrs. Norton*, 247.
18. *Westminster Review* 64 (October 1, 1855), 602, 603.
19. George Eliot, *Middlemarch*, ed. Rosemary Ashton (London: Penguin Books, 1994), chapter 1, p. 10. While my quotations all come from this edition, for the convenience of readers using other editions parenthetical references give the chapter number; then the page number in the Penguin follows.
20. Mary Poovey, *Uneven Developments: The Ideological Work of Gender in Mid-Victorian England* (Chicago: University of Chicago Press, 1988) 64.
21. *Essays of George Eliot*, 156, 157.
22. See, for instance, the Preface and Memorial Introduction in A. B. Grosart's two-volume edition of *The Complete Poems of John Donne, D. D.*, for the Fuller Worthies Library. The volumes were printed privately for subscribers, in 1872–73, shortly after *Middlemarch* was published.
23. Keightley, *An Account*, 35–36.
24. *CPW* 2: 742n.
25. Keightley's account includes Phillips's opinion, pp. 38–39; cf. Charles Symmons, *The Life of John Milton*, 2nd. edn. (London: Nichols and Son, 1810) 251–52. Cf. also William Hayley, who imagined that Miss Davis "had no inclination to reject his suit"; see *The Life of Milton*, 2nd. edn. (1796; rpt., Gainesville, FL: Scholars' Facsimiles and Reprints, 1970) 90–91; Hayley is cited by Nardo, *George Eliot's Dialogue with Milton*, 35–36.
26. Wordsworth expressed much the same aversion to exposing the lives of writers in biographies as George Eliot would. In his *Letter to a Friend of Robert Burns* (1816), for instance, he insisted that the works of poets, "if their words be good, . . . contain within themselves all that is necessary to their being comprehended and relished"; quoted by Eric C. Walker, "Wordsworth as Prose Biographer," *JEGP* 89 (1990): 330–44; quoted from 341.
27. Harold Bloom, *The Anxiety of Influence: A Theory of Poetry* (New York: Oxford University Press, 1973) 32; quoted by Gilbert and Gubar, *The Madwoman in the Attic*, 191; answered by Nardo, *George Eliot's Dialogue with Milton*, 82.

CHAPTER 12

Saying it with flowers: Jane Giraud's ecofeminist Paradise Lost *(1846)*

Wendy Furman-Adams and Virginia James Tufte

> Were I, O God, in churchless lands remaining,
> Far from all voice of teachers and divines,
> My soul would find in Flowers of thy ordaining
> Priests, sermons, shrines.
> (Jane Giraud, frontispiece, *The Floral Months of England*)[1]

> A single flower along the way also can contain the whole ecosystem.
> (John Elder, *Reading the Mountains of Home*)[2]

John Milton's *Paradise Lost* is, after the Bible, the most widely illustrated book in European history. It is also, arguably if controversially, one of the earliest great feminist poems – a poem that, as Joseph Wittreich demonstrated in 1987, has given heart and hope to three centuries of women readers.[3] Yet since 1688, although nearly 200 artists have tried to bring Milton's epic to visual life – among them such well-known figures as William Blake, Henry Fuseli, John Martin, and Gustav Doré – all but four of those artists have been men. Of the four woman artists who have responded in some way to the poem, three have worked during the twentieth century. American artist Carlotta Petrina (1901–97) produced a set of sixteen pencil drawings for a Limited Editions Club issue of *Paradise Lost and Paradise Regained*, which was published in 1936. Working at the same time, but with no knowledge of her American contemporary, Englishwoman Mary Elizabeth Groom (1903–58) produced a set of nineteen wood engravings for the Golden Cockerel Press's rare ten-book edition of *Paradise Lost*, published in honor of the coronation of King George and Queen Elizabeth in 1937. And postmodern conceptual artist Alexis Smith (b. 1949) has used Milton's works intertextually in a number of projects, most notably in her 1992 *Snake Path* at the University of California, San Diego.[4]

Jane Elizabeth Giraud (1810–68) was the first woman to make a visual response to Milton's epic, but her name did not appear on the volume she produced.[5] Moreover, unlike a hundred or more illustrators before her,

Figure 1. Jane Giraud, title page, *The Flowers of Milton*

and unlike Groom and Petrina later, Giraud did not set out to represent characters and events from each book of Milton's narrative. Rather, her illustrations consist of partially hand-colored flower paintings, published in 1846 in *The Flowers of Milton* (figure 1) – a volume attributable to the artist only by tiny initials on a few plates and by a handwritten dedication to Queen Victoria in some copies, in others to the artist's brother. The inscription to her brother reads as follows: "To Herbert Giraud, Esque., M.D., Professor of Chemistry and Materia Medica, in the Grant College, Bombay, this Garland from his Native Land is dedicated by His Sister. Faversham, 1st Jany, 1846."[6] Printed by Day and Haghe, London, lithographers to Queen Victoria, the book is made up of twenty-eight quotations from Milton's poems, each naming one or more flowers or plants. Eight of the pages illustrate *Paradise Lost*, while four more are drawn from *Paradise Regained*, and sixteen from *Poems for Several Occasions*. The *Paradise Lost* sequence follows the narrative, while thematizing flowers mentioned in the text. A botanically correct illustration centers each page, the quotation appearing below it in ornate type. A large, foliate initial letter dramatizes the symbolic nature of each flower in relation to the lines. In several of the letters, tiny figures contribute to both shape and symbol – including one of Eve, as "Each Flow'r of tender stalk . . . / she upstays / Gently with Myrtle band" (*PL* 9:428, 430–31).

As a product of the mid nineteenth century, *Flowers of Milton* both mirrors and embodies a number of intellectual currents. Like many Victorian women with artistic talent and aspirations, Jane Giraud may have become a flower painter because botanical illustration was one of the few acceptable activities for a woman of her time and class. Yet even within this restricted format, she managed to make her illustrations of *Paradise Lost* more than a series of colorful floral decorations. Her choice of quotations and her subtle use of flower symbolism constitute an interpretation of Milton's epic, one that recognizes and celebrates what Diane Kelsey McColley has recently called Milton's "moral and ecological vocabulary" and his role as "a revolutionary epic environmentalist." Jane Giraud, like Milton, represents the natural world as "not only a Book of Nature but a House of Nature, or *oikos*." In some respects at least, she can be considered Milton's first ecofeminist reader.[7]

Jane Giraud was born on June 25, 1810, in the port town of Faversham – nine miles from Canterbury, in the southeastern maritime county of Kent. She was one of the five surviving children of John Thomas Giraud (1764–1836),[8] a Faversham surgeon, and Mary Chapman of Badlesmere, Kent. The Girauds were a prominent family of Huguenot background, whose roots in Faversham went back to the early eighteenth century. Jane's grandfather, Francis Frederick Giraud (1726–1811), served as rector of St. Catherine's parish, in the adjoining rural area of Preston, for some forty-two years, while also serving, for forty-six years, as Head of the Faversham Grammar School. Articles in current issues of *Bygone Kent* provide biographical details not only about him, but also about Jane's public-spirited uncle, nephew, and brothers. One of her brothers, Herbert Giraud, was the professor of chemistry and botany to whom Giraud dedicated her *Flowers of Milton*; the other, Frederick Francis, became, like his father, a surgeon in Faversham.

Giraud's two surviving sisters, Eleanor and Mary Jane, both married; and the "misses Giraud," perhaps including Jane, are said to have presided over a school at some point, although details are entirely lacking. In any case, it would seem that Jane took responsibility for her widowed mother after her father's death: the census of 1841 lists Mary Giraud, age 60, and Jane Elizabeth Giraud, age 30, as living on Court Street, Faversham, both "of independent means."[9]

The only surviving photograph believed to be of Jane Giraud (figure 2) shows an exceedingly proper, seemingly middle-aged woman, standing with her hand placed lightly on the shoulder of a seated, frock-coated man – perhaps her brother Frederick Francis Giraud. To the right of the gentleman stands another, older woman: Jane's mother, or possibly one of Jane's two elder sisters. The artist is heavily and elaborately dressed in the manner of the 1830s and '40s. Her skirt makes a wide whaleboned circle to the floor; her sleeves are trimmed with fringe and embroidery, and reveal voluminous white, lace-trimmed undersleeves. Her right hand clenches slightly, underscoring the formality, if not tension, of the occasion. At her neck Jane wears a white lace collar and a ribbon choker with a brooch at the throat. Her strong, plain face is framed by slightly wavy hair, parted in the middle and drawn back, under a lace cap, into a bun at the nape of the neck. In sum, Giraud's portrait looks remarkably like the one well-known portrait of Emily Dickinson; and together the group appears the very model of Victorian bourgeois respectability, with Jane as its younger feminine exemplar.

Obituaries in the local papers identified Jane Giraud only as the "youngest daughter of John Thomas Giraud, Esq."[10] As is typical of obituaries of the time, no mention was made even of her mother's name, let alone – in spite of her three published works – of her own work as a painter and illustrator. Giraud, like most women of her time, was apparently too ladylike to leave a trace when she died, unmarried, in London, on December 1, 1868, at the age of 58. Faversham, full of public monuments to Giraud's male relatives, holds only one monument to Jane: a monument as modestly hidden away as Giraud's life. It lies in the heart of an enormous Victorian almshouse, built in 1863 and perhaps supported in some way through Giraud's charity. The almshouse is still used today by pensioners, and is closed to the public, as is the tiny chapel set aside for the pensioners and their families. Within that chapel – off to the right, behind a curtain – stands a small organ, later played, apparently, by a later Francis Frederick Giraud (1832–1916).[11] Under its pipes, an inscription in brass very privately recompenses Giraud's earlier, potentially less private, gift of her book to her brother Herbert:

Figure 2. Jane Giraud, family photo

THIS.ORGAN.IS.HUMBLY.DEDICATED.TO.THE.GLORY.OF.
GOD.BY HERBERT J.GIRAUD M.D.IN.MEMORY.OF.HIS.
DEAR.SISTER.JANE.ELIZABETH.GIRAUD.WHO.DEPARTED.
THIS.LIFE.ON.1ST.DEC.R.1868.

Only the woman's name (not her professional status) adorns the organ – along with the brother's name *and* profession. Yet the artist's nearly anonymous flowers remain, and in their quiet way help Milton to sing across the centuries.

"Nineteenth-century reform movements," Whitney Chadwick notes, "were part of a growing middle-class response to widespread social and economic changes following the industrial revolution," a revolution in which "the middle class emerged as the dominant political force." This shift from an aristocratic hegemony to a bourgeois one brought with it, among other things, a new focus on scientific education – a new focus that for the first century, at least, enfranchised women to a certain extent. Yet of all middle-class values of the period, says Chadwick, none was more pervasive than that of "the ideal of modest and pure womanhood that evolved during Queen Victoria's reign" (1837–1901).[12] "Custom and usage" demanded the identification of women and men with very different spheres: the public world of politics and commerce for men, the private sphere of home and garden for women. Chadwick points out, in fact, that "the characterization of women's art as biologically determined or as an extension of their domestic and refining role in society reached its apogee in the nineteenth century." By the 1840s, when Giraud was producing her *Flowers of Milton*, the misogynist Eve of medieval tradition had largely given way to John Ruskin's sentimentalized notion of woman as "angel in the house." As the home was to become a haven for the wounded sensibilities of men, women were to serve as the keepers of their family's spiritual values – values conveniently inscribed in nature, and above all in flowers.

Thus two activities emerged during the century that were deemed especially appropriate for women: botany and watercolor painting, especially of flowering plants. Jane Giraud, like many others, combined the two interests – which were not, at the time, easily separable from one another, as neither was separable from the (similarly gendered) spheres of religion, ethics, and literature. During Giraud's lifetime, in fact, Kent was the home of a number of well-known botanists, including Anne Pratt (1806–93), one of "the best-known women writers of popular botany texts."[13] Pratt was born at Stroud, Kent, daughter of Robert Pratt, a wholesale grocer, and Sarah Bundock, who was known both for her garden and for her Huguenot faith. According to the *Dictionary of National Biography*, Pratt was "educated by Mrs. Roffey at the Eastgate House school, Rochester," learning her botany from a Scottish friend, Dr. Dods. Like her contemporary Jane Giraud, Pratt may have been encouraged to study botany initially because of her poor health as a child. In any case, she took avidly to the subject, and participated in all the ways deemed appropriate for women: collecting specimens, forming a herbarium, and drawing. Between the 1830s and 1850s, she wrote illustrated books of descriptive botany primarily for a scientific laity of women and boys (always, as Ann B. Shteir notes, addressed as "he") – at the exact point at which, as Shteir puts it, "the codes for asserting scientific authority were hardening and when channels for women's writing were narrowing." Her works were at once lyrical and botanically informative. The first, *The Field, the Garden, and the Woodland, or Interesting Facts Respecting Flowers and Plants in General*, appeared anonymously in 1838, when Pratt was thirty-two. She went on, however, to make a living from her books, including her five-volume *Flowering Plants and Ferns of Great Britain* (1855), a work aimed specifically "to the use of the unscientific."[14]

Like Pratt, Giraud lived in a well-educated household of Huguenot descent, where conversations about science would have been normal. We do not know whether Jane introduced her younger brother Herbert to the study of botany or whether he instructed her. We do know, however, that he went on to become not only a professor of chemistry and *materia medica*, but also of botany – the first to introduce the study of botany into western India. About the time Jane Giraud was working on her books, in fact, her brother's article on "Observations of Vegetable Embryology" was published by the Linnaean Society. This and his other works on botanical subjects went on to have lasting influence in the field. He was also well known as a lecturer: "easy and fluent in his address, apt and pertinent in his illustrations, [and] ever prompt to take advantage of any casual circumstance to give effect to his argument." Above all he was famous for his "experiments which always went off with such spontaneity, regularity and brilliant effect that they seemed to be due to the direct action of his volition."[15]

Botany, however, as Pratt's career indicates, was also very much a woman's subject – at least until mid-century, when, because of the field's increasing professionalization and specialization, women began to be edged out by men. "In the 1830s and 1840s," writes Barbara T. Gates, "women joined men in the widespread enthusiasm for natural history. Journals, experiments, and collections were all part of an enterprise that belonged to women as well as men."[16] Yet from the beginning the study of "natural history" was sharply gendered, with women botanists cast in quite different roles from those of their male counterparts. Men were encouraged to study nature as a way of reaching outside themselves – to understand, objectively, phenomena from which they were separate, and over which they exercised dominion. Women, on the other hand, were encouraged to study nature not less rigorously necessarily, but more subjectively – as a way of understanding *themselves*. Linnaeus' sexual classification of plants, in fact, underscored gender difference as an essential property of nature; and women themselves were considered more closely related to nature, biologically connected to the earth they sought to understand through a kind of natural sympathy. Educated mainly at home, they were taught science in the vernacular, spared the rigors of Latin and complex terminology.[17] Although women regularly attended public demonstrations and lectures by leading scientists, like those so successfully given by Giraud's own brother, they were discouraged from *giving* such lectures or from publishing their own findings. They were allowed to contribute to science mainly as collectors, as teachers, as popular authors, and, above all, as botanical illustrators. In fact, women actually dominated the field of botanical drawing at mid-century, largely, no doubt, because they commanded smaller fees than men.[18] Those who came from botanical families often served, Eve-like, as "help-mates and 'fair associates' to fathers, husbands, or brothers."[19] Often their work went uncredited – or was credited to their male protectors.

Another related art form for women was sentimental flower painting, a more literary enterprise, but one nonetheless requiring a keen eye and a very skilled hand. Countless gift books, mostly by women, were produced over the course of the century, juxtaposing colorful, botanically correct images of flowers with appropriate poetic texts.[20] *Flowers of Milton* obviously belongs within this genre, along with Giraud's *Flowers of Shakespeare*. Giraud also ventured, in 1850, into a more purely botanical project called *The Floral Months of England* – some copies of which she actually signed. Here, moreover, the audience addressed in her dedication is not just one person (even the queen), but rather the general public – or at least "All who 'consider the Lilies of the Field, how they grow.'" The book is made up of twelve beautiful and exact paintings of seasonal plants – beginning in March with anemone and periwinkle (listed by both their English and Latin names), and ending in February with daisy, groundsel, and chickweed. An elaborate frontispiece unfurls the book's title and moral on white ribbons, backed with red and blue and hung like banners in a breeze between the stakes and leaves of an arbor, the bottom rung of which sprouts thistles, blackberries, and roses (figure 3). Flowers, Giraud asserts, are teachers, priests, and sermons – suggesting the trope, here an especially self-reflexive one, of nature as God's book. They are also shrines, suggesting the equally important idea of nature as *oikos*, or house: the idea that lies at the root of the word *ecology* and at the center of its originally Christian ethos.[21]

Figure 3. Jane Giraud, title page, *Floral Months of England*

Although, as with the case of *The Floral Months of England*, the names of some women authors and artists appeared on their works, many, if not most, remained anonymous. As Jack Kramer writes in his *Women of Flowers*, "Anonymous was a woman of flowers ... In Victorian England, a lady's name was considered sacred and meant to be held in strict and pure reverence, certainly not to be used for crass, commercial purposes. Only a few women were bold enough to break with this tradition." Kramer goes on to point out that women had another reason to omit their names: "the few pioneering women who published books under their own names were treated harshly by the critics."[22] "Not only," Chadwick notes in *Women, Art, and Society*, "was a woman's work evaluated in terms of what it revealed of its maker's 'femininity,' it was also consigned to media and subjects now considered appropriate and 'natural' to women." Chadwick cites, for instance, the view of Leon Legrange, writing in the *Gazette des Beaux-Arts* in 1860:

Let men conceive of great architectural projects, monumental sculpture, and the most elevated forms of painting ... In a word, let men busy themselves with all that has to do with great art. Let women occupy themselves with those types of art which they have always preferred, such as ... the painting of flowers, those prodigies of grace and freshness which alone can compete with the grace and freshness of women themselves.

Thus Victorian women artists, Chadwick concludes, "existed in a contradictory relationship to the prevailing middle-class ideals of femininity." Although educational and social reform movements had made them in some respects the best-educated generation of women in history, the "public visibility" necessary for success in the arts belonged only to men. Women who entered that competitive fray, whether by publishing their own work or by rejecting flower-painting for heroic subjects, risked being accused of "'unsexing' themselves."[23]

Jane Giraud seems to have taken no such risk – although she may well have needed, in the "hungry forties" and after, to earn a modest living for herself and her widowed mother.[24] Even in *Flowers of Milton*, however, she did transgress the rule of anonymity with sly feminine restraint. In some of her flower paintings she subtly signed her initials – in addition to mentioning her illustrious brother by name and citing *his* public achievement, thereby reclaiming that name for herself, albeit only by reflection. Moreover, while confining herself to the most traditional of ostensible subjects – flowers – she nonetheless managed to produce a remarkably astute reading of Milton's epic, one that stressed ecological concerns just coming to the fore during her time.

At the beginning of their recent *Ecofeminist Literary Criticism*, Greta Gaard and Patrick Murphy define the ecofeminist position as "the recognition and positive identification of 'otherness'" – whether the *other* is defined in terms of race and/or gender, or in terms of the natural world. In contrast to a dominant, masculinist ethic that seeks to dominate and exploit "others" of all kinds, Gaard and Murphy would substitute an ethic of "interanimation" and "mutual co-creation." Two kinds of literature, they argue, have regularly – and not coincidentally – been marginalized in European culture, with its valorization of manipulation and progress: women's writing and environmental writing. The goal of ecofeminist thinking, and of ecofeminist criticism in particular, is to redress this imbalance by recovering and empowering the suppressed voices of women, of ethnic minorities, and of the desperately endangered earth. Ecofeminist criticism, they suggest, can facilitate this process both by giving us a new set of lenses through which to view texts, and by asking the question, "What previously unnoticed elements of a literary text are made visible, or even foregrounded, when one reads from an ecofeminist perspective?"[25] In recent years a number of scholars of early modern literature have taken up the challenge here explicitly posed by Gaard and Murphy. Readings by Diane Kelsey McColley, Richard J. DuRocher, and others have begun to uncover the "previously unnoticed" strands of what we might call ecofeminism and deep ecology in the writings of Vaughan, Marvell, and Milton, while providing new lenses through which to see the work of Milton's illustrators.

The question needs to be raised, of course, of whether a lens first consciously adopted in the 1990s can be applied with integrity to texts produced in the seventeenth and nineteenth centuries.[26] We would argue that for some texts, at least, the lens of ecofeminism might in fact be a more useful one than a number of other modern and postmodern lenses currently and ubiquitously in use. For indeed, although ecofeminists have been at pains to decry the traditional association between woman and earth (rightly seeing that association as a way of subordinating both women and nature to a supposedly superior masculine "culture"), they have also stressed the *analogy* between the two in the "othering," domination, and exploitation both have experienced. As Judith Plant says, "perhaps the essential feature of ecofeminist thought is that all oppressions . . . have their roots in common."[27] In making this analogy the center of their thinking, they have run the risk, as Michael Zimmerman has noted, of being read as antimodern; or the related risk, as Chris Cuomo argues, of being read as neo-essentialists.[28] Yet as Deane Curtin has recently argued, as dangerous as all such analogies are – "women are not essentially more 'natural,' closer to nature, than men, and nature is no more female than male" – the "actual practices typically demanded of women involve mediation between culture and nature."[29] Curtin explicitly calls her approach "nonessentialist"; but in practical terms the lens she proposes is one marvelously suited both to Milton's struggle to envision paradise and to the work of his more ecologically oriented earlier readers.

As a woman living and working in the mid nineteenth century, Jane Giraud was no doubt more than a practical essentialist (as oxymoronic as the term may sound). In fact, as we have seen, essentialist conceptions of sexual difference reached their apex in the botanical classification propounded by the Swedish botanist Carl von Linne, or Linnaeus (1707–78), and in its popular appropriation during the decades of Giraud's productive life. As Pamela Gerrish Nunn puts it in *Problem Pictures*, the Victorians' "linking [of] women and flowers . . . was politically convenient and socially powerful" – as Shirley Hibberd (1856) showed in this admonition to her fellows: "Flowers teach the lessons of patient submission, meek endurance, and innocent cheerfulness under the pressure of adverse circumstances . . . Many are the moral precepts they inculcate, bidding us admire the wisdom of their omnipotent Creator, in their infinite variety of forms and colours, and perfect adaptation to the situation they occupy."[30]

On the other hand, the sense of connectedness, the ethic of flourishing and care, so central to contemporary ecofeminist thinking, is also prominent in much botanical work of Giraud's time. If botanical study had, as Donald Worster has suggested, an "imperial" tradition – a tradition focusing on mastery and dominion – it had equally an anti-imperial, or "Arcadian," tradition – a strain increasingly noted in Milton's epic.[31] For Worster that anti-imperial strain of thought is embodied in Gilbert White's *Natural History of Selbourne*, which was published in 1789 and appeared in numerous editions during the nineteenth century. White's "life program," as Worster puts it, was "to see how many creatures the Selbourne parish contained and to understand how they were all united in an interrelated system."[32] For White and others like him, science and faith were integrated *not* in the masculinist idea of subduing nature, but rather in an appreciation for the fragile interconnectedness of all things – and for an Eve-like deity, creating and sustaining beauty and harmony in the *oikos*, the *house* of nature. As early as the seventeenth century, the term *oeconomy* – predecessor, as Worster demonstrates, to the nineteenth-century neologism *oecology* – was "frequently employed to refer to the divine government of the natural world," a government in which "God was seen both as the Supreme Economist who had designed the earth household and as the housekeeper who kept it functioning productively."[33] Thus, Worster says, "the study of 'ecology' – a word that appeared in the nineteenth century as a more scientific substitute for the older phrase – was in its very origins imbued with a political and economic as well as Christian view of nature."[34] This idea, which in McColley's work has done so much to rehabilitate both Milton's Eve and his ecological ethic,[35] is also central to the work of Jane Giraud.

For her title page to *Paradise Lost*, Giraud chose a telling quotation from book 9 – the only lines she quotes, in fact, that do not mention a specific flower (figure 4). The passage conveys the reaction of nature, at the exact moment Eve plucks and eats the forbidden fruit: "Earth felt the wound, and Nature from her seat / Sighing through all her Works gave signs of woe, / That all was lost" (*PL* 9.782–84). Giraud represents this decisive moment in a vivid symbolic scene. The left side of the page is taken up by a withering tree, enwrapped by a serpent – head dangling, in what appears a mixture of malice and agony, toward the tree's thorn-choked roots. At upper-left, the tree's fruiting foliage wilts – while, to the right, a rose bush rises abruptly into bare thorn. Trapped and felled by the creeping thorns and wilting foliage covering the foreground, a struggling prostrate bird with a snowy white breast brings death into the world and all our woe, as the creation is subjected to futility (Romans 8.22) by invisible human hands. Thus Giraud introduces her reading of *Paradise Lost*, one in which improper action by human beings affects not only the persons involved, but all of nature and the universe. This reading recalls DuRocher's recent argument that:

In Milton's poem, we are shown immediately what Adam and Eve will only later be forced to realize: that the choices of human beings intimately affect the entire scale of being. Chiefly, yet still perhaps mysteriously, Adam and Eve's choice wounds the Earth . . . Milton's focus on the wounded Earth at the pivotal moment of the human drama shows how closely interconnected is the health of human and natural bodies.[36]

By focusing her entire reading of the epic on flowers – and in so doing drawing our attention away from patriarchal strains of the epic, and toward the natural and human (as well as archetypally feminine) realm – Giraud dramatically foregrounds DuRocher's insight. In the story of flowers, she

Figure 4. Jane Giraud, "Earth felt the wound," from *The Flowers of Milton*

suggests, lies the story of an equally precious and vulnerable nature – a story which, in turn, is our *own* story as human beings who are part of nature and are dependent upon it, like every other "fair creature," for our flourishing and survival. Perhaps, in fact, Milton's story of flowers is really more *fundamentally* our story than that of "stern Achilles," and "Not less but more Heroic" for that (*PL* 9.14–15).

Jane Giraud's ecofeminist Paradise Lost

Thus Giraud's reading of *Paradise Lost* functions as Gaard and Murphy suggest ecofeminist criticism functions – drawing us to view the epic from a perspective that: (1) foregrounds connections between human beings and nature; (2) valorizes nature as sacred; (3) treats the text, like nature itself, not as an "it" but as a "thou"; and (4) leads the reader-seer to new levels of "meditative attentiveness."[37] To heighten such awareness, Giraud begins her rendering of Milton's narrative by devoting *two* plates (of a total of seven) to his description of Adam and Eve's bower (figures 5 and 6). In so doing she foregrounds, as does Milton, both the connection between Adam and Eve and their natural and sacred *oikos*, and the connection between prelapsarian human love and human vocation – later to reveal the poignantly related loss of both.

The first actual flower passage Giraud selects from the epic describes the bower's floral roof and walls:

> Laurel and Myrtle, and what higher grew
> Of firm and fragrant leaf; on either side
> *Acanthus*, and each odorous bushy shrub
> Fenc'd up the verdant wall; each beauteous flow'r,
> *Iris* all hues, Roses, and Jessamin
> Rear'd high thir flourisht heads between, and wrought
> Mosaic.   (PL 4.694–700)

This passage is immediately followed in the poem, albeit separately illustrated by Giraud, by the epic voice's description of the bower's floor: "underfoot the Violet, / Crocus, and Hyacinth with rich inlay / Broider'd the ground" (PL 4.700–02). As James Patrick McHenry has pointed out, the mixture of plants Milton has selected to raise the bower are so rich with symbolic resonance that we can give only a few examples here. Acanthus, which, wittily enough, does not merely decorate but actually *forms* the pillars of the bower's walls, "probably symbolized immortality" among the Greeks; it also "appears in early Christian art as a plant of heaven." Laurel and myrtle both carry associations of mourning, but also are revered as tokens of peace and resurrection, as well as being associated with love (laurel) and with Venus (myrtle). All the bower's plants, as McHenry notes, are especially fragrant, and share associations both sacred and medicinal. Jasmine, in addition to its sweet fragrance, is associated with banqueting houses – which McHenry does not relate to the Song of Songs (chapter 4, especially verse 4), but Milton and Giraud well might – and Iris with the rainbow, which so poignantly reappears to Adam near the end of the epic.[38] In fact, for McHenry as for Giraud, a reading of Milton's flowers becomes

238 *Milton and Gender*

> Laurel and **Myrtle** and what higher grew
> Of firm and fragrant leaf: on either side
> **Acanthus**, and each odorous bushy shrub,
> Fenc'd up the verdant wall, each beauteous flower,
> **Iris** all hues, **Roses** and **Jessamine**
> Rear'd high their flourish'd heads between, and wrought
> Mosaic.

Figure 5. Jane Giraud, "Bower 1," from *The Flowers of Milton*

in many ways a reading of the epic itself: a reading grounded in nature, fraught with opportunity for significant moral choice, and encircled with prevenient grace.

The sixteenth- and seventeenth-century "herbals" that McHenry cites – with their sometimes arcane blend of natural history, medicinal theories, moral symbolism, and literary associations – had been largely supplanted

Figure 6. Jane Giraud, "Bower 2," from *The Flowers of Milton*

in Giraud's day by more "scientific" post-Linnaean botanical works. These later works nonetheless shared Milton's assumption of a fundamentally moral universe, designed by a unifying Providence, in which physical forms embodied ethical meanings. Thus a number of the associations Milton would have made with certain plants – e.g. laurel and myrtle with immortality; euphrasy and rue as cures for blindness – would still have had meaning for Giraud, particularly when the symbolic properties were classical and/or biblical as well as early modern in origin. Almost certainly those properties guided her selection from the many possible flower passages in *Paradise Lost*. Even more important – at least to our reading of Giraud's writing of Miltonic gender – is the interpretation of Milton's text she encodes in the decorative capitals that open the Miltonic text on each page. Indeed, these capitals serve as glosses on each selected passage – glosses analogous to those left in classic tomes by medieval reader-artists.

Thus in Giraud's first two flower designs, initial capitals (*L* and *U* respectively) each conceal a small serpentine figure. In the lines describing the bower's walls, he merely weaves the warp of his body through the woof of the grass that creates the horizontal bar of the *L* – a narrow fellow, but "not noxious," necessarily, or threatening. In the lines describing the bower's floor, he reclines against a flower stalk, his body wittily contributing the loop of the *U* of the word *underfoot*. Like Mary Groom nearly a century later, Giraud is not without a sense of humor. And like Groom too, she seems to suggest that nature offers choices to human beings – choices so enmeshed in our environment that they are as difficult as Psyche's seeds to sort out; but choices, nonetheless, with cosmic implications.[39]

Giraud's fourth design (figure 7), borrowing lines from the tender aubade which opens book 5, bypasses Adam's endearments to Eve, moving straight, and with some urgency, to his mention of flowers:

> Awake, the morning shines, and the fresh field
> Calls us; we lose the prime, to mark how spring
> Our tended Plants, how blows the Citron Grove,
> What drops the Myrrh, and what the balmy Reed,
> How Nature paints her colors, how the Bee
> Sits on the Bloom, extracting liquid sweet.
> (*PL* 5.20–25)

Thus Giraud emphasizes not just the romantic "language of flowers" so often celebrated, as Seaton points out, in nineteenth-century parlor games, but rather the serious role of Adam and Eve as custodians of their natural home or *oikos*. As Adam suggests, they have two important Edenic tasks: (1) to care for the garden and (2) to contemplate it – to live, bee-like, in "meditative awareness" of its seasonal glories. Interestingly, Milton has not selected for this passage the most labor intensive of flowers, but rather those known for their thriving in temperate climates and for their glorious fragrances. "The spiritual significance of plants was as real as day or night to many of Milton's contemporary readers," says McHenry; and pleasant fragrances were spiritually significant in a palpable and literal way – as "vital spirits" directly convertible into "spiritual substance."[40] In this design even

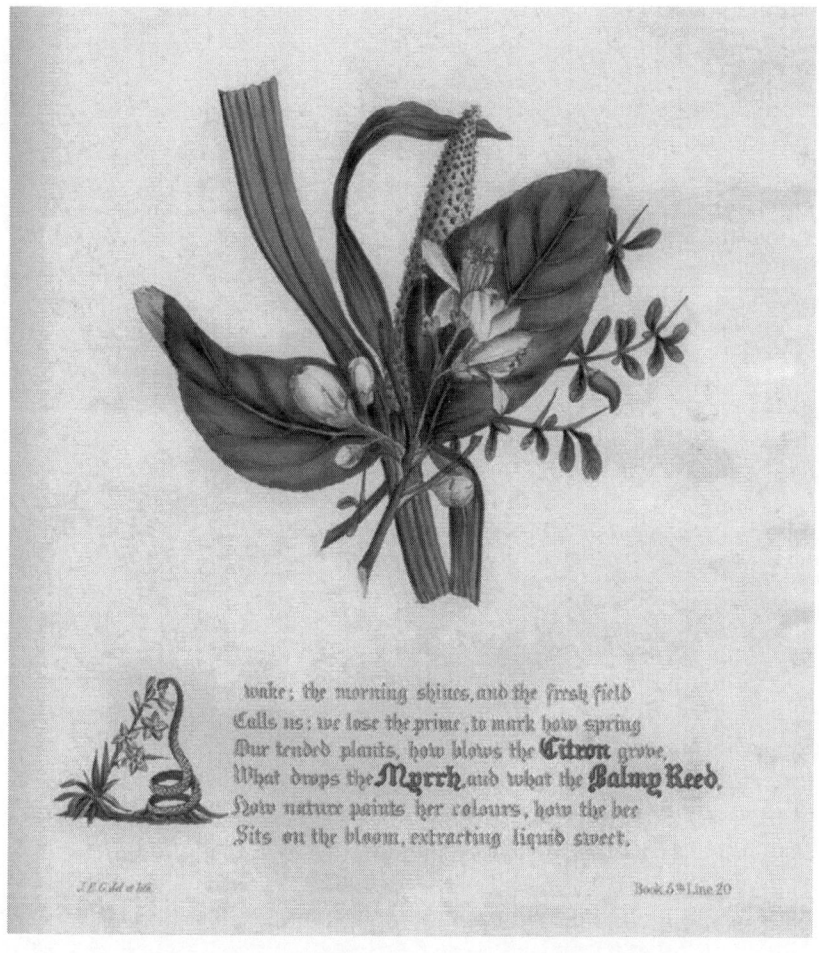

Figure 7. Jane Giraud, "Awake!" from *The Flowers of Milton*

the initial snake becomes a connoisseur of flowers – smelling the lily plant that makes up the other half in the initial *A* in the word *Awake*.[41] Vigilance is no doubt important in this Paradise: one must be awake to danger. Yet just as important to Adam and Eve is the overwhelming counterweight of natural wealth, which they are called not to exploit but to nurture and, above all, to enjoy.

This emphasis gives context to the motive of Eve, as Giraud moves on to her first of three designs based on book 9 (figure 8), where our first mother proposes to work separately from Adam:

Figure 8. Jane Giraud, "Let us divide our labors," from *The Flowers of Milton*

>Let us divide our labors, thou where choice
>Leads thee, or where most needs, whether to wind
>The Woodbine round this Arbor, or direct
>The clasping Ivy where to climb, while I
>In yonder Spring of Roses intermixt
>With Myrtle, find what to redress till Noon.
>   (*PL* 9.214–19)

Mary Groom, in her unambiguously feminist reading of Milton's epic, is one of his few illustrators to completely ignore the separation scene, with its dangerous implication of an Eve insufficient to stand alone. Other artists, such as Blake (along with a number of critics, including Millicent Bell) have represented the scene in a way that suggests that Eve's separation from her partner is the very essence of her fall.[42] Giraud, working in the context of Victorian gender roles, might well have been expected to read the separation in this dubious way. Yet her design suggests that for her, as for McColley, Eve's proposal is a serious and worthy, if always a potentially dangerous, one. The serpent, who has been represented in relatively innocent postures in Giraud's first three designs, now for the first time adopts a somewhat threatening one: looking down from the top of a still-verdant tree which echoes, in miniature, the withering tree of the frontispiece. Yet, if Giraud signals that Eve is in danger, this is no fall before the fall. Here no thorns yet appear upon the ground; the tiny tree of Giraud's *L* still blooms, like the rest of Adam and Eve's garden, all the way to its top leaves. The serpent himself, moreover, if actively curious, also looks cheerful – spying, surely, but without the frightening mien he takes on during and after the fall. He seems still, in short, a part of nature. Whether he, along with the rest of nature, will be consigned to a curse depends on the resolve of Adam and Eve.

In Giraud's second page for book 9 (figures 9 and 10), although the text deals only with Eve's flowers, the serpent of Giraud's initial *E* does in fact "address" his way "toward Eve" – making it plain that the artist has read Milton in full, and with care.[43] The serpent here, like those in Giraud's previous initial letters, is "Mere Serpent in appearance"; but here, as never before, he is, in the epic narrator's words, "on his Quest, where likeliest he might find / The only two of Mankind, but in them / The whole included Race, his purpos'd prey" (*PL* 9.412–16). He is, perhaps, for the first time *not* merely a serpent, but a conscious threat to human happiness – and to the well-being of the entire cosmos, as represented in its floral microcosm. Providing a playful flourish at the bottom right of Eve's capital *E*, he stretches toward her – his forked tongue suggesting "Language of Man pronounc't / By Tongue of Brute" (*PL* 9.553–54) and, perhaps, "Hate . . . under show of Love well feign'd" (492). Eve, moreover – poised innocent but attentive in her tiny capital letter, her entire identity to be vindicated or destroyed by her choice – is able to convey the emotional weight of the passage: its agonized suspension, the world's future hanging in the balance, as "*Eve* separate [the serpent] spies." Sweetly and deftly drawn, even in miniature Eve appears

Figure 9. Jane Giraud, "Eve among her flowers," from *The Flowers of Milton*

> Veil'd in a Cloud of Fragrance, where she stood,[44]
> Half spi'd, so thick the Roses bushing round
> About her glow'd, oft stooping to support
> Each Flow'r of slender stalk, whose head though gay
> Carnation, Purple, Azure, or speckt with Gold,
> Hung drooping unsustain'd, them she upstays
> Gently with Myrtle band.   (*PL* 9.425–31)

Figure 10. Jane Giraud, "Eve and the serpent," from *The Flowers of Milton*

Working, like Eve, within her grammar of flowers, Giraud does not go on to complete the passage – to note that Eve is "mindless the while, / Herself, though fairest unsupported Flow'r, / From her best prop so far, and storm so nigh" (431–33). Yet the Victorian iconography of flowers certainly would have underscored, to Giraud's thinking, a cosmic aptness to the line. As Nunn reminds us, "This peculiar idea, that women were somehow flowers even while they were human beings, surfaced freely in the Victorians' vocabulary."[45] Even so – as clearly as we see Eve propping her flowers, utterly and *literally* one with their forms – it is yet possible to read her at this moment as "sufficient to stand" (*PL* 3.99). Poised, like Mary before the angel Gabriel, and like the Eve in Groom's 1937 design, she has a moment to meditate upon both the book and the house of nature – although both appear distorted in the serpent's fork-tongued verbal appeal – and to choose aright.[46]

That Eve and Adam do not choose aright becomes clear in the passage Giraud next represents (figure 11): the corruption of their natural and God-given sexuality. By this point in the narrative Giraud has sharpened our gaze on flowers and their capacity, not merely emblematic but truly symbolic, to serve as synecdoche for the state of all nature, including the human. Thus, at least for the first time in our reading of the poem, there is something of a shock in Milton's abrupt three-line account beginning with the four-stress assertion that "*Flow'rs* were the Couch, / Pansies, and Violets, and Asphodel, / And Hyacinth, Earth's freshest, softest lap" (*PL* 9.1039–41). Once as innocent as their human companions, the flowers here are suddenly turned unclean by misuse, bearing alone the narrative of human shame and objectification. As Eve, "nothing loath," becomes an *it* (not a thou) to Adam's enflamed appetite, her flowers, too, are exploited by the amorous pair. The "grosser sleep" that immediately "[o]ppresse[s]" our first parents, "wearied with thir amorous play" (*PL* 9.1049, 1045), lies beyond the passage's floral description. Yet Giraud's connected universe can slyly allude to the lines – with a fagged-out little serpent, lying supine in the grass, at the foot of the capital *F* of the flowers that have been pressed into undignified service as Adam and Eve's illicit couch.

Nature then, for Giraud as for Milton, is a fragile and woundable system – one dependent upon human resolve (and perhaps, although less absolutely, upon human solidarity). It is also the ground of significant moral action – for good and ill. A garden, Sue Bennet reminds us, may be a restricted place; but it is also – as for Eve – a "physical and spiritual arena in which individual women strove to assert control, define their identity, struggle with sexual feelings and escape or embrace the world."[47] Finally, as flowers are medicinal as well as aesthetic, so the garden also offers opportunities for reparation and renewal. The final quotation in Giraud's series eloquently suggests that the damage stemming from human misappropriation of nature also finds its antidote in nature (figure 12).

In *Paradise Lost* 11, Michael takes Adam to the Mount of Prophecy – and shows him the spoliation to come, by human agency, of both humanity and nature: the "yet unspoil'd / *Guiana*, whose great City *Geryon's* Sons / Call *El Dorado*" (*PL* 11.409–11). In these painful lines, as throughout the last two books of his epic, Milton clearly embodies Judith Plant's ecofeminist premise of a "single root" to all oppression: the human (and demonic) craving for power divorced from responsibility, at the cost of mutuality

Jane Giraud's ecofeminist Paradise Lost

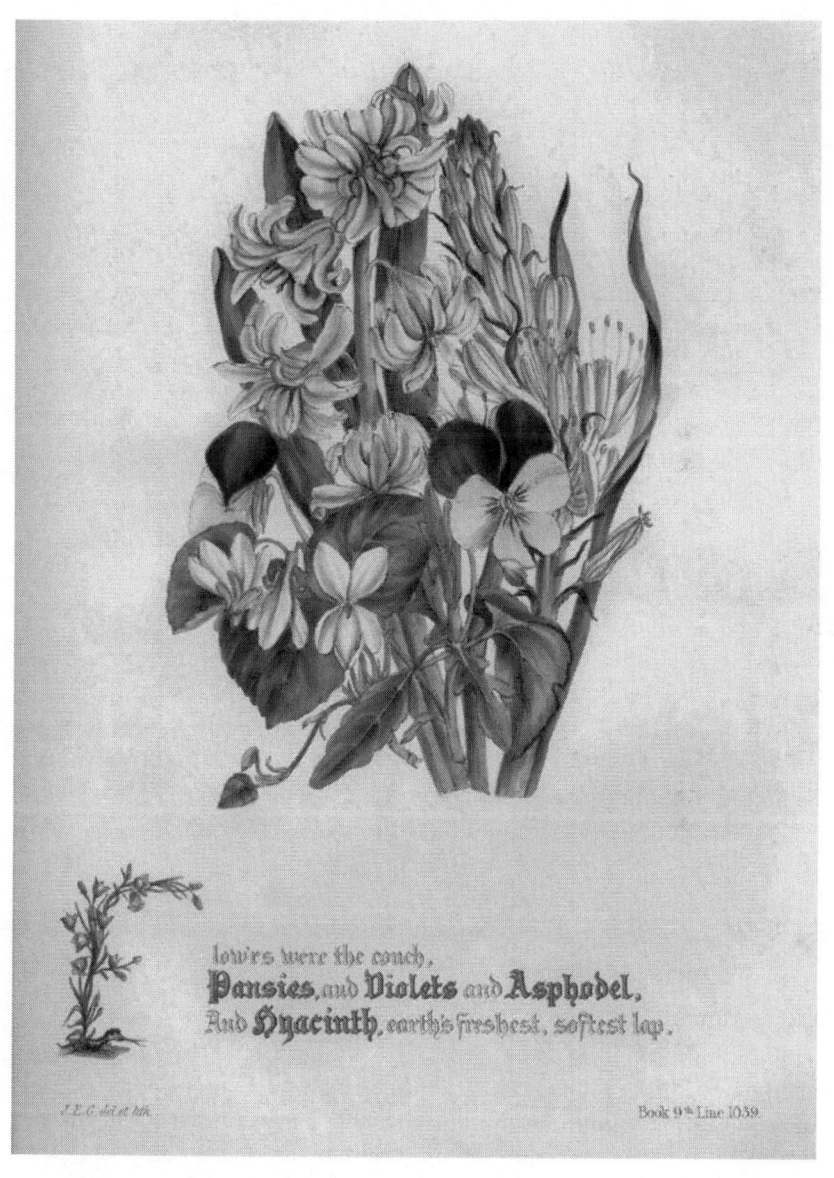

Figure 11. Jane Giraud, "Flowers were the couch," from *The Flowers of Milton*

Figure 12. Jane Giraud, "Euphrasy and rue," from *The Flowers of Milton*

and love.[48] The lines Giraud has chosen come immediately upon this dark image of othering and desecration: the lines in which Michael removes the "Film" from Adam's eyes, "Which that false Fruit that promis'd clearer sight / Had bred; then purg'd with Euphrasy and Rue / The visual Nerve, for he had much to see" (*PL* 11.412–15). Here the lush flowers of all the previous designs give way to two bitter-tasting and austere-looking herbs. Euphrasy, or "eyebright," was "widely reported as a cure for dim eyes" because, as a seventeenth-century herbal asserted, "The Purple and yellow spots and stripes ... doth [sic] very much resemble diseases of the Eyes."[49] Euphrasy was widely used in conjunction with rue, also called the "herb of grace," which was known for having a "very strong and ranke smell, and a biting taste."[50] But "by reason of the signe of the Cross imprest on the Seed," wrote another commentator, rue could cure "Phantasmes," as well as serving as a "remedie against dim eyes" and a repellent for snakes [51] – three remedies much needed in a postlapsarian world. The very commonness and austerity of these herbs (apart from the wonderfully telling pun on *rue*) give vivid visual testimony to the new dispensation within which not only Adam and Eve but all of nature will have to live.

The lushness of paradise, then, gives way to the rigors of history. Anyone who has read the last two books of *Paradise Lost* – and we can be sure Giraud had – will also see a painful ambiguity in the narrator's assertion that there was "much to see." The first thing Adam will see, in fact, will be Abel's murder at the hand of Cain; the last will be the Flood, destroying the entire creation. At that point, he will no longer be able to endure the sight of history, and will settle to hear the rest of the earth's future merely related. For us, however, Giraud seems to suggest, there is still "much to see" in the garden of our minds and the garden of the world. ("Gardens," writes Bennet, "exist in the mind and in reality. Our perceptions of gardens weave together ideas and sensitivities: what we think and what we feel."[52]) As in the capital *B* to the left of Giraud's design, there is still a serpent – immanent in nature and in ourselves – not easily discerned without special grace and endless vigilance. There are plants, useful and beautiful, to be tended, to be preserved, and to be meditated upon with attentiveness and care. Paradoxically, however, in our very "rue" over the loss of Eden's flowers, a hope is born – as it is for our first parents at the poignantly balanced end of Milton's epic – for the renewal of something like them in our lives.

NOTES

1. Faversham, April 26th, 1850. This quotation, unpunctuated, is part of a decorative motif on Giraud's frontispiece. (See figure 3.)
2. (Cambridge, MA: Harvard University Press, 1999) 194.
3. See his *Feminist Milton* (Ithaca: Cornell University Press, 1987).
4. The authors have interviewed Alexis Smith, the late Carlotta Petrina, and relatives of the late Mary Green. Virginia Tufte wrote and co-produced a video-biography of Petrina: *Reaching for Paradise: The Life and Art of Carlotta Petrina* (La Femina Films, 1994; 55 minutes). A visit to Favershan by Wendy Furman-Adams and Charles Adams provided many details of Jane Giraud's background.
5. Joseph Wittreich includes "Giraud's Designs" in his chronological listing of Milton illustrators in *A Milton Encyclopedia*, ed. William B. Hunter, Jr., John

Shawcross, and John M. Steadman (Lewisburg: Bucknell University Press, 1978), 4: 71. Many of the flower watercolors have been cut from the books, sold as prints, and copied for sale.

6. These books were produced at a time when very effective lithographic color printing (called "chromography") was being done, especially in children's books. Giraud's books were in fact printed in color, but many pages also have been touched up by hand. Her *Flowers of Shakespeare* was also anonymous and similarly dedicated to her brother in 1845.

7. We gratefully acknowledge McColley's sharing of her as yet unpublished essay, "Earth and Mother Tongue: Milton's Environmental Poetics."

8. A Giraud descendant, Barry James Price, gives John Thomas Giraud the much later death date of 1851; this date and a wealth of other information about the Giraud family comes from Sydney Clark, "The Girauds of Faversham," a three-part article in *Bygone Kent* 19.11 (Nov. 1998): 677–85; 19.12 (Dec. 1998): 755–60; and 20.1 (Jan. 1999): 25–28.

9. Some details about Giraud's life were searched out by Claire Lloyd, Community Librarian of the Kent County Council Arts and Libraries. Other details were provided by Giraud descendants in the United States, Australia, and Canada – especially Price, who generously shared not only his extensive genealogical knowledge but also family photographs.

10. Thanks are due to Hazel Stanley, of the Sittingbourne Library, for a copy of Giraud's Sittingbourne death record and to reference librarian Joanna Pateman for the opportunity to examine copies of the *South Eastern Gazette* and *Maidstone and Kentish Gazette* for December 7, 1868.

11. See Clark, "The Girauds of Faversham (Part Three)," 28. Thanks are due to Peggy Partis, of Faversham's Fleur De Lis Heritage Centre and Museum, for mentioning the existence of this organ. We are grateful to Arthur Percival, Director of the Centre, for a wealth of background and local history of Kent (and Faversham in particular) during Giraud's time. So secret, however, is Jane Giraud's monument, that even he – the chief local historian – did not know of its existence.

12. Whitney Chadwick, *Women, Art, and Society* (London: Thames and Hudson, 1994) 35, 166–67.

13. Anne B. Shteir, *Cultivating Women, Cultivating Science: Flora's Daughters and Botany in England, 1760 to 1860* (Baltimore: Johns Hopkins University Press, 1996) 202.

14. *Ibid.*, 203, 204.

15. Note no. 8, *Giraud Pedigree*, 2nd. edn. (corrected 1843). Provided to Professor Tufte by Barry Price.

16. *Kindred Nature: Victorian and Edwardian Women Embrace the Living World* (Chicago: University of Chicago Press, 1998) 3.

17. We have been able to find nothing specific about the education Giraud and her sisters enjoyed. Yet given the social class of her family and the professional training of her father and brothers, it is likely that Jane was taught at home by a governess and then, perhaps, attended a nearby day-school for girls in

her early teens. She may have had professional training in flower-painting, but some flower painters were self-instructed, using books that were identified as ways of teaching oneself. Of educated Victorian women, Gaye Tuchman writes, "Women were more likely than men to come from upper-middle-class and upper-class families; their fathers were more likely to be concentrated [as in Giraud's family] in the classic liberal professions of medicine, law, and the clergy. But their formal education was scanty compared to that of men." See *Edging Women Out: Victorian Novelists, Publishers and Social Change* (New Haven: Yale University Press, 1989) 114.
18. Giraud quite possibly earned some of her income by helping anonymously with illustrations in books made by male flower painters. The name *Giraud* is one of those listed as helping with illustrations for a book by a well-known flower artist named Robert Tyas.
19. Shteir, *Cultivating Women*, 50.
20. For a history of the sentimental flower book, see Beverly Seaton, *The Language of Flowers: A History* (Charlottesville: University Press of Virginia, 1995).
21. For a thorough and stimulating history of ecological thought in England, see Donald Worster, *Nature's Economy: A History of Ecological Ideas* (Cambridge: Cambridge University Press, 1994). Worster points out that the word *ecology*, originally spelled "oecology," was first used by Ernst Haeckel, a German disciple of Darwin, in 1866, and was defined as "the science of the relations of living organisms to the external world, their habitat, customs, energies, parasites, etc." Haeckel, however, derived his new word from "the same root found in the older word 'economy': the Greek *oikos*, referring to the family household and its daily operations and maintenance" (192).
22. Jack Kramer, *Women of Flowers: A Tribute to Victorian Women Illustrators* (New York: Stewart, Tabori, and Chang, 1996), 46–49.
23. *Women, Art, and Society*, 35, 165.
24. The phrase comes from Paula Gillett, *The Victorian Painter's World* (New Brunswick, NJ: Rutgers University Press, 1990), 6. Gillett aptly demonstrates that "women – including genteel wives and daughters facing financial adversity . . . benefited significantly from the strong demand for the work of contemporary artists that began to build in the late 1840s and continued for a quarter of a century afterward." They were, however, denied the all-important recognition of membership in the Royal Academy (as in the Royal Society), and had very limited access to education in the arts (133–34).
25. Greta Gaard and Patrick D. Murphy, eds., *Ecofeminist Literary Criticism: Theory, Interpretation, Pedagogy* (Urbana: University of Illinois Press, 1998), 6–7. See also Karen J. Warren, ed. *Ecofeminism: Women, Culture, Nature* (Bloomington: Indiana University Press, 1997). Michael Zimmerman places ecofeminism within the context of other related movements of radical ecology in *Contesting the Earth's Future: Radical Ecology and Postmodernity* (Berkeley: University of California Press, 1994).
26. Barbara Cates traces the movement, or at least its name, to the work of Françoise d'Eaubonne, a Frenchwoman writing in the early 1970s, who coined

the word *ecoféminisme*. Yet she grants that the movement came into its own as a grass-roots phenomenon in the United States only in the 1990s. See "A Root of Ecofeminism: *Ecoféminisme*," in Gaard and Murphy, *Ecofeminist Literary Criticism*, 15–22. Nonetheless, as one of the "new French feminisms," ecofeminism had a somewhat earlier *literary* impact on feminists with an essentialist bent like Stevie Davies. See *The Feminine Reclaimed: The Idea of Woman in Spenser, Shakespeare, and Milton* (Lexington: University of Kentucky Press, 1986). Its philosophical language is not unrelated to that articulated by other French feminists like Luce Irigaray, who also connect, as Edward Casey notes, the "idea of place" to an ethics of sexual difference. See *The Fate of Place: A Philosophical History* (Berkeley: University of California Press, 1997).

27. "Learning to Live with Differences: The Challenge of Ecofeminist Community," in Warren, *Ecofeminism*, 121.
28. Zimmerman, *Contesting Earth's Future*; Chris J. Cuomo, *Feminism and Ecological Communities: An Ethic of Flourishing* (London: Routledge, 1998), 1.
29. Curtin "Women's Knowledge as Expert Knowledge," in Warren, *Ecofeminism*, 83–84.
30. Hibberd, *Rustic Adornments for the House and Recreation for Town folk in the Study and Imitation of Nature* (London: Groombridge, 1856), xii.
31. See *Milton and the Imperial Vision*, ed. Balachandra Rajan and Elizabeth Sauer (Pittsburgh: Duquesne University Press, 1999). Of special interest for our purposes here are Rajan and Sauer's helpful introduction, 1–22; Janel Mueller, "Dominion as Domesticity: Milton's Imperial God and the Experience of History," 25–47; and McColley, "Ecology and Empire," 112–29.
32. Worster, *Nature's Economy*, 2, 7.
33. *Ibid.*, 192.
34. *Ibid.*, 37.
35. We refer here to *Milton's Eve* (Urbana: University of Illinois Press, 1983); to *A Gust for Paradise: Milton's Eden and the Visual Arts* (Urbana: University of Illinois Press, 1993); and to McColley's more recent work cited above (note 31), but also to her forthcoming work on ecofeminism and deep ecology in Milton and other early modern poets.
36. Richard DuRocher, "The Wounded Earth in *Paradise Lost*," *Studies in Philology* 93 (Winter 1996): 93–115.
37. Guard and Murphy, *Ecofeminist Literary Criticism*, 3, 7, 9.
38. James Patrick McHenry, "A Milton Herbal," *Milton Quarterly* 30 (May 1996): 49, 79–80, 82–83, 77, 76. Although we disagree with McHenry's conclusion – one not especially important to his project – that "Milton was no proto-environmentalist" (102), his exhaustive catalogue provides an indispensable overview of Milton's use of flower imagery in *Paradise Lost*.
39. See our reading of Groom's wonderfully analogous headpiece to the 1937 Golden Cockerel *Paradise Lost* in Furman, "'Consider First, that Great / or Bright infers not Excellence': Mapping the Feminine in Mary Groom's Miltonic Cosmos," *Milton Studies* 28 (1992): 128–30.

Jane Giraud's ecofeminist Paradise Lost

40. McHenry, "A Milton Herbal," 47.
41. The lily, of course, is also associated with both the Virgin Annunciate and with the Resurrection – and thus hides another sign of prevenient grace, even in the midst of paradise.
42. On Blake's rendering of Eve's fall, see Furman and Tufte, "'With Other Eyes': Legacy and Innovation in Four Artists' Re-Visions of the Dinner Party in *Paradise Lost*," *Milton Studies* 35 (1997): 156–59.
43. Unable to learn much about Giraud's education, we can nonetheless extrapolate from the reading experience of better-known women of her generation. One such woman, the novelist Harriet Martineau (1802–76), read Milton for the first time at the age of eight, and wrote that "In a few months, I believe there was hardly a line in *Paradise Lost* that I could not have instantly turned to . . . I think this must have been my first experience of moral relief through intellectual resource." See Deirdre David, *Intellectual Women and Victorian Patriarchy: Harriet Martineau, Elizabeth Barrett Browning, George Eliot* (Ithaca: Cornell University Press, 1987) 34–35.
44. In so doing, Eve here poignantly echoes the Son's equally fateful moment of choice in *Paradise Regained* 4.561 – with its vertiginous sequel of Satan's fall. But in her case the real possibility of *standing* is tragically unrealized.
45. Nunn, *Problem Pictures*, 29.
46. For Groom's representation of Eve's fall, see Furman, "Consider First" 147–51.
47. "Escape to Eden," an introductory essay to *Five Centuries of Women and Gardens* (London: National Portrait Gallery, 2000), 12–13.
48. In view of Milton's regular appropriation both as literary arch-imperialist and patriarchal bogey, Plant might well be astonished by our assertion, since many ecofeminist thinkers have tended to blame Christian monotheism itself – with its concept of *dominion*, understood more as domination than as stewardship – for virtually all forms of oppression. Yet some recent readings of Milton, notably in Rajan and Sauer, *Milton and the Imperial Vision*, would corroborate our observation nonetheless.
49. McHenry, "A Milton Herbal," 67.
50. *Ibid.*, 97, here quotes John Gerard's *Herball or Generall Historie of Plantes*, first published in 1597, revised and reprinted in 1633 and 1636 – according to McHenry, the most popular herbal throughout the seventeenth century.
51. McHenry, "A Milton Herbal," 97.
52. "Escape to Eden," in *Five Centuries of Women and Gardens*, 13.

CHAPTER 13

Woolf's Allusion to Comus in The Voyage Out
Lisa Low

In the final chapters of her first novel, *The Voyage Out*, Virginia Woolf's heroine, Rachel Vinrace, slides into a coma carrying the words of Milton's *Comus* with her. Shortly thereafter, she dies. In classic readings of this allusion, Milton is said to kill Rachel off in a book about books. *The Voyage Out* is thus read as a feminist metatext, one that seeks to rewrite the novel's violent marriage plot – a plot that has historically trapped, even "raped" women, denying them full humanity in their status as wives and mothers.[1] Milton is often read as the baleful originator of this marriage plot and as the source of female oppression in the modern west. Having demanded in *Paradise Lost* that women submit to their husband's authority; having sentimentalized the private sphere and so locked early modern women into an asphyxiating domesticity; and, most importantly, having founded in *Paradise Lost* the middle-class novel with its woman-constricting marriage plot, Milton is read as the father of modern female doom. According to this reading, if things are to improve for women, Milton must be slain. So, in her first novel, Woolf takes on Milton in the form of her allusion to *Comus*, a work, like *The Voyage Out*, about the sexual violation of a female heroine. In plotting Milton as her first heroine's murderer, Woolf exposes and deconstructs the soul of the patriarchy Milton establishes, and, by implication at least, herself emerges as a master discourse writer of feminism.

Yet such a reading can be sustained only at the expense of *Comus*'s plot. It is a curious aspect of the history of literary criticism on this subject that the exponents of the most prominent interpretations of the place of *Comus* in *The Voyage Out* have not apparently read *Comus* at all. Rather, critics have assumed Milton to be the arch misogynist, and from that assumption, further false assumptions have followed. But even a brief look at *Comus* will show that the protagonist of Milton's masque, despite living in 1634 in an age when women were expected to be "chaste, silent, and obedient,"[2] is no shrinking violet. On the contrary, she is a powerful heroine who resists her enemy single-handedly. This chapter argues that, for Woolf, *Comus* does not represent the patriarchal plot feminist critics have claimed. Rather, Woolf must go as far back as Milton's *Comus* – before, that is, the fall into the eighteenth- and nineteenth-century novel with its woman-strangling marriage plots – to find an alternative in which the heroine is made mighty. Far from reproaching the masculinist politics of *Comus*, Woolf identified with the masque, turning to it, as she composed her first novel, not to criticize Milton, but to gain insight into the most important moments in her life. Woolf turned to *Comus*, in other words, because she found Miltonic chastity – the Lady's enormous self-confidence, her steely ability to withstand sexual interference – both psychologically therapeutic and politically prescriptive.

The plot of *Comus* is, in many respects, like that of *The Voyage Out*. In *Comus*, an unnamed "Lady" finds herself alone at night in the woods. The Lady is approached by Comus, an orgiast pretending to help her, and she goes with him in search of her brothers. The masque's second half discovers the Lady trapped in Comus's "stately palace" (*Comus* 667), with Comus trying to force her to drink from his glass. Significantly, the Lady's brothers botch an attempt to save her, and only Sabrina, a motherless nymph who has transformed herself into an immortal state to avoid rape, can help the Lady.

Woolf's revolutionary first novel also tells a tale of sexual violation. *The Voyage Out* is the story of Rachel Vinrace, a 24-year-old virgin who travels with her bullying father on a ship to an island in South America.[3] Rachel's mother died when Rachel was a child. Raised by maiden aunts, Rachel remains sexually innocent. Though a brilliant pianist, Rachel is a kind of *tabula rasa* on which the world can imprint itself, which is exactly what happens in the novel. On the boat, Rachel is kissed unexpectedly by an aristocratic parliamentarian named Richard Dalloway. After the kiss, Rachel comes under the solicitous protection of another aunt, Helen Ambrose, who escorts her to Santa Marina, where the bulk of the novel takes place. On Santa Marina, Rachel becomes engaged to a sympathetic novelist, Terence Hewet, but before their marriage can be consummated, Rachel falls ill with a mysterious fever and dies.

Dalloway's kiss occurs early (in the fifth of twenty-seven chapters), but it is a disturbing, and, ultimately, fatal, experience for Rachel. Both drawn to the kiss and horrified by it, Rachel suffers a nightmare afterwards. In her nightmare, Rachel is trapped in a vault with a repulsive dwarf who squats "on the floor gibbering, with long nails."[4] The vault walls are damp, oozing fluids that collect in drops and slide to the floor. This dream motif as well as its theme of sexual repulsion recurs in Rachel's death scene. While her fiancé is reading to her from *Comus*, Rachel's head begins to ache. Over the next few days (and while still thinking and dreaming about *Comus*), Rachel grows increasingly ill, slips into a coma, and dies.

The dwarf appearing in Rachel's nightmares recalls not only the bestiality of *Comus*, but Woolf's own description, in an autobiographical memoir, of early molestation. When she was "very small," Gerald Duckworth felt her "private parts" in front of a looking glass. Afterwards Woolf had a nightmare in which she "was looking [at herself] in a glass when a horrible face – the face of an animal – suddenly showed over [her] shoulder."[5] Both *Comus* and Woolf's allusion to it in her first novel are connected, in other words, to the problem of sexual abuse in Woolf's own life.

The Voyage Out has long been read as an autobiographical novel. Christine Froula writes, for example, that "in seeking Rachel's fortune [Woolf] was also seeking her own," and Louise DeSalvo has argued extensively that in writing her first novel, Woolf was working on the traumas in her own life, each connected to her attempt to become a novelist.[6] In 1912, as the late-blooming, now 29-year-old Woolf was working through draft after draft of the conclusion to the novel, as an emerging feminist, she was not only trying to find a way out of the marriage plot, but also herself trying to decide whether or not to marry Leonard Woolf. While she wanted to be married, in large part for conventional reasons, she was deeply ambivalent about Leonard, about men in general, and about what marriage might mean to herself as an artist. At 29, Woolf was still coming to terms with her mother's death (Woolf was 13 when her mother died, and she suffered depression and attempted suicide in the wake of that death). Also at 29, she remained traumatized by the sexual abuse by her half-brothers, the Duckworths, described in her autobiography as occurring both in early childhood and in adolescence.[7] Sexual abuse contributed to Woolf's lifelong attachment to chastity (demonstrated in *The Voyage Out* and *Mrs. Dalloway*, theorized in the late pamphlet *Three Guineas*, and practiced later in her asexual life with Leonard). It may also have played a significant role in precipitating her suicide by drowning at age 59.

Although relatively brief and one of Milton's earliest compositions, *Comus* has attracted a long list of arguments and counterarguments and at least seven books devoted solely to its interpretation.[8] One of the most important and obsessively recurring questions in the masque's recent critical history is whether or not the "Lady" remains a "Lady" since she is discovered, after making her majestic speech to Comus, "glued" to a chair, "Smear'd with gums of glutinous heat" (916). The central question in this discussion runs as follows: should the reader attribute the "gums of glutinous heat" to Comus's sperm, and thus be convinced that a rape has occurred while the Lady, after brilliant speech, is rendered mysteriously helpless? (From a theological point of view such a rape would destroy her virginity, but leave her chastity intact.[9]) Or are the gums either vaginal or, for William Kerrigan, possibly anal ejaculations of the Lady herself, who, despite her high-flown rhetoric, succumbs to the temptation, drinks the debasing liquor, and is bestialized, albeit against her will? Kerrigan's interpretation seems to suggest that the Lady, however prudish, really "wants it" in the favored locker-room-gossip answer to Freud's famously unanswerable question "what does a woman want?"[10] In any event, the central place which the question of the Lady's virtue holds in the literature indicates the "full sordidness . . . and distinctly seamy [side] of the Lady's [and perhaps of women's in general] situation,"[11] not only within the masque, but within the history of criticism itself. What it does not indicate – in a point critical to my argument of the recuperative role *Comus* plays in *The Voyage Out* – is the seamy side of Milton, for, as I shall suggest, Milton's sympathies are clearly on the side of the Lady with whom he identifies. Indeed, Milton's treatment of the Lady explicitly rejects the fetishized display of female helplessness typical of patriarchal thought.

Feminist readings of *Comus*'s place in *The Voyage Out* have had surprisingly little to say about the masque. Just as Gilbert in the "Milton's Bogey" chapter of *The Madwoman in the Attic* seems not to have read Milton at all, but rather uses him as a metonymic signifier of patriarchy, so feminist readers of *Comus* seem to have substituted the name and reputation of Milton for the masque itself.[12] For DeSalvo *The Voyage Out* is about how *Comus*'s "ideal of virginity murders women, even before they begin to grow."[13] Yet in its exclusive focus on the physical chastity which plays at best a minor role in Milton's masque (the principal theme of *Comus* is chastity, but by chastity Milton means not virginity, per se, but a mental state best defined as the sanctity or integrity of self), DeSalvo's reading completely ignores the question of intellectual chastity which is the thematic center of both the masque and Woolf's feminist program for political reform.

In a conversation with Yeats, Woolf stated that her favorite poem was *Lycidas* for she could return to it again and again without satiety.[14] In 1916, in "Hours in a Library," Woolf writes similarly of *Comus*. Like other classics (notably *Lycidas*, *Antony and Cleopatra*, and *Urn Burial*), *Comus* confers "some consecration" upon her which allows her to return to her life "feeling [it] more keenly than before."[15] Woolf's interest in *Comus* is consistent with feminist literary history as Annette Wheeler Cafarelli tells it, for if some women readers found *Paradise Lost* intimidating, they could "with impunity become enthusiastic revivers of the nonepic Milton." Finding "in the minor poems female characters free of the usual Miltonic reprimand," Cafarelli argues, women writers of gothic narrative found in *Comus* not a parable of virginity, but a story about "the self-reliance and fortitude of women who venture outside the protection of men." Particularly appealing to Romantic women writers may have been the masque's studious disinterest in the sadistic representation of feminine vulnerability. According to Cafarelli, women writers of gothic narratives habitually avoided representing terrorized women, in part because they knew the terror of female entrapment all too well. In contrast to this female tradition, male writers like "Monk" Lewis and Samuel Richardson represent sexual assault explicitly. Again, *Comus* is notable in the history of male-authored literature in its emphasis "on female self-reliance rather than victimization."[16]

Like *The Voyage Out*, *Comus* is often read autobiographically. "Milton criticism has long recognized the weight of empirical evidence in favor of a psychological approach to the masque," Christopher Kendrick writes, one in which "the Lady is a kind of Milton figure." Indeed, "the Lady is . . . one of our main sources of evidence about Milton's cult of chastity."[17] In their psychoanalytical readings of *Comus*, Kendrick and Kerrigan theorize the 26-year-old Milton as a genius who in self-defense against a castigating father identifies with a "cult of chastity." In this reading, Milton – who was called the "Lady" of Christ's, perhaps both for his gentle disposition and his unusual physical, feminine-seeming beauty – *is* the Lady. He is himself the protagonist of a work that dramatizes chastity.

Kerrigan describes the period of *Comus*'s composition (performed in 1634, published anonymously in 1637) as one in which Milton experienced a curious "caesura" or hiatus similar to the paralysis to which the Lady is consigned after brilliant speech. Having graduated from Cambridge and still "gathering knowledge of diverse kinds for a creative achievement in the future," he was nevertheless an "educated man still living at home."[18] A number of Milton's early poems point to the conflict this stasis presented in his life. Sonnet 7 ("How Soon Hath Time") and *Ad Patrem* point to the impatience first of his friend and then of his father that he had not yet blossomed. If Milton himself knew "it took time to become a poet of the highest sort,"[19] he was clearly embarrassed by the discrepancy between what he knew within himself and the present lack of proof. In order to cope psychologically with this embarrassment, Kerrigan argues, Milton identified with his mother (an identification self-evident in the masque) whose modest and chaste deportment guaranteed that the seemingly ineffectual Milton would not be the object of his father's anger.

Milton was early guided toward greatness by his scholarly and indulgent but demanding father. By the age of 21, two portraits had been made of Milton, but not of his younger brother, Christopher. By his own account, he was "destined ... in early childhood for the study of literature" (*CPW* 4.1:612). His father assigned tutors to complete his studies at home after he had been in school all day. He himself stated that in his youth, despite headaches and poor eyesight, he studied by the candle until midnight, since he had an avid thirst for knowledge and fame (*CPW* 4.1:612). He was raised, according to the testimony of his first biographer and nephew, Edward Philips, to be "the ornament and glory of his country" (Hughes 1027).[20] Milton thus seems to have internalized rather than resisted his father's ambitions. Shunning the "broad way and the green" (Sonnet 9), Milton avoided marriage, the "potent inclination of the desire for house and family of his own" (*CPW* 1.319), for what reasons we can only speculate. Milton's pride in his long-suspended chastity was partly religious (by his own confession, Milton was drawn by disposition to the ascetic life), but there may also have been other, more secular reasons for his choice. He wrote that "to me it was always preferable to grow slowly, and as if by the silent lapse of time" (*CPW* 1.819). Milton's hatred of the lewd court is well known and certain autobiographical statements indicate that Milton may have protected his chastity as carefully as a woman – as if his life depended upon it. In *An Apology for a Pamphlet* Milton states that "a certain reserv'dnesse of naturall disposition, and morall discipline learnt out of the noblest Philosophy was anough to keep me in disdain of far less incontinences then this of the burdello" (*CPW* 1.892). His renowned rage in the *Second Defence* at accusations of incontinence is further telling evidence of Milton's defensive attachment to chastity. Milton's early description of his "pure diet and a chaste youth" ("Elegia Sexta") also indicates that he may have shared some of the compulsive asceticism and even anorexia which preoccupied Woolf.[21]

Whether self-imposed chastity led Milton toward identification with women, or whether an identification with women led Milton toward chastity does not matter. In any event, as Kerrigan points out, Milton's cult of chastity is consistent with "such apparent anomalies as the transposed genders in *Areopagitica* (Psyche as Adam, female Truth as Osiris, Britannia as a strong and long-haired Samson)" and the historically unprecedented blurring of gender identities which, as Turner argues, inhabit *Paradise Lost*. (In that poem, Milton's Adam is described as "domestic," for example, and

Eve's intellectual capacity and subjectivity are represented in historically unprecedented ways.[22])

Other motives might have led Milton to a cult of chastity, and to his sustaining, by his own prideful claim, a chaste body into his thirties. John Shawcross has speculated a more than fantasized homosexual relationship between Milton, "the Lady of Christ's," and his best friend Diodati.[23] Certainly Milton's early poems have long been read as carrying more than a trace of homoeroticism. Though Kerrigan dismisses the possibility of a homosexual Milton,[24] a male-identified Milton could still glamorize chastity due to the same fears of marriage Woolf expressed in *The Voyage Out*. Milton may have feared the practical and emotional constraints of intimacy as a drain on the resources which he needed to devote exclusively to his art. Only through chastity could Milton concentrate his energies, store and shore up his talents, develop a reservoir of encyclopedic knowledge, and prepare himself for resistance to his political enemies. Though there is no indication that Milton suffered from childhood sexual abuse (indeed, even the speculation seems absurd), abuse is clearly acknowledged in the rape threat surrounding the Lady with whom Milton identifies and whose body he seems imaginatively to inhabit.

Chastity plays a similarly important role in Woolf's work. Indeed, Jane Marcus describes all of Woolf's works as carrying an underlying "erotics of chastity."[25] Woolf may have used chastity, as Milton did, to defer marriage and to defend herself as she built up her inner self in emotional and intellectual preparation for her battles as a creative artist and political reformer. Yet there may have been, as with Milton, other, differently gendered, reasons for Woolf's interest in chastity.[26]

The drafting of *The Voyage Out* was a complicated, long, even obsessive process.[27] Behind the five drafts of the novel that remain extant there are anywhere from seven to twelve other drafts. Woolf wrote and rewrote her first novel (not finally published until 1915 when Woolf was 33) repeatedly and obsessively over a period of eight years, as if either unable to get it right, or unable to risk exposure. This unusually complicated composition history may show Woolf as a "master" discourse writer of feminism, since the very difficulty of getting the text right points to the complicatedness of her mission. The novel's protracted drafting history may also reflect Woolf's confusion with regard to marriage, sexuality, and her place within the patriarchy generally. As a woman, Woolf seems to have been fearful of both marriage (since it foretold entrapment) and spinsterhood (since it implied social disgrace) and she might have perceived death as an alternative to both. In a letter to her sister, Vanessa, Woolf describes being unmarried in terms that recall Rachel's sexual nausea: "I could not write," Woolf records in June, 1911, "and all the devils came out – hairy black ones. To be 29 and unmarried – to be a failure – childless – insane too, no writer."[28] DeSalvo concludes that though Woolf was not sexually attracted to Leonard, Woolf nevertheless "wanted very much to be married"[29] since life in early twentieth-century England offered respectable women few alternatives. That Woolf's marriage to Leonard was unsatisfactory may be implied by Woolf's suicide attempt within the year. It may be that Woolf was so traumatized by early molestation that the thought of marriage and its inevitable intimacy was unbearably frightening. It may also be that lesbianism made marital dissatisfaction inevitable. In any event, marriage was a subject over which Woolf was impossibly perplexed, and one to which she was later to give sustained attention, describing the marriage of her parents, for example, in the near epic terms of *To the Lighthouse*.

Yet, as with Milton, reasons other than sexual ones may have caused Woolf to preserve her chastity. From an early age, Woolf was engaged in a highly self-disciplined course of study in literature. To write, she stood at a podium in the attic for several hours every morning and she was supervised for years by a famous scholar-father who predestined her for success as a writer, scholar, and historian. The self-discipline required for the "taking of all knowledge to be her province" and the deferred expression of the energy such self-discipline requires may easily have prompted a fear of intimacy. Especially because she was a woman, marriage and childbearing threatened to be drains on the personal resources that success as a writer and political reformer required her to hoard. In any event, in the service of an enormous self-discipline, we can see in Woolf as well as in Milton a determined cultivation of chastity as a personal self-protection against invasion from without which allows the self to, in a sense, seal itself off while it feeds itself on knowledge.

Many aspects of Woolf's early career and psychobiography thus match Milton's and make an underlying identification between them likely. Like Milton, Woolf was groomed by her father to be an intellectual success, an "ornament" for her age. Like Milton, Woolf engaged in a long apprenticeship in which she took "all knowledge to be her province." Like Milton, Woolf was living well after adolescence in the house of her father. Like Milton, Woolf was anxious about heterosexuality, and showed early signs of homoeroticism. Like Milton, Woolf was troubled at the prospect of marriage. If, as DeSalvo has shown, Woolf rejected chastity as a patriarchal ideal, she also may have appropriated it, like Milton, in self-defense. For both Milton and Woolf, chastity may have been a way to say to the world without, "noli me tangere": "thou canst not touch the freedom of my mind" (*Comus* 664).

Woolf's attraction to *Comus*, then, was profound, and I would argue that *Comus*'s placement at the conclusion of *The Voyage Out* is a masterful stroke which serves as shorthand to represent a complex of psychological factors in Woolf: her fear of intimacy and marriage, her love of art and literary ambitions, and, most importantly, her personal goal for herself and women at large of sexual independence and self-reliance. In reading *Comus*, in other words, Woolf tapped into Milton's own psychohistory which she found remarkably like her own.

In making such a case I fight a critical history, especially virulent since the seventies, which commonly pronounces Milton a misogynist. Christopher Kendrick has argued, for example, that *Comus* is the site of the overdetermined construction of female sexuality in the early modern / modern world. Following Foucault (and, interestingly, echoing DeSalvo), Kendrick reads the masque's emphasis on chastity as a representation of the early modern displacement of sexuality onto the female. In Milton, woman becomes the exclusive bearer of the sexual word, unfairly carrying the burden of an overdetermined discourse of specularity/ization. Not *Paradise Lost*, but Milton's *Comus* in this reading becomes the initiator of the novel and all its attendant woes. Kendrick's reading is corroborated by Mary Nyquist's New Historical interpretations of the divorce tracts and *Paradise Lost* as evidence of "the deeply masculinist assumptions at work in Milton's articulation of a radically bourgeois view of marriage."[30] If he opens up a historically new subjectivity for Eve, it is of "the kind . . . required by a new economy's progressive sentimentalization of the private sphere."[31] Both readings would seem to confirm contemporary feminist Woolf scholars (like Froula, DeSalvo, and Gilbert) in their readings of Milton as the master-mind of the patriarchal plot against women. Yet neither Kendrick nor Nyquist fully accounts for *Comus*'s proto-feminist complexity. Nyquist's reading is flawed by the psychoanalytical presumption of Milton as a unified subject, as well as by a largely unsubstantiated claim that Milton was more misogynist than his time. Kendrick's argument recuperates standard sexist complaints against female frigidity (he describes the Lady's final speech as "strident," for example, and he sees her profile as "stony"). Kendrick's reading is flawed in its anti-feminist reading of chastity (espoused by Woolf, for example, as a self-defense against a rapacious patriarchy) as "archaic and asocial," and as emergently capitalistic in its preference for solitude over community.[32]

The most important point in interpreting *Comus* from a feminist poetic is that its protagonist, though seemingly vulnerable, is not. For DeSalvo, *Comus* merely teaches women the importance of chastity, when Milton's text actually teaches self-reliance.[33] Left alone in the woods, the Lady sings. Disabled in Comus's chair, the Lady speaks with undisturbed eloquence, deflating not only Comus but, significantly, patriarchal rapacity itself. In *Comus* Milton may have fathered a line of discourse as powerful in revolutionizing gender as Woolf herself, for through the Lady's heroic example, the whole literary tradition of female helplessness – past and to come – is potentially disabled.

My claim that *The Voyage Out* is a story about sexual violation may take some skeptical readers by surprise. Dalloway, after all, only *kisses* Rachel (and, indeed, for Thomas Caramagno, the neurotic Rachel overreacts to what is, in fact, only a harmless imposition).[34] Yet to minimize the kiss is to misunderstand the Victorian and patriarchal contexts that govern the novel. It is also to ignore what may be Woolf's most subversive theme: the impact on woman of patriarchal sexual violence.

In "Out of the Chrysalis," Froula argues that *The Voyage Out* is most radical in its exposure not of the marriage plot, but of the sexual violence that underwrites it. Dalloway's kiss represents Rachel's "violent [and fatal] abduction into male culture"; it teaches Rachel that "her [proper] place is in the underworld"; and that she is a sexually vulnerable object whose "enclosure by the patriarchy will be enforced."[35] If Dalloway initiates Rachel's training in patriarchal sexual violence, that initiation is only fulfilled in the novel's final chapters, where Rachel slides into a coma and dies as she listens, unsaved, to words from Milton's *Comus*.[36]

At the head of the novel's twenty-fifth chapter, on the day set for her engagement party, Rachel Vinrace becomes mysteriously ill. Hoping to alleviate Rachel's illness, Rachel's fiancé, Terence, offers to read to her as she sits in the garden courtyard. After trying several authors, Terence settles at last on Milton (specifically, *Comus*), for only Milton, Terence claims, can stand up to the heat. Terence says it is not necessary "to understand what he [Milton was] saying." But for Rachel Milton's words are curiously "laden with meaning" (*TVO* 326). Terence reads:

> There is a gentle nymph not far from hence,
> That with moist curb sways the smooth Severn stream.
> Sabrina is her name, a virgin pure;
> Whilom she was the daughter of Locrine,
> That had the sceptre from his father Brute.   (824–28)

For the motherless and unsavable Rachel, a confused heroine vaguely formulating a feminism that does not yet exist, the words are painful to listen to, and her mind goes off on "curious trains of thought" (*TVO* 327), suggested in part by the harsh-sounding words "Locrine" and "Brute." Terence continues:

> Sabrina fair,
> Listen where thou art sitting
> Under the glassy, cool, translucent wave,
> In twisted braids of lilies knitting
> The loose train of thy amber dropping hair,
> Listen for dear honour's sake,
> Goddess of the silver lake,
> Listen and save! (859–66)

At this moment, Rachel's head begins to ache, and she goes inside. Over the next four days (as she grows increasingly ill) Rachel's "chief occupation during the day is to try to remember how the lines [from *Comus*] went." Her mind recites:

> Under the glassy, cool, translucent wave,
> In Twisted braids of lilies knitting
> The loose train of thy amber dropping hair;

but the "adjectives persist . . . in getting in the wrong places" (*TVO* 329). The inability to get the adjectives right signals Rachel's doom – for this "real life" woman, trying alone to invent a feminism not yet available in Victorian England, there will be no Sabrina/mother to come from the waves to save her.

By the second day, Rachel is "completely cut off" (*TVO* 330), unable to communicate with the rest of the world. Feverish and disoriented, she longs for the "glassy, cool translucent wave" (*TVO* 329). There, with Sabrina, she can descend at last into the alien world where women are not forced to live under the patriarchy – half dead, half alive, not yet ready to be born. On the fourth day of her illness, Rachel falls – hallucinogenically – into a pool of "sticky [semen-like?] water" (*TVO* 341) which closes over her head. Shortly thereafter she dies.

Rachel's death is considered mysterious, even unfathomable, by most critics. Although it is possible that she contracted a fever on her journey with Terence up the Amazon River, most critics have read the death as self-willed, and, for Woolf, a symbolic, perhaps somewhat clumsy attempt as feminist novelist to escape the "marriage plot" supposedly originating in Milton and invoked repeatedly in the eighteenth- and nineteenth-century novel. But – as I argue here – the opposite is true, for far from condemning Milton, Woolf turns to him for an alternative to sexual victimization.

In her analysis of the relationship between rape, female silence, and literary culture ("The Daughter's Seduction: Sexual Violence and Literary History"), Froula argues that in literature as well as in life, rape has been traditionally condoned rather than condemned. In examples that range from the abduction of Helen of Troy to Freud's abandonment of the seduction theory,[37] she argues that literary culture reflects a real situation in which silence is "the effect of repression, not of absence." Thus in either case, this repression sanctions sexual violence and prohibits women from telling the story of that violence. Literature, Froula argues, has thus played a *violent* role in the construction of female destiny. The inability to tell the story of rape silences woman, and, where there should be personhood, inserts absence.

But if literature has played its role in silencing, it can also play an equivalent role in liberating women. Indeed, Froula uses Woolf's own prophecy in *A Room of One's Own* that "the woman's freedom to tell [and know] her stories . . . would come . . . once she is no longer the dependent daughter, wife, and servant," to argue that once daughters begin to tell the story of rape – as, for example, the contemporary black writers Maya Angelou and Alice Walker have done in novels such as *I Know Why the Caged Bird Sings* and *The Color Purple* have told it – they will be free.

Rachel is hardly free. She shares the Lady's status as a victim of sexual violence, but she does not share the Lady's success. The Lady rebuffs her assailant and is even strengthened by the experience of sexual assault. Rachel, on the other hand, dies. What explains this difference?

Ultimately, the difference between the fates of Rachel and the Lady is the difference between their male and female subjectivity. Woolf's heroine is born into a Victorian world which silences because it sexualizes women. Interfered with by Dalloway, Rachel wilts like a flower and dies. The revolutionary heroine of Milton's *Comus*, on the other hand, is born into an England on the fiery verge of civil war, and she is invested with the power and revolutionary self-confidence of newfound male speech and subjectivity. Milton's Lady is invested with the privileged male subjecthood of Milton himself: she shares the position of speaking strength that even a revolutionary outsider like Milton occupies. Instead of internalizing the violence of her assailant, she denounces him, speaking in a mighty voice that, charged with the approaching revolutionary fervor of the English civil war, Woolf dimly foresaw as one that could prepare the way for feminism.

Neither Woolf nor Rachel shares the speaking strength of Milton's Lady. Instead of saying self-possessedly, "Thou canst not touch the freedom of my mind" (*Comus* 664) or "Fool do not boast" (*Comus* 663), Woolf recalls her childhood encounter with Gerald Duckworth: "I remember how I hoped that he would stop; how I stiffened and wriggled... But it did not stop" (*MB* 69). Nor did Woolf succeed in freeing herself as an adult. In "Professions for Women," she writes that although she has killed the angel in the house, she *has not yet succeeded in telling the truth about herself as a body* (a truth, she writes, which alone will liberate women). "I doubt," she writes, "that any woman has solved [this problem] yet" for there are "still many ghosts to fight, many prejudices to overcome."[38] Likewise, Woolf is crippled by intellectual guilt. Marcus reminds us, for example, of Woolf's terror of trespassing on the grounds of that male preserve, literary scholarship: "She always feared she would be found out, that the punishment of the fathers for daring to trespass on their territory w[ould be] 'instant dismemberment by wild horses.'"[39] However brave, Woolf internalized the sexual violence and misogyny of her culture, turning it against herself.

Similarly, Rachel Vinrace dies unable to be articulate in sexual self-defense. For the Victorian-born Rachel there is no freedom of mind that Dalloway cannot touch. Sexually innocent (but now spoiled), politically naive, motherless, lacking authority or even credibility in the public sphere, Rachel has no ground to stand on. Subsequent to the kiss, her education descends into the merely sexual realm that for Froula represents the life of the female under the patriarchy. After the kiss, Rachel's life and education are cut short, her tragic ending is set in motion, and she becomes, in a sense, like Coleridge's sea beast, dead while still alive. In some sense, her story ends before it begins.

Woolf's allusion to *Comus* thus serves a double purpose: it reveals the rape story buried in Woolf's actual life and enacts a victory over sexual intimidation that neither the suicidal Rachel Vinrace nor the suicidal Virginia Woolf could accomplish. Through *Comus* Woolf reveals and heals the secret that underlies patriarchal culture – the primal sexual abuse that silences women, curtailing their lives, killing them before they are born into the *Bildung*, making sure that they are submissive, and that, their mouths covered, they never tell their tales.

T. S. Eliot argues in his essay "The Metaphysical Poets" that, following Milton, English literature suffered a dissociation of sensibility, a falling off from its ability to synthesize thought and feeling and that, had Milton not been there to block the progress of English literature, it would have continued to flourish in the Elizabethan mode. In some sense, we can read *The Voyage Out* as Woolf's counter claim, for, in Woolf's reading, culture declines into further sexism *after*, not because of, Milton. If Rachel Vinrace cannot yet follow the path of Milton's intellectually chaste Lady; if she does not yet have the strength to say with her "thou canst not touch the freedom of my mind" (*Comus* 664); if she is as yet unsuccessful in calling upon Sabrina, the mythological woman who would save her – it is not because of Milton but because the tradition Milton's text militates against has educated Rachel in servitude and silence. The Lady of *Comus* both saves herself and is saved (if she needs to be saved) not by a man but by a woman – the mother figure who, according to Christopher Kendrick "must not [continue to] be written out of existence."[40] To Woolf, *Comus* did not represent the epitome of the patriarchal plot against women, but rather its more attractive alternative: female self-reliance, including the self-reliance of a woman-saving-woman community. Woolf uses the strength of the Lady of *Comus* not to condemn Milton, but to break the silence that keeps the patriarchy intact. *Comus* enacts the as-yet-unwritten plot of female liberty that Christine Froula and Rachel Blau DuPlessis would have us believe would have been Rachel Vinrace's had she not died on the threshold of Modernism.

NOTES

1. See Rachel Blau DuPlessis, "'Amor Vin –': Modifications of Romance in Woolf," in *Virginia Woolf: A Collection of Critical Essays*, ed. Margaret Homans (Englewood Cliffs, NJ: Prentice-Hall, 1993), 115–35, and Christine Froula, "Out of the Chrysalis: Female Initiation and Female Authority in Virginia Woolf's *The Voyage Out*," in *Virginia Woolf: A Collection of Critical Essays*, 136–61. See also Louise DeSalvo, *Virginia Woolf's First Voyage* (Totowa, NJ: Rowman & Littlefield, 1980), and "Virginia, Virginius, Virginity," in *Faith of a (Woman) Writer*, ed. Alice Kessler-Harris and William McBrien (Westport, CT: Greenwood, 1988), 179–89. DeSalvo argues that, for Milton, a woman must be a virgin or she will be abandoned or even murdered by her parents.
2. Suzanne Hull, *Chaste, Silent, and Obedient: English Books for Women, 1475–1640* (San Marino, CA: Huntington Library, 1982).
3. See Lisa Tyler, "'Nameless Atrocities' and the Name of the Father: Literary Allusion and Incest in Virginia Woolf's *The Voyage Out*," *Woolf Studies Annual* 1 (1995): 26–46.
4. Virginia Woolf, *The Voyage Out* (rpt. 1915; New York: Harcourt, Brace, and world [Harvest], 1968), 77. All future references to this novel will be cited parenthetically in the text as *TVO*.

5. *Moments of Being* (San Diego and New York: Harcourt Brace, 1985), 69. Referred to hereafter as *MB*.
6. See Froula, "Out of the Chrysalis," 159, and DeSalvo's introductory chapter to *Virginia Woolf's First Voyage*.
7. See especially *MB*. 69.
8. For some of the more interesting interpretations of *Comus* see Annette Wheeler Cafarelli, "How Theories of Romanticism Exclude Women," in *Milton, the Metaphysicals, and Romanticism* (Cambridge: Cambridge University Press, 1994), 84–113; Christopher Kendrick, "Milton and Sexuality: A Symptomatic Reading of *Comus*," in *Re-membering Milton: Essays on the Texts and Traditions*, ed. Mary Nyquist and Margaret W. Ferguson (New York: Methuen, 1988), 43–73; William Kerrigan, *The Sacred Complex: On the Psychogenesis of "Paradise Lost"* (Cambridge, MA: Harvard University Press, 1983); Leah Marcus, "Justice for Margery Evans: A 'Local' Reading of *Comus*," pp. 66–85 in *Milton and the Idea of Woman*, ed. Julia Walker (Urbana: University of Illinois Press, 1988); Mary Nyquist, "The Genesis of Gendered Subjectivity in the Divorce Tracts and in *Paradise Lost*," pp. 99–127 in *Re-membering Milton*; David Aers and Bob Hodge, "'Rational Burning': Milton on Sex and Marriage," *Milton Studies* 12 (1979): 3–33; Tilottama Rajan, "The Other Reading: Transactional Epic in Milton, Blake, and Wordsworth," pp. 20–46 in *Milton, the Metaphysicals, and Romanticism*; James Grantham Turner, *One Flesh: Paradisal Marriage and Sexual Relations in the Age of Milton* (Oxford: Oxford University Press, 1993).
9. William Kerrigan, "The Politically Correct *Comus*: A Reply to John Leonard," *Milton Quarterly* 27 (1993): 149–55 (see esp. p. 152). Leah Marcus, p. 79, also discusses the differences between virginity and chastity.
10. "*Her ritual of undoing implies that the Lady, having figuratively drunk the potion of her tempter, is guilty*" (*Sacred Complex* p. 48; Kerrigan's italics). John Leonard replies to Kerrigan's notorious assertion, "If we think our way to the borderline between Milton and his artistic creation the Lady's 'no' to Comus in some fashion means 'yes.'" See "Saying 'No' to Freud: Milton's A Mask and Sexual Assault," *Milton Quarterly* 25 (1991): 129–40.
11. Marcus, "Justice for Margery Evans," 77.
12. Sandra Gilbert and Susan Gubar, *The Madwoman in the Attic: The Woman Writer and the Nineteenth-Century Literary Imagination* (New Haven: Yale University Press, 1979).
13. "Virginia," 181.
14. *The Diary of Virginia Woolf: 1925–30*, vol. 3, ed. Anne Olivier Bell (New York: Harcourt Brace, 1980), 330.
15. *The Essays of Virginia Woolf: 1912–1918*, vol. 2, ed. Andrew Mc Neillie (San Diego: Harcourt Brace, 1987), 60.
16. "How Theories of Romanticism Exclude Women," 94, 96, 98, 99.
17. "Milton and Sexuality," 45, 48.
18. *Sacred Complex*, 39.
19. *Ibid.*, 40.

20. My reading follows Kerrigan's *Sacred Complex* (42–60) in its characterization of many of the circumstances in Milton's life and psychology during the composition of *Comus*.
21. Madeline Moore, *A Short Season Between Two Silences: The Mystical and the Political in the Novels of Virginia Woolf* (Boston: Allen and Unwin, 1984), 21–24.
22. *Sacred Complex*, 50; *One Flesh*, 237.
23. "Milton and Diodati: An Essay in Psychodynamic Meaning," *Milton Studies* 7 (1975): 141, 156–57. See also Shawcross's discussion of Milton and Diodati in *John Milton: The Self and the World* (Lexington: University of Kentucky Press, 1993), esp. 48, 55–60. In this latter, Shawcross argues that Milton loved Diodati, but that consummation did not necessarily occur.
24. *Sacred Complex*, 49.
25. See Jane Marcus, "The Niece of a Nun: Virginia Woolf, Caroline Stephen, and The Cloistered Imagination," in *Virginia Woolf and the Languages of Patriarchy* (Bloomington: Indiana University Press, 1987) 115–35, for an illuminating discussion of the role of chastity in Woolf's life. See esp. 116 and 133.
26. See *ibid*.
27. See DeSalvo, *First Voyage*, esp. 1–10.
28. Virginia Woolf, *The Letters of Virginia Woolf: Volume One 1888–1912*, ed. Nigel Nicolson and Joanne Trautmann (New York: Harcourt Brace, 1975), 466.
29. *First Voyage*, 5.
30. "The Genesis of Gendered Subjectivity," in *Re-membering Milton*, 106.
31. For Kendrick's argument see "Milton and Sexuality," in *Re-membering Milton*; for Nyquist's, see "The Genesis of Gendered Subjectivity," 106 and 120 in the same volume. See also Shawcross (*John Milton: The Self and the World*, esp. 196–98) on misreadings of Milton as a misogynist, and Michael C. Schoenfeldt, "Gender and Conduct in *Paradise Lost*," in James Grantham Turner's *Sexuality and Gender in Early Modern Europe: Institutions, Texts, Images* (Cambridge: Cambridge University Press, 1993), 310–38 for a discussion of a more feminist Milton than Nyquist's.
32. "Milton and Sexuality," 66, 62. See also Theodora Jankowski, "'The Scorne of Savage People': Virginity as 'Forbidden Sexuality' in John Lyly's *Love's Metamorphosis*," in *Renaissance Drama* (Evanston: Northwestern University Press, 1993), 123–53, esp. 124, 128. Jankowski writes that female chastity, rather than being respected, is often viewed by male critics as "hysterical and antisocial" (124).
33. DeSalvo, "Virginia," 182. In contrast, Catherine Belsey argues that *Comus* is "about rape" but that it resists the implications of its own plot. See *John Milton: Language, Gender, Power* (Oxford: Basic Blackwell, 1988), 47.
34. *The Flight of the Mind: Virginia Woolf's Art and Manic Depressive Illness* (Berkeley: University of California Press, 1992), 158ff.
35. "Out of the Chrysalis," 146–47.

36. Beverly Ann Schlack has described Woolf's allusion to *Comus* at the end of *The Voyage Out* as one of the three most complex and brilliantly successful of all Woolf's allusions. See *Continuing Presences: Virginia Woolf's Use of Literary Allusion* (University Park: Pennsylvania State University Press, 1979), x.
37. Christine Froula, "The Daughter's Seduction: Sexual Violence and Literary History," in *Feminist Theory in Practice and Process*, ed. Micheline R. Malson et al. (Chicago: University of Chicago Press, 1989), 139–62, 148.
38. Virginia Woolf, *The Death of the Moth and Other Essays* (New York: Harcourt Brace [Harvest], 1970), 241.
39. See p. 1 of "Thinking Back through Our Mothers," in *New Feminist Essays on Virginia Woolf*, ed. Jane Marcus (Lincoln: University of Nebraska Press, 1981), 1–30.
40. "Milton and Sexuality," 51.

Index

Achinstein, Sharon, 135, 136, 143–44, 149, 176, 182, 202
Adelman, Janet, 170, 181
Aers, David and Bob Hodge, 268
Agrippa, Cornelius, 132
Ames, William, 68
Angelou, Maya, 265
Anne, Queen [wife of James I], 173
anti-feminism, *see* misogyny
Arundel, Countess, 8
Aquinas, St. Thomas, 73
Attaway, Mrs., 13
Aubrey, John, 216
Audland, Anne, 140
Auerbach, Erich, 165
Augustine, St.
    dualism, 99, 100, 111
    ex nihilo creation (nothingness), 96, 98–99, 112
    on forbidden fruit, 117
    on friendship, 7, 57
    on marriage, 7

Bakhtin, M. M., 152
Bal, Mieke, 111
Barclay, A. R., 151
Barker, Arthur, 71, 92, 203
Baroni, Leonora, 208
Baston, Jane, 150
Behn, Aphra, 62, 133
Bell, Millicent, 243
Belsey, Catherine, 269
Benet, Diana, 72
Bennet, Sue, 246, 249
Bennett, Joan S., 73, 203
Besse, Joseph, 137, 139, 149
Biberman, Matthew, 71, 221
Biddle, Hester, 140
Blake, William, 223, 243, 253
Bland, Jane, 139
Bloom, Harold, 4, 219, 222

Bodenheimer, Rosemarie, 207, 220
Boesky, Amy, 12, 202
Bolton, Robert, 6
Border, David, 137, 150
Boyarin, Daniel, 178, 180, 182, 200, 203
Boyle, Robert, 2
Brathwait, Richard, 168
Breitenberg, Mark, 32, 33
Brontë, Charlotte, 210
Browne, Sir Thomas, 8, 14, 57
    Urn Burial, 257
Browning, Elizabeth Barrett, 253
Brownwell, Anna, 221
Bullinger, Heinrich, 68
Bunyan, John, 135
Burrough, Edward, 152
Butler, Judith, 161–62, 166

Cafarelli, Annette Wheeler, 257–58, 268
Calvin, Jean, 121–22, 131
Campbell, Gardner, 130
Capp, Bernard S., 136, 137, 149
Caramagno, Thomas, 263, 269
Carey, John, 203
Cary, Mary, 133, 134, 137–38, 139, 150
Casey, Edward, 252
Cates, Barbara, 251–52
Cavendish, Margaret, 91
Chadwick, Whitney, 228, 232, 250
Channel, Elinor, 140
Chaplin, Gregory, 8, 14, 57, 61, 71, 72
Charles I, 23, 25, 26–27, 45, 139, 182, 186
    Eikon Basilike, 26, 187
Charles II, 28, 196
chastity, *see* virginity
Chevers, Sarah, 140
Christian liberty, 3, 54, 57, 60, 67, 68, 69–70, 71, 102, 184, 188, 189, 196–99, 200, 203
Chrysotom, 58
Cicero, 73
Clark, Sidney, 250

271

classical republicanism, 25, 26, 27–29, 172
  civic virtue in, 19
  masculinity in, 19–23, 29
Clinton, Elizabeth, 173, 182
Coiro, Anne Baynes, 182
Cole, Margaret, 139–40, 152
Coleridge, Samuel T., 13, 266
Cotton, Priscilla, 139–40, 152
courtesy books, 7, 8
Cowley, Abraham, 196
Cranworth, Lord, 211–12, 217
Crawford, Patricia, 134, 148, 150
Cristin, Renato, 111
Cromwell, Oliver, 138, 139, 150, 151, 173–74, 178, 179
Cross, Claire, 182
Cross, Frank, 73
Cuomo, Chris, 234, 252
Curtin, Deane, 234
Curtius, Ernest Robert, 92
Cutland, Elizabeth, 139

Dalila (Milton's character), 9, 53–54, 56, 58–71, 72, 74, 159, 175–76, 191–92
Dante, 44, 82
David, Deirdre, 253
Davies, Stevie, 252
Davis, Dr., 218
Davis, Michael, 94
Davis, Miss, 57, 218, 222
Day and Haghe, 225
DeSalvo, Louise, 256, 257, 261, 262, 263, 267, 268, 269
Dickens, Charles, 211, 221
  Hard Times, 212
Dickinson, Emily, 226
Diodati, Charles, 260, 269
DiSalvo, Jackie, 70, 202
divorce, 1, 3, 13, 57, 115, 207–08, 209–15, *see also* divorce tracts, marriage; misogyny; women
divorcers [sect of], 1
Dod, John, and Robert Cleaver, 68, 170, 171, 172, 181
Dods, Dr., 228
Donne, John, 2, 93, 216, 222
Doré, Gustav, 223
Dryden, John, 14, 196
  All for Love, 9–10, 14
  "A Learned Wife," 9, 14
  The State of Innocence, 9
Duckworth, Gerald, 256, 266
DuPlessis, Rachel Blau, 267
DuRocher, Richard, 233, 235–37, 252
Dzelzainis, Martin, 25, 33

ecofeminism, 13, 230, 233–49, 251–52, 253
effeminacy, 23–24, 27, 55, 191, 195, *see also* masculinism; misogyny
Eaubonne, Francoise d', 251
Egerton, Alice, 77, 79, 81–82
Egerton, John, Lord Brackley, 81, 91
Elder, John, 223
Eliot, George (Mary Ann Evans), 12, 13, 15, 207–19, 221, 222, 253
  Middlemarch, 12, 207, 208–09, 214, 215–20
  Romola, 208
Eliot, T. S., 6, 13, 266–67
Elizabeth I, Queen, 1
Empson, William, 70, 130
Erasmus, Desiratus, 68
Erbery, Mary, 139
Escher, M. C., 41
Evans, Katharine, 139–40
Eve
  biblical, 7, 10, 23, 127
  Milton's character, 2, 4, 9, 10, 14, 32, 35, 39, 40, 42, 64, 72, 105–06, 108–09, 121–22, 123–26, 127–29, 225, 235, 245, 262

Fallon, Stephen, 13, 51, 71, 99–100, 112, 221
Feake, Christopher, 138
Fell, Margaret, 10, 62, 133, 134, 136, 137, 140, 145, 149, 151
feminism
  Dalila's, 66
  seventeenth-century, 223
  twentieth-century, 1–2, 3, 4–5, 254, 257–58, 262–63
  Victorian, 264
  Virginia Woolf's, 256
  see also ecofeminism; Eliot, George
Ferguson, Margaret, 133, 148
Ficino, Marsilio, 112
Field, Lucy, 139
Figes, Eva, 152
Fineman, Joel, 165
Fish, Stanley, 64, 68, 74, 182, 203
Fixler, Michael, 201
Flannagan, Roy, 160, 166
Fletcher, Angus, 79, 92
Fletcher, Anthony, 25, 33, 92
Forster, Mary, 136
Foucault, Michel, 262
Fowler, Alastair, 52, 113
Fox, George, 135, 136, 149, 150, 151
Foxe, John, 137, 140
Freud, Sigmund, 84, 87–88, 93, 105, 109, 113, 257, 265, 270
Froula, Christine, 2, 262, 263, 265, 266, 267, 268, 269

Index

Frye, Northrop, 58–59, 72
Furman-Adams, Wendy, 12
    Furman-Adams, Wendy, and Virginia James Tufte, 253
Fuseli, Henry, 223

Gaard, Greta, 233, 237, 251, 252
Galen, 171–72, 181
Gallagher, Phillip J., 113
Gardiner, Judith, 151
Gataker, Thomas, 31, 33
Gates, Barbara T., 229
Gauden, John, 22–23
gender, language of, 5, 11, 38–40, 184, 188–89, *see also* effeminacy; masculinism
Gilbert, Sandra, 2, 35, 36, 51, 220, 257, 262
    and Susan Gubar, *The Madwoman in the Attic*, 4, 5, 11, 12, 53–54, 58, 70, 71, 220, 222
Gilbert, William, 101, 112
Gillett, Paula, 251
Gilman, Sander, 157–58, 166
Gerard, John, 253
Giraud, Eleanor, 226
Giraud, Francis (Sr.), 225
Giraud, Francis (Jr.), 226
Giraud, Frederick, 225, 226
Giraud, Herbert, 224, 225, 226, 229
Giraud, Jane, 13, 223, 225
Giraud, John Thomas, 225, 226, 250
Giraud, Mary Chapman, 225, 226
Giraud, Mary Jane, 226
Gottlieb, Sidney, 149
Gouge, William, 168, 170, 173, 181
Graham, Jean E., 92
Grantham, Caleb, 21, 33
Greenblatt, Stephen, 172, 181
Gregerson, Linda, 151, 169, 180, 181, 183
Gregory, Francis, 202
Greville, Robert, Lord Brooke, 9, 10, 14
Groom, Mary, 223, 224, 240, 243, 245
Grossman, Marshall, 5, 12, 14, 112, 113, 114
Gubar, Susan, 2, 4
Guibbory, Achsah, 12, 71, 177–78, 182, 201, 202
Guillimeau, James, 172, 181
Guillory, John, 72, 92, 124, 132, 166

Halkett, John, 4, 6–7, 13, 14, 71, 72, 74
Haller, William, 71, 201
    and Maleville, 6
Halpern, Richard, 91
Hardy, Nathaniel, 21, 33
Harrison, Anne, 139
Hartlib Circle, 11
Haskin, Dayton, 12, 73, 74, 166, 182, 201
Hauskneckt, Gina, 11, 36, 43

Hayley, William, 222
Hebrew prophets, 185, 188–89, 193, 199, *see also* Jews
Hegel, Georg Wilhelm Friedrich, 161–62
Heidegger, Martin, 5, 95, 97–98, 101–02, 108, 111
Helmont, Jean Baptiste van, 118, 130
Henrietta Maria, Queen, 22, 23, 27
Henry, Nathaniel H., 13
Henry, Prince of Wales, 173
Hesiod, 113
heterosexuality, 3, 8, 11, 30–31, 38, 45, 66
Heydon, John, 9
Hibberd, Shirley, 234
Hill, Christopher, 133–34, 135, 137, 147, 148, 149, 150, 152, 201, 202
Hinds, Hilary, 136, 150
Hobby, Elaine, 8, 14, 151
Holstun, James, 178, 179, 183
Hooker, Richard, 121, 122, 131, 214
Hookes, Ellis, 136, 149
Hooton, Elizabeth, 140
Howgill, Mary, 139, 151
Hull, Suzanne, 267
Hunt, Thorton, 209, 210, 211
husbands, 21, *see also* marriage, wives

Ingram, Jane, 139
Irigaray, Luce, 5, 14, 252

James I, 173
    Basilikon Doron, 173, 182
Jameson, Anna Brownwell, 71, 208
Jameson, Fredric, 93
Jankowski, Theodora, 269
Jefferson, Thomas, 72
Jeffries, Anne, 140
Jessey, Hugh, 138
Jews, 12, 157–58, 177, 178–79, 184, 185
Johnson, Samuel, 13
    Life of Milton, 1, 2, 11, 35, 53–54, 70, 71, 208, 215, 216, 221
Jones, Edward, 2
Jonson, Ben, 86, 93, 94
Jordon, Matthew, 33
Jose, Nicholas, 202

Katz, David, 150, 183, 201
Keats, John, 98, 208
Keeble, N. H., 152
Keightley, Thomas, 209, 211, 212, 213, 214, 215, 216, 218, 221, 222
Kelly, Joan, 133, 148
Kendrick, Christopher, 92, 258, 262, 268, 269
Kerrigan, William, 83, 92, 114, 130, 257, 259–60, 268–69

Kezar, Dennis, 203
Knoppers, Laura Lunger, 73–74, 201
Knott, James R., 146, 152
Kramer, Jack, 232, 251
Kristeva, Julia, 5, 14, 88, 93
Krouse, Michael, 154, 165
Kunze, Bonnelyn, 151

Lacan, Jacques, 14, 80, 84–85, 92, 93, 111, 113
Laplanche, L. and J. B. Pontalis, 93
Laquer, Thomas, 181, 201
Laud, Archbishop William, 24, 137
Lead, Jane, 74
Leavis, F. R., 6
Legrange, Leon, 232
Lehnhof, Kent R., 52
Leibniz, Gottfried Wilhelm Freiherr von, 97–98, 111
Leonard, John, 93, 268
Leverenz, David, 172, 181
Lewalski, Barbara K., 146, 152
Lewes, George Henry, 207, 209, 210–11, 214, 221
Lewis, Matthew Gregory "Monk," 258
Lieb, Michael, 91, 127, 130, 132, 203
Linnaeus, Carolus, 230, 234
Lobb, Judge, 139
Loeffelhoz, Mary, 92
Loewenstein, David, 135, 143–44, 149, 152, 203
Loscocco, Paula, 202
Low, Anthony, 154, 209, 221
Low, Lisa, 12
Luther, Martin, 121, 131
Luxon, Thomas, 165

MacCallum, Hugh, 202
Madsen, William, 154
Makin, Bathsua, 8, 10–11, 15, 62
Manchester, William, 182
Manheim, Ralph, 111
Marcus, Jane, 260, 266, 269, 270
Marcus, Leah, 151, 268
marriage, 1, 3, 14, 65, 68, 115–17, 119–23, 125–27, 209, 214, 215, 220
  companionate, 54–55
  conversation in, 3, 49, 57
  "marriage plot," 254–55, 260–61
  polygamy, 115
  proto-modern, 7
Martia, Queen, 1
Martin, Catherine Gimelli, 14, 73, 100, 105, 112, 113
Martin, John, 223
Martineau, Harriet, 253
Marvell, Andrew, 233

masculinism, 1, 3, 11, 19–23, 25, 30–33, 34, 35–41, 43, 46, 61–62, 73, 184, 189, *see also* patriarchy
maternity, 210
  nursing, nurture, 167–76, 180
  surrogate, 12, 161, 180
Maus, Katharine Eisaman, 94
McColley, Diane, 4, 13, 225, 233, 235, 243, 250, 252
McHenry, James Patrick, 237–38, 240, 248–49, 252, 253
Menand, Louis, 58, 72
Michie, Elsie, 220, 221
Miller, Jacqueline T., 173, 182
Milton, John
  family
    brother Christopher, 259
    daughters, 2, 12, 54, 57, 208, 213, 217
    nephews Edward and John Phillips, 2
    sister Anne Phillips, 2
    wives, 2
    see also Powell, Mary; Woodcock, Katherine
  Poetry
    "At a Solemn Music," 43
    "Elegia Sexta," 259
    Lycidas, 82, 257
    A Maske Presented at Ludlow Castle [*Comus*], 11, 12, 32, 77–91, 254–55, 256–58, 262
    Nativity Ode, 82
    Paradise Lost, 11, 12, 34–36, 38–39, 41, 43, 46–51, 57, 95–96, 98, 99–111, 116, 117–20, 122–30, 134–35, 140, 144–46, 147–48, 209, 214, 220, 223, 225, 233, 235, 236, 237, 240, 242, 243, 244, 245, 246, 248, 249, 252, 253, 254, 258, 259–60, 262
    Paradise Regained, 90, 144, 154, 155, 160, 177, 192, 223, 225, 253
    Poems (1645), 78
    Samson Agonistes, 11, 12, 44, 45, 53–56, 58–59, 62–70, 153–55, 156–65, 167–68, 173, 174–80, 184, 186, 189
    Sonnet 9, 57, 259
    Sonnet 10, 57
    Sonnet 14, 57
    Sonnet 19, 142–43, 147
    Sonnet 23, 65, 70
  politics, ideas of nationhood, 6, 12, 19–29, 64–65, 142–43, 146, 148, 186
    universalism, 169, 170, 176, 177, 178–79, 180
  Prose
    Animadversions, 137
    Apology for a Pamphlet, 44, 62, 259
    Areopagitica, 10, 11, 22, 60, 79, 118, 138, 143, 174, 177, 259

Index

Colasterion, 7, 49, 56, 57, 60
Commonplace Book, 1
De Doctrina Christiana, 12, 38, 115–18, 119–21, 122, 123, 127, 130, 131, 198, 200
divorce tracts, 2, 8, 10–11, 19–20, 23, 26, 29–32, 36–42, 43–45, 49, 51, 54, 58–62, 63–66, 69, 118–19, 128, 209, 213, 219–20,
see also individual titles
Doctrine and Discipline of Divorce, 13, 20, 30, 32, 41, 44, 50, 54–55, 56, 63, 64, 145, 146, 209, 214–15, 217
Of Education, 24–25, 168, 214
Eikonoklastes, 19, 21, 22, 23, 25–27, 28, 186, 187, 191, 195
History of Britain, 26, 187
Pro Populo Anglicano [Defence of the English People], 26, 186, 187, 192, 195
Readie and Easie Way, 19, 20, 21, 27–29, 143, 188, 189, 190, 192, 195
The Reason of Church Government, 23, 25, 197, 212
Of Reformation, 24, 143, 169, 181
Second Defence, 217, 259
The Tenure of Kings and Magistrates, 19, 20, 21–23, 26, 186
Tetrachordon, 11, 29–32, 36–41, 42, 44, 45, 46–47, 48, 58, 59, 61–62, 73, 118–19, 120, 126, 128, 131
misogyny, 2, 4, 5, 7, 8, 10, 11, 53–54, 58–59, 65, 67–68, 254–55, 262
Mohl, Ruth, 1
Mollenkott, Virginia, 70
Mollineux, Mary, 149
Montaigne, Michel de, 8, 57
Moore, Madeline, 269
Morland, Samuel, 152
Mueller, Janel, 173, 182, 252
Munda, Constantia, 9
Murphy, Patrick, 233, 237, 251, 252

Nardo, Anna, 12, 15, 208–09, 221, 222
Newcome, Henry, 202
Newton, Sir Isaac, 210
Nietzsche, Friedrich, 94
Norton, Carolyn Sheridan, 210, 211–15, 221
Nunn, Pamela Gerrish, 234
Nuttall, Geoffrey, 150
Nyquist, Mary, 29, 33, 52, 61, 72, 202, 262, 268, 269

Ostovich, Helen and Elizabeth Sauer, 150
Ovid, 44, 88, 89, 93

Paglia, Camille, 80, 92, 94
Paraeus, David, 68

Parker, William Riley, 13
Pascal, Blaise, 45
Pask, Kevin, 152
patriarchy, 11, 81–82, 168–69, 173, 207, 266
marital, 68, 255, 262–63
Milton as patriarchal poet, 1, 11, 34–36, 160, 257
see also masculinism
Patterson, Annabel, 13, 220–21
Pauline doctrine
on Jews, 169, 185, 188–89, 196–99, 202
on marriage, 3, 10, 11, 31, 36, 37–38, 45, 46, 60, 61, 132
on universalism, 169, 176, 177, 178, 179, 180
Peacham, Henry, 92
Pell, John, 11
Perkins, Jane Grey, 221
Perkins, William, 68
Perry, Ruth, 171, 172, 181
Peter, Hugh, 137–38
Petrina, Carlotta, 223, 224, 249
Petto, Samuel, 135
Phillips, Edward, 216, 218, 222, 259
Plant, Judith, 233, 246–48, 253
Plato, Platonism, 25, 42, 44, 45
Phaedrus, 8
Symposium, 8
Polydou, Desma, 14, 52
Poole, Kristen, 135, 144, 149, 152
Poovey, Mary, 214, 222
Postlethwaite, Diana, 220
Powell, Mary, 2, 3, 13, 42, 44, 54, 57, 216, 218
Pratt, Anne, 228–29
Pratt, Robert, 228
Pratt, Sarah Bundock, 228
Puritanism, 177–78
marriage doctrine, 6–7
views on nursing mothers, 168, 172–73, 174, 180
Puttenham, Richard, 92

Quilligan, Maureen, 91

Radzinowicz, Mary Ann, 72–73, 154, 203
Ragussis, Michael, 177, 182
Rajan, Tillottama, 268
Ranelagh, Lady Katherine, 2
Rapaport, Herman, 113
Revard, Stella
Richardson, Samuel, 258
Ricoeur, Paul, 112
Roffey, Mrs., 228
Rogers, John, 12, 91, 92, 112, 113, 130
Rogers, John (seventeenth century), 134, 135, 149
Rose, Mary Beth, 202

Rosenblatt, Jason, 166, 201
Rowe, Elizabeth, 149
Ruether, Rosemary Radford, 201
Rumrich, John, 71, 100, 112, 114
Ruskin, John, 228

Sallust, 26
Samuel, Irene, 70
Sandys, George, 84, 85–86, 87, 88–89, 93, 94
Sauer, Elizabeth, 12, 72, 178, 179, 182
Scarry, Elaine, 155–56, 159, 160–61, 162, 164
Schlack, Beverly Ann, 270
Schoenfeldt, Michael C., 269
Schwartz, Regina, 112
Schwarz, Kathryn, 91, 171–72, 181
Schwoerer, Lois, 148
Scroop, Lady, 1
Seaton, Beverly, 240, 251
Selden, John, 55, 71, 73
sexuality, *see* heterosexuality
Shakespeare, William
  Antony and Cleopatra, 257
  Romantic heroines, 80
  The Tempest, 80
Shapiro, James, 185, 201
Shawcross, John T., 33, 92, 260, 269
Shoaf, R. A., 113
Shoulson, Jeffrey, 142, 149, 182
Shteir, Ann, 229, 230, 250
Shullenberger, William, 5, 11, 14, 152
Simpson, Margaret, 221
Smith, Alexis, 223
Smith, Joseph H., 93
Smith, Nigel, 135, 141, 149
Sokol, B. J., 91
Sowernam, Esther, 9
Speght, Rachel, 9, 10, 14
Spenser, Edmund
  The Faerie Queene, 80, 168
Spinoza, Benedict de, 66
Sprat, Thomas, 10
Stackhouse, Amy Dunham, 114
Stanton, Elizabeth Cady, 72
Staten, Henry, 52
Stein, Arnold, 73
Stevens, Paul, 169, 177, 180, 182, 201
Stevens, Wallace, 95, 111
Stouppe, J. B., 152
Sumers, Alinda, 14
Swetnam, Joseph, 8, 10
Swiss, Margo, 152

Tasso, Torquato, 1, 112
Teskey, Gordon, 113

Tims, Sarah, 140
Tosh, John, 21, 33
Trapnel, Anna, 133, 134, 138–39, 140, 145, 150
Trubowitz, Rachel, 12, 181, 202
Tuchman, Gaye, 251
Tufte, Virginia, 13, 249
Turner, James Grantham, 11, 13, 14, 30, 33, 52, 61, 72
  One Flesh, 46, 52, 72, 73, 130, 259–60, 268, 269
Turner, Jane, 135
Tyler, Lisa, 267

Ulreich, John, 71

Vaughan, Henry, 233
Vicary, Thomas, 171–72, 181
Victoria, Queen, 224–25, 228
virginity, 77–91, 92, 257, 258, 259–60, 262
Vivers, Margaret, 140
Vives, Ludovicus, 7

Walker, Alice, 265
Walker, Eric C., 222
Walker, George, 121–22, 131
Walker, Henry, 135
Walker, Julia C., 5, 93, 191, 202
Wall, Kathleen, 83, 93
Waller, Edmund, 196
Walton, Izaac, 216
Walzer, Michael, 6, 14, 134, 149
Waugh, Dorothy, 140
Wayne, Valerie, 182
Webber, Joan, 51
Wentworth, Anne, 134, 141–42, 151
Whately, William, 20, 21, 33
White, Gilbert, 234
White, R. S., 73
Wilden, Anthony, 93
Wilding, Michael, 135, 149
Witte, John Jr., 131
Wittreich, Joseph, 4, 13, 51, 72, 74, 112–13, 140, 151, 152, 203, 249
wives, *see* marriage; patriarchy
  Stepford wives, 8
Wollstonecraft, Mary, 58
women
  eighteenth-century, 62
  nineteenth-century, 211–13
  seventeenth-century, 8, 12, 62, 133–34
    querelle des femmes, 8–11
  Victorian, 13, 225, 232
  see also divorce; feminism; marriage
Woodcock, Katherine, 2, 13
Woods, Derek N. C., 199, 202, 203

Woolf, Leonard, 256, 261
Woolf, Virginia, 5, 12, 13, 36, 39, 41, 44, 45, 46, 48, 58, 207, 214
 Diary, 34–36, 51
 Letters, 51
 Moments of Being, 268
 Mrs. Dalloway, 256
 Professions for Women, 266
 A Room of One's Own, 58, 70, 72, 265
 Three Guineas, 256
 To the Lighthouse, 261
 The Voyage Out, 12, 260–61, 262
Wordsworth, William, 219, 222
Worster, David, 234–35, 251

Yeats, William Butler, 257

Zagorin, Perez, 71
Zimmerman, Michael, 234, 251
Zimmerman, Shari, 61–62, 72